Praise for React Quickly

"React Quickly *is a one-stop shop for anyone who wants a guided introduction to React and the ecosystem of tools, concepts, and libraries around it. Follow Azat's walkthroughs, work on the projects given, and you'll soon understand React, Redux, GraphQL, Webpack, and Jest, as well as how to put them to work.*"

—Peter Cooper, editor of *JavaScript Weekly*

"React Quickly *teaches the reader the most valuable and buzz-worthy concepts in building modern web applications with React including GraphQL, Webpack, and server-side rendering. After reading* React Quickly, *you should feel confident in your ability to create a production-grade web application with React.*"

—Stan Bershadskiy, author of *React Native Cookbook*

"*Azat is one of the most authoritative voices in the programming space. This book goes far beyond the basics by deep diving into React's foundation and architecture. It's a must read for any developer!*"

—Erik Hanchett, author of *Ember.js Cookbook*

"*This book is simple to follow. It uses very basic language that makes you understand each concept step by step.*"

—Israel Morales, front-end developer and web designer at SavvyCard

"*Simple language with simple logical examples to get you up and running quickly is why this book truly justifies its title,* React Quickly. *This book covers all the major topics that any developer new to React needs in order to start writing apps using React. And the author's sense of humor will keep you engaged until the end. I am thankful Azat took time to share his React journey with us.*"

—Suhas Deshpande, software engineer at Capital One

"React Quickly *is a great resource for coming up to speed with React. Very thorough and relevant. I'll be using it as a reference for my next app.*"

—Nathan Bailey, full stack developer at SpringboardAuto.com

React Quickly

PAINLESS WEB APPS WITH REACT, JSX, REDUX, AND GRAPHQL

AZAT MARDAN
FOREWORD BY JOHN SONMEZ

MANNING
SHELTER ISLAND

Manning Publications Co.
20 Baldwin Road
PO Box 761
Shelter Island, NY 11964

Development editor:	Dan Maharry
Technical development editor:	Anto Aravinth
Review editor:	Ivan Martinović
Project editor:	Tiffany Taylor
Copyeditor:	Tiffany Taylor
Proofreader:	Katie Tennant
Technical proofreader:	German Frigerio
Typesetter:	Gordan Salinovic
Cover designer:	Leslie Haimes

ISBN 9781617293344
Printed in the United States of America
1 2 3 4 5 6 7 8 9 10 – EBM – 22 21 20 19 18 17

To my grandfather, Khalit Khamitov. Thank you for being such a kind and just person. You will always stay in my memory, along with the crafts you taught me, the trips we took to the dacha, and the chess games we played.

brief contents

contents

foreword

I keep hoping that JavaScript will die. Seriously. Die brutally and painfully.

It's not that I completely dislike JavaScript—it has improved quite a bit over the years. It's that I have a severe distaste for complexity—so much so that I named my blog and my business *Simple Programmer*. My tagline has always been, "Making the complex simple."

Making the complex simple isn't easy. It takes a special set of skills. You have to be able to understand the complex, and understand it so well that you can distill it down to the core—because everything is simple at the core. This is exactly what Azat has done with this book, *React Quickly*.

Now, I'll admit Azat had a little help. You see, one of the reasons I personally like ReactJS so much is that it's simple. It was designed to be simple. It was designed to deal with the increasing complexity of JavaScript frameworks and reduce that complexity by going back to the basics: plain old JavaScript. (At least, for the most part. ReactJS does have a JSX language that's compiled into JavaScript, but I'll let Azat tell you about that.)

The point is, although I like Angular, Backbone, and some other JavaScript frameworks because they've helped make it much easier for web developers to create asynchronous web applications and single-page applications, they've also added a great deal of complexity. Using templates and understanding the syntax and subtleties of these frameworks increased productivity, but they moved the complexity from the backend to the frontend. ReactJS starts over, gets rid of templates, and gives you a way to apply component-based architecture to your UI using JavaScript. I like this. It's simple. But even the simplest thing can be difficult to explain—or worse yet, made complex by a teacher who lacks this skill.

This is where Azat comes in. He knows how to teach. He knows how to simplify. He begins this book by explaining React through contrasting it with something you probably already know: Angular. Even if you don't know Angular, his explanation of ReactJS will quickly help you understand the basics and its purpose. Then Azat quickly demonstrates how to create a basic ReactJS application, so you can see and do it for yourself. After that, he takes you through the 20% you need to know in order to accomplish 80% of what you'll do in React, using real-world examples that anyone can grasp easily. Finally—and this is my favorite part—he includes examples and projects galore. The absolute best way to learn is by doing, and Azat walks you through creating six—yes, six—nontrivial projects using ReactJS.

In keeping with my theme of simplicity, I'll leave off here by saying that *React Quickly* is simply the best way I know of to learn ReactJS.

JOHN SONMEZ
AUTHOR OF *Soft Skills* (http://amzn.to/2hFHXAu)
AND FOUNDER OF *Simple Programmer* (https://simpleprogrammer.com)

preface

It was 2008, and banks were closing left and right. I was working at the Federal Deposit Insurance Corporation (FDIC), whose primary task is to pay back depositors of closed, failed, and insolvent banks. I admit that, in terms of job security, my job was on par with working at Lehman Brothers or being a ticket salesman for the *Titanic*. But when my department's eventual budget cuts were still far in the future, I had the chance to work on an app called Electronic Deposit Insurance Estimator (EDIE). The app became hugely popular for a simple reason: people were anxious to find out how much of their savings was insured by the United States federal government, and EDIE estimated that amount.

But there was a catch: people don't like to tell the government about their private accounts. To protect their privacy, the app was made entirely in front-end JavaScript, HTML, and CSS, without any back-end technologies. This way, the FDIC wasn't collecting any financial information.

The app was a hot mess of spaghetti code left by dozens of iterations of consultants. Developers came and went, leaving no documentation and nothing resembling any logical, simple algorithms. It was like trying to use the New York City subway without a map. There were myriads of functions to call other functions, strange data structures, and more functions. In modern terminology, the app was pure user interface (UI), because it had no backend.

I wish I'd had React.js back then. React brings joy. It's a new way of thinking—a new way of developing. The simplicity of having your core functionality in one place, as opposed to splitting it into HTML and JS, is liberating. It reignited my passion for front-end development.

React is a fresh way of looking at developing UI components. It's a new generation of presentation layer libraries. Together with a model and routing library, React can replace Angular, Backbone, or Ember in the web and mobile tech stack. This is the reason I wrote this book. I never liked Angular: it's too complex and opinionated. The template engine is very domain specific, to the point that it's not JavaScript anymore; it's another language. I have used Backbone.js and like it for its simplicity and DIY approach. Backbone.js is mature and more like a foundation for your own framework than a full-blown, opinionated framework in itself. The problem with Backbone is the increased complexity of interactions between models and views: multiple views update various models, which update other views, which trigger events on models.

My personal experience from doing a Kickstarter campaign for my React.js online course (http://mng.bz/XgkO) and from going to various conferences and events has shown me that developers are hungry for a better way to develop UIs. Most business value now lies in UIs. The backend is a commodity. In the Bay Area, where I live and work, most job openings in software engineering are for front-end or (a trendy new title) generalist/fullstack developers. Only a few big companies like Google, Amazon, and Capital One still have relatively strong demand for data scientists and back-end engineers.

The best way to ensure job security or get a great job in the first place is to become a generalist. The fastest way to do so is to use an isomorphic, scalable, developer-friendly library like React on the front end, paired with Node.js on the backend in case you ever need to mess with server-side code.

For mobile developers, HTML5 was a dirty word two or three years ago. Facebook dropped its HTML5 app in favor of a more performant native implementation. But this unfavorable view is quickly changing. With React Native, you can render for mobile apps: you can keep your UI components but tailor them to different environments, another point in favor of learning React.

Programming can be creative. Don't get bogged down by mundane tasks, complexity, and fake separation of concerns. Cut out all the unnecessary junk, and *unleash your creative power with the simplistic beauty of modular, component-based UIs powered by React.* Throw in some Node for isomorphic/universal JavaScript, and you'll achieve Zen.

Happy reading, and let me know how you like the book by leaving a review on Amazon.com (http://amzn.to/2gPxv9Q).

acknowledgments

I'd like to acknowledge the internet, the universe, and the human ingenuity that brought us to the point that telepathy is possible. Without opening my mouth, I can share my thoughts with millions of people around the globe via social media such as Twitter, Facebook, and Instagram. Hurray!

I feel humongous gratitude to my teachers, both intentional at schools and universities, and accidental and occasional, whose wisdom I grasped from books and from learning by osmosis.

As Stephen King once wrote, "To write is human, to edit is divine." Thus, my endless gratitude to the editors of this book and even more so to the readers who will have to deal with the inevitable typos and bugs they'll encounter in this volume. This is my 14th book, and I know there will be typos, no mater what [sic].

I thank the people at Manning who made this book possible: publisher Marjan Bace and everyone on the editorial and production teams, including Janet Vail, Kevin Sullivan, Tiffany Taylor, Katie Tennant, Gordan Salinovic, Dan Maharry, and many others who worked behind the scenes.

I can't thank enough the amazing group of technical peer reviewers led by Ivan Martinovic: James Anaipakos, Dane Balia, Art Bergquist, Joel Goldfinger, Peter Hampton, Luis Matthew Heck, Ruben J. Leon, Gerald Mack, Kamal Raj, and Lucas Tettamanti. Their contributions included catching technical mistakes, errors in terminology, and typos, and making topic suggestions. Each pass through the review process and each piece of feedback implemented through the forum topics shaped and molded the manuscript.

On the technical side, special thanks go to Anto Aravinth, who served as the book's technical editor; and German Frigerio, who served as the book's technical proofreader. They are the best technical editors I could have hoped for.

Many thanks go to John Sonmez of Pluralsight, Manning, and SimpleProgrammer.com fame, for writing the foreword to this book. Thank you, Peter Cooper, Erik Hanchett, and Stan Bershadskiy for your reviews and for giving the book extra credibility. Readers who haven't heard of John, Peter, Erik, or Stan should subscribe and follow their work around software engineering.

Finally, a thank you to all the MEAP readers for your feedback. Revising the book based on your reviews delayed publication by a year, but the result is the best book currently available about React.

about this book

This book is intended to cure the troubles of front-end developers, make their lives more meaningful and happier, and help them earn more money by introducing them to React.js—and doing so in a fast manner (hence the word *Quickly* in the title). *It's the work of one and a half years and about a dozen people.* At the very least, the book is meant to open your mind to some unusual concepts like JSX, unidirectional data flow, and declarative programming.

Roadmap

The book is split into two parts: "Core React" (chapters 1–11) and "React and friends" (chapters 12–20). Each chapter includes descriptive text supplemented with code examples and diagrams where they're applicable. Each chapter also has an optional introductory video that will help you decide whether you need to read the chapter or can skip it. Chapters are written in a standalone manner, meaning you should have no trouble if you don't read the book in order—although I do recommend reading it sequentially. At the end of each chapter is a quiz, to reinforce your retention of the material, and a summary.

Each part ends with a series of larger projects that will give you more experience with React and solidify your new understanding by building on the concepts and knowledge introduced in the previous chapters. The projects are supplemented by optional screencast videos to reinforce your learning and show you dynamic things like creating files and installing dependencies (there are a *lot* of moving parts in web development!). These projects are an integral part of the book's flow—avoid skipping them.

I encourage you to type each line of code yourself and abstain from copying and pasting. Studies have shown that typing and writing increase learning effectiveness.

The book ends with five appendixes that provide supplemental material. Check them out, along with the table of contents, before you begin reading.

The websites for this book are www.manning.com/books/react-quickly and http://reactquickly.co. If you need up-to-date information, most likely you'll find it there.

The source code is available on the Manning website (www.manning.com/books/react-quickly) and on GitHub (https://github.com/azat-co/react-quickly). See the "Source code" section for more details. I show full listings of the code in the book—this is more convenient than jumping to GitHub or a code editor to look at the files.

Who this book is for (read this!)

This book is for web and mobile developers and software engineers with two to three years of experience, who want to start learning and using React.js for web or mobile development. Basically, it's for people who know the shortcut for the Developer Tools by heart (Cmd-Opt-J or Cmd-Opt-I on Macs). The book targets readers who know and are on a first-name basis with these concepts:

- Single-page applications (SPAs)
- RESTful services and API architecture
- JavaScript, especially closures, scopes, and string and array methods
- HTML, HTML5, and their elements and attributes
- CSS and its styles and JavaScript selectors

Having experience with jQuery, Angular, Ember.js, Backbone.js, or other MVC-like frameworks is a plus, because you'll be able to contrast them with the React way. But it's not necessary and to some degree may be detrimental, because you'll need to unlearn certain patterns. React is not exactly MVC.

You'll be using command-line tools, so if you're afraid of them, this is the best time to fight your phobia of the command line/Terminal/command prompt. Typically, CLIs are more powerful and versatile than their visual (GUI) versions (for example, the Git command line versus the GitHub desktop—the latter confuses the heck out of me).

Having some familiarity with Node.js will allow you to learn React much more quickly than someone who's never heard of Node.js, npm, Browserify, CommonJS, Gulp, or Express.js. I've authored several books on Node.js for those who want to brush up on it, the most popular being *Practical Node.js* (http://practicalnodebook.com). Or, you can go online for a free NodeSchool adventure (http://nodeschool.io) (free does not always mean worse).

What this book is not (read this too!)

This book is *not* a comprehensive guide to web or mobile development. I assume that you already know about those. If you want help with basic programming concepts or JavaScript fundamentals, there are plenty of good books on those topics. *You Don't*

Know JS by Kyle Simpson (free to read at https://github.com/getify/You-Dont-Know-JS), *Secrets of the JavaScript Ninja, Second Edition* (www.manning.com/books/secrets-of-the-javascript-ninja-second-edition), and *Eloquent JavaScript* by Marijn Haverbeke (free to read at http://eloquentjavascript.net) come to mind. So, there's no need for me to duplicate existing content with this book.

How to use this book

First of all, *you should read this book.* That is *not* a joke. Most people buy books but never read them. It's even easier to do so with digital copies, because they hide on drives and in the cloud. *Read the book,* and work through the projects, chapter by chapter.

Each chapter covers either a topic or a series of topics that build on each other. For this reason, *I recommend that you read this book from beginning to end* and then go back to individual chapters for reference. But as I said earlier, you can also read individual chapters out of order, because the projects in the chapters stand alone.

There are many links to external resources. Most of them are optional and provide additional details about topics. Therefore, I suggest that you read the book at your computer, so you can open links as I refer to them.

Some text appears in a monospace font, like this: `getAccounts()`. That means it's code, inline or in blocks. Sometimes you'll see code with weird indentation:

```
document.getElementById('end-of-time').play()
}
```

This means I'm annotating a large chunk of code and broke it into pieces. This piece belongs to a bigger listing that started from position 0; this small chunk won't run by itself.

Other times, code blocks aren't indented. In such cases, it's generally safe to assume that the snippet is the whole thing:

```
ReactDOM.render(
<Content />,
  document.getElementById('content')
)
```

If you see a dollar sign ($), it's a Terminal/command prompt command. For example:

```
$ npm install -g babel@5.8.34
```

The most important thing to know and remember while using this book is that you must have fun. If it's not fun, it's not JavaScript!

Source code

All of the book's code is available at www.manning.com/books/react-quickly and https://github.com/azat-co/react-quickly. Follow the folder-naming convention ch*NN*, where *NN* is the chapter number with a leading 0 if needed (for example, ch02 for chapter 2's code).The source code in the GitHub repository will evolve by including patches, bug fixes, and maybe even new versions and styles (ES2020?).

Errata

I'm sure there are typos in this book. Yes, I had editors—a bunch of them, all professionals provided by Manning. But thanks for finding that typo. No need to leave nasty Amazon reviews or send me hate mail about it, or about grammar.

Please don't email me bugs and typos. Instead, you can report them on the book's forum at https://forums.manning.com/forums/react-quickly or create a GitHub issue at https://github.com/azat-co/react-quickly/issues. This way, other people can benefit from your findings.

Also, please don't email me technical questions or errata. Post them on the book's forum, the book's GitHub page (https://github.com/azat-co/react-quickly), or Stack Overflow. Other people may help you more quickly (and better) than I can.

Book forum

Purchase of *React Quickly* includes free access to a private web forum run by Manning Publications where you can make comments about the book, ask technical questions, and receive help from the author and from other users. To access the forum, go to https://forums.manning.com/forums/react-quickly. You can also learn more about Manning's forums and the rules of conduct at https://forums.manning.com/forums/about.

Manning's commitment to our readers is to provide a venue where a meaningful dialogue between individual readers, and between readers and the author, can take place. It is not a commitment to any specific amount of participation on the part of the author, whose contribution to the forum remains voluntary (and unpaid). We suggest you try asking the author some challenging questions lest his interest stray! The forum and the archives of previous discussions will be accessible from the publisher's website as long as the book is in print.

about the author

I've published more than 14 books and 17 online courses (https://node.university), most of them on the cloud, React, JavaScript, and Node.js. (One book is about how to write books, and another is about what to do after you've written a few books.) Before focusing on Node, I programmed in other languages (Java, C, Perl, PHP, Ruby), pretty much ever since high school (more than a dozen years ago) and definitely more than the 10,000 hours prescribed.[1]

Right now, I'm a Technology Fellow at one of the top 10 U.S. banks, which is also a Fortune 500 company: Capital One Financial Corporation, in beautiful San Francisco. Before that, I worked for small startups, giant corporations, and even the U.S. federal government, writing desktop, web, and mobile apps; teaching; and doing developer evangelism and project management.

I don't want to take too much of your time telling you about myself; you can read more on my blog (http://webapplog.com/about) and social media (www.linkedin.com/in/azatm). Instead, I want to write about my experience that's relevant to this book.

When I moved to the sunny state of California in 2011 to join a startup and go through a business accelerator (if you're curious, it was 500 Startups), I started to use modern JavaScript. I learned Backbone.js to build a few apps for the startup, and I was

---

[1] See https://en.wikipedia.org/wiki/Outliers_(book).

impressed. The framework was a huge improvement in code organization over other SPAs I'd built in prior years. It had routes and models. Yay!

I had another chance to see the astounding power of Backbone and isomorphic JavaScript during my work as software engineering team lead at DocuSign, the Google of e-signatures (it has a 70% market share). We reengineered a seven-year-old monolithic ASP.NET web app that took four weeks for each minor release into a snappy Backbone-Node-CoffeeScript-Express app that had great user experience and took only one or two weeks for its release. The design team did great work with usability. Needless to say, there were boatloads of UI views with various degrees of interactivity.

The end app was isomorphic before such a term even existed. We used Backbone models on the server to prefetch the data from APIs and cache it. We used the same Jade templates on the browser and the server.

It was a fun project that made me even more convinced of the power of having one language across the entire stack. Developers versed in C# and front-end JavaScript (mostly jQuery) from the old app would spend a sprint (one release cycle, typically a week or two) and fall in love with the clear structure of CoffeeScript, the organization of Backbone, and the speed of Node (both the development and the running speed).

My decade in web development exposed me to the good, the bad, and the ugly (mostly ugly) of front-end development. This turned out to be a blessing in disguise, because I came to appreciate React even more, once I switched to it.

If you'd like to receive updates, news, and tips, then connect with me online by following, subscribing, friending, stalking, whatever:

- Twitter—https://twitter.com/azat_co
- Website—http://azat.co
- LinkedIn—http://linkedin.com/in/azatm
- Professional blog—http://webapplog.com
- Publications—http://webapplog.com/books

For in-person workshops and courses, visit http://NodeProgram.com or https://Node.University, or send me a message via https://webapplog.com/azat.

about the cover

An email from an early reader asked about the dervish on the cover. Yes, the character could easily be a Persian or any one of many Turko-nomadic people inhabiting the Middle East and central Asia. This is due to the fact that trade and travel were highly developed and frequent among those regions for many centuries. But, according to the illustrator who drew this picture, he was depicting a Siberian Bashkir. Most of the modern-day Bashkirs live in the Republic of Bashkortostan (a.k.a. Bashkiria). Bashkirs are close ethnic and geographical neighbors of the Volga Bulgars (improperly named Tatars); Bashkirs and Tatars are the second-most-populous ethnic group in the Russian Federation. (The first is Russians, if you're curious.)

The figure comes from an eighteenth-century illustration, "Gravure Homme Baschkir," by Jacques Grasset de Saint-Sauveur. Fascination with faraway lands and travel for pleasure were relatively new phenomena at the time, and collections of drawings such as this one were popular, introducing both the tourist as well as the armchair traveler to the inhabitants of other countries. The rich variety of drawings reminds us vividly of how culturally apart the world's regions, towns, villages, and neighborhoods were just 200 years ago. Isolated from each other, people spoke different dialects and languages. In the streets or in the countryside, it was easy to identify where they lived and what their trade or station in life was, just by their dress.

Dress codes have changed since then and the diversity by region, so rich at the time, has faded away. It is now hard to tell apart the inhabitants of different continents, let alone different towns or regions. Perhaps we have traded cultural diversity for a more varied personal life—certainly for a more varied and fast-paced technological life.

At a time when it is hard to tell one computer book from another, Manning celebrates the inventiveness and initiative of the computer business with book covers based on the rich diversity of regional life of two centuries ago, brought back to life by pictures such as this one.

Part 1

React foundation

Hello! My name is Azat Mardan, and I'm going to take you on a journey into the wonderful world of React. It will make your front-end development more enjoyable and your code easier to write and maintain, and your users will be delighted at the speed of your web apps. React is a game changer in web development: the React community has pioneered many approaches, terms, and design patterns, and other libraries have followed the path forged by React.

I've taught this material more than 20 times in my live-online and in-person workshops to hundreds of software engineers from very different backgrounds and varied levels of seniority. Thus, this material has been battle tested on my students: you're getting the distilled, most effective version of my React foundation course in a written format. These chapters are critical to get you on familiar terms with React.

Chapters 1–11 are the result of almost two years of work by several people, but they read as a fast sequence of topics that build on each other. The best way to consume these chapters is to start with chapter 1 and proceed in order. Each chapter includes a video message from me; chapters 1–8 have a quiz at the end; and chapters 9–11, which are projects, contain homework for self-guided development.

All in all, this part of the book builds a solid foundation of React concepts, patterns, and features. Can you go to a foreign country and understand the language without studying? No—and that's why you must learn the React "language" before you attempt to build complex apps. Thus, it's paramount that you study these basic React concepts—that you learn the React language—which is exactly what you'll do in the next 11 chapters.

Let's get started with React—and learn to speak fluent React-ese.

Watch this chapter's introductory video by scanning this QR code with your phone or going to http://reactquickly.co/videos/ch01.

Meeting React

This chapter covers

- Understanding what React is
- Solving problems with React
- Fitting React into your web applications
- Writing your first React app: Hello World

When I began working on web development in early 2000, all I needed was some HTML and a server-side language like Perl or PHP. Ah, the good old days of putting in `alert()` boxes just to debug your front-end code. It's a fact that as the internet has evolved, the complexity of building websites has increased dramatically. Websites have become web applications with complex user interfaces, business logic, and data layers that require changes and updates over time—and often in real time.

Many JavaScript template libraries have been written to try to solve the problems of dealing with complex user interfaces (UIs). But they still require developers to adhere to the old separation of concerns—which splits style (CSS), data and structure (HTML), and dynamic interactions (JavaScript)—and they don't meet modern-day needs. (Remember the term *DHTML?*)

In contrast, React offers a new approach that streamlines front-end development. React is a powerful UI library that offers an alternative that many big firms such as Facebook, Netflix, and Airbnb have adopted and see as the way forward. Instead of defining a one-off template for your UIs, React allows you to create reusable UI components in JavaScript that you can use again and again in your sites.

Do you need a captcha control or date picker? Then use React to define a `<Captcha />` or `<DatePicker />` component that you can add to your form: a simple drop-in component with all the functionality and logic to communicate with the back end. Do you need an autocomplete box that asynchronously queries a database once the user has typed four or more letters? Define an `<Autocomplete charNum="4"/>` component to make that asynchronous query. You can choose whether it has a text box UI or has no UI and instead uses another custom form element—perhaps `<Autocomplete textbox="..." />`.

This approach isn't new. Creating *composable UIs* has been around for a long time, but React is the first to use pure JavaScript without templates to make this possible. And this approach has proven easier to maintain, reuse, and extend.

React is a great library for UIs, and it should be part of your front-end web toolkit; but it isn't a complete solution for all front-end web development. In this chapter, we'll look at the pros and cons of using React in your applications and how you might fit it into your existing web-development stack.

Part 1 of the book focuses on React's primary concepts and features, and part 2 looks at working with libraries related to React to build more-complex front-end apps (a.k.a. *React stack* or *React and friends*). Each part demonstrates both greenfield and brownfield development[1] with React and the most popular libraries, so you can get an idea of how to approach working with it in real-world scenarios.

Chapter videos and source code

We all learn differently. Some people prefer text and others video, and others learn best via in-person instruction. Each chapter of this book includes a short video that explains the chapter's gist in less than 5 minutes. Watching them is totally *optional*. They'll give you a summary if you prefer a video format or need a refresher. After watching each video, you can decide whether you need to read the chapter or can skip to the next one.

The source code for the examples in this chapter is at www.manning.com/books/react-quickly and at https://github.com/azat-co/react-quickly/tree/master/ch01 (in the ch01 folder of the GitHub repository https://github.com/azat-co/react-quickly). You can also find some demos at http://reactquickly.co/demos.

---

[1] *Brownfield* is a project with legacy code and existing systems, while *greenfield* is a project without any legacy code or systems; see https://en.wikipedia.org/wiki/Brownfield_(software_development).

1.1 What is React?

To introduce React.js properly, I first need to define it. So, what is React? It's a UI component library. The UI components are created with React using JavaScript, not a special template language. This approach is called *creating composable UIs*, and it's fundamental to React's philosophy.

React UI components are highly self-contained, concern-specific blocks of functionality. For example, there could be components for date-picker, captcha, address, and ZIP code elements. Such components have both a visual representation and dynamic logic. Some components can even talk to the server on their own: for example, an autocomplete component might fetch the autocompletion list from the server.

User interfaces

In a broad sense, a user interface[2] is everything that facilitates communication between computers and humans. Think of a punch card or a mouse: they're both UIs. When it comes to software, engineers talk about graphical user interfaces (GUIs), which were pioneered for early personal computers such as Macs and PCs. A GUI consists of menus, text, icons, pictures, borders, and other elements. Web elements are a narrow subset of the GUI: they reside in browsers, but there are also elements for desktop applications in Windows, OS X, and other operating systems.

Every time I mention a *UI* in this book, I mean a *web GUI*.

Component-based architecture (CBA)—not to be confused with web components, which are just one of the most recent implementations of CBA—existed before React. Such architectures generally tend to be easier to reuse, maintain, and extend than monolithic UIs. What React brings to the table is the use of pure JavaScript (without templates) and a new way to look at composing components.

1.2 The problem that React solves

What problem does React solve? Looking at the last few years of web development, note the problems in building and managing complex web UIs for front-end applications: React was born primarily to address those. Think of large web apps like Facebook: one of the most painful tasks when developing such applications is managing how the views change in response to data changes.

Let's refer to the official React website for more hints about the problem React addresses: "We built React to solve one problem: building large applications with data that changes over time."[3] Interesting! We can also look at the history of React for more information. A discussion on the React Podcast[4] mentions that the creator of

---

2 https://en.wikipedia.org/wiki/User_interface.
3 React official website, "Why React?" March 24, 2016, http://bit.ly/2mdCJKM.
4 *React Podcast*, "8. React, GraphQL, Immutable & Bow-Ties with Special Guest Lee Byron," December 31, 2015, http://mng.bz/W1X6.

React—Jordan Walke—was solving a problem at Facebook: having multiple data sources update an autocomplete field. The data came asynchronously from a back end. It was becoming more and more complicated to determine where to insert new rows in order to reuse DOM elements. Walke decided to generate the field representation (DOM elements) anew each time. This solution was elegant in its simplicity: UIs as functions. Call them with data, and you get rendered views predictably.

Later, it turned out that generating elements in memory is extremely fast and that the actual bottleneck is rendering in the DOM. But the React team came up with an algorithm that avoids unnecessary DOM pain. This made React very fast (and cheap in terms of performance). React's splendid performance and developer-friendly, component-based architecture are a winning combination. These and other benefits of React are described in the next section.

React solved Facebook's original problem, and many large firms agreed with this approach. React adoption is solid, and its popularity is growing every month. React emerged from Facebook[5] and is now used not only by Facebook but also by Instagram, PayPal, Uber, Sberbank, Asana,[6] Khan Academy,[7] HipChat,[8] Flipboard,[9] and Atom,[10] to name just a few.[11] Most of these applications originally used something else (typically, template engines with Angular or Backbone) but switched to React and are extremely happy about it.

1.3   Benefits of using React

Every new library or framework claims to be better than its predecessors in some respect. In the beginning, we had jQuery, and it was leaps and bounds better for writing cross-browser code in native JavaScript. If you remember, a single AJAX call taking many lines of code had to account for Internet Explorer and WebKit-like browsers. With jQuery, this takes only a single call: `$.ajax()`, for example. Back in the day, jQuery was called a framework—but not anymore! Now a *framework* is something bigger and more powerful.

Similarly with Backbone and then Angular, each new generation of JavaScript frameworks has brought something new to the table. React isn't unique in this. What *is* new is that React challenges some of the core concepts used by most popular front-end frameworks: for example, the idea that you need to have templates.

The following list highlights some of the benefits of React versus other libraries and frameworks:

[5]   "Introduction to React.js," July 8, 2013, http://mng.bz/86XF.

[6]   Malcolm Handley and Phips Peter, "Why Asana Is Switching to TypeScript," *Asana Blog*, November 14, 2014, http://mng.bz/zXKo.

[7]   Joel Burget, "Backbone to React," http://mng.bz/WGEQ.

[8]   Rich Manalang, "Rebuilding HipChat with React.js," *Atlassian Developers*, February 10, 2015, http://mng.bz/r0w6.

[9]   Michael Johnston, "60 FPS on the Mobile Web," *Flipboard*, February 10, 2015, http://mng.bz/N5F0.

[10] Nathan Sobo, "Moving Atom to React," *Atom*, July 2, 2014, http://mng.bz/K94N.

[11] See also the JavaScript usage stats at http://libscore.com/#React.

- *Simpler apps*—React has a CBA with pure JavaScript; a declarative style; and powerful, developer-friendly DOM abstractions (and not just DOM, but also iOS, Android, and so on).
- *Fast UIs*—React provides outstanding performance thanks to its virtual DOM and smart-reconciliation algorithm, which, as a side benefit, lets you perform testing without spinning up (starting) a headless browser.
- *Less code to write*—React's great community and vast ecosystem of components provide developers with a variety of libraries and components. This is important when you're considering what framework to use for development.

Many features make React simpler to work with than most other front-end frameworks. Let's unpack these items one by one, starting with its simplicity.

1.3.1 Simplicity

The concept of simplicity in computer science is highly valued by developers and users. It doesn't equate to ease of use. Something simple can be hard to implement, but in the end it will be more elegant and efficient. And often, an easy thing will end up being complex. Simplicity is closely related to the KISS principle (keep it simple, stupid).[12] The gist is that simpler systems work better.

React's approach allows for simpler solutions via a dramatically better web-development experience for software engineers. When I began working with React, it was a considerable shift in a positive direction that reminded me of switching from using plain, no-framework JavaScript to jQuery.

In React, this simplicity is achieved with the following features:

- *Declarative over imperative style*—React embraces declarative style over imperative by updating views automatically.
- *Component-based architecture using pure JavaScript*—React doesn't use domain-specific languages (DSLs) for its components, just pure JavaScript. And there's no separation when working on the same functionality.
- *Powerful abstractions*—React has a simplified way of interacting with the DOM, allowing you to normalize event handling and other interfaces that work similarly across browsers.

Let's cover these one by one.

DECLARATIVE OVER IMPERATIVE STYLE

First, React embraces declarative style over imperative. Declarative style means developers write how it *should* be, not what to do, step-by-step (imperative). But why is declarative style a better choice? The benefit is that declarative style reduces complexity and makes your code easier to read and understand.

Consider this short JavaScript example, which illustrates the difference between declarative and imperative programming. Let's say you need to create an array (arr2)

---

[12] https://en.wikipedia.org/wiki/KISS_principle.

whose elements are the result of doubling the elements of another array (arr). You can use a for loop to iterate over an array and tell the system to multiply by 2 and create a new element (arr2[i]=):

```
var arr = [1, 2, 3, 4, 5],
  arr2 = []
for (var i=0; i<arr.length; i++) {
  arr2[i] = arr[i]*2
}
console.log('a', arr2)
```

The result of this snippet, where each element is multiplied by 2, is printed on the console as follows:

```
a [2, 4, 6, 8, 10]
```

This illustrates imperative programming, and it works—until it doesn't work, due to the complexity of the code. It becomes too difficult to understand what the end result is supposed to be when you have too many imperative statements. Fortunately, you can rewrite the same logic in declarative style with map():

```
var arr = [1, 2, 3, 4, 5],
  arr2 = arr.map(function(v, i){ return v*2 })
console.log('b', arr2)
```

The output is b [2, 4, 6, 8, 10]; the variable arr2 is the same as in the previous example. Which code snippet is easier to read and understand? In my humble opinion, the declarative example.

Look at the following imperative code for getting a nested value of an object. The expression needs to return a value based on a string such as account or account.number in such a manner that these statements print true:

```
var profile = {account: '47574416'}
var profileDeep = {account: { number: 47574416 }}
console.log(getNestedValueImperatively(profile, 'account') === '47574416')
console.log(getNestedValueImperatively(profileDeep, 'account.number')
➥ === 47574416)
```

This imperative style literally tells the system what to do to get the results you need:

```
var getNestedValueImperatively = function getNestedValueImperatively
➥ (object, propertyName) {
  var currentObject = object
  var propertyNamesList = propertyName.split('.')
  var maxNestedLevel = propertyNamesList.length
  var currentNestedLevel

  for (currentNestedLevel = 0; currentNestedLevel < maxNestedLevel;
  ➥ currentNestedLevel++) {
```

```
    if (!currentObject || typeof currentObject === 'undefined')
    ➥ return undefined
    currentObject = currentObject[propertyNamesList[currentNestedLevel]]
  }

  return currentObject
}
```

Contrast this with declarative style (focused on the result), which reduces the number of local variables and thus simplifies the logic:

```
var getValue = function getValue(object, propertyName) {
  return typeof object === 'undefined' ? undefined : object[propertyName]
}

var getNestedValueDeclaratively = function getNestedValueDeclaratively(object,
➥ propertyName) {
  return propertyName.split('.').reduce(getValue, object)
}
console.log(getNestedValueDeclaratively({bar: 'baz'}, 'bar') === 'baz')
console.log(getNestedValueDeclaratively({bar: { baz: 1 }}, 'bar.baz')=== 1)
```

Most programmers have been trained to code imperatively, but usually the declarative code is simpler. In this example, having fewer variables and statements makes the declarative code easier to grasp at first glance.

That was just some JavaScript code. What about React? It takes the same declarative approach when you compose UIs. First, React developers describe UI elements in a declarative style. Then, when there are changes to views generated by those UI elements, React takes care of the updates. Yay!

The convenience of React's declarative style fully shines when you need to make changes to the view. Those are called changes of the *internal state*. When the state changes, React updates the view accordingly.

NOTE I cover how states work in chapter 4.

Under the hood, React uses a *virtual DOM* to find differences (the delta) between what's already in the browser and the new view. This process is called *DOM diffing* or *reconciliation of state and view* (bringing them back to similarity). This means developers don't need to worry about explicitly changing the view; all they need to do is update the state, and the view will be updated automatically as needed.

Conversely, with jQuery, you'd need to implement updates imperatively. By manipulating the DOM, developers can programmatically modify the web page or parts of the web page (a more likely scenario) without rerendering the entire page. DOM manipulation is what you do when you invoke jQuery methods.

Some frameworks, such as Angular, can perform automatic view updates. In Angular, it's called *two-way data binding*, which basically means views and models have two-way communication/syncing of data between them.

The jQuery and Angular approaches aren't great, for two reasons. Think about them as two extremes. At one extreme, the library (jQuery) isn't doing anything, and a developer (you!) needs to implement all the updates manually. At the other extreme, the framework (Angular) is doing everything.

The jQuery approach is prone to mistakes and takes more work to implement. Also, this approach of directly manipulating the regular DOM works fine with simple UIs, but it's limiting when you're dealing with a lot of elements in the DOM tree. This is the case because it's harder to see the results of imperative functions than declarative statements.

The Angular approach is difficult to reason about because with its two-way binding, things can spiral out of control quickly. You insert more and more logic, and all of a sudden, different views are updating models, and those models update other views.

Yes, the Angular approach is somewhat more readable than imperative jQuery (and requires less manual coding!), but there's another issue. Angular relies on templates and a DSL that uses ng directives (for example, ng-if). I discuss its drawbacks in the next section.

COMPONENT-BASED ARCHITECTURE USING PURE JAVASCRIPT

Component-based architecture[13] existed before React came on the scene. Separation of concerns, loose coupling, and code reuse are at the heart of this approach because it provides many benefits; software engineers, including web developers, love CBA. A building block of CBA in React is the component class. As with other CBAs, it has many benefits, with code reuse being the main one (you can write less code!).

What was lacking before React was a pure JavaScript implementation of this architecture. When you're working with Angular, Backbone, Ember, or most of the other MVC-like front-end frameworks, you have one file for JavaScript and another for the template. (Angular uses the term *directives* for components.) There are a few issues with having two languages (and two or more files) for a single component.

The HTML and JavaScript separation worked well when you had to render HTML on the server, and JavaScript was only used to make your text blink. Now, single page applications (SPAs) handle complex user input and perform rendering on the browser. This means HTML and JavaScript are closely coupled functionally. For developers, it makes more sense if they don't need to separate between HTML and JavaScript when working on a piece of a project (component).

Consider this Angular code, which displays different links based on the value of userSession:

```
<a ng-if="user.session" href="/logout">Logout</a>
<a ng-if="!user.session" href="/login">Login</a>
```

You can read it, but you may have doubts about what ng-if takes: a Boolean or a string. And will it hide the element or not render it at all? In the Angular case, you can't be sure whether the element will be hidden on true or false, unless you're familiar with how this particular ng-if directive works.

---

[13] http://mng.bz/a65r.

Compare the previous snippet with the following React code, which uses JavaScript `if/else` to implement conditional rendering. It's absolutely clear what the value of `user.session` must be and what element (`logout` or `login`) is rendered if the value is true. Why? Because it's just JavaScript:

```
if (user.session) return React.createElement('a', {href: '/logout'}, 'Logout')
else return React.createElement('a', {href: '/login'}, 'Login')
```

Templates are useful when you need to iterate over an array of data and print a property. We work with lists of data all the time! Let's look at a `for` loop in Angular. As mentioned earlier, in Angular, you need to use a DSL with directives. The directive for a `for` loop is `ng-repeat`:

```
<div ng-repeat="account in accounts">
  {{account.name}}
</div>
```

One of the problems with templates is that developers often have to learn yet another language. In React, you use pure JavaScript, which means you don't need to learn a new language! Here's an example of composing a UI for a list of account names with pure JavaScript:

Regular JavaScript method that takes an iterator expression as a parameter[14]

```
accounts.map(function(account)  {
  return React.createElement('div', null, account.name)
})
```

Iterator expression that returns a <div> with the account name

Imagine a situation where you're making some changes to the list of accounts. You need to display the account number and other fields. How do you know what fields the account has in addition to `name`?

You need to open the corresponding JavaScript file that calls and uses this template, and then you have to find `accounts` to see its properties. So the second problem with templates is that the logic about the data and the description of how that data should be rendered are separated.

It's much better to have the JavaScript and the markup in one place so you don't have to switch between file and languages. This is exactly how React works; and you'll see how React renders elements shortly in a Hello World example.

NOTE Separation of concerns generally is a good pattern. In a nutshell, it means separation of different functions such as the data service, the view layer, and so on. When you're working with template markup and corresponding JavaScript code, you're working on *one functionality*. That's why having two files (.js and .html) isn't a separation of concerns.

---

[14] http://mng.bz/555J.

Now, if you want to explicitly set the method by which to keep track of items (for example, to ensure there are no duplicates) in the rendered list, you can use Angular's track by feature:

```
<div ng-repeat="account in accounts track by account._id">
  {{account.name}}
</div>
```

If you want to track by an index of the array, there's $index:

```
<div ng-repeat="account in accounts track by $index">
  {{account.name}}
</div>
```

But what concerns me and many other developers is, what is this magic $index? In React, you use an argument from map() for the value of the key attribute:

Uses an array element value (account) and its index provided by Array.map()

```
accounts.map(function(account, index)   {
  return React.createElement('div', {key: index}, account.name)
})
```

Returns a React element <div/> with an attribute key with the value index and inner text set to account.name

It's worth noting that map() isn't exclusive to React. You can use it with other frameworks because it's part of the language. But the declarative nature of map() makes it and React a perfect pair.

I'm not picking on Angular—it's a great framework. But the bottom line is that if a framework uses a DSL, you need to learn its magic variables and methods. In React, you can use pure JavaScript.

If you use React, you can carry your knowledge to the next project even if it's not in React. On the other hand, if you use an X template engine (or a Y framework with a built-in DSL template engine), you're locked into that system and have to describe yourself as an X/Y developer. Your knowledge isn't transferable to projects that don't use X/Y. To summarize, the pure JavaScript component-based architecture is about using discrete, well-encapsulated, reusable components that ensure better separation of concerns based on functionality without the need for DSLs, templates, or directives.

Working with many developer teams, I've observed another factor related to simplicity. React has a better, shallower, more gradual learning curve compared to MVC frameworks (well, React isn't an MVC, so I'll stop comparing them) and template engines that have special syntax—for example, Angular directives or Jade/Pug. The reason is that instead of using the power of JavaScript, most template engines build abstractions with their own DSL, in a way reinventing things like an if condition or a for loop.

POWERFUL ABSTRACTIONS

React has a powerful abstraction of the document model. In other words, it hides the underlying interfaces and provides normalized/synthesized methods and properties. For example, when you create an `onClick` event in React, the event handler will receive not a native browser-specific event object, but a synthetic event object that's a wrapper around native event objects. You can expect the same behavior from synthetic events regardless of the browser in which you run the code. React also has a set of synthetic events for touch events, which are great for building web apps for mobile devices.

Another example of React's DOM abstraction is that you can render React elements on the server. This can be handy for better search engine optimization (SEO) and/or improving performance.

There are more options when it comes to rendering React components than just DOM or HTML strings for the server back end. We'll cover them in section 1.5.1. And, speaking of the DOM, one of the most sought-after benefits of React is its splendid performance.

1.3.2 Speed and testability

In addition to the necessary DOM updates, your framework may perform unnecessary updates, which makes the performance of complex UIs even worse. This becomes especially noticeable and painful for users when you have a lot of dynamic UI elements on your web page.

On the other hand, React's virtual DOM exists only in the JavaScript memory. Every time there's a data change, React first compares the differences using its virtual DOM; only when the library knows there has been a change in the rendering will it update the actual DOM. Figure 1.1 shows a high-level overview of how React's virtual DOM works when there are data changes.

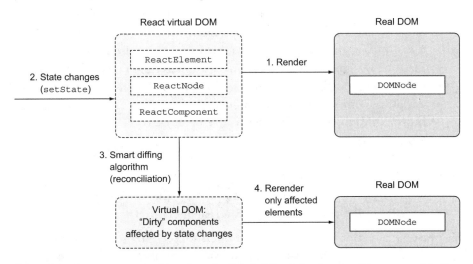

Figure 1.1 Once a component has been rendered, if its state changes, it's compared to the in-memory virtual DOM and rerendered if necessary.

Ultimately, React updates only those parts that are absolutely necessary so that the internal state (virtual DOM) and the view (real DOM) are the same. For example, if there's a `<p>` element and you augment the text via the state of the component, only the text will be updated (that is, `innerHTML`), not the element itself. This results in increased performance compared to rerendering entire sets of elements or, even more so, entire pages (server-side rendering).

> **NOTE** If you like to geek out on algorithms and Big Os, these two articles do a great job of explaining how the React team managed to turn an O(n3) problem into an O(n) one: "Reconciliation," on the React website (http://mng.bz/PQ9X) and "React's Diff Algorithm" by Christopher Chedeau (http://mng.bz/68L4).

The added benefit of the virtual DOM is that you can do unit testing without headless browsers like PhantomJS (http://phantomjs.org). There's a Jasmine (http://jasmine.github.io) layer called Jest (https://facebook.github.io/jest) that lets you test React components right on the command line!

1.3.3 *Ecosystem and community*

Last, but not least, React is supported by the developers of a juggernaut web application called Facebook, as well as by their peers at Instagram. As with Angular and some other libraries, having a big company behind the technology provides a sound testing ground (it's deployed to millions of browsers), reassurance about the future, and an increase in contribution velocity.

The React community is incredible. Most of the time, developers don't even have to implement much of the code. Look at these community resources:

- List of React components: https://github.com/brillout/awesome-react-components and http://devarchy.com/react-components
- Set of React components that implement the Google Material Design specification (https://design.google.com): http://react-toolbox.com
- Material Design React components: www.material-ui.com
- Collection of React components for Office and Office 360 experiences (http://dev.office.com/fabric#/components) using the Office Design Language: https://github.com/OfficeDev/office-ui-fabric-react
- Opinionated catalog of open source JS (mostly React) packages: https://js.coach
- Catalog of React components: https://react.rocks
- Khan Academy React components: https://khan.github.io/react-components
- Registry of React components: www.reactjsx.com

My personal anecdotal experience with open source taught me that the marketing of open source projects is as important to its wide adoption and success as the code itself. By that, I mean that if a project has a poor website, lacks documentation and examples, and has an ugly logo, most developers won't take it seriously—especially now, when there are so many JavaScript libraries. Developers are picky, and they won't use an ugly duckling library.

My teacher used to say, "Don't judge a book by its cover." This might sound controversial; but, sadly, most people, including software engineers, are prone to biases such as good branding. Luckily, React has a great engineering reputation backing it. And, speaking of book covers, I hope you didn't buy this book just for its cover!

1.4   Disadvantages of React

Of course, almost everything has its drawbacks. This is true with React, but the full list of cons depends on whom you ask. Some of the differences, like declarative versus imperative, are highly subjective. So, they can be both pros and cons. Here's my list of React disadvantages (as with any such list, it may be biased because it's based on opinions I've heard from other developers):

- React isn't a full-blown, Swiss Army knife–type of framework. Developers need to pair it with a library like Redux or React Router to achieve functionality comparable to Angular or Ember. This can also be an advantage if you need a minimalistic UI library to integrate with your existing stack.
- React isn't as mature as other frameworks. React's core API is still changing, albeit very little after the 0.14 release; the best practices for React (as well as the ecosystem of components, plug-ins, and add-ons) are still developing.
- React uses a somewhat new approach to web development, and JSX and Flux (often used with React as the data library) can be intimidating to beginners. There's a lack of best practices, good books, courses, and resources available for mastering React.
- React only has a one-way binding. Although one-way binding is better for complex apps and removes a lot of complexity, some developers (especially Angular developers) who got used to a two-way binding will find themselves writing a bit more code. I'll explain how React's one-way binding works compared to Angular's two-way binding in chapter 14, which covers working with data.
- React isn't reactive (as in reactive programming and architecture, which are more event-driven, resilient, and responsive) out of the box. Developers need to use other tools such as Reactive Extensions (RxJS, https://github.com/Reactive-Extensions/RxJS) to compose asynchronous data streams with Observables.

To continue with this introduction to React, let's look at how it fits into a web application.

1.5   How React can fit into your web applications

In a way, the React library by itself, without React Router or a data library, is less comparable to frameworks (like Backbone, Ember, and Angular) and more comparable to libraries for working with UIs, like template engines (Handlebars, Blaze) and DOM-manipulation libraries (jQuery, Zepto). In fact, many teams have swapped traditional template engines like Underscore in Backbone or Blaze in Meteor for React, with great success. For example, PayPal switched from Dust to Angular, as did many other companies listed earlier in this chapter.

You can use React for just part of your UI. For example, let's say you have a load-application form on a web page built with jQuery. You can gradually begin to convert this front-end app to React by first converting the city and state fields to populate automatically based on the ZIP code. The rest of the form can keep using jQuery. Then, if you want to proceed, you can convert the rest of the form elements from jQuery to React, until your entire page is built on React. Taking a similar approach, many teams successfully integrated React with Backbone, Angular, or other existing front-end frameworks.

React is back-end agnostic for the purposes of front-end development. In other words, you don't have to rely on a Node.js back end or MERN (MongoDB, Express.js, React.js, and Node.js) to use React. It's fine to use React with any other back-end technology like Java, Ruby, Go, or Python. React is a UI library, after all. You can integrate it with any back end and any front-end data library (Backbone, Angular, Meteor, and so on).

To summarize how React fits into a web app, it's most often used in these scenarios:

- As a UI library in React-related stack SPAs, such as React+React and Router+Redux
- As a UI library (*V* in MVC) in non-fully React-related stack SPAs, such as React+Backbone
- As a drop-in UI component in *any* front-end stack, such as a React autocomplete input component in a jQuery+server-side rendering stack
- As a server-side template library in a purely thick-server (traditional) web app or in a hybrid or isomorphic/universal web app, such as an Express server that uses `express-react-views`
- As a UI library in mobile apps, such as a React Native iOS app
- As a UI description library for different rendering targets (discussed in the next section)

React works nicely with other front-end technologies, but it's mostly used as part of single-page architecture because SPA seems to be the most advantageous and popular approach to building web apps. I cover how React fits into an SPA in section 1.5.2.

In some extreme scenarios, you can even use React *only on the server* as a template engine of sorts. For example, there's an `express-react-views` library (https://github.com/reactjs/express-react-views). It renders the view server-side from React components. This server-side rendering is possible because React lets you use different rendering targets.

1.5.1   *React libraries and rendering targets*

In versions 0.14 and higher, the React team split the library into two packages: React Core (`react` package on npm) and ReactDOM (`react-dom` package on npm). By doing so, the maintainers of React made it clear that React is on a path to become not just a library for the web, but a universal (sometimes called *isomorphic* because it can be used in different environments) library for describing UIs.

For example, in version 0.13, React had a `React.render()` method to mount an element to a web page's DOM node. In versions 0.14 and higher, you need to include `react-dom` and call `ReactDOM.render()` instead of `React.render()`.

Having multiple packages created by the community to support various rendering targets made this approach of separating writing components and rendering logical. Some of these modules are as follows:

- Renderer for the blessed (https://github.com/chjj/blessed) terminal interface: http://github.com/Yomguithereal/react-blessed
- Renderer for the ART library (https://github.com/sebmarkbage/art): https://github.com/reactjs/react-art
- Renderer for <canvas>: https://github.com/Flipboard/react-canvas
- Renderer for the 3D library using three.js (http://threejs.org): https://github.com/Izzimach/react-three
- Renderer for virtual reality and interactive 360 experiences: https://facebook.github.io/react-vr

In addition to the support of these libraries, the separation of React Core from React-DOM makes it easier to share code between React and React Native libraries (used for native mobile iOS and Android development). In essence, when using React for web development, you'll need to include at least React Core and ReactDOM.

Moreover, there are additional React utility libraries in React and npm. (Before React v15.5, some of them were part of React as React *add-ons*.[15] These utility libraries allow you to enhance functionality, work with immutable data (https://github.com/kolodny/immutability-helper), and perform testing.

Finally, React is almost always used with JSX—a tiny language that lets developers write React UIs more eloquently. You can transpile JSX into regular JavaScript by using Babel or a similar tool.

As you can see, there's a lot of modularity—the functionality of React-related things is split into different packages. This gives you power and choice, which is a good thing. No monolith or opinionated library dictates to you the only possible way to implement things. More on this in section 1.5.3.

If you're a web developer reading this book, you probably use SPA architecture. Either you already have a web app built using this and want to reengineer it with React (brownfield), or you're starting a new project from scratch (greenfield). Next, we'll zoom in on React's place in SPAs as the most popular approach to building web apps.

---

[15] See the version 15.5 change log with the list of add-ons and npm libraries: https://facebook.github.io/react/blog/2017/04/07/react-v15.5.0.html. See also the page on add-ons: https://facebook.github.io/react/docs/addons.html.

1.5.2 Single-page applications and React

Another name for SPA architecture is *thick client*, because the browser, being a client, holds more logic and performs functions such as rendering of the HTML, validation, UI changes, and so on. Figure 1.2 is basic: it shows a bird's-eye view of a typical SPA architecture with a user, a browser, and a server. The figure depicts a user making a request, and input actions like clicking a button, drag-and-drop, mouse hovering, and so on:

1 The user types a URL in the browser to open a new page.
2 The browser sends a URL request to the server.
3 The server responds with static assets such as HTML, CSS, and JavaScript. In most cases, the HTML is bare-bones—that is, it has only a skeleton of the web page. Usually there's a "Loading ..." message and/or rotating spinner GIF.
4 The static assets include the JavaScript code for the SPA. When loaded, this code makes additional requests for data (AJAX/XHR requests).
5 The data comes back in JSON, XML, or any other format.
6 Once the SPA receives the data, it can render missing HTML (the User Interface block in the figure). In other words, UI rendering happens on the browser by means of the SPA hydrating templates with data.[16]
7 Once the browser rendering is finished, the SPA replaces the "Loading ..." message, and the user can work with the page.
8 The user sees a beautiful web page. The user may interact with the page (Inputs in the figure), triggering new requests from the SPA to the server, and the cycle of steps 2–6 continues. At this stage, browser routing may happen if the SPA implements it, meaning navigation to a new URL will trigger not a new page reload from the server, but rather an SPA rerender in the browser.

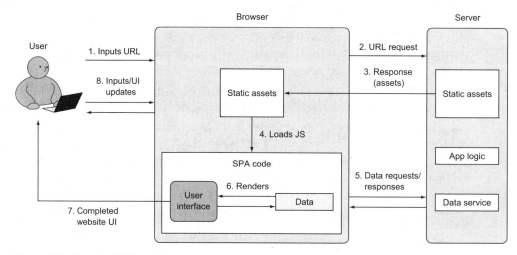

Figure 1.2   A typical SPA architecture

---

[16] "What does it mean to hydrate an object?" *Stack Overflow*, http://mng.bz/uP25.

To summarize, in the SPA approach, most rendering for UIs happens on the browser. Only data travels to and from the browser. Contrast that with a thick-server approach, where all the rendering happens on the server. (Here I mean *rendering* as in generating HTML from templates or UI code, not as in rendering that HTML in the browser, which is sometimes called *painting* or *drawing* the DOM.)

Note that the MVC-like architecture is the most popular approach, but it isn't the only one. React doesn't require you to use an MVC-like architecture; but, for the sake of simplicity, let's assume that your SPA is using an MVC-like architecture. You can see its possible distinct parts in figure 1.3. A navigator or routing library acts as a controller of sorts in the MVC paradigm; it dictates what data to fetch and what template to use. The navigator/controller makes a request to get data and then hydrates/populates the templates (views) with this data to render the UI in the form of the HTML. The UI sends actions back to the SPA code: clicks, mouse hovers, keystrokes, and so on.

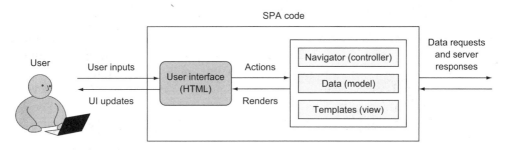

Figure 1.3   Inside a single-page application

In an SPA architecture, data is interpreted and processed in the browser (browser rendering) and is used by the SPA to render additional HTML or to change existing HTML. This makes for nice interactive web applications that rival desktop apps. Angular.js, Backbone.js, and Ember.js are examples of front-end frameworks for building SPAs.

> **NOTE** Different frameworks implement navigators, data, and templates differently, so figure 1.3 isn't applicable to all frameworks. Rather, it illustrates the most widespread separation of concerns in a typical SPA.

React's place in the SPA diagram in figure 1.3 is in the Templates block. React is a view layer, so you can use it to render HTML by providing it with data. Of course, React does much more than a typical template engine. The difference between React and other template engines like Underscore, Handlebars, and Mustache is in the way you develop UIs, update them, and manage their states. We'll talk about states in chapter 4 in more detail. For now, think of states as data that can change and that's related to the UI.

1.5.3   *The React stack*

React isn't a full-blown, front-end JavaScript framework. React is minimalistic. It doesn't enforce a particular way of doing things like data modeling, styling, or routing (it's non-opinionated). Because of that, developers need to pair React with a routing and/or modeling library.

For example, a project that already uses Backbone.js and the Underscore.js template engine can switch to Underscore for React and keep existing data models and routing from Backbone. (Underscore also has utilities, not just template methods. You can use these Underscore utilities with React as a solution for a clear declarative style.) Other times, developers opt to use the *React stack*, which consists of data and routing libraries created to be used specifically with React:

- *Data-model libraries and back ends*—RefluxJS (https://github.com/reflux/refluxjs), Redux (http://redux.js.org), Meteor (https://www.meteor.com), and Flux (https://github.com/facebook/flux)
- *Routing library*—React Router (https://github.com/reactjs/react-router)
- *Collection of React components to consume the Twitter Bootstrap library*—React-Bootstrap (https://react-bootstrap.github.io)

The ecosystem of libraries for React is growing every day. Also, React's ability to describe composable components (self-contained chunks of the UI) is helpful in reusing code. There are many components packaged as npm modules. Just to illustrate the point that having small composable components is good for code reuse, here are some popular React components:

- Datepicker component: https://github.com/Hacker0x01/react-datepicker
- Set of tools to handle form rendering and validation: https://github.com/prometheusresearch/react-forms
- WAI-ARIA-compliant autocomplete (combo box) component: https://github.com/reactjs/react-autocomplete

Then there's JSX, which is probably the most frequent argument for not using React. If you're familiar with Angular, then you've already had to write a lot of JavaScript in your template code. This is because in modern web development, plain HTML is too static and is hardly any use by itself. My advice: give React the benefit of the doubt, and give JSX a fair run.

JSX is a little syntax for writing React objects in JavaScript using <> as in XML/HTML. React pairs nicely with JSX because developers can better implement and read the code. Think of JSX as a mini-language that's compiled into native JavaScript. So, JSX isn't run on the browser but is used as the source code for compilation. Here's a compact snippet written in JSX:

```
if (user.session)
  return <a href="/logout">Logout</a>
else
  return <a href="/login">Login</a>
```

Even if you load a JSX file in your browser with the runtime transformer library that compiles JSX into native JavaScript on the run, you still don't run the JSX; you run

JavaScript instead. In this sense, JSX is akin to CoffeeScript. You compile these languages into native JavaScript to get better syntax and features than that provided by regular JavaScript.

I know that to some of you, it looks bizarre to have XML interspersed with JavaScript code. It took me a while to adjust, because I was expecting an avalanche of syntax error messages. And yes, using JSX is optional. For these two reasons, I'm not covering JSX until chapter 3; but trust me, it's powerful once you get a handle on it.

By now, you have an understanding of what React is, its stack, and its place in the higher-level SPA. It's time to get your hands dirty and write your first React code.

1.6   *Your first React code: Hello World*

Let's explore your first React code—the quintessential example used for learning programming languages—the Hello World application. (If we don't do this, the gods of programming might punish us!) You won't be using JSX yet, just plain JavaScript. The project will print a "Hello world!!!" heading (`<h1>`) on a web page. Figure 1.4 shows how it will look when you're finished (unless you're not quite that enthusiastic and prefer a single exclamation point).

Figure 1.4   Hello World

Learning React first without JSX

Although most React developers write in JSX, browsers will only run standard JavaScript. That's why it's beneficial to be able to understand React code in pure JavaScript. Another reason we're starting with plain JS is to show that JSX is optional, albeit the de facto standard language for React. Finally, preprocessing JSX requires some tooling.

I want to get you started with React as soon as possible without spending too much time on setup in this chapter. You'll perform all the necessary setup for JSX in chapter 3.

The folder structure of the project is simple. It consists of two JavaScript files in the js folder and one HTML file, index.html:

```
/hello-world
  /js
    react.js
    react-dom.js
  index.html
```

The two files in the js folder are for the React library version 15.5.4:[17] react-dom.js (web browser DOM renderer) and react.js (React Core package). First, you need to download the aforementioned React Core and ReactDOM libraries. There are many ways to do it. I recommend using the files provided in the source code for this book, which you can find at www.manning.com/books/react-quickly and https://github.com/azat-co/react-quickly/tree/master/ch01/hello-world. This is the most reliable and easiest approach, because it doesn't require a dependency on any other service or tool. You can find more ways to download React in appendix A.

> **WARNING** Prior to version 0.14, these two libraries were bundled together. For example, for version 0.13.3, all you needed was react.js. This book uses React and React DOM version 15.5.4 (the latest as of this writing) unless noted otherwise. For most of the projects in part 1, you'll need two files: react.js and react-com.js. In chapter 8, you'll need prop-types (www.npmjs.com/package/prop-types), which was part of React until version 15.5.4 but is now a separate module.

After you place the React files in the js folder, create the index.html file in the hello-world project folder. This HTML file will be the entry point of the Hello World application (meaning you'll need to open it in the browser).

The code for index.html is simple and starts with the inclusion of the libraries in <head>. In the <body> element, you create a <div> container with the ID content and a <script> element (that's where the app's code will go later), as shown in the following listing.

Listing 1.1   Loading React libraries and code (index.html)

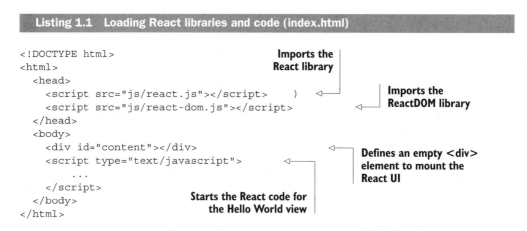

Why not render the React element directly in the <body> element? Because doing so can lead to conflict with other libraries and browser extensions that manipulate the

---

[17] v15.5.4 is the latest as of this writing. Typically, major releases like 14, 15, and 16 incorporate significant differences, whereas minor releases like 15.5.3 and 15.5.4 have fewer breaking changes and conflicts. The code for this book was tested for v15.5.4. The code may work with future versions, but I can't guarantee that it will work because no one knows what will be in the future versions—not even the core contributors.

document body. In fact, if you try attaching an element directly to the body, you'll get this warning:

```
Rendering components directly into document.body is discouraged...
```

This is another good thing about React: it has great warning and error messages!

> **NOTE** React warning and error messages aren't part of the production build, in order to reduce noise, increase security, and minimize the distribution size. The production build is the minified file from the React Core library: for example, react.min.js. The development version with the warnings and error messages is the unminified version: for example, react.js.

By including the libraries in the HTML file, you get access to the React and ReactDOM global objects: `window.React` and `window.ReactDOM`. You'll need two methods from those objects: one to create an element (React) and another to render it in the `<div>` container (ReactDOM), as shown in listing 1.2.

To create a React element, all you need to do is call `React.createElement(element-Name, data, child)` with three arguments that have the following meanings:

- `elementName`—HTML as a string (for example, `'h1'`) or a custom component class as an object (for example, `HelloWorld`; see section 2.2)
- `data`—Data in the form of attributes and properties (we'll cover properties later); for example, `null` or `{name: 'Azat'}`
- `child`—Child element or inner HTML/text content; for example, `Hello world!`

Listing 1.2 Creating and rendering an `h1` element (index.html)

```
var h1 = React.createElement('h1', null, 'Hello world!')     ◁─┐  Creates and saves in a
ReactDOM.render(                              ◁──────────────┐ │  variable a React element
  h1,                                                        │ │  of h1 type
  document.getElementById('content')                         │
)

                                            Renders the h1 element in the real
                                            DOM element with ID "content"
```

This listing gets a React element of the h1 type and stores the reference to this object into the h1 variable. The h1 variable isn't an actual DOM node; rather, it's an instantiation of the React h1 component (element). You can name it any way you want: `helloWorldHeading`, for example. In other words, React provides an abstraction over the DOM.

> **NOTE** The h1 variable name is arbitrary. You can name this variable anything you want (such as `bananza`), as long as you use the same variable in `React-DOM.render()`.

Once the element is created and stored in h1, you render it to the DOM node/element with ID content using the ReactDOM.render() method shown in listing 1.2. If you prefer, you can move the h1 variable to the render call. The result is the same, except you don't use an extra variable:

```
ReactDOM.render(
  React.createElement('h1', null, 'Hello world!'),
  document.getElementById('content')
)
```

Now, open the index.html file served by a static HTTP web server in your favorite browser. I recommend using an up-to-date version of Chrome, Safari, or Firefox. You should see the "Hello world!" message on the web page, as shown in figure 1.5.

This figure shows the Elements tab in Chrome DevTools with the <h1> element selected. You can observe the data-reactroot attribute; it indicates that this element was rendered by ReactDOM.

One quick note: you can abstract the React code (listing 1.2) into a separate file instead of creating elements and rendering them with ReactDOM.render() all in the index.html file (listing 1.1). For example, you can create script.js and copy and paste the h1 element and ReactDOM.render() call into that file. Then, in index.html, you need to include script.js after the <div> with ID content, like this:

```
<div id="content"></div>
<script src="script.js"></script>
```

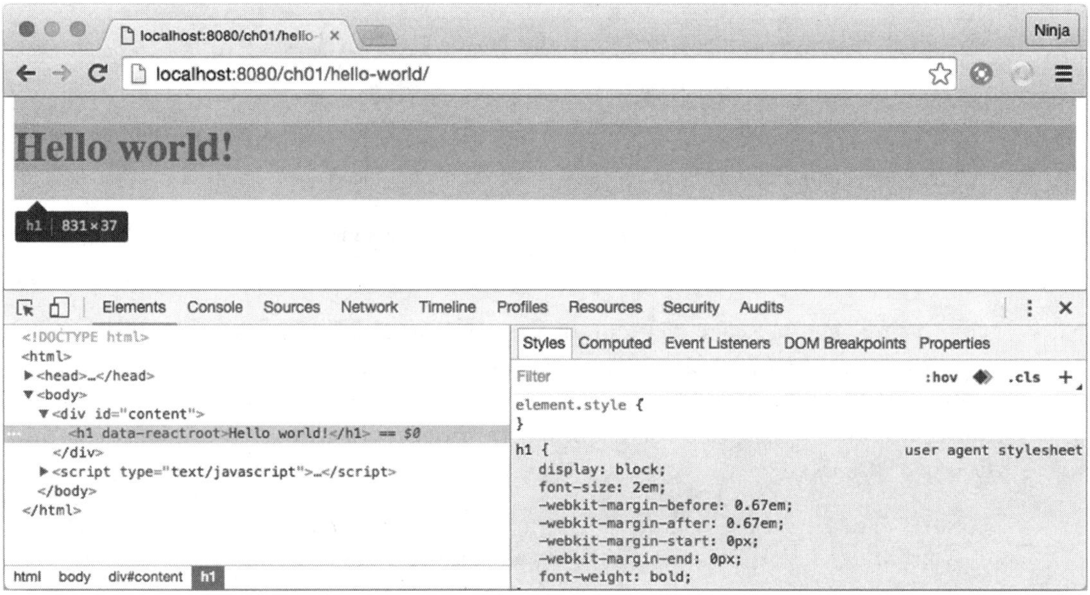

Figure 1.5   Inspecting the Hello World app as rendered by React

> **Local dev web server**
>
> It's better to use a local web server instead of opening an index.html file in the browser directly, because with a web server, your JavaScript apps will be able to make AJAX/XHR requests. You can tell whether it's a server or a file by looking at the URL in the address bar. If the address starts with *file*, then it's a file; and if the address starts with *http*, then it's a server. You'll need this feature for future projects. Typically, a local HTTP web server listens to incoming requests on 127.0.0.1 or localhost.
>
> You can get any open source web server, such as Apache, MAMP, or (my favorites because they're written in Node.js) node-static (https://github.com/cloud-head/node-static) or http-server (www.npmjs.com/package/http-server). To install node-static or http-server, you must have Node.js and npm installed. If you don't have them, you can find installation instructions for Node and npm in appendix A or by going to http://nodejs.org.
>
> Assuming you have Node.js and npm on your machine, run `npm i -g node-static` or `npm i -g http-server` in your terminal or command prompt. Then, navigate to the folder with the source code, and run `static` or `http-server`. In my case, I'm launching `static` from the react-quickly folder, so I need to put the path to Hello World in my browser URL bar: http://localhost:8080/ch01/hello-world/ (see figure 1.5).

Congratulations! You've just implemented your first React code!

1.7 *Quiz*

1 The declarative style of programming doesn't allow for mutation of stored values. It's "this is what I want" versus the imperative style's "this is how to do it." True or false?

2 React components are rendered into the DOM with which of the following methods? (Beware, it's a tricky question!) `ReactDOM.renderComponent`, `React.render`, `ReactDOM.append`, or `ReactDOM.render`

3 You have to use Node.js on the server to be able to use React in your SPA. True or false?

4 You must include react-com.js in order to render React elements on a web page. True or false?

5 The problem React solves is that of updating views based on data changes. True or false?

1.8 *Summary*

- React is declarative; it's only a view or UI layer.
- React uses components that you bring into existence with `ReactDOM.render()`.
- React component classes are created with `class` and its mandatory `render()` method.
- React components are reusable and take immutable properties that are accessible via `this.props.NAME`.

- You use pure JavaScript to develop and compose UIs in React.
- You don't need to use JSX (an XML-like syntax for React objects); JSX is optional when developing with React!
- To summarize the definition of React: React for the web consists of the React Core and ReactDOM libraries. React Core is a library geared toward building and sharing composable UI components using JavaScript and (optionally) JSX in an isomorphic/universal manner. On the other hand, to work with React in the browser, you can use the ReactDOM library, which has methods for DOM rendering as well as for server-side rendering.

1.9   *Quiz answers*

5 True. This is the primary problem that React solves.

4 True. You need the ReactDOM library.

3 False. You can use any back-end technology.

2 ReactDOM.render.

1 True. Declarative is a "what I want" style, and imperative is a "this is how to do it" style.

Watch this chapter's introduction video by scanning this QR code with your phone or going to http://reactquickly.co/videos/ch02.

Baby steps with React

2

This chapter covers

- Nesting elements
- Creating a component class
- Working with properties

This chapter will teach you how to take baby steps with React and lays the foundation for the following chapters. It's crucial for understanding React concepts such as elements and components. In a nutshell, *elements* are instances of *components* (also called *component classes*). What are their use cases, and why do you use them? Read on!

> **NOTE** The source code for the examples in this chapter is at www.manning .com/books/react-quickly and https://github.com/azat-co/react-quickly/ tree/master/ch02 (in the ch02 folder of the GitHub repository https://github.com/azat-co/react-quickly). You can also find some demos at http://reactquickly.co/demos.

2.1 Nesting elements

In the last chapter, you learned how to create a React element. As a reminder, the method you use is `React.createElement()`. For example, you can create a link element like this:

```
let linkReactElement = React.createElement('a',
  {href: 'http://webapplog.com'},
  'Webapplog.com'
)
```

The problem is that most UIs have more than one element (such as a link inside a menu). For example, in figure 2.1, there are buttons in the section, video thumbnails, and a YouTube player.

The solution to creating more-complex structures in a hierarchical manner is nesting elements. In the previous chapter, you implemented your first React code by creating an h1 React element and rendering it in the DOM with ReactDOM.render():

```
let h1 = React.createElement('h1', null, 'Hello world!')
ReactDOM.render(
  h1,
  document.getElementById('content')
)
```

It's important to note that ReactDOM.render() takes only one element as an argument, which is h1 in the example (the view is shown in figure 2.2).

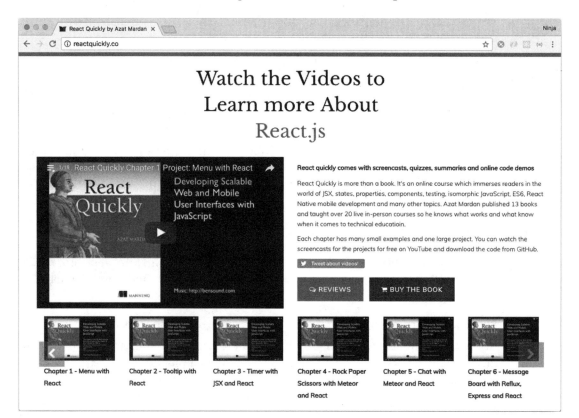

Figure 2.1   The *React Quickly* website has many nested UI elements.

Figure 2.2   Rendering a single heading element

As I mentioned at the beginning of this section, the problem arises when you need to render two same-level elements (for example, two h1 elements). In this case, you can wrap the elements in a visually neutral element, as shown in figure 2.3. The <div> container is usually a good choice, as is <span>.

You can pass an unlimited number of parameters to createElement(). All the parameters after the second one become child elements. Those child elements (h1, in this case) are siblings—that is, they're on the same level relative to each other, as you can see in figure 2.4, which shows Dev-Tools open in Chrome.

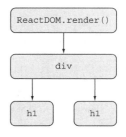

Figure 2.3   Structuring a React render by using a wrapper <div> container to render sibling headings

Figure 2.4   React DevTools shows a <div> wrapper for nested sibling h1 elements.

React Developer Tools

In addition to the Elements tab, which is included by default in Chrome DevTools, you can install an extension (or plug-in) called React Developer Tools. It's the last tab in figure 2.4. React Developer Tools is available for Firefox as well. It lets you inspect the results of React rendering closely, including the component's hierarchy, name, properties, states, and more.

Here's the GitHub repository: https://github.com/facebook/react-devtools. You can also find React Developer Tools for Chrome at http://mng.bz/V276 and for Firefox at http://mng.bz/59V9.

Knowing this, let's use `createElement()` to create the `<div>` element with two `<h1>` child elements (ch02/hello-world-nested/index.html).

Listing 2.1 Creating a `<div>` element with two `<h1>` children

```
let h1 = React.createElement('h1', null, 'Hello world!')
ReactDOM.render(
  React.createElement('div', null, h1, h1),
  document.getElementById('content')
)
```

If the third parameter of createElement() is a string, it specifies the text value of the element being created.

If the third and subsequent parameters aren't text, they specify the child elements of the element being created.

The HTML code can stay the same as in the Hello World example from chapter 1, as long as you include the necessary React and ReactDOM libraries and have the content node (ch02/hello-world-nested/index.html).

Listing 2.2 HTML for the nested elements example without the React code

```
<!DOCTYPE html>
<html>
  <head>
    <script src="js/react.js"></script>
    <script src="js/react-dom.js"></script>
  </head>
  <body>
    <div id="content"></div>
    <script type="text/javascript">
    ...
    </script>
  </body>
</html>
```

So far, you've only provided string values as the first parameter of `createElement()`. But the first parameter can have two types of input:

- Standard HTML tag as a string; for example, `'h1'`, `'div'`, or `'p'` (without the angle brackets). The name is lowercase.
- React component classes as an object; for example, `HelloWorld`. The name is capitalized.

The first approach renders standard HTML elements. React goes through its list of standard HTML elements and, when and if it finds a match, uses it as a type for the React element. For example, when you pass `'p'`, React will find a match because p is a paragraph tag name. This will produce <p> in the DOM when/if you render this React element.

Now let's look at the second type of input: creating and providing custom component classes.

2.2 *Creating component classes*

After nesting elements with React, you'll stumble across the next problem: soon, there are a lot of elements. You need to use the component-based architecture described in chapter 1, which lets you reuse code by separating the functionality into loosely coupled parts. Meet *component classes*, or just *components*, as they're often called for brevity (not to be confused with web components).

Think of standard HTML tags as building blocks. You can use them to compose your own React component classes, which you can use to create custom elements (instances of classes). By using custom elements, you can encapsulate and abstract logic in portable classes (composable reusable components). This abstraction allows teams to reuse UIs in large, complex applications as well as in different projects. Examples include autocomplete components, toolboxes, menus, and so on.

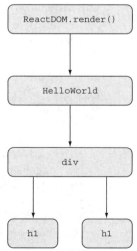

Creating the `'Hello world!'` element with an HTML tag in the `createElement()` method was straightforward: `(createElement('h1', null, 'Hello World!')`. But what if you need to separate Hello World into its own class, as shown in figure 2.5? Let's say you need to reuse Hello World in 10 different projects! (You probably wouldn't use it that many times, but a good autocomplete component will definitely be reused.)

Interestingly, you create a React component class by extending the `React.Component` class with `class CHILD extends PARENT` ES6 syntax. Let's create a custom `Hello-World` component class using `class HelloWorld extends React.Component`.

The one mandatory thing you must implement for this new class is the `render()` method. This method *must* return a single React element, `createElement()`, which is created from another custom component class or an HTML tag. Both can have nested elements.

Figure 2.5 Rendering a <div> element created from a custom component class instead of rendering it directly

Listing 2.3 (ch02/hello-world-class/js/script.js) shows how you can refactor the nested Hello World example (listing 2.1) into an app with a custom React component class, `HelloWorld`. The benefit is that with a custom class, you can reuse this UI better. The mandatory `render()` method of the `HelloWorld` component returns the same `<div>` element from the previous example. Once you've created the custom `HelloWorld` class, you can pass it as an object (not as a string) to `ReactDOM.render()`.

Listing 2.3   Creating and rendering a React component class

Creates a render() method as an expression (function returning a single element)

Defines a React component class with the capitalized name

```
let h1 = React.createElement('h1', null, 'Hello world!')
class HelloWorld extends React.Component {
  render() {
    return React.createElement('div', null, h1, h1)
  }
}
ReactDOM.render(
  React.createElement(HelloWorld, null),
  document.getElementById('content')
)
```

Attaches the React element to the real DOM element with ID "content"

Implements a return statement with a single React element so the React class can invoke render() and receive the `<div>` element with two h1 elements

Uses the HelloWorld class to create an element by passing the object, instead of a string, as the first argument

---

By convention, the names of variables containing React components are capitalized. This isn't required in regular JS (you can use the lowercase variable name `helloWorld`); but because it's necessary in JSX, you apply this convention here. (In JSX, React uses uppercase and lowercase to differentiate a custom component like `<HelloWorld/>` from a regular HTML element such as `<h1/>`. But in regular JS, it's differentiated by passing either a variable such as `HelloWorld` or a string such as `'h1'`. It's a good idea to start using capitalization convention for custom components now.) More about JSX in chapter 3.

ES6+/ES2015+ and React

The component class example defines `render()` using ES6 style, in which you omit the colon and the word `function`. It's exactly the same as defining an attribute (a.k.a. key or object property) with a value that's a function: that is, typing `render: function()`. My personal preference, and my recommendation to you, is to use the ES6 method style because it's shorter (the less you type, the fewer mistakes you make).

Historically, React had its own method to create a component class: `React.createClass()`. There are slight differences between using the ES6 class to extend `React.Component` and using `React.createClass()`. Typically, you'd use either `class` (recommended) or `createClass()`, but not both. Moreover, in React 15.5.4, `createClass()` is deprecated (that is, no longer supported).

Analogous to `ReactDOM.render()`, the `render()` method in `createClass()` can *only return a single element*. If you need to return multiple same-level elements, wrap them in a `<div>` container or another unobtrusive element such as `<span>`. You can run the code in your browser; the result is shown in figure 2.6.

Figure 2.6 Rendering an element created from a custom `HelloWorld` component class

You may think you didn't gain much with the refactoring; but what if you need to print more Hello World statements? You can do so by reusing the `HelloWorld` component multiple times and wrapping them in a `<div>` container:

```
...
ReactDOM.render(
  React.createElement(
    'div',
    null,
    React.createElement(HelloWorld),
    React.createElement(HelloWorld),
```

---

[1] ECMAScript 6 Compatibility Table, https://kangax.github.io/compat-table/es6.

```
      React.createElement(HelloWorld)
    ),
    document.getElementById('content')
)
```

This is the power of component reusability! It leads to faster development and fewer bugs. Components also have lifecycle events, states, DOM events, and other features that let you make them interactive and self-contained; these are covered in the following chapters.

Right now, the HelloWorld elements will all be the same. Is there a way to customize them? What if you could set element attributes and modify their content and/or behavior? Meet properties.

2.3   *Working with properties*

Properties are a cornerstone of the declarative style that React uses. Think of properties as unchangeable values within an element. They allow elements to have different variations if used in a view, such as changing a link URL by passing a new value for a property:

```
React.createElement('a', {href: 'http://node.university'})
```

One thing to remember is that properties are *immutable within their components*. A parent assigns properties to its children upon their creation. The child element isn't supposed to modify its properties. (A *child* is an element nested inside another element; for example, <h1/> is a child of <HelloWorld/>.) For instance, you can pass a property PROPERTY_NAME with the value VALUE, like this:

```
<TAG_NAME PROPERTY_NAME=VALUE/>
```

Properties closely resemble HTML attributes. This is one of their purposes, but they also have another: you can use the properties of an element in your code as you wish. Properties can be used as follows:

- To render standard HTML attributes of an element: href, title, style, class, and so on
- In the JavaScript code of a React component class via this.props values; for example, this.props.PROPERTY_NAME (replacing PROPERTY_NAME with your arbitrary name)

Under the hood, React will match the property name (PROPERTY_NAME) with the list of standard attributes. If there's a match, the property will be rendered as an attribute of an element (the first scenario). The value of this attribute is also accessible in this.props.PROPERTY_NAME in the component class code.

If there's no match with any of the standard HTML attribute names (the second scenario), then the property name isn't a standard attribute. It won't be rendered as an attribute of an element. But the value will still be accessible in the this.props object; for example, this.props.PROPERTY_NAME. It can be used in your code or rendered explicitly in the render() method. This way, you can pass different data to

> **Object.freeze() and Object.isFrozen()**
>
> Internally, React uses `Object.freeze()`[2] from the ES5 standard to make the `this.props` object immutable. To check whether an object is frozen, you can use the `Object.isFrozen()` method.[3] For example, you can determine whether this statement will return `true`:
>
> ```
> class HelloWorld extends React.Component {
>   render() {
>     console.log(Object.isFrozen(this.props))
>     return React.createElement('div', null, h1, h1)
>   }
> }
> ```
>
> If you're interested in more details, I encourage you to read the React changelog[4] and search on React's GitHub repository.[5]

different instances of the same class. This allows you to reuse components, because you can programmatically change how elements are rendered by providing different properties.

You can even take this feature of properties a step further and completely modify the rendered elements based on the value of a property. For example, if `this.props.heading` is true, you render "Hello" as a heading. If it's false, you render "Hello" as a normal paragraph:

```
render() {
  if (this.props.heading) return <h1>Hello</h1>
  else return <p>Hello</p>
}
```

In other words, you can use the same component—but provided with different properties, the elements rendered by the component can be different. Properties can be rendered by `render()`, used in components' code, or used as HTML attributes.

To demonstrate the properties of components, let's slightly modify `HelloWorld` with props. The goal is to reuse the `HelloWorld` component such that each instance of this class renders different text and different HTML attributes. You'll enhance the `HelloWorld` headings (`<h1>` tag) with three properties (see figure 2.7):

- `id`—Matches the standard attribute `id` and is automatically rendered by React
- `frameworkName`—Doesn't match any standard attributes for `<h1>`, but is explicitly printed in the text of headings
- `title`—Matches the standard attribute `title` and is automatically rendered by React

---

[2] Mozilla Developer Network, Object.freeze(), http://mng.bz/p6Nr.
[3] Mozilla Developer Network, Object.isFrozen(), http://mng.bz/0P75.
[4] GitHub, 2016-04-07-react-v15, http://mng.bz/j6c3.
[5] GitHub, "freeze" search results, http://mng.bz/2l0Z.

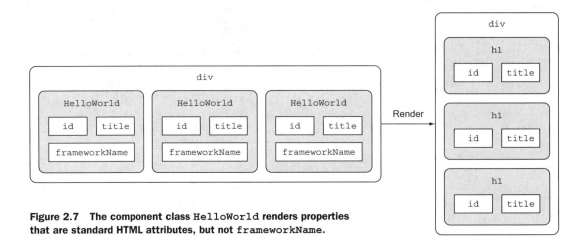

Figure 2.7   The component class `HelloWorld` renders properties that are standard HTML attributes, but not `frameworkName`.

If a property's name matches a standard HTML attribute, it will be rendered as an attribute of the `<h1>` element, as shown in figure 2.7. So the two properties `id` and `title` will be rendered as `<h1>` attributes, but not `frameworkName`. You may even get a warning about the unknown `frameworkName` property (because it's not in the HTML specification). How nice!

Let's zoom in on the `<div>` element implementation (figure 2.8). Obviously, it needs to render three child elements of the `HelloWorld` class, but the text and attributes of the resulting headings (`<h1/>`) must be different. For example, you pass `id`, `frameworkName`, and `title`. They'll be part of the `HelloWorld` class.

Before you implement `<h1/>`, you need to pass the properties to `HelloWorld`. How do you do this? By passing these properties in an object literal in the second argument to `createElement()` when you create `HelloWorld` elements in the `<div>` container:

```
ReactDOM.render(
  React.createElement(
    'div',
    null,
    React.createElement(HelloWorld, {
      id: 'ember',
      frameworkName: 'Ember.js',
      title: 'A framework for creating ambitious web applications.'}),
    React.createElement(HelloWorld, {
      id: 'backbone',
      frameworkName: 'Backbone.js',
      title: 'Backbone.js gives structure to web applications...'}),
    React.createElement(HelloWorld, {
      id: 'angular',
      frameworkName: 'Angular.js',
      title: 'Superheroic JavaScript MVW Framework'})
  ),
  document.getElementById('content')
)
```

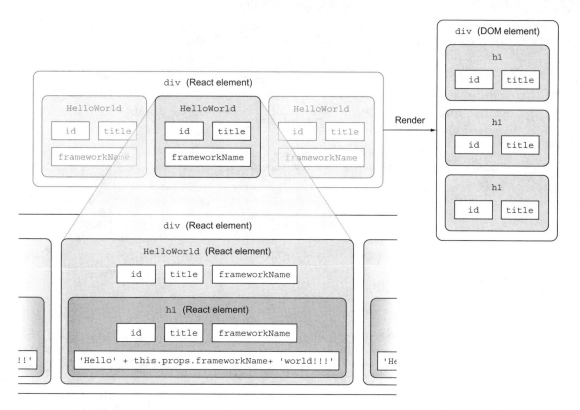

Figure 2.8 The HelloWorld **class is used three times to generate three** h1 **elements that have different attributes and** innerHTML.

Now let's look at the HelloWorld component implementation. The way React works is that the second parameter to createElement() (for example, {id: 'ember'...}) is an object whose properties are accessible via the this.props object inside the component's render() method. Therefore, you can access the value of frameworkName as shown in the following listing.

Listing 2.4   Using the frameworkName **property in the** render() **method**

```
class HelloWorld extends React.Component {
  render() {
    return React.createElement(
      'h1',
      null,
      'Hello ' + this.props.frameworkName + ' world!!!'
    )
  }
}
```

> **Concatenates (combines) three strings: "Hello", "this.props.frameworkName", and "world!!!"**

The keys of the this.props object are exactly the same as the keys of the object passed to createElement() as the second parameter. That is, this.props has id, frameworkName, and `title` keys. The number of key/value pairs you can pass in the second argument to `React.createElement()` is unlimited.

In addition, you may have already guessed that it's possible to pass all the properties of `HelloWorld` to its child `<h1/>`. This can be extremely useful when you don't know what properties are passed to a component; for example, in `HelloWorld`, you want to leave the style attribute value up to a developer instantiating `HelloWorld`. Therefore, you don't limit what attributes to render in `<h1/>`.

Listing 2.5   Passing all the properties from `HelloWorld` to `<h1>`

```
class HelloWorld extends React.Component {
  render() {
    return React.createElement(
      'h1',
      this.props,
      'Hello ' + this.props.frameworkName + ' world!!!'
    )
  }
}
```

> Passes all the properties to the child heading element

Then, you render three `HelloWorld` elements into the `<div>` with the ID content, as shown in the following listing (ch02/hello-js-world/js/script.js) and figure 2.9.

Listing 2.6   Using properties passed during element creation

Outputs the frameworkName property as text in `<h1>`

Any properties passed into HelloWorld when createElement is called are passed into this `<h1>` element.

frameworkName isn't a standard HTML attribute for `<h1>`, so it won't be rendered unless you do something with it.

id and title correspond to standard HTML attributes for `<h1>` and are rendered as those attributes.

```
class HelloWorld extends React.Component {
  render() {
    return React.createElement(
      'h1',
      this.props,
      'Hello ' + this.props.frameworkName + ' world!!!'
    )
  }
}
ReactDOM.render(
  React.createElement(
    'div',
    null,
    React.createElement(HelloWorld, {
      id: 'ember',              3((CO5-3))
      frameworkName: 'Ember.js',
      title: 'A framework for creating ambitious web applications.'}),
    React.createElement(HelloWorld, {
      id: 'backbone',
      frameworkName: 'Backbone.js',
      title: 'Backbone.js gives structure to web applications...'}),
    React.createElement(HelloWorld, {
      id: 'angular',
      frameworkName: 'Angular.js',
      title: 'Superheroic JavaScript MVW Framework'})
  ),
  document.getElementById('content')
)
```

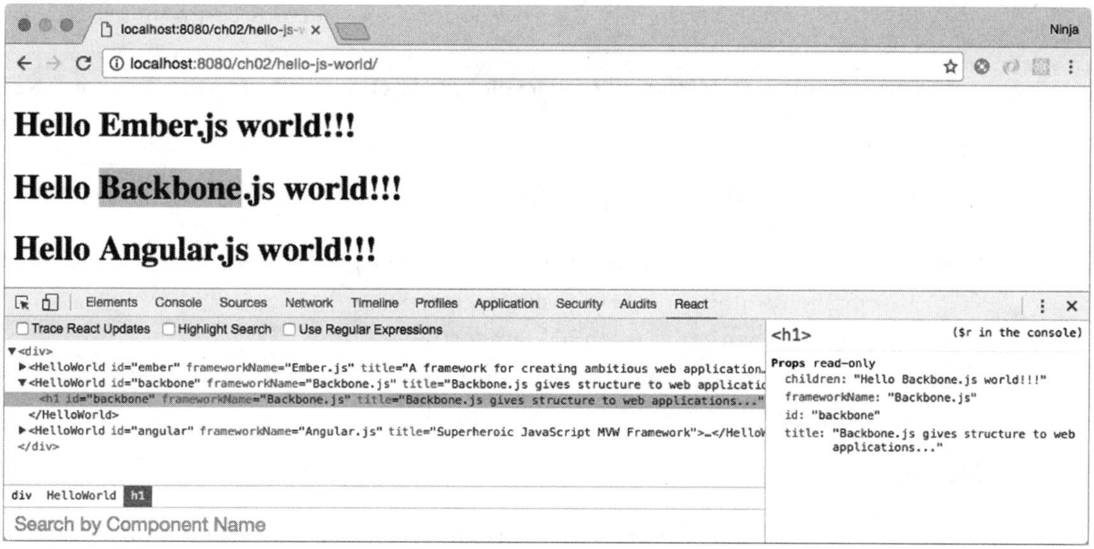

Figure 2.9 Result of reusing `HelloWorld` with different properties to render three different headings

As usual, you can run this code via a local HTTP web server. The result of reusing the `HelloWorld` component class is three different headings (see figure 2.9).

You used `this.props` to render different text for the headings. You used properties to render different titles and IDs. Thus, you effectively reused most of the code, which makes you the master of React `HelloWorld` component classes!

We've covered several permutations of Hello World. Yes, I know, it's still the boring, good-old Hello World. But by starting small, we're building a solid foundation for future, more-advanced topics. Believe me, you can achieve a lot of great things with component classes.

It's very important to know how React works in regular JavaScript events if you (like many React engineers) plan to use JSX. This is because in the end, browsers will still run regular JS, and you'll need to understand the results of the JSX-to-JS transpilation from time to time. Going forward, we'll be using JSX, which is covered in the next chapter.

2.4 Quiz

1 A React component class can be created with which of the following? `createComponent()`, `createElement()`, `class NAME extends React.Component`, `class NAME extends React.Class`

2 The only mandatory attribute or method of a React component is which of the following? `function`, `return`, `name`, `render`, `class`

3 To access the `url` property of a component, you use which of the following? `this.properties.url`, `this.data.url`, `this.props.url`, `url`

4   React properties are immutable in a context of a current component. True or false?

5   React component classes allows developers to create reusable UIs. True or false?

2.5   *Summary*

- You can nest React elements using third, fourth, and so on arguments in `create-Element()`.
- Create elements from custom component classes.
- Modify the resulting elements using properties.
- You can pass properties to child element(s).
- To use a component-based architecture (one of the features of React), you create components.

2.6   *Quiz answers*

1   `class NAME extends React.Component`, because there's no `React.Class` and others will fail due to ReferenceError (not defined).

2   `render()` because it's the *only* required method; also, because function, return, render, and class are not valid, and name is optional.

3   `this.props.url` because only `this.props` gives the properties object.

4   True. It's impossible to change a property.

5   True. Developers use new components to create reusable UIs.

Introduction to JSX

3

This chapter covers

- Understanding JSX and its benefits
- Setting up JSX transpilers with Babel
- Being aware of React and JSX gotchas

Welcome to JSX! It's one of the greatest things about React, in my opinion—and one of the most controversial subjects related to React in the minds of a few developers I spoke with (who, not surprisingly, haven't yet built anything large in React).

Thus far, we've covered how to create elements and components so that you can use custom elements and better organize your UIs. You used JavaScript to create React elements, instead of working with HTML. But there's a problem. Look at this code, and see if you can tell what's happening:

```
render() {
  return React.createElement(
    'div',
    { style: this.styles },
    React.createElement(
      'p',
      null,
      React.createElement(
        reactRouter.Link,
        { to: this.props.returnTo },
```

```
        'Back'
      )
    ),
    this.props.children
  );
}
```

Were you able to tell that there are three elements, that they're nested, and that the code uses a component from React Router? How readable is this code, compared to standard HTML? Do you think this code is eloquent? The React team agrees that reading (and typing, for that matter) a bunch of `React.createElement()` statements isn't fun. JSX is the solution to this problem.

> **NOTE**   The source code for the examples in this chapter is at www.manning .com/books/react-quickly and https://github.com/azat-co/react-quickly/ tree/master/ch03 (in the ch03 folder of the GitHub repository https://github.com/azat-co/react-quickly). You can also find some demos at http://reactquickly.co/demos.

3.1   What is JSX, and what are its benefits?

JSX is a JavaScript extension that provides syntactic sugar (sugar-coating) for function calls and object construction, particularly `React.createElement()`. It may look like a template engine or HTML, but it isn't. JSX produces React elements while allowing you to harness the full power of JavaScript.

JSX is a great way to write React components. Its benefits include the following:

- *Improved developer experience (DX)*—Code is easier to read because it's more eloquent, thanks to an XML-like syntax that's better at representing nested declarative structures.
- *More-productive team members*—Casual developers (such as designers) can modify code more easily, because JSX looks like HTML, which is already familiar to them.
- *Fewer wrist injuries and syntax errors*—Developers have less code to type (that is, less sugar-coating), which means they make fewer mistakes and are less likely to develop repetitive-stress injuries.

Although JSX isn't required for React, it fits in nicely and is highly recommended by me and React's creators. The official "Introducing JSX" page[1] states, "We recommend using [JSX] with React."

To demonstrate the eloquence of JSX, this is the code to create `HelloWorld` and an a link element:

```
<div>
  <HelloWorld/>
  <br/>
  <a href="http://webapplog.com">Great JS Resources</a>
</div>
```

---

[1] https://facebook.github.io/react/docs/introducing-jsx.html.

That's analogous to the following JavaScript:

```
React.createElement(
  "div",
  null,
  React.createElement(HelloWorld, null),
  React.createElement("br", null),
  React.createElement(
    "a",
    { href: "http://webapplog.com" },
    "Great JS Resources"
  )
)
```

And if you use Babel v6 (one of the tools for JSX; more on Babel in a few pages), the JS code becomes this:

```
"use strict";

React.createElement(
  "div",
  null,
  " ",
  React.createElement(HelloWorld, null),
  " ",
  React.createElement("br", null),
  " ",
  React.createElement(
    "a",
    { href: "http://webapplog.com" },
    "Great JS Resources"
  ),
  " "
);
```

In essence, JSX is a small language with an XML-like syntax; but it has changed the way people write UI components. Previously, developers wrote HTML—and JS code for controllers and views—in an MVC-like manner, jumping between various files. That stemmed from the separation of concerns in the early days. This approach served the web well when it consisted of static HTML, a little CSS, and a tiny bit of JS to make text blink.

This is no longer the case; today, we build highly interactive UIs, and JS and HTML are tightly coupled to implement various pieces of functionality. React fixes the broken separation of concerns (SoC) principle by bringing together the description of the UI and the JS logic; and with JSX, the code looks like HTML and is easier to read and write. If for no other reason, I'd use React and JSX just for this new approach to writing UIs.

JSX is compiled by various *transformers* (tools) into standard ECMAScript (see figure 3.1). You probably know that JavaScript is ECMAScript, too; but JSX isn't part of the specification, and it doesn't have any defined semantics.

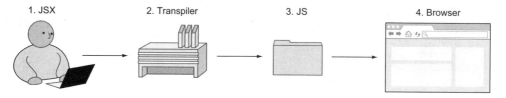

Figure 3.1   JSX is transpiled into regular JavaScript.

NOTE According to https://en.wikipedia.org/wiki/Source-to-source_compiler, "*A source-to-source compiler, transcompiler,* or *transpiler* is a type of compiler that takes the source code of a program written in one programming language as its input and produces the equivalent source code in another programming language."

You may wonder, "Why should I bother with JSX?" That's a great question. Considering how counterintuitive JSX code looks to begin with, it's no surprise that many developers are turned off by this amazing technology. For example, this JSX shows that there are angle brackets in the JavaScript code, which looks bizarre at first:

```
ReactDOM.render(<h1>Hello</h1>, document.getElementById('content'))
```

What makes JSX amazing are the shortcuts to `React.createElement(NAME, ...)`. Instead of writing that function call over and over, you can instead use `<NAME/>`. And as I said earlier, the less you type, the fewer mistakes you make. With JSX, DX is as important as user experience (UX).

The main reason to use JSX is that many people find code with angle brackets (< >) easier to read than code with a lot of `React.createElement()` statements (even when they're aliased). And once you get into the habit of thinking about `<NAME/>` not as XML, but as an alias to JavaScript code, you'll get over the perceived weirdness of JSX syntax. Knowing and using JSX can make a big difference when you're developing React components and, subsequently, React-powered applications.

Alternative shortcuts

To be fair, there are a few alternatives to JSX when it comes to avoiding typing verbose `React.createElement()` calls. One of them is to use the alias `React.DOM.*`. For example, instead of creating an `<h1/>` element with

```
React.createElement('h1', null, 'Hey')
```

the following will also suffice and requires less space and time to implement:

```
React.DOM.h1(null, 'Hey')
```

You have access to all the standard HTML elements in the `React.DOM` object, which you can inspect like any other object:

```
console.log(React.DOM)
```

```
const E = React.createElement
E('h1', null, 'Hey')
```

As I mentioned earlier, JSX needs to be transpiled (or compiled, as it's often called) into regular JavaScript before browsers can execute its code. We'll explore various available methods for doing so, as well as the recommended method, in section 3.3.

3.2 Understanding JSX

Let's explore how to work with JSX. You can read this section and keep it bookmarked for your reference, or (if you prefer to have some of the code examples running on your computer) you have the following options:

- Set up a JSX transpiler with Babel on your computer, as shown in section 3.3.
- Use the online Babel REPL service (https://babeljs.io/repl), which transpiles JSX into JavaScript in the browser.

The choice is up to you. I recommend reading about the main JSX concepts first, and then doing the proper Babel setup on your computer.

3.2.1 Creating elements with JSX

Creating `ReactElement` objects with JSX is straightforward. For example, instead of writing the following JavaScript (where `name` is a string—h1—or component class object—HelloWorld)

```
React.createElement(
  name,
  {key1: value1, key2: value2, ...},
  child1, child2, child3, ..., childN
)
```

you can write this JSX:

```
<name key1=value1 key2=value2 ...>
  <child1/>
  <child2/>
  <child3/>
  ...
  <childN/>
</name>
```

In the JSX code, the attributes and their values (for example, key1=value1) come from the second argument of createElement(). We'll focus on working with properties later in this chapter. For now, let's look at an example of a JSX element without properties. Here's our old friend Hello World in JavaScript (ch03/hello-world/index.html).

Listing 3.1   Hello World in JavaScript

```
ReactDOM.render(
  React.createElement('h1', null, 'Hello world!'),
  document.getElementById('content')
)
```

The JSX version is much more compact (ch03/hello-world-jsx/js/script.jsx).

Listing 3.2   Hello World in JSX

```
ReactDOM.render(
  <h1>Hello world!</h1>,
  document.getElementById('content')
)
```

You can also store objects created with JSX syntax in variables, because JSX is just a syntactic improvement of React.createElement(). This example stores the reference to the Element object in a variable:

```
let helloWorldReactElement = <h1>Hello world!</h1>
ReactDOM.render(
  helloWorldReactElement,
  document.getElementById('content')
)
```

3.2.2   *Working with JSX in components*

The previous example used the <h1> JSX tag, which is also a standard HTML tag name. When working with components, you apply the same syntax. The only difference is that the component class name must start with a capital letter, as in <HelloWorld/>.

Here's a more advanced iteration of Hello World, rewritten in JSX. In this case, you create a new component class and use JSX to create an element from it.

Listing 3.3   Creating a HelloWorld class in JSX

```
class HelloWorld extends React.Component {
  render() {
    return (
      <div>
        <h1>1. Hello world!</h1>
        <h1>2. Hello world!</h1>
      </div>
```

```
    )
  }
}
ReactDOM.render(
  <HelloWorld/>,
  document.getElementById('content')
)
```

Can you read listing 3.3 more easily than the following JavaScript code?

```
class HelloWorld extends React.Component {
  render() {
    return React.createElement('div',
      null,
      React.createElement('h1', null, '1. Hello world!'),
      React.createElement('h1', null, '2. Hello world!'))
  }
}
ReactDOM.render(
  React.createElement(HelloWorld, null),
  document.getElementById('content')
)
```

> **NOTE** As I said earlier, seeing angle brackets in JavaScript code may be strange for experienced JavaScript developers. My brain went bananas when I first saw this, because for years I trained myself to spot JS syntax errors! The brackets are the primary controversy regarding JSX and one of the most frequent objections I hear; this is why we dive into JSX early in the book, so you can get as much experience with it as possible.

Notice the parentheses after `return` in the JSX code in listing 3.3; you must include them if you don't type anything on the same line after `return`. For example, if you start your top element, `<div>`, on a new line, you must put parentheses (`()`) around it. Otherwise, JavaScript will finish the `return` with nothing. This style is as follows:

```
render() {
  return (
    <div>
    </div>
  )
}
```

Alternatively, you can start your top element on the same line as `return` and avoid the necessary `()`. For example, this is valid as well:

```
render() {
  return <div>
  </div>
}
```

A downside of the second approach is the reduced visibility of the opening <div> tag: it may be easy to miss in the code.[2] The choice is up to you. I use *both* styles in this book to give you a deeper perspective.

3.2.3   *Outputting variables in JSX*

When you compose components, you want them to be smart enough to change the view based on some code. For example, it would be useful if a current date-time component used a current date and time, not a hardcoded value.

When working with JavaScript-only React, you have to resort to concatenation (+) or, if you're using ES6+/ES2015+, string templates marked by a backtick and ${varName}, where varName is the name of a variable. The official name for this feature is *template literal*, according to the specification.[3] For example, to use a property in text in a DateTimeNow component in regular JavaScript React, you'd write this code:

```
class DateTimeNow extends React.Component {
  render() {
    let dateTimeNow = new Date().toLocaleString()
    return React.createElement(
      'span',
      null,
      `Current date and time is ${dateTimeNow}.`
    )
  }
}
```

Conversely, in JSX, you can use curly braces {} notation to output variables dynamically, which reduces code bloat substantially:

```
class DateTimeNow extends React.Component {
  render() {
    let dateTimeNow = new Date().toLocaleString()
    return <span>Current date and time is {dateTimeNow}.</span>
    )
  }
}
```

The variables can be properties, not just locally defined variables:

```
<span>Hello {this.props.userName}, your current date and time is
  {dateTimeNow}.</span>
```

Moreover, you can execute JavaScript expressions or any JS code inside of {}. For example, you can format a date:

```
<p>Current time in your locale is
  {new Date(Date.now()).toLocaleTimeString()}</p>
```

---

[2] For more about this behavior in JavaScript, see James Nelson, "Why Use Parenthesis [sic] on JavaScript Return Statements?" August 11, 2016, http://jamesknelson.com/javascript-return-parenthesis; and "Automated Semicolon Insertion," *Annotated ECMAScript 5.1*, http://es5.github.io/#x7.9.

[3] "Template Literals," *ECMAScript 2015 Language Specification*, June 2015, http://mng.bz/i8Bw.

Now, you can rewrite the `HelloWorld` class in JSX using the dynamic data that JSX stores in a variable (ch03/hello-world-class-jsx).

Listing 3.4 Outputting variables in JSX

```
let helloWorldReactElement = <h1>Hello world!</h1>
class HelloWorld extends React.Component {
  render() {
    return <div>
      {helloWorldReactElement}
      {helloWorldReactElement}
    </div>
  }
}
ReactDOM.render(
  <HelloWorld/>,
  document.getElementById('content')
)
```

Let's discuss how you work with properties in JSX.

3.2.4 *Working with properties in JSX*

I touched on this topic earlier, when I introduced JSX: element properties are defined using attribute syntax. That is, you use `key1=value1 key2=value2…` notation inside of the JSX tag to define both HTML attributes and React component properties. This is similar to attribute syntax in HTML/XML.

In other words, if you need to pass properties, write them in JSX as you would in normal HTML. Also, you render standard HTML attributes by setting element properties (discussed in section 2.3). For example, this code sets a standard HTML attribute `href` for the anchor element `<a>`:

```
ReactDOM.render((
  <div>
    <a href="http://reactquickly.co">Time for React?</a>      ⟵  Renders a
    <DateTimeNow userName='Azat'/>      ⟵                          standard HTML
  </div>                                                            attribute href
  ),
  document.getElementById('content')           Sets a value for the
)                                              userName property
```

Using hardcoded values for attributes isn't flexible. If you want to reuse the link component, then the `href` must change to reflect a different address each time. This is called *dynamically setting* values versus hardcoding them. So, next we'll go a step further and consider a component that can use dynamically generated values for attributes. Those values can come from component properties (`this.props`). After that, everything's easy. All you need to do is use curly braces (`{}`) inside angle braces (`<>`) to pass dynamic values of properties to elements.

For example, suppose you're building a component that will be used to link to user accounts. `href` and `title` must be different and not hardcoded. A dynamic component

ProfileLink renders a link <a> using the properties url and label for href and title, respectively. In ProfileLink, you pass the properties to <a> using { }:

```
class ProfileLink extends React.Component {
  render() {
    return <a href={this.props.url}
      title={this.props.label}
      target="_blank">Profile
    </a>
  }
}
```

Where do the property values come from? They're defined when the ProfileLink is created—that is, in the component that creates ProfileLink, a.k.a. its parent. For example, this is how the values for url and label are passed when a ProfileLink instance is created, which results in the render of the <a> tag with those values:

```
<ProfileLink url='/users/azat' label='Profile for Azat'/>
```

From the previous chapter, you should remember that when rendering standard elements (<h>, <p>, <div>, <a>, and so on), React renders all attributes from the HTML specification and omits all other attributes that aren't part of the specification. This isn't a JSX gotcha; it's React's behavior.

But sometimes you want to add custom data as an attribute. Let's say you have a list item; there's some information that's essential to your app but not needed by users. A common pattern is to put this information in the DOM element as an attribute. This example uses the attributes react-is-awesome and id:

```
<li react-is-awesome="true" id="320">React is awesome!</li>
```

Storing data in custom HTML attributes in the DOM is generally considered an anti-pattern, because you don't want the DOM to be your database or a front-end data store. Getting data from the DOM is slower than getting it from a virtual/in-memory store.

In cases when you *must* store data as elements' attributes, and you use JSX, you need to use the data-NAME prefix. For example, to render the <li> element with a value of this.reactIsAwesome in an attribute, you can write this:

```
<li data-react-is-awesome={this.reactIsAwesome}>React is awesome!</li>
```

Let's say this.reactIsAwesome is true. Then, the resulting HTML is

```
<li data-react-is-awesome="true">React is awesome!</li>
```

But if you attempt to pass a nonstandard HTML attribute to a standard HTML element, the attribute won't render (as covered in section 2.3). For example, this code

```
<li react-is-awesome={this.reactIsAwesome}>React is orange</li>
```

and this code

```
<li reactIsAwesome={this.reactIsAwesome}>React is orange</li>
```

both produce only the following:

```
<li>React is orange</li>
```

Obviously, because custom elements (component classes) don't have built-in renderers and rely on standard HTML elements or other custom elements, this issue of using data- isn't important for them. They get all attributes as properties in this.props.

Speaking of component classes, this is the code from Hello World (section 2.3) written in regular JavaScript:

```
class HelloWorld extends React.Component {
  render() {
    return React.createElement(
      'h1',
      this.props,
      'Hello ' + this.props.frameworkName + ' world!!!'
    )
  }
}
```

In the HelloWorld components, you pass the properties through to <h1> no matter what properties are there. How can you do this in JSX? You don't want to pass each property individually, because that's more code; and when you need to change a property, you'll have tightly coupled code that you'll need to update as well. Imagine having to pass each property manually—and what if you have two or three levels of components to pass through? That's an antipattern. Don't do this:

```
class HelloWorld extends React.Component {
  render() {
    return <h1 title={this.props.title} id={this.props.id}>
      Hello {this.props.frameworkName} world!!!
    </h1>
  }
}
```

Don't pass the properties individually when your intention is to pass *all* of them; JSX offers a spread solution that looks like ellipses, ..., as you can see in the following listing (ch03/jsx/hello-js-world-jsx).

Listing 3.5 Working with properties

```
class HelloWorld extends React.Component {
  render() {
    return <h1 {...this.properties}>
      Hello {this.props.frameworkName} world!!!
    </h1>
  }
}

ReactDOM.render(
  <div>
```

```
    <HelloWorld
      id='ember'
      frameworkName='Ember.js'
      title='A framework for creating ambitious web applications.'/>,
    <HelloWorld
      id='backbone'
      frameworkName= 'Backbone.js'
      title= 'Backbone.js gives structure to web applications...'/>
    <HelloWorld
      id= 'angular'
      frameworkName= 'Angular.js'
      title= 'Superheroic JavaScript MVW Framework'/>
  </div>,
  document.getElementById('content')
)
```

With {...this.props}, you can pass every property to the child. The rest of the code is just converted to the JSX example from section 2.3.

Ellipses in ES6+/ES2015+: rest, spread, and destructuring

Speaking of ellipses, there are similar-looking operators in ES6+, called *destructuring*, *spread*, and *rest*. This is one of the reasons React's JSX uses ellipses!

If you've ever used or written a JavaScript function with a variable or unlimited number of arguments, you know the arguments object. This object contains all parameters passed to the function. The problem is that this arguments object isn't a real array. You have to convert it to an array if you want to use functions like sort() and map() explicitly. For example, this request function converts arguments using call():

```
function request(url, options, callback) {
  var args = Array.prototype.slice.call(arguments, request.length)
  var url = args[0]
  var callback = args[2]
  // ...
}
```

Is there a better way in ES6 to access an indefinite number of arguments as an array? Yes! It's the rest parameter syntax, defined with ellipses (...). For example, following is the ES6 function signature with the rest parameter callbacks, which become an array (a real array, not the arguments pseudoarray) with the rest of the parameters:[4]

```
function(url, options, ...callbacks) {
  var callback1 = callbacks[0]
  var callback2 = callbacks[1]
  // ...
}
```

---

[4] In the rest array, the first parameter is the one that doesn't have a name: for example, the callback is at index 0, not 2, as in ES5's arguments. Also, putting other named arguments after the rest parameter will cause a syntax error.

(continued)

Rest parameters can be *destructured*, meaning they can be extracted into separate variables:

```
function(url, options, ...[error, success]) {
  if (!url) return error(new Error('ooops'))
  // ...
  success(data)
}
```

What about spread? In brief, spread allows you to expand arguments or variables in the following places:

- *Function calls*—For example, `push()` method: `arr1.push(...arr2)`
- *Array literals*—For example, `array2 = [...array1, x, y, z]`
- new *function calls (constructors)*—For example, `var d = new Date(...dates)`

In ES5, if you wanted to use an array as an argument to a function, you'd have to use the `apply()` function:

```
function request(url, options, callback) {
  // ...
}
var requestArgs = ['http://azat.co', {...}, function(){...}]
request.apply(null, requestArgs)
```

In ES6, you can use the spread parameter, which looks similar to the rest parameter in syntax and uses ellipses (...):

```
function request(url, options, callback) {
  // ...
}
var requestArgs = ['http://azat.co', {...}, function(){...}]
request(...requestArgs)
```

The spread operator's syntax is similar to that of the rest parameter's, but rest is used in a function definition/declaration, and spread is used in calls and literals. They save you from typing extra lines of imperative code, so knowing and using them is a valuable skill.

3.2.5 Creating React component methods

As a developer, you're free to write any component methods for your applications, because a React component is a class. For example, you can create a helper method, `getUrl()`:

```
class Content extends React.Component {
  getUrl() {
    return 'http://webapplog.com'
  }
```

```
  render() {
    ...
  }
}
```

The getUrl() method isn't sophisticated, but you get the idea: you can create your own arbitrary methods, not just render(). You can use the getUrl() method to abstract a URL to your API server. Helper methods can have reusable logic, and you can call them anywhere within other methods of the component, including render().

If you want to output the return from the custom method in JSX, use {}, just as you would with variables (see the following listing, ch03/method/jsx/scrch03/meipt.jsx). In this case, the helper method is invoked in render, and the method's return values will be used in the view. Remember to invoke the method with ().

Listing 3.6   Invoking a component method to get a URL

```
class Content extends React.Component {
  getUrl() {
    return 'http://webapplog.com'
  }
  render() {
    return (
      <div>
        <p>Your REST API URL is:
          <a href={this.getUrl()}>          ⟵  Invokes the class method
            {this.getUrl()}                      in the curly braces
          </a>
        </p>
      </div>
    )
  }
}
...
```

Once again, it's possible to invoke component methods directly from {} and JSX. For example, using {this.getUrl()} in the helper method getUrl: when you use the method in listing 3.6, you'll see http://webapplog.com as its returned value in the link in the paragraph <p> (see figure 3.2).

You should now understand component methods. My apologies if you found this section too banal; these methods are important as a foundation for React event handlers.

Figure 3.2   Results of rendering a link with the value from a method

3.2.6 *if/else in JSX*

Akin to rendering dynamic variables, developers need to compose their components so that components can change views based on the results of `if/else` conditions. Let's start with a simple example that renders the elements in a component class; the elements depend on a condition. For example, some link text and a URL are determined by the `user.session` value. This is how you can code this in plain JS:

```
...
render() {
  if (user.session)
    return React.createElement('a', {href: '/logout'}, 'Logout')
  else
    return React.createElement('a', {href: '/login'}, 'Login')
}
...
```

You can use a similar approach and rewrite this with JSX like so:

```
...
render() {
  if (this.props.user.session)
    return <a href="/logout">Logout</a>
  else
    return <a href="/login">Login</a>
}
...
```

Let's say there are other elements, such as a `<div>` wrapper. In this case, in plain JS, you'd have to create a variable or use an expression or a ternary operator (also known as the *Elvis operator* by the younger generation of JavaScript developers; see http://mng.bz/92Zg), because you can't use an `if` condition inside the `<div>`'s `createElement()`. The idea is that you must get the value at runtime.

Ternary operators

The following ternary condition works such that if `userAuth` is true, then `msg` will be set to `welcome`. Otherwise, the value will be `restricted`:

```
let msg = (userAuth) ? 'welcome' : 'restricted'
```

This statement is equivalent to the following:

```
let session = ''
if (userAuth) {
  session = 'welcome'
} else {
  session = 'restricted'
}
```

> **(continued)**
>
> In some cases, the ternary (?) operator is a shorter version of `if/else`. But there's a big difference between them if you try to use the ternary operator as an expression (where it returns a value). This code is valid JS:
>
> ```
> let msg = (userAuth) ? 'welcome' : 'restricted'
> ```
>
> But `if/else` won't work because this isn't an expression, but a statement:
>
> ```
> let msg = if (userAuth) {'welcome'} else {'restricted'} // Not valid
> ```
>
> You can use this quality of a ternary operator to get a value from it at runtime in JSX.

To demonstrate the three different styles (variable, expression, and ternary operator), look at the following regular JavaScript code before it's converted to JSX:

```
// Approach 1: Variable
render() {
  let link
  if (this.props.user.session)                                    Uses a variable link
    link = React.createElement('a', {href: '/logout'}, 'Logout')
  else
    link = React.createElement('a', {href: '/login'}, 'Login')
  return React.createElement('div', null, link)
}
// Approach 2: Expression
render() {
  let link = (sessionFlag) => {          ◄──── Creates an expression
    if (sessionFlag)
      return React.createElement('a', {href: '/logout'}, 'Logout')
    else
      return React.createElement('a', {href: '/login'}, 'Login')
  }
  return React.createElement('div', null, link(this.props.user.session))
}
// Approach 3: Ternary operator
render() {                                               Uses a ternary operator
  return React.createElement('div', null,
    (this.props.user.session) ? React.createElement('a', {href: '/logout'},
    ➥ 'Logout') : React.createElement('a', {href: '/login'}, 'Login')
  )
}
```

Not bad, but kind of clunky. Would you agree? With JSX, the {} notation can print variables and execute JS code. Let's use it to achieve better syntax:

```
// Approach 1: Variable
render() {
  let link
  if (this.props.user.session)
    link = <a href='/logout'>Logout</a>
  else
    link = <a href='/login'>Login</a>
  return <div>{link}</div>
```

```
}
// Approach 2: Expression
render() {
  let link = (sessionFlag) => {
    if (sessionFlag)
      return <a href='/logout'>Logout</a>
    else
      return <a href='/login'>Login</a>
  }
  return <div>{link(this.props.user.session)}</div>
}
// Approach 3: Ternary operator
render() {
  return <div>
    {(this.props.user.session) ? <a href='/logout'>Logout</a> :
    <a href='/login'>Login</a>}
  </div>
}
```

If you look more closely at the expression/function style example (Approach 2: a function outside the JSX before `return`), you can come up with an alternative. You can define the same function using an immediately invoked function expression (IIFE, http://mng.bz/387u) inside the JSX. This lets you avoid having an extra variable (such as `link`) and execute the `if/else` at runtime:

```
render() {
  return <div>{                           Defines
    (sessionFlag) => {                     an IIFE
      if (sessionFlag)
        return <a href='/logout'>Logout</a>
      else
        return <a href='/login'>Login</a>       Invokes an IIFE
    }(this.props.user.session)                  with a parameter
  }</div>
}
```

Furthermore, you can use the same principles for rendering not just entire elements (`<a>`, in these examples), but also text and the values of properties. All you need to do is use one of the approaches shown here, inside curly braces. For example, you can augment the URL and text and not duplicate the code for element creation. Personally, this is my favorite approach, because I can use a single `<a>`:

```
render() {                                  Creates a local variable to store the
  let sessionFlag = this.props.user.session session Boolean value, resulting in
  return <div>                              less code and better performance
    <a href={(sessionFlag)?'/logout':'/login'}>
      {(sessionFlag)?'Logout':'Login'}            Uses the ternary
    </a>                                          operator to render
  </div>                  Uses the ternary operator different URLs based on
}                        to render different text     the sessionFlag value
```

As you can see, unlike in template engines, there's no special syntax for these conditions in JSX—you just use JavaScript. Most often, you'll use a ternary operator, because it's one of the most compact styles. To summarize, when it comes to implementing if/else logic in JSX, you can use these options:

- Variable defined outside of JSX (before return) and printed with {} in JSX
- Expression (function that returns a value) defined outside of JSX (before return) and invoked in {} in JSX
- Conditional ternary operator
- IIFE in JSX

This is my rule of thumb when it comes to conditions and JSX: use if/else outside of JSX (before return) to generate a variable that you'll print in JSX with {}. Or, skip the variable, and print the results of the Elvis operator (?) or expressions using {} in JSX:

```
class MyReactComponent extends React.Component {
  render() {
    // Not JSX: Use a variable and if/else or ternary
    return (
      // JSX: Print result of ternary or expression with {}
    )
  }
}
```

We've covered the important conditions for building interactive UIs with React and JSX. Occasionally, you may want to narrate the functionality of your beautiful, intelligent code so that other people can quickly understand it. To do so, you use comments.

3.2.7   Comments in JSX

Comments in JSX work similar to comments in regular JavaScript. To add JSX comments, you can wrap standard JavaScript comments in {}, like this:

```
let content = (
  <div>
    {/* Just like a JS comment */}
  </div>
)
```

Or, you can use comments like this:

```
let content = (
  <div>
    <Post
      /* I
      am
      multi
      line */
      name={window.isLoggedIn ? window.name : ''} // We are inside of JSX
    />
  </div>
)
```

You've now had a taste of JSX and its benefits. The rest of this chapter is dedicated to JSX tools and potential traps to avoid. That's right: tools and gotchas.

Because before we can continue, you must understand that for any JSX project to function properly, the JSX needs to be *compiled*. Browsers can't run JSX—they can run only JavaScript, so you need to take the JSX and transpile it to normal JS (see figure 3.1).

3.3 *Setting up a JSX transpiler with Babel*

As I mentioned, in order to execute JSX, you need to convert it to regular JavaScript code. This process is called *transpilation* (from *compilation* and *transformation*), and various tools are available to do the job. Here are some recommended ways to do this:

- *Babel command-line interface (CLI) tool*—The `babel-cli` package provides a command for transpilation. This approach requires less setup and is the easiest to start.
- *Node.js or browser JavaScript script (API approach)*—A script can import the `babel-core` package and transpile JSX programmatically (`babel.transform`). This allows for low-level control and removes abstractions and dependencies on the build tools and their plug-ins.
- *Build tool*—A tool such as Grunt, Gulp, or Webpack can use the Babel plug-in. This is the most popular approach.

All of these use Babel in one way or another. Babel is mostly an ES6+/ES2015+ compiler, but it also can convert JSX to JavaScript. In fact, the React team stopped development on its own JSX transformer and recommends using Babel.

Can I use something other than Babel 6?

Although there are various tools to transpile JSX, the most frequently used tool—and the one recommended by the React team on the official React website, as of August 2016—is Babel (formerly, 5to6). Historically, the React team maintained `react-tools` and JSXTransformer (transpilation in the browser); but, since version 0.13, the team has recommended Babel and stopped evolving `react-tools` and JSXTransformer.[5]

For in-browser runtime transpilation, Babel version 5.x has browser.js, which is a ready-to-use distribution. You can drop it in the browser, like JSXTransformer, and it will convert any `<script>` code into JS (use `type="text/babel"`). The latest Babel version that has browser.js is 5.8.34, and you can include it from the CDN directly (https://cdnjs.com/libraries/babel-core/5.8.34).

Babel 6.x switched to not having default presets/configs (such as JSX) and removed browser.js. The Babel team encourages developers to create their own distributions or use the Babel API. There's also a `babel-standalone` library (https://github.com/Daniel15/babel-standalone), but you still have to tell it which presets/configs to use.

---

[5] Paul O'Shannessy, "Deprecating JSTransform and react-tools," *React*, June 12, 2015, http://mng.bz/8yGc.

(continued)

Traceur (https://github.com/google/traceur-compiler) is another tool that you can use as a replacement for Babel.

Finally, TypeScript (www.typescriptlang.org) seems to support JSX compilation via `jsx-typescript` (https://github.com/fdecampredon/jsx-typescript),[6] but that's a whole new toolchain and language (a superset of regular JavaScript).

You *probably* can use the JSXTransformer, Babel v5, babel-standalone, TypeScript, and Traceur tools with the examples in this book (I use React v15). TypeScript and Traceur should be relatively safe bets, because they're supported as of the time of this writing. But if you end up using anything other than Babel 6 for the book's examples, you do so at your own risk. Manning's tech reviewers and I didn't test the code in this book to see if it works with these tools!

By using Babel for React, you can get extra ES6/ES2015 features to streamline your development just by adding an extra configuration and a module for ES6. The sixth iteration of the ECMAScript standard has a myriad of improvements, and is mostly available as of this writing in all *modern* browsers. But, older browsers will have a hard time interpreting the new ES6 code. Also, if you want to use ES7, ES8, or ES27, then some browsers might not have all the features implemented yet.

To solve the lag in ES6 or ES.Next (collective name for the most cutting-edge features) implementation by browsers, Babel comes to the rescue. It offers support for the next generation of JavaScript languages (many languages … get the hint from the name?). This section covers the recommended approach used in the next few chapters—the Babel CLI—because it involves minimal setup and doesn't require knowledge of Babel's API (unlike the API approach).

To use the Babel CLI (http://babeljs.io), you need Node v6.2.0, npm v3.8.9, `babel-cli` v6.9.0 (www.npmjs.com/package/babel-cli), and `babel-preset-react` v6.5.0 (www.npmjs.com/package/babel-preset-react). Other versions aren't guaranteed to work with this book's code, due to the fast-changing nature of Node and React development.

If you need to install Node and npm, the easiest way to do so is to download the installer (just one for both Node and npm) from the official website: http://nodejs.org. For more options and detailed installation instructions regarding Babel installation, please see appendix A.

If you think you have these tools installed, or you're not sure, check the versions of Node and npm with these shell/terminal/command prompt commands:

```
node -v
npm -v
```

---

[6]   www.typescriptlang.org/docs/handbook/jsx.html.

You need to have the Babel CLI and React preset locally. Using the Babel CLI globally (-g, when installing with npm) is discouraged, because you might run into conflict when your projects rely on different versions of the tool. Here's a short version of the instructions found in appendix A:

1   Create a new folder, such as ch03/babel-jsx-test.
2   Create a package.json file in the new folder and enter an empty object { } in it, or use `npm init` to generate the file.
3   Define your Babel presets in package.json (used in this book and explained in the next section) or .babelrc (not used in this book).
4   Optionally, fill package.json with information such as the project name, license, GitHub repository, and so on.
5   Install the Babel CLI and React preset *locally*, using `npm i babel-cli@6.9.0 babel-preset-react@6.5.0 --save-dev` to save these dependencies in devDependencies in package.json.
6   Optionally, create an npm script with one of the Babel commands described shortly.

Babel ES6 preset

In the unfortunate event that you have to support an older browser such as IE9, but you still want to write in ES6+/ES2015+ because that's the future standard, you can add the `babel-preset-es2015` (www.npmjs.com/package/babel-preset-es2015) transpiler. It will convert your ES6 into ES5 code. To do so, install the library:

```
npm i babel-preset-es2015 --save-dev
```

Then, add it to the `presets` configuration next to `react`:

```
{
  "presets": ["react", "es2015"]
}
```

I don't recommend using this ES2015 transpiler if you don't have to support older browsers, for several reasons. First, you'll be running old ES5 code, which is less optimized than ES6 code. Second, you're adding an additional dependency and more complexity. And third, if most people continue to run ES5 code in their browser, why did we—meaning browser teams and regular JavaScript developers—bother with ES6? You could use TypeScript (www.typescriptlang.org), ClojureScript (http://clojurescript.org), or CoffeeScript (http://coffeescript.org), which give you more bang for your buck!

To repeat what's written in appendix A, you need a package.json file with at least this preset:

```
{
  ...
  "babel": {
    "presets": ["react"]
  },
  ...
}
```

Then, running this command (from your newly created project folder) to check the version should work:

```
$ ./node_modules/.bin/babel --version
```

After installation, issue a command to process your js/script.jsx JSX into js/script.js JavaScript:

```
$ ./node_modules/.bin/babel js/script.jsx -o js/script.js
```

This command is long because you're using a path to Babel. You can store this command in a package.json file to use a shorter version: npm run build. Open the file with your editor, and add this line to scripts:

```
"build": "./node_modules/.bin/babel js/script.jsx -o js/script.js"
```

You can automate this command with the watch option (-w or --watch):

```
$ ./node_modules/.bin/babel js/script.jsx -o js/script.js -w
```

The Babel command watches for any changes in script.jsx and compiles it to script.js when you save the updated JSX. When this happens, the terminal/command prompt will display the following:

```
change js/script.jsx
```

As you accumulate more JSX files, use the command with -d (--out-dir) and folder names to compile JSX source files (source) into many regular JS files (build):

```
$ ./node_modules/.bin/babel source --d build
```

Often, having a single file to load is better for the performance of a front-end app than loading many files. This is because each request adds a delay. You can compile all the files in the source directory into a single regular JS file with -o (--out-file):

```
$ ./node_modules/.bin/babel src -o script-compiled.js
```

Depending on the path configuration on your computer, you may be able to run babel instead of ./node_modules/.bin/babel. In both cases, you're executing locally. If you have an older babel-cli installed globally, delete it with npm rm -g babel-cli.

If you're unable to run babel when you install babel-cli locally in your project, then consider adding either one of these path statements into your shell profile:

~/.bash_profile, ~/.bashrc, or ~/.zsh, depending on your shell (bash, zsh, and so on) if you're on POSIX (Unix, Linux, macOS, and the like).

This shell statement will add a path—so you can launch locally installed npm CLI packages without typing the path—if there's ./node_modules/.bin in the current folder:

```
if [ -d "$PWD/node_modules/.bin" ]; then
    PATH="$PWD/node_modules/.bin"
fi
```

The shell script checks whether there's a ./node_modules/.bin folder in your terminal bash environment current folder, and then adds that folder to the path to enable npm CLI tools like Babel, Webpack, and so on by name: babel, webpack, and so on.

You can opt to have the path set all the time, not just when there's a subfolder. This shell statement will *always* add the path ./node_modules/.bin to your PATH environment variable (also in profile):

```
export PATH="./node_modules/.bin:$PATH"
```

Bonus: This setting will also allow you to run *any npm CLI tool* locally with just its name, not the path and the name.

> **TIP** For working examples of Babel package.json configurations, open the projects in the ch03 folder in the source code accompanying this book. They follow the same approach used in the chapters that follow. The package.json file in ch03 has npm build scripts for each project (subfolder) that needs compilation, unless the project has its own package.json.

When you run a build script—for example, npm run build-hello-world—it'll compile the JSX from ch03/PROJECT_NAME/jsx into regular JavaScript and put that compiled file into ch03/PROJECT_NAME/js. Therefore, all you need to do is install the necessary dependencies with npm i (it will create a ch03/node_modules folder), check whether a build script exists in package.json, and then run npm run build-PROJECT_NAME.

Thus far, you've learned the easiest way to transpile JSX into regular JS, in my humble opinion. But I want you to be aware of some tricky parts when it comes to React and JSX.

3.4 *React and JSX gotchas*

This section covers some edge cases. There are a few gotchas to be aware of when you use JSX.

For instance, JSX requires you to have a closing slash (/) either in the closing tag or, if you don't have any children and use a single tag, in the end of that single tag. For example, this is correct:

```
<a href="http://azat.co">Azat, the master of callbacks</a>
<button label="Save" className="btn" onClick={this.handleSave}/>
```

This is *not* correct, because the slashes are missing:

```
<a href="http://azat.co">Azat<a>
<button label="Save" className="btn" onClick={this.handleSave}>
```

Conversely, HTML is more fault tolerant. Most browsers will ignore the missing slash and render the element just fine without it. Go ahead: try `<button>Press me` for yourself!

There are other differences between HTML and JSX, as well.

3.4.1 *Special characters*

HTML entities are codes that display special characters such as copyright symbols, em dashes, quotation marks, and so on. Here are some examples:

```
&copy;
&mdash;
&ldquo;
```

You can render those codes as any string in `<span>` or in the string attribute `<input>`. For example, this is static JSX (text defined in code without variables or properties):

```
<span>&copy;&mdash;&ldquo;</span>
<input value="&copy;&mdash;&ldquo;"/>
```

But if you want to dynamically output HTML entities (from a variable or a property) with `<span>`, all you'll get is the direct output (`&copy;&mdash;&ldquo;`), not the special characters. Thus, the following code won't work:

```
// Anti-pattern. Will NOT work!
var specialChars = '&copy;&mdash;&ldquo;'

<span>{specialChars}</span>
<input value={specialChars}/>
```

React/JSX will auto-escape the dangerous HTML, which is convenient in terms of security (security by default rocks!). To output special characters, you need to use one of these approaches:

- Break them into multiple strings by outputting an array; for example, `<span>{[<span>&copy;&mdash;&ldquo;</span>]}</span>`. You can also set key, as in key="specialChars", to suppress a warning about the missing key.
- Copy the special character directly into your source code (make sure you use a UTF-8 character set).
- Escape the special character with \u, and use a unicode number (search www.fileformat.info/info/unicode/char/search.htm, if you don't remember it; who does?).

- Convert from a character code to a character number with `String` `.fromCharCode(charCodeNumber)`.
- Use the internal method `__html` to dangerously set inner HTML (http:// mng.bz/TplO; not recommended).

To illustrate the last approach (as a last resort—when all else fails on the Titanic, run for the boats!), look at this code:

```
var specialChars = {__html: '&copy;&mdash;&ldquo;'}

<span dangerouslySetInnerHTML={specialChars}/>
```

Obviously, the React team has a sense of humor, to name a property `dangerouslySetInnerHTML`. Sometimes React naming makes me laugh to myself!

3.4.2 *data- attributes*

Section 2.3 covered properties in a non-JSX way, but let's look at how to create custom attributes in HTML one more time (this time with JSX). Chiefly, React will blissfully ignore any nonstandard HTML attributes that you add to components. It doesn't matter whether you use JSX or native JavaScript—that's React's behavior.

But sometimes, you want to pass additional data using DOM nodes. This is an anti-pattern because your DOM shouldn't be used as a database or local storage. If you still want to create custom attributes and get them rendered, use the `data-` prefix.

For example, this is a valid custom `data-object-id` attribute that React will render in the view (HTML will be the same as this JSX):

```
<li data-object-id="097F4E4F">...</li>
```

If the input is the following React/JSX element, React won't render `object-id`, because it's not a standard HTML attribute (HTML will miss `object-id`, unlike this JSX):

```
<li object-id="097F4E4F">...</li>
```

3.4.3 *style attribute*

The `style` attribute in JSX works differently than in plain HTML. With JSX, instead of a string, you need to pass a JavaScript object, and CSS properties need to be in camel-Case. For example:

- `background-image` becomes `backgroundImage`.
- `font-size` becomes `fontSize`.
- `font-family` becomes `fontFamily`.

You can save the JavaScript object in a variable or render it inline with double curly braces (`{{...}}`). The double braces are needed because one set is for JSX and the other is for the JavaScript object literal.

Suppose you have an object with this font size:

```
let smallFontSize = {fontSize: '10pt'}
```

In your JSX, you can use the `smallFontSize` object:

```
<input style={smallFontSize} />
```

Or you can settle for a larger font (30 point) by passing the values directly without an extra variable:

```
<input style={{fontSize: '30pt'}} />
```

Let's look at another example of passing styles directly. This time, you're setting a red border on <span>:

```
<span style={{borderColor: 'red',
  borderWidth: 1,
  borderStyle: 'solid'}}>Hey</span>
```

Alternatively, the following border value will also work:

```
<span style={{border: '1px red solid'}}>Hey</span>
```

The main reason classes are not opaque strings but JavaScript objects is so React can work with them more quickly when it applies changes to views.

3.4.4   *class and for*

React and JSX accept any attribute that's a standard HTML attribute, except `class` and `for`. Those names are reserved words in JavaScript/ECMAScript, and JSX is converted into regular JavaScript. Use `className` and `htmlFor` instead. For example, if you have a class `hidden`, you can define it in a <div> this way:

```
<div className="hidden">...</div>
```

If you need to create a label for a form element, use `htmlFor`:

```
<div>
    <input type="radio" name={this.props.name} id={this.props.id}>
    </input>
    <label htmlFor={this.props.id}>
      {this.props.label}
    </label>
</div>
```

3.4.5   *Boolean attribute values*

Last but not least, some attributes (such as `disabled`, `required`, `checked`, `autofocus`, and `readOnly`) are specific only to form elements. The most important thing to remember here is that the attribute value *must* be set in the JavaScript expression (that is, inside {}) and not set in strings.

For example, use {false} to enable the input:

```
<input disabled={false} />
```

But don't use a "false" value, because it'll pass the truthy check (a non-empty string is truthy in JavaScript—see the sidebar) and render the input as disabled (disabled will be true):

```
<input disabled="false" />
```

> **Truthiness**
> In JavaScript/Node, a *truthy* value translates to true when evaluated as a Boolean; for example, in an if statement. The value is truthy if it's not falsy. (That's the official definition. Brilliant, right?) And there are only six falsy values:
>
> - false
> - 0
> - "" (empty string)
> - null
> - Undefined
> - NaN (not a number)
>
> I hope you can see that the string "false" is a non-empty string, which is truthy and translates to true. Hence, you'll get disabled=true in HTML.

If you omit the value, React will assume the value is true:

```
<input disabled />
```

The subsequent chapters use JSX exclusively. But knowing the underlying regular JavaScript that will be run by browsers is a great skill to have in your toolbox.

3.5 *Quiz*

1 To output a JavaScript variable in JSX, which of the following do you use? =, <%= %>, {}, or <?= ?>
2 The class attribute isn't allowed in JSX. True or false?
3 The default value for an attribute without a value is false. True or false?
4 The inline style attribute in JSX is a JavaScript object and not a string like other attributes. True or false?
5 If you need to have if/else logic in JSX, you can use it inside {}. For example, class={if (!this.props.admin) return 'hide'} is valid JSX code. True or false?

3.6   *Summary*

- JSX is just syntactic sugar for React methods like `createElement`.
- You should use `className` and `htmlFor` instead of the standard HTML `class` and `for` attributes.
- The `style` attribute takes a JavaScript object, not a string like normal HTML.
- Ternary operators and IIFE are the best ways to implement `if`/`else` statements.
- Outputting variables, comments, and HTML entities, and compiling JSX code into native JavaScript are easy.
- There are a few choices to turn JSX into regular JavaScript; compiling with the Babel CLI requires minimal setup compared to configuring build processing with a tool like Gulp or Webpack or writing Node/JavaScript scripts to use the Babel API.

3.7   *Quiz answers*

you should use a ternary operator.

5 False. First, `class` isn't a proper attribute. Then, instead of `if` return (not valid),

4 True. `style` is an object for performance reasons.

Boolean values explicitly.

3 False. It's recommended that you use attribute `name={false/true}` to set the

`className` in JSX.

2 True. `class` is a reserved or special JavaScript statement. For this reason, you use

1 You use `{ }` for variables and expressions.

Making React interactive with states

4

If you read only one chapter in this book, this should be it! Without states, your React components are just glorified static templates. I hope you're as excited as I am, because understanding the concepts in this chapter will allow you to build much more interesting applications.

Imagine that you're building an autocomplete input field (see figure 4.1). When you type in it, you want to make a request to the server to fetch information about matches to show on the web page. So far, you've worked with properties, and you've learned that by changing properties, you can get different views. But properties can't change in the context of the current component, because they're passed on this component's creation.

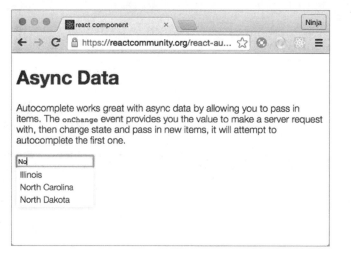

Figure 4.1
**The `react-autocomplete`
component in action**

To put it another way, properties are immutable in the current component, meaning you don't change properties in this component unless you re-create the component by passing new values from a parent (figure 4.2). But you must store the information you receive from the server somewhere and then display the new list of matches in the view. How do you update the view if the properties are unchangeable?

One solution is to render an element with new properties each time you get the new server response. But then you'll have to have logic outside the component—the component stops being self-contained. Clearly, if you can't change the values of properties, and the autocomplete needs to be self-contained, you can't use properties. Thus the

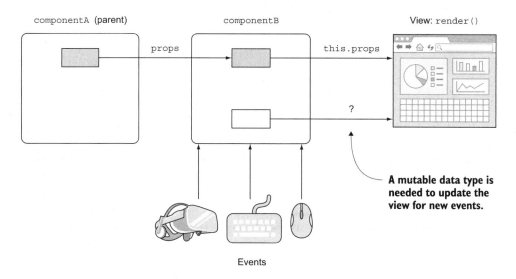

Figure 4.2   We need another data type that's mutable in the component to make the view change.

question is, how do you update views in response to events without re-creating a component (`createElement()` or JSX `<NAME/>`)? This is the problem that states solve.

Once the response from the server is ready, your callback code will augment the component state accordingly. You'll have to write this code yourself. Once the state is updated, though, React will intelligently update the view for you (only in the places where it needs to be updated; that's where you use the state data).

With React component states, you can build meaningful, interactive React applications. *State* is the core concept that lets you build React components that can store data and automagically augment views based on data changes.

> **NOTE** The source code for the examples in this chapter is at www.manning .com/books/react-quickly and at https://github.com/azat-co/react-quickly/ tree/master/ch04 (in the ch04 folder of the GitHub repository https:// github.com/azat-co/react-quickly). You can also find some demos at http:// reactquickly.co/demos.

4.1   *What are React component states?*

A React *state* is a mutable data store of components—self-contained, functionality-centric blocks of UI and logic. *Mutable* means state values can change. By using state in a view (`render()`) and changing values later, you can affect the view's representation.

Here's a metaphor: if you think of a component as a function that has properties and state as its input, then the result of this function is the UI description (view). Or, as React teams phrase it, "Components are state machines." Properties and state both augment views, but they're used for different purposes (see section 4.3).

To work with states, you access them by name. This name is an attribute (a.k.a. an object key or an object property—not a component property) of the `this.state` object: for example, `this.state.autocompleMatches` or `this.state.inputFieldValue`.

> **NOTE** Generally speaking, the word *states* refers to the attributes of the `this.state` object in a component. Depending on the context, *state* (singular) can refer to the `this.state` object or an individual attribute (such as `this.state.inputFieldValue`). Conversely, *states* (plural) almost always refers to the multiple attributes of the `state` object in a single component.

State data is often used to display dynamic information in a view to augment the rendering of views. Going back to the earlier example of an autocomplete field, the state changes in response to the XHR request to the server, which is, in turn, triggered by a user typing in the field. React takes care of keeping views up to date when the state used in the views changes. In essence, when state changes, *only* the *corresponding parts* of views change (down to single elements or even an attribute value of a single element).

Everything else in the DOM remains intact. This is possible due to the virtual DOM (see section 1.1.1), which React uses to determine the delta using the reconciliation process. This is how you can write declaratively. React does all the magic for you. The steps in the view change and how it happens are discussed in chapter 5.

React developers use states to generate new UIs. Component properties (this.props), regular variables (inputValue), and class attributes (this.inputValue) won't do it, because they don't trigger a view change when you alter their values (in the current component context). For instance, the following is an antipattern, showing that if you change a value in anything except the state, you won't get view updates:

```
// Anti-pattern: Stay away from it!
let inputValue = 'Texas'
class Autocomplete extends React.Component {           ┐ Triggered as a result of
  updateValues() {                                     ◁─┘ a user action (typing)
    this.props.inputValue = 'California'
    inputValue = 'California'
    this.inputValue = 'California'
  }
  render() {
    return (
      <div>
        {this.props.inputValue}
        {inputValue}
        {this.inputValue}
      </div>
    )
  }
}
```

Next, you'll see how to work with React component states.

NOTE As mentioned earlier (repetition is the mother of skills), properties will change the view if you pass a new value from a parent, which in turn will create a new instance of the component you're currently working with. In the context of a given component, changing properties as in this.props.inputValue = 'California' won't cut it.

4.2   *Working with states*

To be able to work with states, you need to know how to access values, update them, and set the initial values. Let's start with accessing states in React components.

4.2.1   *Accessing states*

The state object is an attribute of a component and can be accessed with a this reference; for example, this.state.name. You'll recall that you can access and print variables in JSX with curly braces ({}). Similarly, you can render this.state (like any other variable or custom component class attribute) in render(); for example, {this.state.inputFieldValue}. This syntax is similar to the way you access properties with this.props.name.

Let's use what you've learned so far to implement a clock, as shown in figure 4.3. The goal is to have a self-contained component class that anyone can import and use in their application without having to jump through hoops. The clock must render the current time.

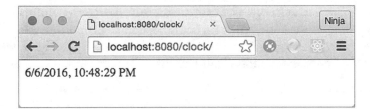

Figure 4.3   The clock component shows the current time in digital format and is updated every second.

The structure of the clock project is as follows:

```
/clock
   index.html
   /jsx
      script.jsx
      clock.jsx
   /js
      script.js
      clock.js
      react.js
      react-dom.js
```

I'm using the Babel CLI with a watch (-w) and a directory flag (-d) to compile all source JSX files from clock/jsx to a destination folder, clock/js, and recompile on changes. Moreover, I have the command saved as an npm script in my package.json in a parent folder, ch04, in order to run `npm run build-clock` from ch04:

```
"scripts": {
    "build-clock": "./node_modules/.bin/babel clock/jsx -d clock/js -w"
},
```

Obviously, time is always changing (for good or for bad). Because of that, you'll need to update the view—and you can do so by using state. Give it the name `currentTime`, and try to render this state as shown in the following listing.

Listing 4.1   Rendering state in JSX

```
class Clock extends React.Component {
  render() {
    return <div>{this.state.currentTime}</div>
  }
}

ReactDOM.render(
  <Clock />,
  document.getElementById('content')
)
```

You'll get an error: `Uncaught TypeError: Cannot read property 'currentTime' of null`. Normally, JavaScript error messages are as helpful as a glass of cold water to a drowning man. It's good that, at least in this case, JavaScript gives you a helpful message. This one means you don't have a value for `currentTime`. Unlike properties, states aren't set on a parent. You can't `setState` in `render()` either, because it'll create a circular (`setState → render → setState...`) loop—and, in this case, React will throw an error.

4.2.2 Setting the initial state

Thus far, you've seen that before you use state data in `render()`, you must initialize the state. To set the initial state, use `this.state` in the constructor with your ES6 class `React.Component` syntax. Don't forget to invoke `super()` with properties; otherwise, the logic in the parent (`React.Component`) won't work:

```
class MyFancyComponent extends React.Component {
  constructor(props) {
    super(props)
    this.state = {...}
  }
  render() {
    ...
  }
}
```

You can also add other logic while you're setting the initial state. For example, you can set the value of `currentTime` using `new Date()`. You can even use `toLocaleString()` to get the proper date and time format for the user's location, as shown next (ch04/clock).

Listing 4.2 `Clock` component constructor

```
class Clock extends React.Component {
  constructor(props) {
    super(props)
    this.state = {currentTime: (new Date()).toLocaleString()}
  }
  ...
}
```

The value of `this.state` must be an object. We won't get into a lot of detail here about the ES6 `constructor()`; see appendix E and the ES6 cheatsheet at https://github.com/azat-co/cheatsheets/tree/master/es6. The gist is that as with other OOP languages, `constructor()` is invoked when an instance of this class is created. The constructor method name must be exactly `constructor`. Think of it as an ES6 convention. Furthermore, if you create a `constructor()` method, you'll almost always need to invoke `super()` inside it; otherwise, the parent's constructor won't be executed. On the other hand, if you don't define a `constructor()` method, then the call to `super()` will be assumed under the hood.

Class attributes

Hopefully, Technical Committee 39 (TC39: the people behind the ECMAScript standard) will add attributes to the class syntax in future versions of ECMAScript! This way, we'll be able to set `state` not just in the constructor, but also in the body of a class:

```
class Clock extends React.Component {
  state = {
    ...
  }
}
```

The proposal for class fields/attributes/properties is at https://github.com/jeffmo/es-class-fields-and-static-properties. It's been there for many years, but as of this writing (March 2017), it's only a stage 2 proposal (stage 4 means final and in the standard), meaning it's not widely available in browsers. That is, this feature won't work natively. (As of this writing, exactly zero browsers support class fields.)

Most likely, you'll have to use a transpiler (such as Babel, Traceur, or TypeScript) to ensure that the code will work in all browsers. Check out the current compatibility of class properties in the ECMAScript compatibility table (http://kangax.github.io/compat-table/esnext), and, if needed, use the ES.Next Babel preset.

Here, `currentTime` is an arbitrary name; you'll need to use the same name later when accessing and updating this state. You can name the state anything you want, as long as you refer to it later using this name.

The `state` object can have nested objects or arrays. This example adds an array of my books to the state:

```
class Content extends React.Component {
  constructor(props) {
    super(props)
    this.state = {
      githubName: 'azat-co',
      books: [
        'pro express.js',
        'practical node.js',
        'rapid prototyping with js'
      ]
    }
  }
  render() {
    ...
  }
}
```

The `constructor()` method is called just once, when a React element is created from this class. This way, you can set state directly by using `this.state` just once, in the constructor() method. Avoid setting and updating state directly with this.state = ... anywhere else, because doing so may lead to unintended consequences.

> **NOTE** With React's own createClass() method to define a component, you'll need to use getInitialState(). For more information on create-Class() and an example in ES5, see the sidebar in section 2.2, "ES6+/ES2015+ and React."

This will only get you the first value, which will be outdated very soon—like, in 1 second. What's the point of a clock that doesn't show the current time? Luckily, there's a way to update the state.

4.2.3 Updating states

You change state with the this.setState(data, callback) class method. When this method is invoked, React merges the data with current states and calls render(). After that, React calls callback.

Having the callback in setState() is important because the method works *asynchronously*. If you're relying on the new state, you can use the callback to make sure this new state is available.

If you rely on a new state without waiting for setState() to finish its work—that is, working synchronously with an asynchronous operation—then you may have a bug when you rely on new state values to be updated, but the state is still an old state with old values.

So far, you've rendered the time from a state. You also set the initial state, but you need to update the time every second, right? To do so, you can use a browser timer function, setInterval() (http://mng.bz/P2d6), which will execute the state update every *n* milliseconds. The setInterval() method is implemented in virtually all modern browsers as a global, which means you can use it without any libraries or prefixes. Here's an example:

```
setInterval(()=>{
  console.log('Updating time...')
  this.setState({
    currentTime: (new Date()).toLocaleString()
  })
}, 1000)
```

To kick-start the clock, you need to invoke setInterval() once. Let's create a launchClock() method to do just that; you'll call launchClock() in the constructor. The final clock is shown in the following listing (ch04/clock/jsx/clock.jsx).

> **Listing 4.3   Implementing a clock with state**

```
class Clock extends React.Component {
        constructor(props) {
            super(props)
            this.launchClock()                    Triggers
                                                  launchClock()
```

```
                    this.state = {
                      currentTime: (new Date()).toLocaleString()     Sets the initial state
                    }                                                 to the current time
                  }
                  launchClock() {
Updates the         setInterval(()=>{
state with the        console.log('Updating time...')
current time          this.setState({
every second            currentTime: (new Date()).toLocaleString()
                            })
                    }, 1000)
                  }
                  render() {
                    console.log('Rendering Clock...')                 Renders
                    return <div>{this.state.currentTime}</div>        the state
                  }
                }
```

You can use `setState()` anywhere, not just in `launchClock()` (which is invoked by constructor), as shown in the example. Typically, `setState()` is called from the event handler or as a callback for incoming data or data updates.

> **TIP** Changing a state value in your code using `this.state.name= 'new name'` won't do any good. This won't trigger a rerender and a possible real DOM update, which you want. For the most part, changing state directly without `setState()` is an antipattern and should be avoided.

It's important to note that `setState()` updates only the states you pass to it (partially or merged, but not a complete replace). It doesn't replace the entire `state` object each time. So, if you have three states and change one, the other two will remain unchanged. In the following example, `userEmail` and `userId` will remain intact:

```
constructor(props) {
  super(props)
  this.state = {
    userName: 'Azat Mardan',
    userEmail: 'hi@azat.co',
    userId: 3967
  }
}
updateValues() {
  this.setState({userName: 'Azat'})
}
```

If your intention is to update all three states, you need to do so explicitly by passing the new values for these states to `setState()`. (Another method you may still see in old React code but that's no longer working and has been deprecated is the `this.replaceState()` method.[1] As you can guess from the name, it replaced the entire `state` object with all its attributes.)

---

[1] https://github.com/facebook/react/issues/3236.

Keep in mind that `setState()` triggers `render()`. It works in most cases. In some edge-case scenarios where the code depends on external data, you can trigger a rerender with `this.forceUpdate()`. But this approach should be avoided as a bad practice, because relying on external data and not state makes components more fragile and depends on external factors (tight coupling).

As mentioned earlier, you can access the `state` object with `this.state`. As you'll recall, you output values with curly braces (`{}`) in JSX; therefore, to declare a state property in the view (that is, render's return statement), apply `{this.state.NAME}`.

React magic happens when you use state data in a view (for example, to print, in an `if/else` statement, as a value of an attribute, or as a child's property value) and then give `setState()` new values. Boom! React updates the necessary HTML for you. You can see this in your DevTools console. It should show cycles of "Updating …" and then "Rendering …." And the best part is that *only* the absolute minimum required DOM elements will be affected.

Binding this in JavaScript

In JavaScript, `this` mutates (changes) its value depending on the place from which a function is called. To ensure that `this` refers to your component class, you need to bind the function to the proper context (`this` value: your component class).

If you're using ES6+/ES2015+, as I do in this book, you can use fat-arrow function syntax to create a function with autobinding:

```
setInterval(()=>{
  this.setState({
    currentTime: (new Date()).toLocaleString()
  })
}, 1000)
```

Autobinding means the function created with a fat arrow gets the current value of `this`, which in this case is `Clock`.

The manual approach uses the `bind(this)` method on the closure:

```
function() {...}.bind(this)
```

It looks like this for your clock:

```
setInterval(function(){
  this.setState({
    currentTime: (new Date()).toLocaleString()
  })
}.bind(this), 1000)
```

This behavior isn't exclusive to React. The `this` keyword mutates in a function's closure, so you need do some sort of binding; you can also save the context (`this`) value so you can use it later.

> **(continued)**
>
> Typically, you'll see variables like `self`, `that`, and `_this` used to save the value of the original `this`. You've probably seen statements like the following:
>
> ```
> var that = this
> var _this = this
> var self = this
> ```
>
> The idea is straightforward: you create a variable and use it in the closure instead of referring to `this`. The new variable isn't a copy but rather a reference to the original `this` value. Here's `setInterval()`:
>
> ```
> var _this = this
> setInterval(function(){
>   _this.setState({
>     currentTime: (new Date()).toLocaleString()
>   })
> }, 1000)
> ```

You have a clock, and it's working, as shown in figure 4.4. Tadaaa!

One more quick thing before we move on. You can see how React is reusing the same DOM `<div>` element and only changes the text inside it. Go ahead and use DevTools to modify the CSS of this element. I added a style to make the text blue: `color: blue`, as shown in figure 4.5 (you can see the color in electronic versions of the book). I created an inline style, not a class. The element and its new inline style stayed the same (blue) while the time kept ticking.

React will only update the inner HTML (the content of the second `<div>` container). The `<div>` itself, as well as all other elements on this page, remain intact. Neat.

Figure 4.4   The `Clock` is ticking.

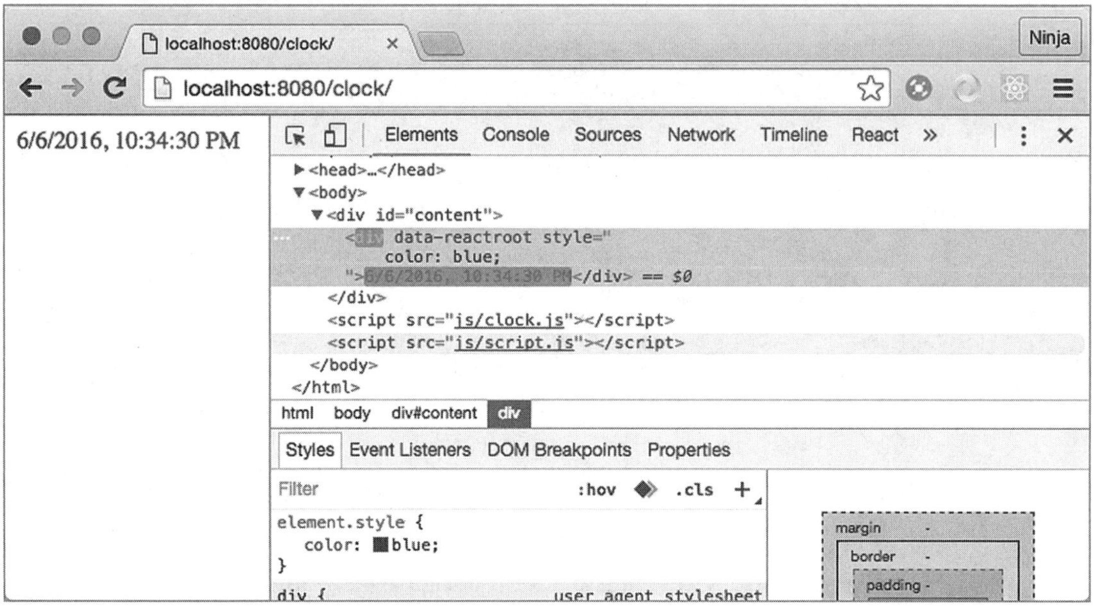

Figure 4.5 React is updating the time's text, not the `<div>` element (I manually added `color: blue`, and the `<div>` remained blue).

4.3 States and properties

States and properties are both attributes of a class, meaning they're `this.state` and `this.props`. That's the only similarity! One of the primary differences between states and properties is that the former are mutable, whereas the latter are immutable.

Another difference between properties and states is that you pass properties from parent components, whereas you define states in the component itself, not its parent. The philosophy is that you can only change the value of a property from the parent, not the component. So properties determine the view upon creation, and then they remain static (they don't change). The state, on the other hand, is set and updated by the object.

Properties and states serve different purposes, but both are accessible as attributes of the component class, and both help you to compose components with a different representation (view). There are differences between properties and states when it comes to the component lifecycle (more in chapter 5). Think of properties and states as inputs for a function that produces different outputs. Those outputs are views. So you can have different UIs (views) for each set of different properties and states (see figure 4.6).

Not all components need to have state. In the next section, you'll see how to use properties with stateless components.

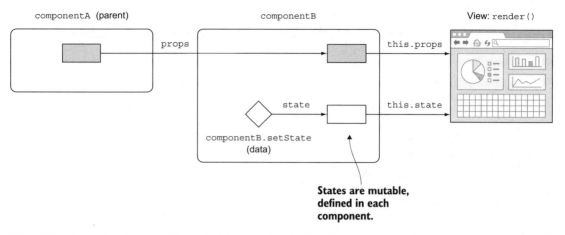

States are mutable, defined in each component.

Figure 4.6 New values for properties and states can change the UI. New property values come from a parent, and new state values come from the component.

4.4 Stateless components

A *stateless* component has no states or components or any other React lifecycle events/methods (see chapter 5). The purpose of a stateless component is just to render the view. The only thing it can do is take properties and do something with them—it's a simple function with the input (properties) and the output (UI element).

The benefit of using stateless components is that they're predictable, because you have one input that determines the output. Predictability means they're easier to understand, maintain, and debug. In fact, not having a state is the most desired React practice—the more stateless components you use and the fewer stateful ones you use, the better.

You wrote a lot of stateless components in the first three chapters of this book. For example, Hello World is a stateless component (ch03/hello-js-world-jsx/jsx/script.jsx).

Listing 4.4 Stateless Hello World

```
class HelloWorld extends React.Component {
  render() {
    return <h1 {...this.props}>Hello {this.props.frameworkName} world!!!
    </h1>
  }
}
```

To provide a smaller syntax for stateless components, React uses this function style: you create a function that takes properties as an argument and returns the view. A stateless component renders like any other component. For example, the HelloWorld component can be rewritten as a function that returns <h1>:

```
const HelloWorld = function(props){
  return <h1 {...props}>Hello {props.frameworkName} world!!!</h1>
}
```

You can use ES6+/ES2015+ arrow functions for stateless components. The following snippet is analogous to the previous one (return can be omitted too, but I like to include it):

```
const HelloWorld = (props)=>{
  return <h1 {...props}>Hello {props.frameworkName} world!!!</h1>
}
```

As you can see, you can also define functions as React components when there's no need for state. In other words, to create a stateless component, define it as a function. Here's an example in which Link is a stateless component:

```
function Link (props) {
  return <a href={props.href} target="_blank" className="btn btn-primary">
  ➥ {props.text}</a>
}
ReactDOM.render(
  <Link text='Buy React Quickly'
  ➥ href='https://www.manning.com/books/react-quickly'/>,
  document.getElementById('content')
)
```

Although there's no need for autobinding, you can use the fat-arrow function syntax for brevity (when there's a single statement, the notation can be a one-liner):

```
const Link = props => <a href={props.href}
  target="_blank"
  className="btn btn-primary">
    {props.text}
  </a>
```

Or you can use the same arrow function but with curly braces ({}), explicit return, and parentheses (()) to make it *subjectively* more readable:

```
const Link = (props)=> {
  return (
    <a href={props.href}
      target="_blank"
      className="btn btn-primary">
        {props.text}
    </a>
  )
}
```

In a stateless component, you can't have a state, but you can have two properties: propTypes and defaultProps (see sections 8.1 and 8.2, respectively). You set them on the object. And, by the way, it's okay to *not* have an opening parenthesis after return as long as you start an element on the same line:

```
function Link (props) {
  return <a href={props.href}
    target="_blank"
    className="btn btn-primary">
      {props.text}
  </a>
}
Link.propTypes = {...}
Link.defaultProps = {...}
```

You also *cannot* use references (refs) with stateless components (functions).[2] If you need to use refs, you can wrap a stateless component in a normal React component. More about references in section 7.2.3.

4.5   *Stateful vs. stateless components*

Why use stateless components? They're more declarative and work better when all you need to do is render some HTML without creating a backing instance or lifecycle components. Basically, stateless components reduce duplication and provide better syntax and more simplicity when all you need to do is mesh together some properties and elements into HTML.

My suggested approach, and the best practice according to the React team, is to use stateless components instead of normal components as often as possible. But as you saw in the clock example, it's not always possible; sometimes you have to resort to using states. So, you have a handful of stateful components on top of the hierarchy to handle the UI states, interactions, and other application logic (such as loading data from a server).

Don't think that stateless components must be static. By providing different properties for them, you can change their representation. Let's look at an example that refactors and enhances Clock into three components: a stateful clock that has the state and the logic to update it; and two stateless components, DigitalDisplay and AnalogDisplay, which only output time (but do it in different ways). The goal is something like figure 4.7. Pretty, right?

The structure of the project is as follows:

```
/clock-analog-digital
  /jsx
    analog-display.jsx
    clock.jsx
    digital-display.jsx
    script.jsx
  /js
    analog-display.js
    clock.js
    digital-display.js
    script.js
    react.js
    react-dom.js
  index.html
```

---

[2] "React stateless component this.refs..value?" http://mng.bz/Eb91.

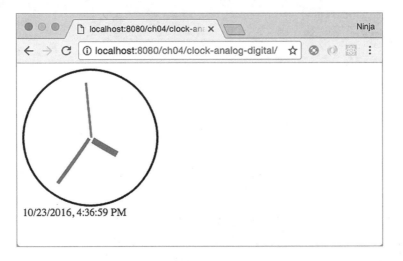

Figure 4.7   Clock with two ways to show time: analog and digital

The code for `Clock` renders the two child elements and passes the `time` property with the value of the `currentTime` state. The state of a parent becomes a property of a child.

Listing 4.5   Passing state to children

```
...
  render() {
    console.log('Rendering...')
    return <div>
      <AnalogDisplay time={this.state.currentTime}/>
      <DigitalDisplay time={this.state.currentTime}/>
    </div>
  }
```

Now, you need to create `DigitalDisplay`, which is simple. It's a function that takes the properties and displays `time` from that property argument (`props.time`), as shown next (ch04/clock-analog-digital/jsx/digital-display.jsx).

Listing 4.6   Stateless digital display component

```
const DigitalDisplay = function(props) {
  return <div>{props.time}</div>
}
```

`AnalogDisplay` is also a function that implements a stateless component; but in its body is some fancy animation to rotate the hands. The animation works based on the `time` property, not based on any state. The idea is to take the time as a string; convert it to a Date object; get minutes, hours, and seconds; and convert those to degrees. For example, here's how to get seconds as angle degrees:

```
let date = new Date('1/9/2007, 9:46:15 AM')
console.log((date.getSeconds()/60)*360 )  // 90
```

Once you have the degrees, you can use them in CSS, written as an object literal. The difference is that in the React CSS, the style properties are camelCased, whereas in regular CSS, the dashes (-) make style properties invalid JavaScript. As mentioned earlier, having objects for styles allows React to more quickly determine the difference between the old element and the new element. See section 3.4.3. for more about style and CSS in React.

The following listing shows the stateless analog display component with CSS that uses values from the time property (ch04/clock-analog-digital/jsx/analog-display.jsx).

Listing 4.7 Stateless analog display component

```
const AnalogDisplay = function AnalogDisplay(props) {
  let date = new Date(props.time)          ◁─── Converts the string date
  let dialStyle = {                             into an object so you can
    position: 'relative',                       parse it later
    top: 0,
    left: 0,
    width: 200,
    height: 200,
    borderRadius: 20000,        ◁─── Uses borderRadius (border-radius in
    borderStyle: 'solid',            regular CSS) on a <div> with a high
    borderColor: 'black'             number relative to the width, to make
  }                                  it a circle
  let secondHandStyle = {
    position: 'relative',
    top: 100,
    left: 100,
    border: '1px solid red',
    width: '40%',
    height: 1,
    transform: 'rotate(' + ((date.getSeconds()/60)*360 - 90 )
    ➥ .toString() + 'deg)',        ◁─── Calculates the angle and rotates the
    transformOrigin: '0% 0%',    ◁───     second hand with minus 90 to offset for
    backgroundColor: 'red'                the hand's starting horizontal position
  }
  let minuteHandStyle = {
    position: 'relative',
    top: 100,               Uses transformOrigin to offset
    left: 100,              the center of the rotation
    border: '1px solid grey',
    width: '40%',
    height: 3,
    transform: 'rotate(' + ((date.getMinutes()/60)*360 - 90 )
    ➥ .toString() + 'deg)',
```

```
      transformOrigin: '0% 0%',
      backgroundColor: 'grey'
  }
  let hourHandStyle = {
    position: 'relative',
    top: 92,
    left: 106,
    border: '1px solid grey',
    width: '20%',
    height: 7,
    transform: 'rotate(' + ((date.getHours()/12)*360 - 90 ).toString() + 'deg)',
    transformOrigin: '0% 0%',
    backgroundColor: 'grey'
  }
  return <div>
    <div style={dialStyle}>
      <div style={secondHandStyle}/>
      <div style={minuteHandStyle}/>
      <div style={hourHandStyle}/>
    </div>
  </div>
}
```

> Renders the containers with applicable styles relative to the clock dial (large circle)

If you have React Developer Tools for Chrome or Firefox (available at http://
mng.bz/mt5P and http://mng.bz/DANq), you can open the React pane in your
DevTools (or an analog in Firefox). Mine shows that the <Clock> element has two
children (see figure 4.8). Notice that React DevTools tells you the names of the
components along with the state, currentTime. What a great tool for debugging!

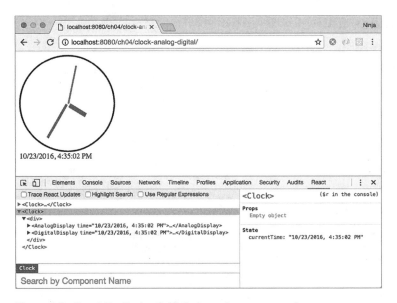

Figure 4.8   React DevTools v0.15.4 shows two components.

Note that in this example, I used anonymous expressions stored as `const` variables. Another approach is to use a syntax with named function declarations:

```
function AnalogDisplay(props) {...}
```

Or you can use the named function declaration referenced from a variable:

```
const AnalogDisplay = function AnalogDisplay(props) {...}
```

About function declarations in JavaScript

In JavaScript, there are several way to define a function. You can write an anonymous function expression that's used right away (typically as a callback):

```
function() { return 'howdy'}
```

Or you can create an IIFE:

```
(function() {
  return('howdy')
}) ()
```

An anonymous function expression can be referenced in a variable:

```
let sayHelloInMandarin = function() { return 'nǐ hǎo'}
```

This is a named or *hoisted* function expression:

```
function sayHelloInTatar() { return 'sălam'}
```

And this is a named or hoisted function expression referenced in a variable:

```
let sayHelloInSpanish = function digaHolaEnEspanol() { return 'hola'}
```

Finally, you can use an immediately invoked, named function expression:

```
(function sayHelloInTexan() {
    return('howdy')
}) ()
```

There's no fat-arrow syntax for named/hoisted functions.

As you can see, the `AnalogDisplay` and `DigitalDisplay` components are stateless: they have no states. They also don't have any methods, except for the body of the function, which is not like `render()` in a normal React class definition. All the logic and states of the app are in `Clock`.

In contrast, the only logic you put into the stateless components is the animation, but that's closely related to the analog display. Clearly, it would have been a bad design to include analog animation in `Clock`. Now, you have two components, and you can render either or both of them from Clock. Using stateless components properly with a handful of stateful components allows for more flexible, simpler, better design.

Usually, when React developers say *stateless*, they mean a component created with a function or fat-arrow syntax. It's possible to have a stateless component created with a class, but this approach isn't recommended because then it's too easy for someone else (or you in six months) to add a state. No temptation, no way to complicate code!

You may be wondering whether a stateless component can have methods. Obviously, if you use classes, then yes, they can have methods; but as I mentioned, most developers use functions. Although you can attach methods to functions (they're also objects in JavaScript), the code isn't elegant, because you can't use this in a function (the value isn't the component; it's window):

```
// Anti-pattern: Don't do this.
const DigitalDisplay = function(props) {
  return <div>{DigitalDisplay.locale(props.time)}</div>
}
DigitalDisplay.locale = (time)=>{
  return (new Date(time)).toLocaleString('EU')
}
```

If you need to perform some logic related to the view, create a new function right in the stateless component:

```
// Good pattern
const DigitalDisplay = function(props) {
  const locale = time => (new Date(time)).toLocaleString('EU')
  return <div>{locale(props.time)}</div>
}
```

Keep your stateless components simple: no states and no methods. In particular, don't have any calls to external methods or functions, because their results may break predictability (and violate the concept of purity).

4.6   Quiz

1 You can set state in a component method (not a constructor) with which syntax? this.setState(a), this.state = a, or this.a = a
2 If you want to update the render process, it's normal practice to change properties in components like this: this.props.a=100. True or false?
3 States are mutable, and properties are immutable. True or false?
4 Stateless components can be implemented as functions. True or false?
5 How do you define the first state variables when an element is created? setState(), initialState(), this.state =... in the constructor, or setInitialState()

4.7 Summary

- States are mutable; properties are immutable.
- `getInitialState` allows components to have an initial `state` object.
- `this.setState` updates only the properties you pass to it, not all `state` object properties.
- `{}` is a way to render variables and execute JavaScript in JSX code.
- `this.state.NAME` is the way to access state variables.
- Stateless components are the preferred way of working with React.

4.8 Quiz answers

1 `this.setState(a)`, because we never, never, never assign `this.state` directly except in `constructor()`. `this.a` will not do anything with state. It'll only create an instance field/attribute/property.

2 False. Changing a property in the component won't trigger a rerender.

3 True. There's no way to change a property from a component—only from its parent. Conversely, states are changed only by the component.

4 True. You can use the arrow function or the traditional `function()` `{}` definition, but both must return an element (single element).

5 `this.state = ...` in the constructor, or `getInitialState()` if you're using `createClass()`.

Watch this chapter's introduction video by scanning this QR code with your phone or going to http://reactquickly.co/videos/ch05.

React component lifecycle events

5

This chapter covers

- Getting a bird's-eye view of React component lifecycle events
- Understanding event categories
- Defining an event
- Mounting, updating, and unmounting events

Chapter 2 provided information about how to create components, but there are certain situations in which you need more granular control over a component. For instance, you may be building a custom radio button component that can change in size depending on the screen width. Or perhaps you're building a menu that needs to get information from the server by sending an XHR request.

One approach would be to implement the necessary logic before instantiating a component and then re-create it by providing different properties. Unfortunately, this won't create a self-contained component, and thus you'll lose React's benefit of providing a component-based architecture.

The best approach is to use component lifecycle events. By mounting events, you can inject the necessary logic into components. Moreover, you can use other events to make components smarter by providing specific logic about whether or not to rerender their views (overwriting React's default algorithm).

Going back to the examples of a custom radio button and menu, the button can attach event listeners to `window` (`onResize`) when the button component is created, and detach them when the component is removed. And the menu can fetch data from the server when the React element is mounted (inserted) into the real DOM.

Onward to learning about component lifecycle events!

NOTE The source code for the examples in this chapter is at www.manning .com/books/react-quickly and https://github.com/azat-co/react-quickly/ tree/master/ch05 (in the ch05 folder of the GitHub repository https:// github.com/azat-co/react-quickly). You can also find some demos at http:// reactquickly.co/demos.

5.1   *A bird's-eye view of React component lifecycle events*

React provides a way for you to control and customize a component's behavior based on its lifecycle events (think of *hooking* [https://en.wikipedia.org/wiki/Hooking] in computer programming). These events belong to the following categories:

- *Mounting events*—Happen when a React element (an instance of a component class) is attached to a DOM node
- *Updating events*—Happen when a React element is updated as a result of new values of its properties or state
- *Unmounting events*—Happen when a React element is detached from the DOM

Each and every React component has *lifecycle events* that are triggered at certain moments depending on what a component has done or will do. Some of them execute just once, whereas others can be executed continuously.

Lifecycle events allow you to implement custom logic that will enhance what components can do. You can also use them to modify the behavior of components: for example, to decide when to rerender. This enhances performance, because unnecessary operations are eliminated. Another usage is to fetch data from the back end or integrate with DOM events or other front-end libraries. Let's look more closely at how categories of events operate, what events they possess, and in what sequence those events are executed.

5.2   *Categories of events*

React defines several component events in three categories (see figure 5.1 and also table 5.1, later in the chapter). Each category can fire events various number of times:

- *Mounting*—React invokes events only once.
- *Updating*—React can invoke events many times.
- *Unmounting*—React invokes events only once.

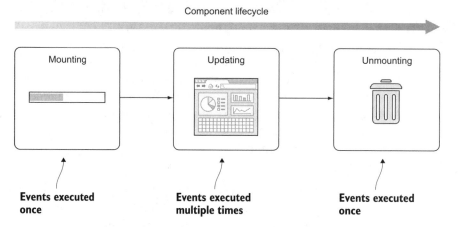

Figure 5.1   Categories of lifecycle events as a component proceeds through its lifecycle, and how many times events in a category can be called

In addition to lifecycle events, I'll include `constructor()`, to illustrate the order of execution from start to finish during the component's lifecycle (updating can happen multiple times):

- `constructor()`—Happens when an element is created and lets you set the default properties (chapter 2) and the initial state (chapter 4)
- Mounting
  - `componentWillMount()`—Happens before mounting to the DOM
  - `componentDidMount()`—Happens after mounting and rendering
- Updating
  - `componentWillReceiveProps(nextProps)`—Happens when the component is about to receive properties
  - `shouldComponentUpdate(nextProps, nextState)-> bool`—Lets you optimize the component's rerendering by determining when to update and when to not update
  - `componentWillUpdate(nextProps, nextState)`—Happens right before the component is updated
  - `componentDidUpdate(prevProps, prevState)`—Happens right after the component updated
- Unmounting
  - `componentWillUnmount function()`—Lets you unbind and detach any event listeners or do other cleanup work before the component is unmounted

Usually, an event's name makes clear to developers when the event is triggered. For example, `componentDidUpdate()` is fired when the component is updated. In other cases, there are subtle differences. Table 5.1 shows the sequence of lifecycle events (from top to bottom) and how some of them depend on changes of properties or state (the Component Properties and Component State columns).

Table 5.1   Lifecycle events (and their relation with state and properties)

Mounting	Updating component properties	Updating component state	Updating using forceUpdate()	Unmounting
constructor()				
componentWillMount()				
	componentWillReceiveProps()			
	shouldComponentUpdate()	shouldComponentUpdate()		
	componentWillUpdate()	componentWillUpdate()	componentWillUpdate()	
render()	render()	render()	render()	
componentDidMount()	componentDidUpdate()	componentDidUpdate()	componentDidUpdate()	
				componentWillUnmount()

There's one more case in which a component might be rerendered: when `this.forceUpdate()` is called. As you can guess from the name, it forces updates. You may need to resort to using it when, for one reason or another, updating state or properties won't trigger a desired rerender. For example, this might happen when you use data in `render()` that isn't part of the state or properties, and that data changes—hence, the need to manually trigger an update. Generally (and according to the React core team), the `this.forceUpdate()` method (http://mng.bz/v5sU) should be avoided, because it makes components impure (see the following sidebar).

Next, let's define an event to see it in action.

Pure functions

In computer science in general—not just in React—a *pure* function is a function that

- Given the same input, will *always* return the same output
- Has no side effects (doesn't alter external states)
- Doesn't rely on any external state

For example, here's a pure function that doubles the value of the input: $f(x) = 2x$ or, in JavaScript/Node, `let f= (n) ⇒2*n`. Here it is in action:

```
let f = (n)=>2*n
consoleg.log(f(7))
```

An impure function to double numbers looks like this in action (adding curly braces removes the implicit return of the one-liner fat-arrow function):

```
let sharedStateNumber = 7
let double
let f = ()=> {double =2*sharedStateNumber}
f()
console.log(double)
```

Pure functions are the cornerstone of functional programming (FP), which minimizes state as much as possible. Developers (especially functional programmers) prefer pure functions primarily because their usage mitigates shared state, which in turn simplifies development and decouples different pieces of logic. In addition, using them makes testing easier. When it comes to React, you already know that having more stateless components and fewer dependencies is better; that's why the best practice is to create pure functions.

In some ways, FP contradicts OOP (or is it OOP that contradicts FP?), with FP fans saying that Fortran and Java were programming dead ends and that Lisp (and nowadays, Clojure and Elm) is the way to go. It's a fascinating debate to follow. Personally, I'm slightly biased toward the functional approach.

Many good books have been written about FP, because the concept has been around for decades. For this reason, I won't get into much detail here; but I highly recommend learning more about FP, because it will make you a better programmer even if you never plan to use it at your job.

5.3   *Implementing an event*

To implement lifecycle events, you define them on a class as methods (see section 3.2.5)—this is a convention that React expects you to follow. React checks to see whether there's a method with an event name; if React finds a method, it will call that method. Otherwise, React will continue its normal flow. Obviously, event names are case sensitive like any name in JavaScript.

To put it differently, under the hood, React calls certain methods during a component's lifecycle if they're defined. For example, if you define `componentDidMount()`, then React will call this method when an element of this component class is mounted. `componentDidMount()` belongs to the mounting category listed in table 5.1, and it will be called once per instance of the component class:

```
class Clock extends React.Component {
  componentDidMount() {
  }
  ...
}
```

If no `componentDidMount()` method is defined, React won't execute any code for this event. Thus, the name of the method must match the name of the event. Going forward, I'll use the terms *event, event handler,* and *method* interchangeably in this chapter.

As you might have guessed from its name, the `componentDidMount()` method is invoked when a component is inserted into the DOM. This method is a recommended place to put code to integrate with other front-end frameworks and libraries as well as to send XHR requests to a server, because at this point in the lifecycle, the component's element is in the real DOM and you get access to all of its elements, including children.

Let's go back to the issues I mentioned at the beginning of the chapter: resizing, and fetching data from a server. For the first, you can create an event listener in `componentDidMount()` that will listen for `window.resize` events. For the second, you can make an XHR call in `componentDidMount()` and update the state when you have a response from the server.

Equally important, `componentDidMount()` comes in handy in isomorphic/universal code (where the same components are used on the server and in the browser). You can put browser-only logic in this method and rest assured that it'll only be called for browser rendering, and not on the server side. There's more on isomorphic JavaScript with React in chapter 16.

Most developers learn best by looking at examples. For this reason, let's consider a trivial case that uses `componentDidMount()` to print the DOM information to the console. This is feasible because this event is fired after all the rendering has happened; thus, you have access to the DOM elements.

Creating event listeners for component lifecycle events is straightforward: you define a method on the component/class. For the fun of it, let's add `componentWillMount()` to contrast the absence of the real DOM for this element at this stage.

The DOM node information is obtained via the React DOM's utility function `ReactDOM.findDOMNode()`, to which you pass the class. Note that DOM isn't camelCase, but rather is in all-caps:

```
class Content extends React.Component {
  componentWillMount() {
    console.log(ReactDOM.findDOMNode(this))        ⟵ Expects the DOM
  }                                                    node to be null
  componentDidMount() {
    console.dir(ReactDOM.findDOMNode(this))         ⟵ Expects the DOM
  }                                                     node to be <div>
  render() {
    return (

    )
  }
}
```

The result is this output in the developer console, which reassures you that `componentDidMount()` is executed when you have real DOM elements (see figure 5.2):

```
html
null
div
```

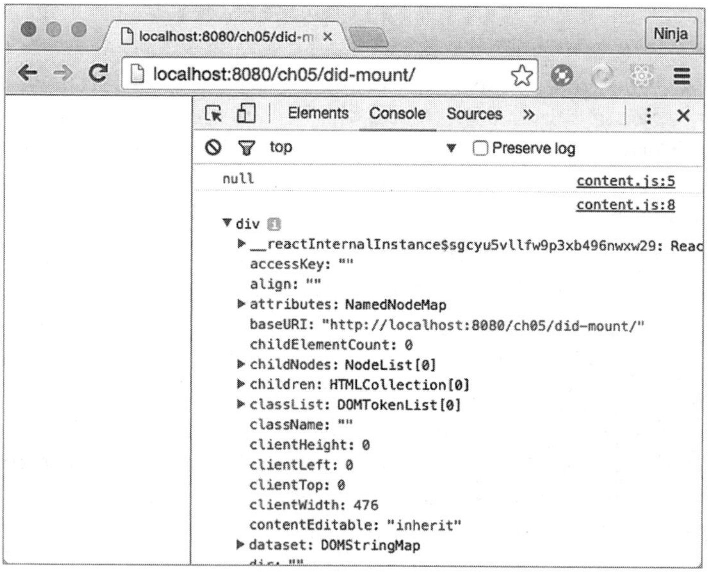

Figure 5.2   The second log shows the DOM node because `componentDidMount()` was fired when the element was rendered and mounted to the real DOM. Thus, you have the node.

5.4   *Executing all events together*

Listing 5.1 (ch05/logger/jsx/content.jsx) and listing 5.2 (ch05/logger/jsx/logger.jsx) show all the events in action at once. For now, all you need to know is that they're like classes in the sense that they allow you to reuse code. This logger mixin can be useful for debugging; it displays all the events, properties, and state when the component is about to be rerendered and after it's been rerendered.

Listing 5.1   Rendering and updating a `Logger` component three times

```
class Content extends React.Component {
  constructor(props) {
    super(props)
    this.launchClock()
    this.state = {
      counter: 0,
      currentTime: (new Date()).toLocaleString()
    }
  }
  launchClock() {
    setInterval(()=>{
      this.setState({
        counter: ++this.state.counter,
        currentTime: (new Date()).toLocaleString()
      })
    }, 1000)
  }
  render() {
    if (this.state.counter > 2) return
    return <Logger time="{this.state.currentTime}"></Logger>
  }
}
```

Listing 5.2   Observing component lifecycle events

```
class Logger extends React.Component {
  constructor(props) {
    super(props)
    console.log('constructor')
  }
  componentWillMount() {
    console.log('componentWillMount is triggered')
  }
  componentDidMount(e) {
    console.log('componentDidMount is triggered')
    console.log('DOM node: ', ReactDOM.findDOMNode(this))
  }
  componentWillReceiveProps(newProps) {
    console.log('componentWillReceiveProps is triggered')
    console.log('new props: ', newProps)
  }
  shouldComponentUpdate(newProps, newState) {
```

```
      console.log('shouldComponentUpdate is triggered')
      console.log('new props: ', newProps)
      console.log('new state: ', newState)
      return true
    }
    componentWillUpdate(newProps, newState) {
      console.log('componentWillUpdate is triggered')
      console.log('new props: ', newProps)
      console.log('new state: ', newState)
    }
    componentDidUpdate(oldProps, oldState) {
      console.log('componentDidUpdate is triggered')
      console.log('new props: ', oldProps)
      console.log('old props: ', oldState)
    }
    componentWillUnmount() {
      console.log('componentWillUnmount')
    }
    render() {
      // console.log('rendering... Display')
      return (
        {this.props.time}
      )
    }
  }
}
```

The functions and lifecycle events from the `Display` component give you console logs
when you run this web page. Don't forget to open your browser console, because all
the logging happens there, as shown in figure 5.3!

As noted in the text and shown in the figure, the mounting event fires only once. You
can clearly see this in the logs. After the counter in `Context` reaches 3, the render function won't use `Display` anymore, and the component is unmounted (see figure 5.4).

Now that you've learned about component lifecycle events, you can use them when
you need to implement logic for components, such as fetching data.

Figure 5.3   The logger has been mounted.

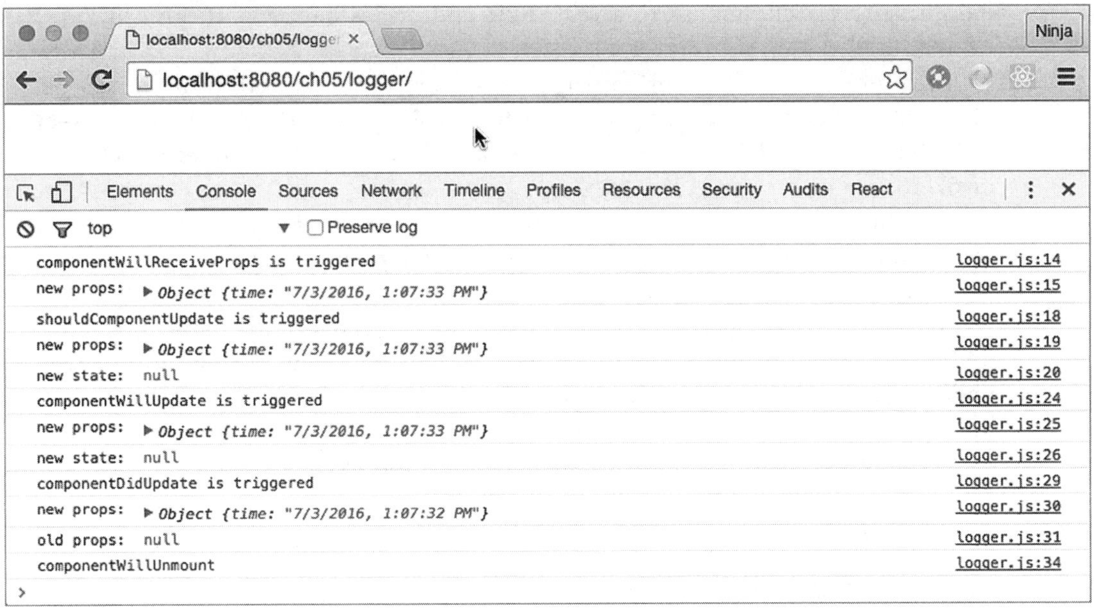

Figure 5.4 Content was removed from the logger after 2 seconds; hence, the `componentWillUnmount()` log entry right before the removal.

5.5 Mounting events

The mounting category of events is all about a component being attached to the real DOM. Think of mounting as a way for a React element to see itself in the DOM. This typically happens when you use a component in `ReactDOM.render()` or in the `render()` of another, higher-order component that will be rendered to the DOM. The mounting events are as follows:

- `componentWillMount()`—React knows that this element will be in the real DOM.
- `componentDidMount()`—React has "inserted" the React element into the real DOM; and `element` is the DOM node.

`constructor()` execution happens prior to `componentWillMount()`. Also, React first renders and then mounts elements. (Rendering in this context means calling a class's `render()`, not painting the DOM.) Refer to table 5.1 for events in between `componentWillMount()` and `componentDidMount()`.

5.5.1 componentWillMount()

It's worth mentioning that `componentWillMount()` is invoked only once in the component's lifecycle. The timing of the execution is just before the initial rendering.

The lifecycle event `componentWillMount()` is executed when you render a React element on the browser by calling `ReactDOM.render()`. Think of it as attaching (or mounting) a React element to a real DOM node. This happens in the browser: the front end.

If you render a React component on a server (the back end, using isomorphic/ universal JavaScript; see chapter 16), which basically gets an HTML string, then—even though there's no DOM on the server or mounting in that case—this event will also be invoked!

You saw in chapter 4 how to update the `currentTime` state using `Date` and `setInterval()`. You triggered the series of updates in `constructor()` by calling `launchClock()`. You can do so in `componentWillMount()` as well.

Typically, a state change triggers a rerender, right? At the same time, if you update the state with `setState()` in the `componentWillMount()` method or trigger updates as you did with `Clock`, then `render()` will get the updated state. The best thing is that even if the new state is different, there will be no rerendering because `render()` will get the new state. To put it another way, you can invoke `setState()` in `componentWillMount()`. `render()` will get the new values, if any, and there will be no extra rerendering.

5.5.2   *componentDidMount()*

In contrast, `componentDidMount()` is invoked after the initial rendering. It's executed only once and only in the browser, not on the server. This comes in handy when you need to implement code that runs only for browsers, such as XHR requests.

In this lifecycle event, you can access any references to children (for example, to access the corresponding DOM representation). Note that the `componentDidMount()` method of child components is invoked before that of parent components.

As mentioned earlier, the `componentDidMount()` event is the best place to integrate with other JavaScript libraries. You can fetch a JSON payload that has a list of users with their info. Then, you can print that information, using a Twitter Bootstrap table to get the page shown in figure 5.5.

The structure of the project is as follows:

```
/users
  /css
    bootstrap.css
  /js
    react.js
    react-dom.js
    script.js
    - users.js
  /jsx
    script.jsx
    users.jsx
  index.html
  real-user-data.json
```

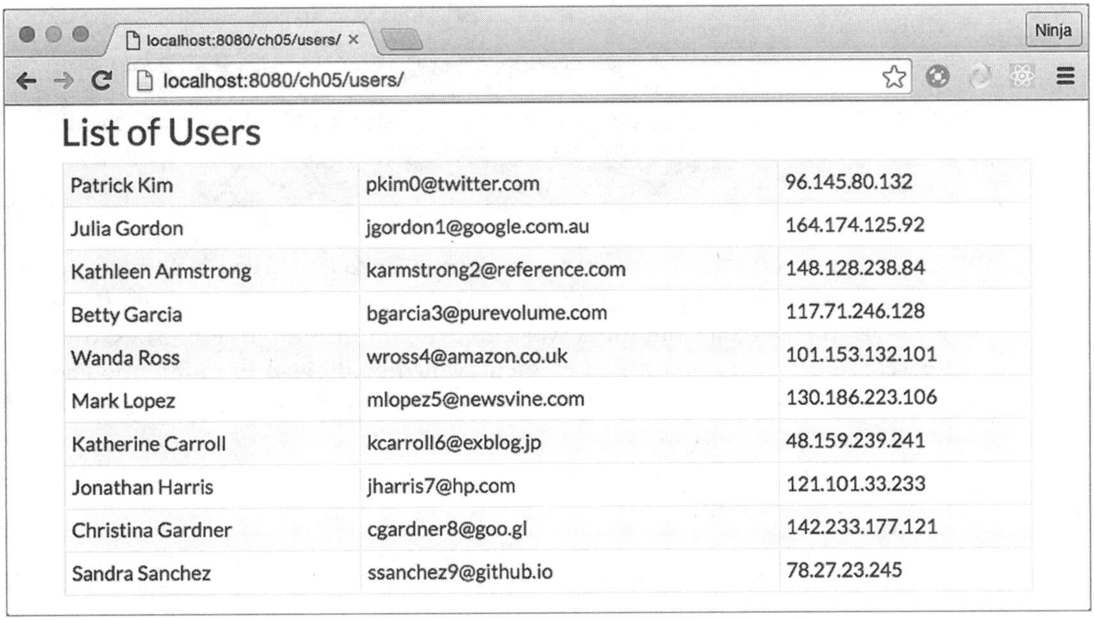

Figure 5.5   Showing a list of users (fetched from a data store) styled with Twitter Bootstrap

You have the DOM element in the event, and you can send XHR/AJAX requests to fetch the data with the new `fetch()` API:

```
fetch(this.props['data-url'])
  .then((response)=>response.json())
  .then((users)=>this.setState({users: users}))
```

Fetch API

The Fetch API (http://mng.bz/mbMe) lets you make XHR request using promises in a unifying manner. It's available in most modern browsers, but refer to the specs (https://fetch.spec.whatwg.org) and the standard (https://github.com/whatwg/fetch) to find out if the browsers you need to support for your apps implement it. The usage is straightforward—you pass the URL and define as many promise `then` statements as needed:

```
fetch('http://node.university/api/credit_cards/')
  .then(function(response) {
    return response.blob()
  })
  .then(function(blob) {
    // Process blob
  })
  .catch(function(error) {
    console.log('A problem with your fetch operation: ' +
      error.message)
  })
```

> **(continued)**
> If the browser you develop for doesn't support `fetch()` yet, you can shim it, or use any other HTTP agent library such as superagent (https://github.com/visionmedia/super-agent); request (https://github.com/request/request); axios (https://github.com/mzabriskie/axios); or even jQuery's `$.ajax()` (http://api.jquery.com/jquery.ajax) or `$.get()`.

You can put your XHR fetch request in `componentDidMount()`. You may think that by putting the code in `componentWillMount()`, you can optimize loading, but there are two issues: if you get data from the server faster than your rendering finishes, you may trigger rerender on an unmounted element, which could lead to unintended consequences. Also, if you're planning to use a component on the server, then `component-WillMount()` will fire there as well.

Now, let's look at the entire component, with fetch happening in `component-DidMount()` (ch05/users/jsx/users.jsx).

Listing 5.3   Fetching data to display in a table

```
class Users extends React.Component {
  constructor(props) {
    super(props)
    this.state = {
      users: []                              ◁—— Initializes users'
    }                                               state with an
  }                                               empty array
  componentDidMount() {
    fetch(this.props['data-url'])            ◁—— Performs a GET XHR request
      .then((response)=>response.json())          using the URL from the
      .then((users)=>this.setState({users: users}))   property to fetch user data
  }
  render() {                                 ◁—— Retrieves user info
    return <div className="container">            from the response and
    <h1>List of Users</h1>                        assigns it to the state
    <table className="table-striped table-condensed table table-bordered
    ➥ table-hover">
      <tbody>{this.state.users.map((user)=>   ◁—— Iterates over users'
        <tr key={user.id}>                          state to create table
          <td>{user.first_name} {user.last_name}</td>   rows
          <td> {user.email}</td>
          <td> {user.ip_address}</td>
        </tr>)}
      </tbody>
    </table>
  </div>
  }
}
```

Notice that users is set to an empty array (`[]`) in the constructor. This gets around the need to check for existence later in `render()`. Repetitive checks and bugs due to undefined values—what a great way to waste time and get a repetitive-stress injury from excessive typing. Setting your initial values will help you avoid lots of pain later! In other words, this is an antipattern:

```
// Anti-pattern: Don't try this at home!
class Users extends React.Component {
  constructor(props) {                       ◁─┐  Doesn't set the empty
    super(props)                                │  value initially
  }
  ...
  render() {
    return <div className="container">
      <h1>List of Users</h1>
      <table className="table-striped table-condensed table table-bordered
      ▶ table-hover">
        <tbody>{(this.state.users && this.state.users.length>0) ?    ◁─┐
          this.state.users.map((user)=>                                │
          <tr key={user.id}>                              Checks for existence
            <td>{user.first_name} {user.last_name}</td>   (no need with initial
            <td> {user.email}</td>                                    values)
            <td> {user.ip_address}</td>
          </tr>) : ''}
        </tbody>
      </table>
    </div>
  }
}
```

5.6 *Updating events*

As noted earlier, mounting events are often used to integrate React with the outside world: other frameworks, libraries, or data stores. *Updating events* are associated with updating components. These events are as follows, in order from the component life-cycle's beginning to its end (see table 5.2 for just the updating lifecycle events and table 5.1 for all events).

1 componentWillReceiveProps(newProps)
2 shouldComponentUpdate()
3 componentWillUpdate()
4 componentDidUpdate()

Table 5.2 Lifecycle events invoked/called on component update

Updating component properties	Updating component state	Updating using forceUpdate()
componentWillReceiveProps()		
shouldComponentUpdate()	shouldComponentUpdate()	
componentWillUpdate()	componentWillUpdate()	componentWillUpdate()
render()	render()	render()
componentDidUpdate()	componentDidUpdate()	componentDidUpdate()

5.6.1   *componentWillReceiveProps(newProps)*

componentWillReceiveProps(newProps) is triggered when a component receives new properties. This stage is called an *incoming property transition*. This event allows you to intercept the component at the stage between getting new properties and before render(), in order to add some logic.

The componentWillReceiveProps(newProps) method takes the new prop(s) as an argument. It isn't invoked on the initial render of the component. This method is useful if you want to capture the new property and set the state accordingly before the rerender. The old property value is in the this.props object. For example, the following snippet sets the opacity state, which in CSS is 0 or 1, depending on the Boolean property isVisible (1 = true, 0 = false):

```
componentWillReceiveProps(newProps) {
  this.setState({
    opacity: (newProps.isVisible) ? 1 : 0
  })
}
```

Generally speaking, the setState() method in componentWillReceiveProps-(newProps) won't trigger extra rerendering.

In spite of receiving new properties, these properties may not necessarily have new values (meaning values different from current properties), because React has no way of knowing whether the property values have changed. Therefore, componentWill-ReceiveProps(NewProps) is invoked each time there's a rerendering (of a parent structure or a call), regardless of property-value changes. Thus, you can't assume that newProps always has values that are different from the current properties.

At the same time, rerendering (invoking render()) doesn't necessarily mean changes in the real DOM. The decision whether to update and what to update in the real DOM is delegated to shouldComponentUpdate() and the reconciliation process.[1]

5.6.2   *shouldComponentUpdate()*

Next is the shouldComponentUpdate() event, which is invoked right before rendering. Rendering is preceded by the receipt of new properties or state. The should-ComponentUpdate() event isn't triggered for the initial render or for forceUpdate() (see table 5.1).

You can implement the shouldComponentUpdate() event with return false to prohibit React from rerendering. This is useful when you're checking that there are no changes and you want to avoid an unnecessary performance hit (when dealing with hundreds of components). For example, this snippet uses the + binary

---

[1] For more reasons why React can't perform smarter checks before calling componentWillReceiveProps-(newProps), read the extensive article "(A ⇒ B) !⇒ (B ⇒ A)," by Jim Sproch, *React*, January 8, 2016, http://mng.bz/3WpG.

operator to convert the Boolean isVisible into a number and compare that to the opacity value:

```
shouldComponentUpdate(newProps, newState) {
  return this.state.opacity !== + newProps.isVisible
}
```

When isVisible is false and this.state.opacity is 0, the entire render() is skipped; also, componentWillUpdate() and componentDidUpdate() aren't called. In essence, you can control whether a component is rerendered.

5.6.3 componentWillUpdate()

Speaking of componentWillUpdate(), this event is called just before rendering, preceded by the receipt of new properties or state. This method isn't called for the initial render. Use the componentWillUpdate() method as an opportunity to perform preparations before an update occurs, and avoid using this.setState() in this method! Why? Well, can you imagine trying to trigger a new update while the component is being updated? It sounds like a bad idea to me!

If shouldComponentUpdate() returns false, then componentWillUpdate() isn't invoked.

5.6.4 componentDidUpdate()

The componentDidUpdate() event is triggered immediately after the component's updates are reflected in the DOM. Again, this method isn't called for the initial render. componentDidUpdate() is useful for writing code that works with the DOM and its other elements after the component has been updated, because at this stage you'll get all the updates rendered in the DOM.

Every time something is mounted or updated, there should be a way to unmount it. The next event provides a place for you to put logic for unmounting.

5.7 Unmounting event

In React, *unmounting* means detaching or removing an element from the DOM. There's only one event in this category, and this is the last category in the component lifecycle.

5.7.1 componentWillUnmount()

The componentWillUnmount() event is called just before a component is unmounted from the DOM. You can add any necessary cleanup to this method; for example, invalidating timers, cleaning up any DOM elements, or detaching events that were created in componentDidMount.

5.8   *A simple example*

Suppose you're tasked with creating a Note web app (to save text online). You've implemented the component, but initial feedback from users is that they lose their progress if they close the window (or a tab) unintentionally. Let's implement the confirmation dialog shown in figure 5.6.

To implement a dialog like that, we need to listen to a special window event. The tricky part is to clean up after the element is no longer needed, because if the element is removed but its event is not, memory leaks could be the result! The best way to approach this problem is to attach the event on mounting and remove the event on dismounting.

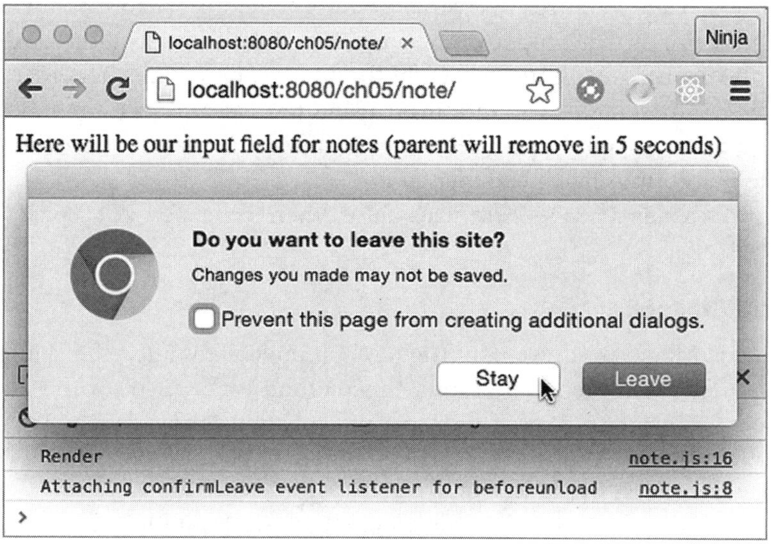

Figure 5.6   A dialog confirmation when the user tries to leave the page

The structure of the project is as follows:

```
/note
  /jsx
    note.jsx
    script.jsx
  /js
    note.jsx
    react.js
    react-dom.js
    script.js
  index.html
```

The `window.onbeforeunload` native browser event (with additional code for cross-browser support) is straightforward:

```
window.addEventListener('beforeunload',function () {
  let confirmationMessage = 'Do you really want to close?'
  e.returnValue = confirmationMessage      // Gecko, Trident, Chrome 34+
  return confirmationMessage               // Gecko, WebKit, Chrome < 34
})
```

The following approach will work, too:

```
window.onbeforeunload = function () {
  ...
  return confirmationMessage
}
```

Let's put this code in an event listener in `componentDidMount()` and remove the event listener in `componentWillUnmount()` (ch05/note/jsx/note.jsx).

Listing 5.4 Adding and removing an event listener

```
class Note extends React.Component {
  confirmLeave(e) {
    let confirmationMessage = 'Do you really want to close?'
    e.returnValue = confirmationMessage      // Gecko, Trident, Chrome 34+
    return confirmationMessage               // Gecko, WebKit, Chrome <34
  }
  componentDidMount() {
    console.log('Attaching confirmLeave event listener for beforeunload')
    window.addEventListener('beforeunload', this.confirmLeave)
  }
  componentWillUnmount() {
    console.log('Removing confirmLeave event listener for beforeunload')
    window.removeEventListener('beforeunload', this.confirmLeave)
  }
  render() {
    console.log('Render')
    return Here will be our input field for notes (parent will remove in
    ➥ {this.props.secondsLeft} seconds)
  }
}
```

You want to check how your code works when the `Note` element is removed, right? For this reason, you need to remove the `Note` element so that it's dismounted. Therefore, the next step is to implement the parent in which you not only create `Note` but remove it. Let's use a timer for that (`setInterval()` all the way!), as shown in the following listing (ch05/note/jsx/script.jsx) and figure 5.7.

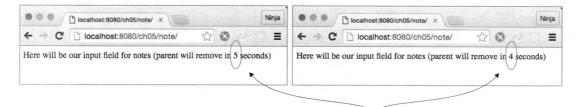

A timer counts down the seconds.

Each event is shown in the Console tab.

Figure 5.7   Note will be replaced by another element in 5, 4, … seconds.

Listing 5.5   Rendering Note **before removing it**

```
let secondsLeft = 5

let interval = setInterval(()=>{
  if (secondsLeft == 0) {
    ReactDOM.render(
      <div>
        Note was removed after {secondsLeft} seconds.
      </div>,
      document.getElementById('content')
    )
    clearInterval(interval)
  } else {
    ReactDOM.render(
      <div>
        <Note secondsLeft={secondsLeft}/>
      </div>,
      document.getElementById('content')
    )
  }
  secondsLeft--
}, 1000)
```

Figure 5.8 shows the result (with console logs): render, attach event listener, render four more times, remove event listener.

If you don't remove the event listener in componentWillUnmount() (you can comment out this method to see), the page will still have a pesky dialog even though the

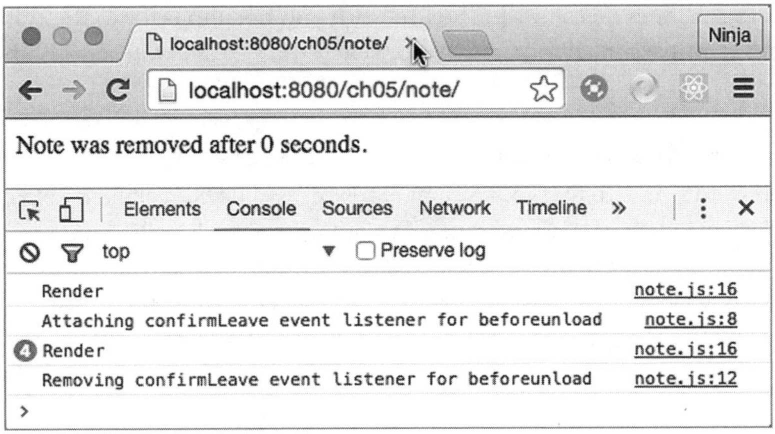

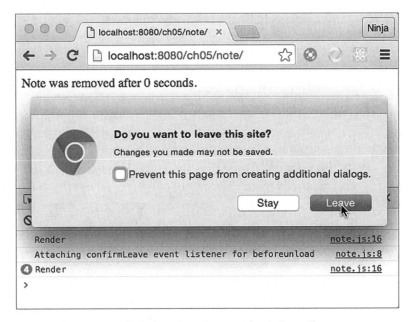

Figure 5.8 Note **is replaced by a** div, **and there will be no dialog confirmation when the user tries to leave the page.**

Note element is long gone, as shown in figure 5.9. This isn't a good UX and may lead to bugs. You can use this lifecycle event to clean up after components.

The React team is listening to feedback from React developers. Most of these lifecycle events allow developers to tweak the behavior of their components. Think of lifecycle events as black-belt-Ninja-Matrix-Jedi skills. You can code without them, but boy your code will be more powerful with them. What's interesting is that there's still conversation about the best practices and usage. React is still evolving, and there may be changes

Figure 5.9 Dialog confirmation when the user tries to leave the page

or additions to the lifecycle events in the future. If you need to refer to the official documentation, see https://facebook.github.io/react/docs/react-component.html.

5.9 Quiz

1 `componentWillMount()` will be rendered on the server. True or false?

2 Which event will fire first, `componentWillMount()` or `componentDidMount()`?

3 Which of the following is a good place to put an AJAX call to the server to get some data for a component? `componentWillUnmount()`, `componentHasMounted()`, `componentDidMount()`, `componentWillReceiveData()`, or `componentWillMount()`

4 `componentWillReceiveProps()` means there was a rerendering of this element (from a parent structure), and you know for sure that you have new values for the properties. True or false?

5 Mounting events happen multiple times on each rerendering. True or false?

5.10 Summary

- `componentWillMount()` is invoked on both the server and the client, whereas `componentDidMount()` is invoked only on the client.

- Mounting events are typically used to integrate React with other libraries and get data from stores or servers.

- You use `shouldComponentUpdate()` to optimize rendering.

- You use `componentWillReceiveProps()` to perform a state change with new properties.

- Unmounting events are typically used for cleanup.

- Updating events provide a place to put logic that relies on new properties or state, and they give you more granular control over when to update a view.

5.11 Quiz answers

1 True. Although there's no DOM, this event will be triggered on the server rendering, but `componentDidMount()` won't.

2 `componentWillMount` is first, followed by `componentDidMount()`.

3 `componentDidMount()`, because it won't be triggered on the server.

4 False. You can't guarantee new values. React doesn't know if the values have been changed.

5 False. Mounting isn't triggered on rerender to optimize performance, because excessive mounting is a relatively expensive operation.

Watch this chapter's introduction video by scanning this QR code with your phone or going to http://reactquickly.co/videos/ch06.

Handling events in React

6

This chapter covers

- Working with DOM events in React
- Responding to DOM events that aren't supported by React
- Integrating React with other libraries: jQuery UI events

So far, you've learned how to render UIs that have zero user interaction. In other words, you're just displaying data. For example, you've built a clock that doesn't accept user inputs, such as setting the time zone.

Most of the time, you don't have static UIs; you need to build elements that are smart enough to respond to user actions. How do you respond to user actions such as clicking and dragging a mouse?

This chapter provides the solution to how to handle events in React. Then, in chapter 7, you'll apply this knowledge of events to working with web forms and their elements. I've mentioned that React supports only certain events; in this chapter, I'll show you how to work with events that aren't supported by React.

> **NOTE** The source code for the examples in this chapter is at https://www.manning.com/books/react-quickly and https://github.com/azat-co/react-quickly/tree/master/ch06 (in the ch06 folder of the GitHub repository https://github.com/azat-co/react-quickly). You can also find some demos at http://reactquickly.co/demos.

111

6.1   *Working with DOM events in React*

Let's look how you can make React elements respond to user actions by defining event handlers for those actions. You do this by defining the event handler (function definition) as the value of an element attribute in JSX and as an element property in plain JavaScript (when `createElement()` is called directly without JSX). For attributes that are event names, you use standard W3C DOM event names in camelCase, such as `onClick` or `onMouseOver`, as in

```
onClick={function() {...}}
```

or

```
onClick={() => {...}}
```

For example, in React, you can define an event listener that's triggered when a user clicks a button. In the event listener, you're logging the `this` context. The event object is an enhanced version of a native DOM event object (called `SyntheticEvent`):

```
<button onClick={(function(event) {
    console.log(this, event)
  }).bind(this)}>
  Save
</button>
```

`bind()` is needed so that in the event-handler function, you get a reference to the instance of the class (React element). If you don't bind, `this` will be `null` (use `strict` mode). You don't bind the context to the class using `bind(this)` in the following cases:

- When you don't need to refer to this class by using `this`
- When you're using the older style, `React.createClass()`, instead of the newer ES6+ class style, because `createClass()` autobinds it for you
- When you're using fat arrows (`() ⇒ {}`)

You can also make things neater by using a class method as event handler (let's name it `handleSave()`) for the `onClick` event. Consider a `SaveButton` component that, when clicked, prints the value of `this` and `event`, but uses a class method as shown in figure 6.1 and the following listing (ch06/button/jsx/button.jsx).

Listing 6.1   Declaring an event handler as a class method

```
class SaveButton extends React.Component {
  handleSave(event) {
    console.log(this, event)
  }
  render() {
    return <button onClick={this.handleSave.bind(this)}>
```

Passes the function definition returned by bind() to onClick

```
      Save
    </button>
  }
}
```

This is how the save button will log the output of `this` and `event`.

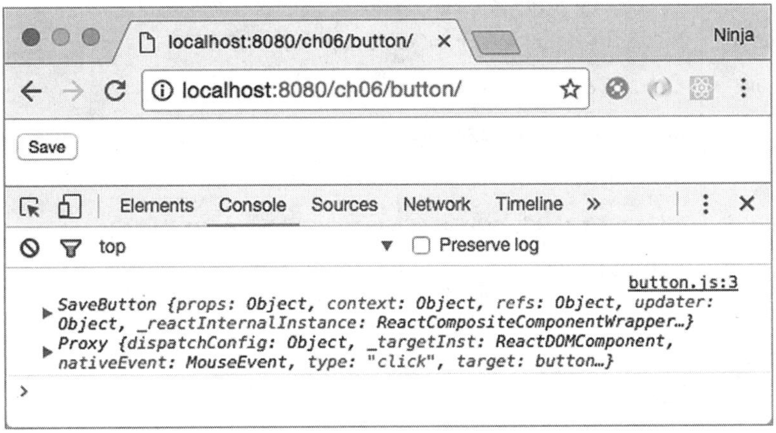

Figure 6.1 Clicking the button prints the value of `this`: `SaveButton`.

Moreover, you can bind an event handler to the class in the class's `constructor`. Functionally, there's no difference; but if you're using the same method more than once in `render()`, then you can reduce duplication by using the constructor binding. Here's the same button, but with constructor binding for the event handler:

```
class SaveButton extends React.Component {
  constructor(props) {
    super(props)
    this.handleSave = this.handleSave.bind(this)     ◁┐  Binds the "this" context to the
  }                                                     │  class to use "this" in the event
  handleSave(event) {                                   │  handler to refer to this class
    console.log(this, event)
  }
  render() {
    return <button onClick={this.handleSave}>    ◁┐  Passes the function
      Save                                        │  definition to onClick
    </button>
  }
}
```

Binding event handlers is my favorite and recommended approach, because it eliminates duplication and puts all the binding neatly in one place.

Table 6.1 lists the current event types supported by React v15. Notice the use of camelCase in the event names, to be consistent with other attribute names in React.

Table 6.1 DOM events supported by React v15

Event group	Events supported by React
Mouse events	onClick, onContextMenu, onDoubleClick, onDrag, onDragEnd, onDragEnter, onDragExit, onDragLeave, onDragOver, onDragStart, onDrop, onMouseDown, onMouseEnter, onMouseLeave, onMouseMove, onMouseOut, onMouseOver, onMouseUp
Keyboard events	onKeyDown, onKeyPress, onKeyUp
Clipboard events	onCopy, onCut, onPaste
Form events	onChange, onInput, onSubmit
Focus events	onFocus, onBlur
Touch events	onTouchCancel, onTouchEnd, onTouchMove, onTouchStart
UI events	onScroll
Wheel events	onWheel
Selection events	onSelect
Image events	onLoad, onError
Animation events	onAnimationStart, onAnimationEnd, onAnimationIteration
Transition events	onTransitionEnd

As you can see, React supports several types of normalized events. If you contrast this with the list of standard events at https://developer.mozilla.org/en-US/docs/Web/Events, you'll see that React's support is extensive—and you can be sure that team React will add more events in the future! For more information and event names, visit the documentation page at http://facebook.github.io/react/docs/events.html.

6.1.1 Capture and bubbling phases

As I've noted, React is declarative, not imperative, which removes the need to manipulate objects; and you don't attach events to your code as you would with jQuery (for example, $('.btn').click(handleSave)). Instead, you declare an event in the JSX as an attribute (for instance, onClick={handleSave}). If you're declaring mouse events, the attribute name can be any of the supported events from table 6.1. The value of the attribute is your event handler.

For example, if you want to define a mouse-hover event, you can use onMouseOver, as shown in the following code. Hovering will display "mouse is over" in your DevTools or Firebug console when you move your cursor over the <div>'s red border:

```
<div
  style={{border: '1px solid red'}}
  onMouseOver={()=>{console.log('mouse is over')}} >
    Open DevTools and move your mouse cursor over here
</div>
```

The events shown previously, such as onMouseOver, are triggered by an event in the bubbling phase (*bubble up*). As you know, there's also a capture phase (*trickle down*), which precedes the bubbling and target phases. First is the capture phase, from the window down to the target element; next is the target phase; and only then comes the bubbling phase, when an event travels up the tree back to the window, as shown in figure 6.2.

The distinction between phases becomes important when you have the same event on an element and its ancestor(s). In bubbling mode, the event is first captured and handled by the innermost element (target) and then propagated to outer elements (*ancestors,* starting with the target's parent). In capture mode, the event is first captured by the outermost element and then propagated to the inner elements.

To register an event listener for the capture phase, append Capture to an event name. For example, instead of using onMouseOver, you use onMouseOverCapture to handle the mouseover event in the capture phase. This applies to all the event names listed in table 6.1.

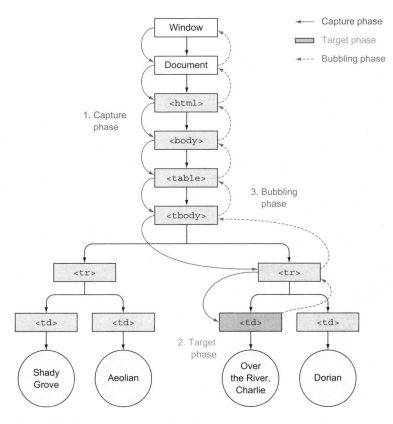

Figure 6.2 Capture, target, and bubbling phases

To illustrate, suppose you have a <div> with a regular (bubbling) event and a capture event. Those events are defined with onMouseOver and onMouseOverCapture, respectively (ch06/mouse-capture/jsx/mouse.jsx).

Listing 6.2   Capture event following by bubbling event

```
class Mouse extends React.Component {
  render() {
    return <div>
      <div
        style={{border: '1px solid red'}}
        onMouseOverCapture={((event)=>{
          console.log('mouse over on capture event')
          console.dir(event, this)}).bind(this)}
        onMouseOver={((event)=>{
          console.log('mouse over on bubbling event')
          console.dir(event, this)}).bind(this)} >
          Open DevTools and move your mouse cursor over here
      </div>
    </div>
  }
}
```

The container has a red border 1 pixel wide; it contains some text, as shown in figure 6.3, so you know where to hover the cursor. Each mouseover event will log what type of event it is as well as the event object (hidden under Proxy in DevTools in figure 6.3 due to the use of console.dir()).

Not surprisingly, the capture event is logged first. You can use this behavior to stop propagation and set priorities between events.

It's important to understand how React implements events, because events are the cornerstone of UIs. Chapter 7 dives deeper into React events.

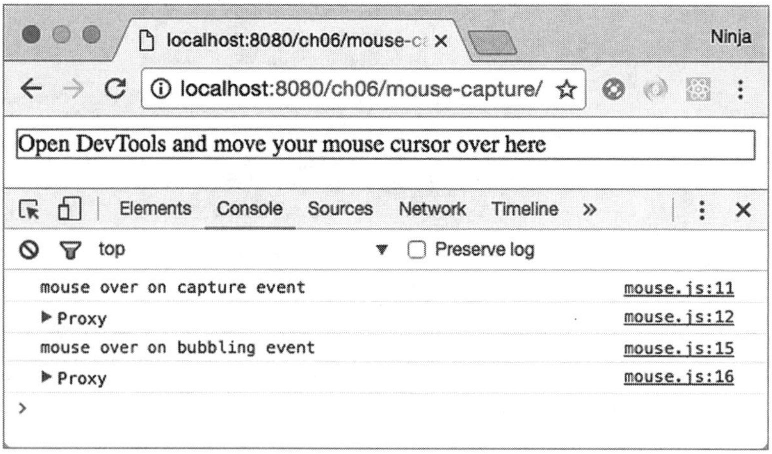

Figure 6.3   The capture event happens before the regular event.

6.1.2 React events under the hood

Events work differently in React than in jQuery or plain JavaScript, which typically put the event listener directly on the DOM node. When you put events directly on nodes, there may be problems removing and adding events during the UI lifecycle. For example, suppose you have a list of accounts, and each can be removed or edited, or new accounts can be added to the list. The HTML might look something like this, with each account element `<li>` uniquely identified by ID:

```
<ul id="account-list">
    <li id="account-1">Account #1</li>
    <li id="account-2">Account #2</li>
    <li id="account-3">Account #3</li>
    <li id="account-4">Account #4</li>
    <li id="account-5">Account #5</li>
    <li id="account-6">Account #6</li>
</ul>
```

If accounts are removed from or added to the list frequently, then managing events will become difficult. A better approach is to have one event listener on a parent (`account-list`) and to listen for bubbled-up events (an event bubbles higher up the DOM tree if nothing catches it on a lower level). Internally, React keeps track of events attached to higher elements and target elements in a mapping. This allows React to trace the target from the parent (`document`), as shown in figure 6.4.

Let's see how this event delegation to the parent looks in action in the example `Mouse` component from listing 6.2. There's a `<div>` element with the `mouseover` React event. You want to inspect the events on this element.

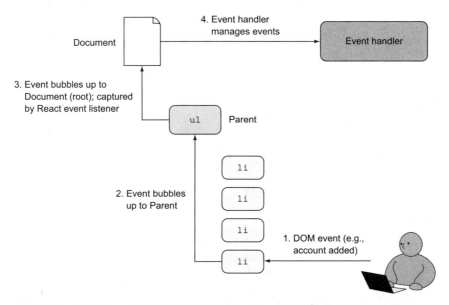

Figure 6.4 A DOM event (1) bubbling to its ancestors (2-3), where it's captured by a regular (bubbling-stage) React event listener (4), because in React, events are captured at the root (`Document`)

If you open Chrome DevTools or Firefox Tools and select the `data-reactroot` element in the Elements or Inspector tab (or use Inspect in the Chrome context menu or Inspect Element in the Firefox context menu), then you can refer to the `<div>` in the console (another tab in DevTools/Firebug) by typing `$0` and pressing Enter. This is a nice little trick.

Interestingly, this DOM node `<div>` doesn't have any event listeners. `$0` is the `<div>` and a `reactroot` element; see figure 6.5. Therefore, you can check what events are attached to this particular element (DOM node) by using the global `getEventListeners()` method in the DevTools console:

```
getEventListeners($0)
```

The result is an empty object `{}`. React didn't attach event listeners to the `reactroot` node `<div>`. Hovering the mouse on the element logs the statements—you can clearly see that the event is being captured! Where did it go?

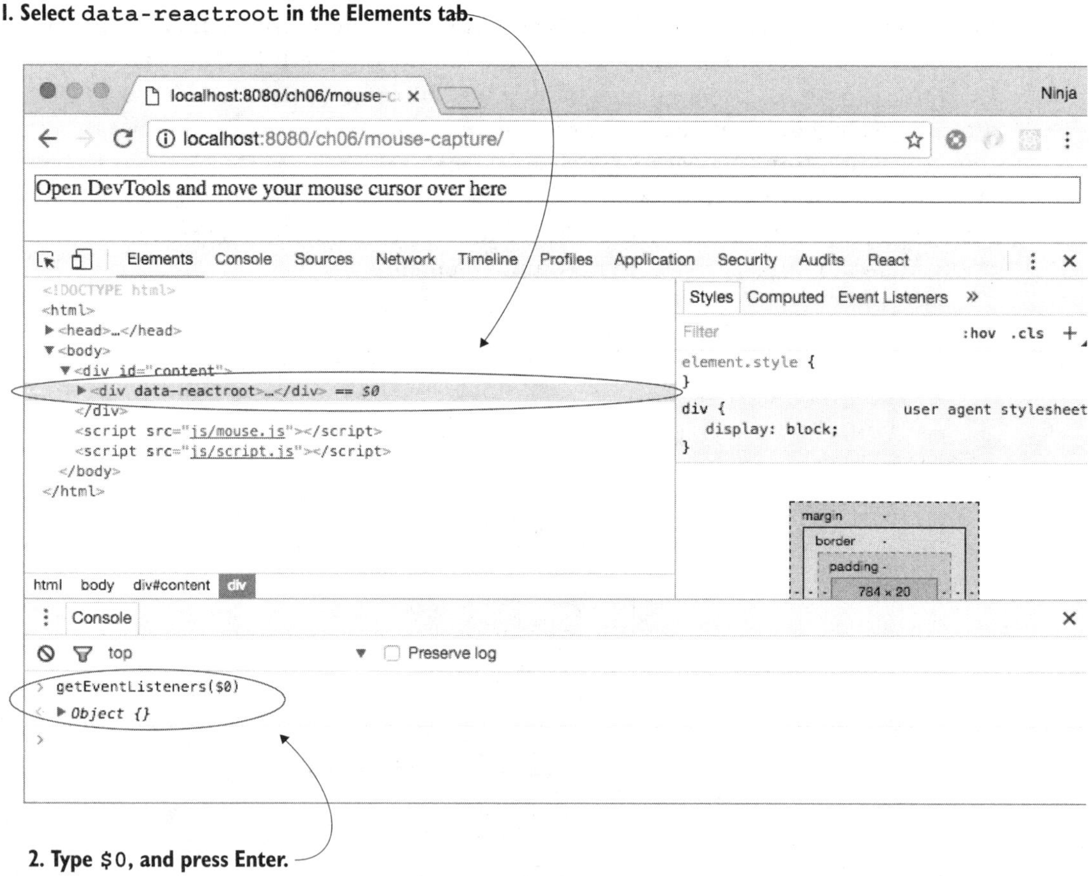

1. Select `data-reactroot` in the Elements tab.

2. Type `$0`, and press Enter.

Figure 6.5   Inspecting events on the `<div>` element (there are none)

Feel free to repeat the procedure with `<div id="content">` or perhaps with the red-bordered `<div>` element (child of `reactroot`). For each currently selected element on the Elements tab, `$0` will be the selected element, so select a new element and repeat `getEventListeners($0)`. Still nothing?

Okay. Let's examine the events on `document` by calling this code from the console:

```
getEventListeners(document)
```

Boom! You have your event: `Object {mouseover: Array[1]}`, as shown in figure 6.6. Now you know that React attached the event listener to the *ultimate* parent, the grand-daddy of them all—the `document` element. The event was not attached to an individual node like `<div>` or an element with the `data-reactroot` attribute.

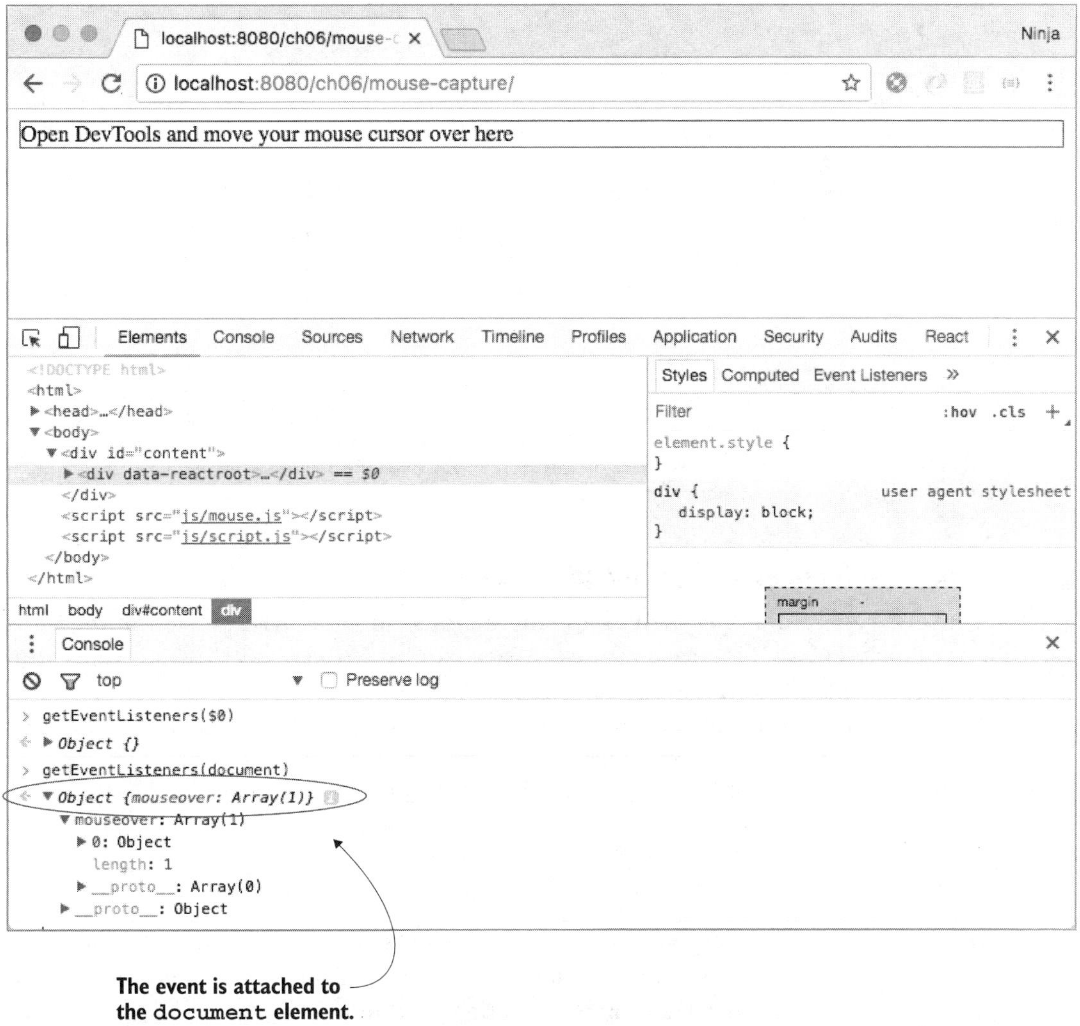

The event is attached to
the `document` element.

Figure 6.6   Inspecting events on the `document` element (there is one)

Next, you can remove this event by invoking the following line in the console:

```
getEventListeners(document).mouseover[0].remove()
```

Now the message "mouse is over" won't appear when you move the cursor. The event listener that was attached to document is gone, illustrating that React attaches events to document, not to each element. This allows React to be faster, especially when working with lists. This is contrary to how jQuery works: with that library, events are attached to individual elements. Kudos to React for thinking about performance.

If you have other elements with the same type of event—for example, two mouse-overs—then they're attached to one event and handled by React's internal mapping to the correct child (target element), as shown in figure 6.7. And speaking of target elements, you can get information about the target node (where the event originated) from the event object.

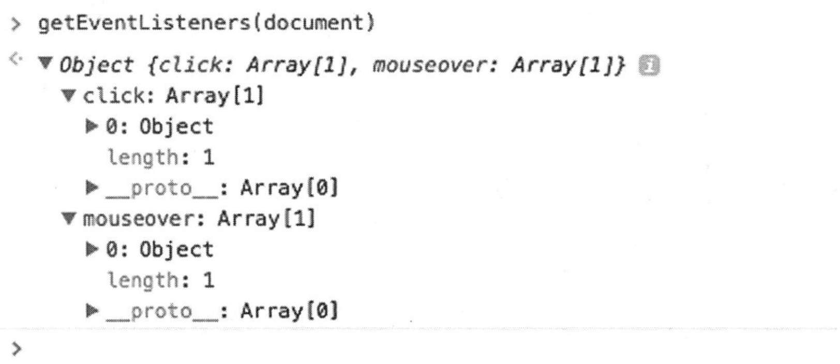

```
>  getEventListeners(document)
<  ▼ Object {click: Array[1], mouseover: Array[1]} ⓘ
      ▼ click: Array[1]
        ▶ 0: Object
          length: 1
        ▶ __proto__: Array[0]
      ▼ mouseover: Array[1]
        ▶ 0: Object
          length: 1
        ▶ __proto__: Array[0]
   >
```

Figure 6.7   React reuses event listeners on the root, so you see only one of each type even when you have one or more elements with mouseover.

6.1.3   *Working with the React SyntheticEvent event object*

Browsers can differ in their implementations of the W3C specification (see www.w3.org/TR/DOM-Level-3-Events). When you're working with DOM events, the event object passed to the event handler may have different properties and methods. This can lead to cross-browser issues when you're writing event-handling code. For example, to get the target element in IE version 8, you'd need to access event.srcElement, whereas in Chrome, Safari, and Firefox, you'd use event.target:

```
var target = event.target || event.srcElement
console.log(target.value)
```

Of course, things are better in terms of cross-browser issues in 2016 than in 2006. But still, do you want to spend time reading specs and debugging issues due to obscure discrepancies between browser implementations? I don't.

Cross-browser issues aren't good because users should have the same experience on different browsers. Typically, you need to add extra code, such as if/else statements, to account for the difference in browser APIs. You also have to perform more testing in different browsers. In short, working around and fixing cross-browser issues is worse on the annoyance scale than CSS issues, IE8 issues, or scrupulous designers in hipster glasses.

React has a solution: a wrapper around browsers' native events. This makes events consistent with the W3C specification regardless of the browser on which you run your pages. Under the hood, React uses its own special class for *synthetic events* (Synthetic-Event). Instances of this SyntheticEvent class are passed to the event handler. For example, to get access to a synthetic event object, you can add an argument event to the event-handler function, as shown in the following listing (ch06/mouse/jsx/mouse.jsx). This way, the event object is output in the console, as shown in figure 6.8.

Listing 6.3   Event handler receiving a synthetic event

```
class Mouse extends React.Component {
  render() {
    return <div>
      <div
        style={{border: '1px solid red'}}
        onMouseOver={((event)=>{
          console.log('mouse is over with event')
          console.dir(event)})} >
          Open DevTools and move your mouse cursor over here
      </div>
    </div>
  }
}
```

Defines an event argument → (points to the `onMouseOver` line)

Accesses the SyntheticEvent object to log interactively (dir) ← (points to the `console.dir(event)` line)

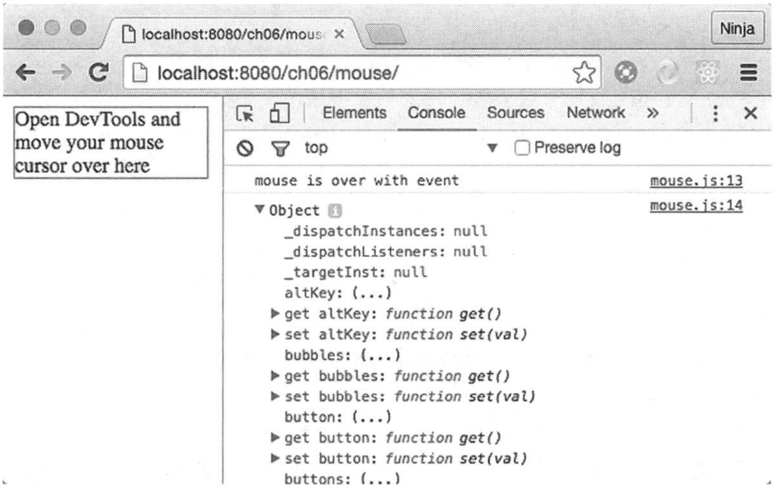

Figure 6.8   Hovering the mouse over the box prints the event object in the DevTools console.

As you've seen before, you can move the event-handler code into a component method or a standalone function. For example, you can create a handleMouseOver() method using ES6+/ES2015+ class method syntax and refer to it from the return of render() with {this.handleMouseOver.bind(this)}. The bind() is needed to transfer the proper value of this into the function. When you use fat-arrow syntax as you did in the previous example, this happens automatically. It also happens automatically with createClass() syntax. Not with class, though. Of course, if you don't use this in the method, you don't have to bind it; just use onMouseOver={this.handleMouseOver}.

The name handleMouseOver() is arbitrary (unlike the names of lifecycle events, covered in chapter 5) and doesn't have to follow any convention as long as you and your team understand it. Most of the time in React, you prefix an event handler with handle to distinguish it from a regular class method, and you include either an event name (such as mouseOver) or the name of the operation (such as save).

Listing 6.4   Event handler as a class method; binding in render()

```
class Mouse extends React.Component {
  handleMouseOver(event) {
    console.log('mouse is over with event')
    console.dir(event.target)
  }
  render(){
    return <div>
      <div
        style={{border: '1px solid red'}}
        onMouseOver={this.handleMouseOver.bind(this)} >
          Open DevTools and move your mouse cursor over here
        </div>
    </div>
  }
}
```

The event has the same properties and methods as most native browser events, such as stopPropagation(), preventDefault(), target, and currentTarget. If you can't find a native property or method, you can access a native browser event with nativeEvent:

```
event.nativeEvent
```

Following is a list of some of the attributes and methods of React's v15.x Synthetic-Event interface:

- currentTarget—DOMEventTarget of the element that's capturing the event (can be a target or the parent of a target)
- target—DOMEventTarget, the element where the event was triggered
- nativeEvent—DOMEvent, the native browser event object

- preventDefault()—Prevents the default behavior, such as a link or a form-submit button
- isDefaultPrevented()—A Boolean that's true if the default behavior was prevented
- stopPropagation()—Stops propagation of the event
- isPropagationStopped()—A Boolean that's true if propagation was stopped
- type—A string tag name
- persist()—Removes the synthetic event from the pool and allows references to the event to be retained by user code
- isPersistent—A Boolean that's true if SyntheticEvent was taken out of the pool

The aforementioned target property of the event object has the DOM node of the object on which the event happened, not where it was captured, as with currentTarget (https://developer.mozilla.org/en-US/docs/Web/API/Event/target). Most often, when you build UIs, in addition to capturing, you need to get the text of an input field. You can get it from event.target.value.

The synthetic event is *nullified* (meaning it becomes unavailable) once the event handler is done. So you can use the same event reference in a variable to access it later or to access it asynchronously (in the future) in a callback function. For example, you can save the reference of the event object in a global e as follows (ch06/mouse-event/jsx/mouse.jsx).

Listing 6.5　Nullifying a synthetic event

```
class Mouse extends React.Component {
  handleMouseOver(event) {
    console.log('mouse is over with event')
    window.e = event  // Anti-pattern          ◁─── Uses the event object and its
    console.dir(event.target)                       attributes in the method
    setTimeout(()=>{
      console.table(event.target)
      console.table(window.e.target)         ◁─── By default, you can't use an event
    }, 2345)                                       in an asynchronous callback or
  }                                                by calling window.e.
  render() {
    return <div>
      <div
        style={{border: '1px solid red'}}
        onMouseOver={this.handleMouseOver.bind(this)}>
        Open DevTools and move your mouse cursor over here
      </div>
    </div>
  }
}
```

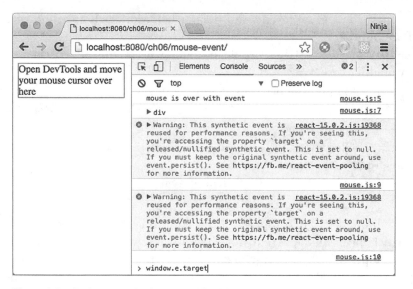

Figure 6.9   Saving a synthetic event object for later use isn't possible by default—hence, the warning.

You'll get a warning saying that React is reusing the synthetic event for performance reasons (see figure 6.9):

```
This synthetic event is reused for performance reasons. If you're seeing this,
➥ you're accessing the property `target` on a released/nullified synthetic
➥ event. This is set to null.
```

If you need to keep the synthetic event after the event handler is over, use the `event.persist()` method. When you apply it, the event object won't be reused and nullified.

You've seen that React will even synthesize (or normalize) a browser event for you, meaning that React will create a cross-browser wrapper around the native event objects. The benefit of this is that events work identically in virtually all browsers. And in most cases, you have all the native methods on the React event, including `event.stopPropagation()` and `event.preventDefault()`. But if you still need to access a native event, it's in the `event.nativeEvent` property of the synthetic event object. Obviously, if you work with native events directly, you'll need to know about and work with any cross-browser differences you encounter.

6.1.4   *Using events and state*

Using states with events, or, to put it differently, being able to change a component's state in response to an event, will give you interactive UIs that respond to user actions. This is going to be fun, because you'll be able to capture any events and change views based on these events and your app logic. This will make your components self-contained, because they won't need any external code or representation.

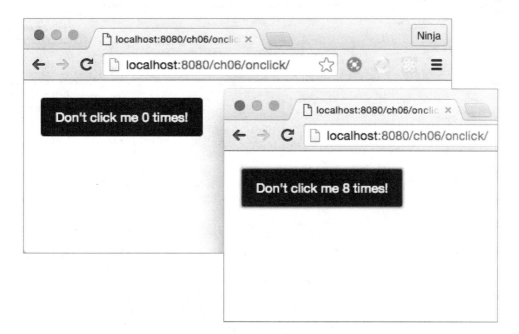

Figure 6.10 Clicking the button increments the counter, which has an initial value of 0.

For example, let's implement a button with a label that has a counter starting at 0, as shown in figure 6.10. Each click of the button increments the number shown on a button (1, 2, 3, and so on).

You start by implementing the following:

- `constructor()`—`this.state` equals 1 because you must set the counter to 0 before you can use it in the view.
- `handleClick()`—Event handler that increments the counter.
- `render()`—Render method that returns the button JSX.

The `click()` method is not unlike any other React component method. Remember `getUrl()` in chapter 3 and `handleMouseOver()` earlier in this chapter? This component method is declared similarly, except that you have to manually bind the `this` context. The `handleClick()` method sets the `counter` state to the current value of counter, incremented by 1 (ch06/onclick/jsx/content.jsx).

Listing 6.6   Updating state as a result of a click action

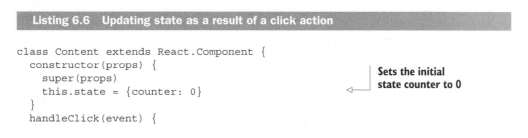

```
class Content extends React.Component {
  constructor(props) {
    super(props)
    this.state = {counter: 0}                    Sets the initial
  }                                              state counter to 0
  handleClick(event) {
```

```
      this.setState({counter: ++this.state.counter})          ◁─┐  Increases the
    }                                                              counter value by 1
    render() {
      return (
        <div>
          <button
            onClick={this.handleClick.bind(this)}           ◁───  Attaches the onClick
            className="btn btn-primary">                           event listener to the
            Don't click me {this.state.counter} times!            handleClick trigger
          </button>
        </div>
      )
    }
}
```

Displays the value of the state counter → points to `Don't click me {this.state.counter} times!`

Invocation vs. definition

Just a reminder: did you notice that although `this.handleClick()` is a method in listing 6.6, you don't invoke it in JSX when you assign it to `onClick` (that is, `<button onClick={this.handleClick}>`)? In other words, there are *no* parentheses (`()`) after `this.handleClick()` inside the curly braces. That's because you need to *pass a function definition, not invoke it*. Functions are first-class citizens in JavaScript, and in this case, you pass the function definition as a value to the `onClick` attribute.

On the other hand, `bind()` is invoked because it lets you use the proper value of `this`, but `bind()` *returns a function definition*. So you still get the function definition as the value of `onClick`.

Keep in mind, as noted previously, `onClick` isn't a real HTML attribute, but syntactically it looks just like any other JSX declaration (for example, `className={btnClassName}` or `href={this.props.url}`).

When you click the button, you'll see the counter increment with each click. Figure 6.10 shows that I clicked the button eight times: the counter is now at 8 but initially was at 0. Brilliant, isn't it?

Analogous to `onClick` or `onMouseOver`, you can use any DOM events supported by React. In essence, you define the view and an event handler that changes the state. You don't imperatively modify the representation. This is the power of declarative style!

The next section will teach you how to pass event handlers and other objects to children elements.

6.1.5 *Passing event handlers as properties*

Consider this scenario: you have a button that's a stateless component. All it has is styling. How do you attach an event listener so this button can trigger some code?

Let's go back to properties for a moment. Properties are immutable, which means they don't change. They're passed by parent components to their children. Because functions are first-class citizens in JavaScript, you can have a property in a child element that's a function and use it as an event handler.

The solution to the problem outlined earlier—triggering an event from a stateless component—is to pass the event handler as a property to this stateless component and use the property (event-handler function) in the stateless component (invoke the function). For example, let's break down the functionality of the previous example into two components: `ClickCounterButton` and `Content`. The first will be dumb (stateless) and the second smart (stateful).

Presentational/Dumb vs. container/smart components

Dumb and *smart* components are sometimes called *presentational* and *container* components, respectively. This dichotomy is related to statelessness and statefulness but isn't always exactly the same.

Most of the time, presentational components don't have states and can be stateless or function components. That's not always the case, because you may need to have some state that relates to the presentation.

Presentational/dumb components often use `this.props.children` and render DOM elements. On the other hand, container/smart components describe how things work without DOM elements, have states, typically use higher-order component patterns, and connect to data sources.

Using a combination of dumb and smart components is the best practice. Doing so keeps things clean and allows for better separation of concerns.

When you run the code, the counter increases with each click. Visually, nothing has changed from the previous example with the button and the counter (figure 6.10); but internally, there's an extra component `ClickCounterButton` (stateless and pretty much logic-less) in addition to `Content`, which still has all the logic.

`ClickCounterButton` doesn't have its own `onClick` event handler (that is, it has no `this.handler` or `this.handleClick`). It uses the handler passed down to it by its parent in a `this.props.handler` property. Generally, using this approach is beneficial for handling events in a button, because the button is a stateless presentational/dumb component. You can reuse this button in other UIs.

The following listing shows the code for the presentational component that renders the button (ch06/onclick-props/jsx/click-counter-button.jsx); the `Content` parent that renders this element is shown shortly, in listing 6.8.

Listing 6.7 Stateless button component

```
class ClickCounterButton extends React.Component {
  render() {
    return <button
      onClick={this.props.handler}
```

```
        className="btn btn-danger">
        Increase Volume (Current volume is {this.props.counter})
      </button>
    }
}
```

The `ClickCounterButton` component, shown in figure 6.11, is dumber than *Dumb &
Dumber,*[1] but that's what's good about this architecture. The component is simple and
easy to grasp.

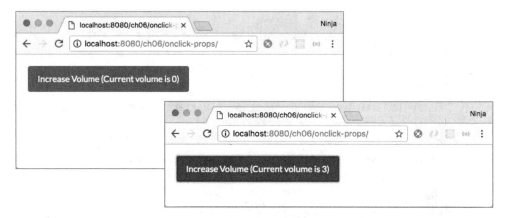

**Figure 6.11   Passing an event handler as a property to a button (presentational component) enables
the incrementing of the counter in the button label, which is also a property of a button.**

The `ClickCounterButton` component also uses the `counter` property, which is rendered with `{this.props.counter}`. Supplying properties to children like `ClickCoun-
terButton` is straightforward if you remember the examples from chapter 2. You use
the standard attribute syntax: `name=VALUE`.

For example, to provide `counter` and `handler` properties to the `ClickCounter-
Button` component, specify the attributes in the JSX declaration of the parent's `render`
parameter (the parent here is `Content`):

```
<div>
  <ClickCounterButton
    counter={this.state.counter}
    handler={this.handleClick}/>
</div>
```

`counter` in `ClickCounterButton` is a property and thus *immutable,* but in the `Content`
parent, it's a state and thus *mutable.* (For a refresher on properties versus state, see
chapter 4.) Obviously, the names can differ. You don't have to keep the names the
same when you pass properties to children. But I find that keeping the same name
helps me understand that the data is related between different components.

---

[1] www.imdb.com/title/tt0109686.

What's happening? The initial `counter` (the state) is set to 0 in the `Content` parent. The event handler is defined in the parent as well. Therefore, the child (`Click-CounterButton`) triggers the event on a parent. The code for the `Content` parent com ponent with `constructor()` and `handleClick()` is shown next (ch06/onclick-props/jsx/content.jsx).

Listing 6.8   Passing an event handler as a property

```
class Content extends React.Component {
  constructor(props) {
    super(props)
    this.handleClick = this.handleClick.bind(this)
    this.state = {counter: 0}
  }
  handleClick(event) {
    this.setState({counter: ++this.state.counter})
  }
  render() {
    return (
      <div>
        <ClickCounterButton
          counter={this.state.counter}
          handler={this.handleClick}/>
      </div>
    )
  }
}
```

> ◁─┐ **Binds the context in the constructor so you can use this.setState(), which refers to the instance of this Content class**

As I said earlier, in JavaScript, functions are first-class citizens, and you can pass them as variables or properties. Thus, there should be no big surprises here. Now the question arises, where do you put logic such as event handlers—in a child or parent?

6.1.6   *Exchanging data between components*

In the previous example, the click event handler was in the parent element. You can put the event handler in the child, but using the parent allows you to exchange information among child components.

Let's use a button as an example but this time remove the counter value from `render()` (1, 2, 3, and so on). The components are single-minded, granular pieces of representation (remember?), so the counter will be in another component: `Counter`. Thus, you'll have three components in total: `ClickCounterButton`, `Content`, and `Counter`.

As you can see in figure 6.12, there are now two components: the button and the text below it. Each has properties that are states in the `Content` parent. In contrast to the previous example (figure 6.11), here you need to communicate between the button and the text to count clicks. In other words, `ClickCounterButton` and `Counter` need to talk to each other. They'll do it via `Content`, *not directly* (communicating directly would be a bad pattern because it would create tight coupling).

Figure 6.12   Splitting state and working with two stateless child components (by allowing them to exchange data via a parent): one for the counter (text) and another for the button

ClickCounterButton remains stateless as in the previous example, just like most React components should be: no thrills, just properties and JSX.

Listing 6.9   Button component using an event handler from `Content`

```
class ClickCounterButton extends React.Component {
  render() {
    return <button
      onClick={this.props.handler}
      className="btn btn-info">
      Don't touch me with your dirty hands!
    </button>
  }
}
```

Of course, you can also write ClickCounterButton as a function instead of a class to simplify the syntax a little:

```
const ClickCounterButton = (props) => {
  return <button
    onClick={props.handler}
    className="btn btn-info">
    Don't touch me with your dirty hands!
  </button>
}
```

The following new component, Counter, displays the value property that's the counter (names can be different—you don't have to always use counter):

```
class Counter extends React.Component {
  render() {
    return <span>Clicked {this.props.value} times.</span>
  }
}
```

Finally, we get to the parent component that provides the properties: one is the event handler, and the other is a counter. You need to update the render parameter accordingly, but the rest of the code remains intact (ch06/onclick-parent/jsx/content.jsx).

Listing 6.10　Passing an event handler and state to two components

```
class Content extends React.Component {
  constructor(props) {
    super(props)
    this.handleClick = this.handleClick.bind(this)
    this.state = {counter: 0}
  }
  handleClick(event) {
    this.setState({counter: ++this.state.counter})
  }
  render() {
    return (
      <div>
        <ClickCounterButton handler={this.handleClick}/>
        <br/>
        <Counter value={this.state.counter}/>
      </div>
    )
  }
}
```

To answer the initial question of where to put the event-handling logic, the rule of thumb is to put it in the parent or wrapper component if you need interaction between child components. If the event concerns only the child components, there's no need to pollute the components higher up the parent chain with event-handling methods.

6.2　*Responding to DOM events not supported by React*

Table 6.1 listed events supported by React. You may wonder about DOM events not supported by React. For example, suppose you're tasked with creating a scalable UI that needs to become bigger or smaller depending on a window size (resize) event. But this event isn't supported! There's a way to capture resize and any other event, and you already know the React feature to implement it: lifecycle events.

In this example, you'll implement radio buttons. As you may know, standard HTML radio button elements scale (become larger or smaller) badly and inconsistently across browsers. For this reason, back when I worked at DocuSign, I implemented scalable CSS radio buttons (http://mng.bz/kPMu) to replace standard HTML radio inputs. I did that in jQuery. These CSS buttons can be scaled via jQuery by manipulating their CSS. Let's see how to create a scalable radio button UI in React. You'll make the same CSS buttons scale with React when you resize the screen, as shown in figure 6.13.

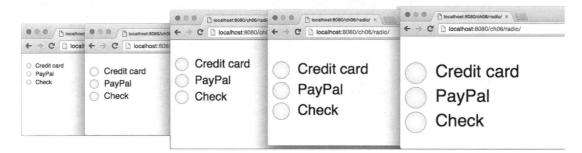

Figure 6.13   Scalable CSS radio buttons managed by React, which is listening to a window resize event. As the window size changes, so does the size of the radio buttons.

As I said earlier, the `resize` event isn't supported by React—adding it to the element as shown here won't work:

```
...
  render() {
    return <div>
      <div onResize={this.handleResize}
        className="radio-tagger"
        style={this.state.taggerStyle}>
      ...
```

There's a simple way to attach unsupported events like `resize` and most custom elements you need to support: using React component lifecycle events. Listing 6.11 (ch06/radio/jsx/radio.jsx) adds `resize` event listeners to `window` in `componentDidMount()` and then removes the same event listeners in `componentWillUnmount()` to make sure nothing is left after this component is gone from the DOM. Leaving event listeners hanging after their components are removed is a great way to introduce memory leaks that might crash your app at some point. Believe me, memory leaks can be a source of sleepless, red-eyed, Red Bull–fueled nights spent debugging and cursing.

Listing 6.11   Using lifecycle events to listen to DOM events

```
class Radio extends React.Component {
  constructor(props) {
    super(props)
    this.handleResize = this.handleResize.bind(this)
    let order = props.order
    let i = 1
    this.state = {                                    ⟵  Saves styles
      outerStyle: this.getStyle(4, i),                    in the state
      innerStyle: this.getStyle(1, i),
      selectedStyle: this.getStyle(2, i),
      taggerStyle: {top: order*20, width: 25, height: 25}
    }
```

```
  }
  getStyle(i, m) {                                          ◁──┐   Uses a function to create various
    let value = i*m                                               styles from width (which will
    return {                                                      change later) and a multiplier
      top: value,
      bottom: value,
      left: value,
      right: value,
    }                                                     Attaches an unsupported
  }                                                       event listener to window
  componentDidMount() {
    window.addEventListener('resize', this.handleResize)  ◁──┐   Removes the
  }                                                               unsupported
  componentWillUnmount() {                                        event listener
    window.removeEventListener('resize', this.handleResize)  ◁──┘  from window
  }
  handleResize(event) {                                                          ◁──
    let w = 1+ Math.round(window.innerWidth / 300)
    this.setState({
      taggerStyle: {top: this.props.order*w*10, width: w*10, height: w*10},
      textStyle: {left: w*13, fontSize: 7*w}
    })                                                  Implements a magic function to
  }                                                       handle radio button resizing
  ...                                                     based on the new screen size
```

The helper function getStyle() abstracts some of the styling because there's repetition in the CSS, such as top, bottom, left, and right, but with different values that depend on the width of the window. Hence, getStyle() takes the value and the multiplier m and returns pixels. (Numbers in React's CSS become pixels.)

The rest of the code is easy. All you need to do is implement the render() method, which uses the states and properties to render four <div/> elements. Each one has a special style, defined earlier in constructor().

Listing 6.12   Using state values for styles to resize elements

```
...
  render() {
    return <div>
      <div className="radio-tagger" style={this.state.taggerStyle}>
        <input type="radio" name={this.props.name} id={this.props.id}>
        </input>
        <label htmlFor={this.props.id}>
          <div className="radio-text" style={this.state.textStyle}>
          ➥ {this.props.label}</div>
          <div className="radio-outer" style={this.state.outerStyle}>
            <div className="radio-inner" style={this.state.innerStyle}>
              <div className="radio-selected"
              ➥ style={this.state.selectedStyle}>
              </div>
            </div>
          </div>
        </label>
```

```
      </div>
    </div>
  }
}
```

That's it for the `Radio` component implementation. The gist of this example is that by using lifecycle events in your components, you can create custom event listeners. In this example, you did so by using `window`. This is similar to how React's event listeners work: React attaches events to `document`, as you remember from the beginning of this chapter. And don't forget to remove the custom event listeners on the `unmount` event.

If you're interested in the scalable radio buttons and their non-React implementation (jQuery), I wrote a separate blog post at http://mng.bz/kPMu and created an online demo at http://jsfiddle.net/DSYz7/8. Of course, you can find the React implementation in the source code for this book.

This brings us to the topic of integrating React with other UI libraries, such as jQuery.

6.3   *Integrating React with other libraries: jQuery UI events*

As you've seen, React provides standard DOM events; but what if you need to integrate with another library that uses (triggers or listens to) nonstandard events? For example, suppose you have jQuery components that use `slide` (as in the slider control element). You want to integrate a React widget into your jQuery app. You can attach any DOM events not provided by React, using the component lifecycle events `component-DidMount` and `componentWillUnmount`.

As you may have guessed from the choice of the lifecycle events, you'll be attaching an event listener when the component is mounted and detaching the event listener when the component is unmounted. Detaching (you can think of it as a cleanup) is important so that no event listeners are causing conflicts or performance issues by hanging around as orphans. (*Orphaned* event handlers are handlers that don't have DOM nodes that created them—potential memory leaks.)

For example, suppose you're working at a music-streaming company, and you're tasked with implementing volume controls on the new version of the web player (think Spotify or iTunes). You need to add a label and buttons in addition to the legacy jQuery slider (http://plugins.jquery.com/ui.slider).

You want to implement a label with a numeric value, and two buttons to decrease and increase the value by 1. The idea is to make these pieces work together: when a user slides the pin (the square peg on a slider) left or right, the numeric value and the values on the buttons should change accordingly. In the same fashion, the user should be able to click either button, and the slider pin should move left or right correspondingly. In essence, you want to create not just a slider, but the widget shown in figure 6.14.

Figure 6.14   React components (buttons and the text "Value: ...") can be integrated with other libraries, such as jQuery Slider, to make all elements from all libraries communicate with each other.

6.3.1   Integrating buttons

You have at least two options when it comes to integration: first, attaching events for jQuery Slider in a React component; and second, using `window`. Let's start with the first approach and use it for buttons.

> **NOTE** This approach for integrating buttons is tightly coupled. Objects depend on each other. Generally, you should avoid tightly coupled patterns. The other, more loosely coupled option, will be implemented for integrating labels after we cover this approach.

When there's a `slide` event on the jQuery slider (meaning there's a change in that value), you want to update the button values (text on buttons). You can attach an event listener to the jQuery slider in `componentDidMount` and trigger a method on a React component (`handleSlide`) when there's a `slide` event. With every slide and change in value, you'll update the state (`sliderValue`). `SliderButtons` implements this approach, as shown in the following listing (ch06/slider/jsx/slider-buttons.jsx).

Listing 6.13   Integrating with a jQuery plug-in via its events

Sets the initial value to 0 →

Defines a method to update the slider when a button is clicked →

Uses a jQuery method to set the new value →

```
class SliderButtons extends React.Component {
  constructor(props) {
    super(props)
    this.state = {sliderValue: 0}
  }
  handleSlide(event, ui) {
    this.setState({sliderValue: ui.value})
  }
  handleChange(value) {
    return () => {
      $('#slider').slider('value', this.state.sliderValue + value)
      this.setState({sliderValue: this.state.sliderValue + value})
    }
  }
  componentDidMount() {
    $('#slider').on('slide', this.handleSlide)
  }
```

jQuery will pass two arguments: a jQuery event and the ui object with the current value, which you use to update the state.

Uses the Factory Function pattern for the -1 and +1 buttons

Updates the state to a new value

```
      componentWillUnmount() {
        $('#slider').off('slide', this.handleSlide)     ◁──┐ Removes the
      }                                                     │ event listener
      ...                                                   │ on unmount
    })
```

The `render()` method of `SliderButtons` has two buttons with `onClick` events; a dynamic `disabled` attribute so you don't set values less than 0 (see figure 6.15) or greater than 100; and Twitter Bootstrap classes for buttons (ch06/slider/jsx/slider-buttons.jsx).

Listing 6.14   Rendering slider buttons

```
                      ...                                   Uses the ternary operator to
  Invokes     ┌──── render() {                              disable buttons when the value
this.handleChange        return <div>                       is less than 1 or greater than 99
  with -1 to get a        <button disabled={(this.state.sliderValue<1)?true:false}
function from the           className="btn default-btn"
function factory  └──▷     onClick={this.handleChange(-1)}>
                             1 Less ({this.state.sliderValue-1})
                         </button>
                         <button disabled={(this.state.sliderValue>99) ? true : false}  ◁─┘
  Applies Twitter  ┌──▷     className="btn default-btn"
    Bootstrap      │        onClick={this.handleChange(1)}>
  classes using    │         1 More ({this.state.sliderValue+1})      ◁──┐ Renders the next
    className       │       </button>                                    │ value for the slider
                         </div>                                         │ as button labels
                      }
                    })
```

The end result is that if the value is less than or greater than the set range (minimum of 0, maximum of 100), the buttons become disabled. For example, when the value is 0, the Less button is disabled, as shown in figure 6.15.

Dragging the slider changes the text on the buttons and disables/enables them as needed. Thanks to the call to the slider in `handleChange()`, clicking the buttons moves the slider left or right. Next, you'll implement the Value label, which is a `SliderValue` React component.

Figure 6.15   Programmatically disabling the Less button to prevent negative values

6.3.2   Integrating labels

You read about calling jQuery directly from React methods. At the same time, you can decouple jQuery and React by using another object to catch events. This is a *loosely coupled pattern* and is often preferable, because it helps avoid extra dependencies. In other words, different components don't need to know the details of each others' implementation. Thus, the `SliderValue` React component won't know how to call a jQuery slider. This is good, because later you can more easily change Slider to Slider 2.0 with a different interface.

You can implement this by dispatching events to `window` in jQuery events and defining event listeners for `window` in React component lifecycle methods. The following listing shows `SliderValue` (ch06/slider/jsx/slider-value.jsx).

Listing 6.15 Integrating with a jQuery plug-in via `window`

```
class SliderValue extends React.Component {
  constructor(props) {
    super(props)
    this.handleSlide = this.handleSlide.bind(this)
    this.state = {sliderValue: 0}
  }
  handleSlide(event) {
    this.setState({sliderValue: event.detail.ui.value})
  }
  componentDidMount() {
    window.addEventListener('slide', this.handleSlide)
  }
  componentWillUnmount() {
    window.removeEventListener('slide', this.handleSlide)
  }
  render() {
    return <div className="" >
      Value: {this.state.sliderValue}
    </div>
  }
}
```

> Attaches the slide event listener to the window object to trigger handleSlide()

> Removes slide from window to avoid orphan event handlers and memory leaks

In addition, you need to dispatch a custom event. In the first approach (`Slider-Buttons`), you didn't need to do this, because you used existing plug-in events. In this implementation, you have to create an event and dispatch it to `window` with data. You can implement the dispatchers of the `slide` custom event alongside the code that creates the jQuery `slider` object, which is a script tag in index.html (ch06/slider/index.html).

Listing 6.16 Setting up event listeners on a jQuery UI plug-in

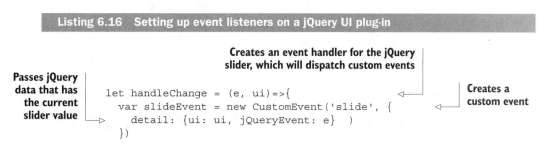

> Creates an event handler for the jQuery slider, which will dispatch custom events

> Passes jQuery data that has the current slider value

> Creates a custom event

```
let handleChange = (e, ui)=>{
  var slideEvent = new CustomEvent('slide', {
    detail: {ui: ui, jQueryEvent: e}  )
})
```

```
                    window.dispatchEvent(slideEvent)                 ◁──┐ Dispatches an event
                  }                                                      │ to window
  Creates a   ┌─▷ $( '#slider' ).slider({
slider using a │     'change': handleChange,         ◁──┐ Attaches event listeners on
  container    │     'slide': handleChange               │ change (programmatic) and
with ID slider │   })                                    │ slide (UI)
```

When you run the code, both buttons and the value label will work seamlessly. You used two approaches: one loosely coupled and the other tightly coupled. The latter's implementation is shorter, but the former is preferable because it will allow you to modify the code more easily in the future.

As you can see from this integration, React can work nicely with other libraries by listening to events in its `componentDidMount()` lifecycle method. React acts in a very un-opinionated way. React can play nicely with others! React's easy integration with other libraries is a great advantage because developers can switch to React gradually instead of rewriting an entire application from scratch, or they can just continue to use their favorite good-old libraries with React indefinitely.

6.4   Quiz

1 Select the correct syntax for the event declaration: `onClick=this.doStuff`, `onclick={this.doStuff}`, `onClick="this.doStuff"`, `onClick={this.doStuff}`, or `onClick={this.doStuff()}`

2 `componentDidMount()` won't be triggered during server-side rendering of the React component on which it's declared. True or false?

3 One way to exchange information among child components is to move the object to the parent of the children. True or false?

4 You can use `event.target` asynchronously and outside the event handler by default. True or false?

5 You can integrate with third-party libraries and events not supported by React by setting up event listeners in the component lifecycle events. True or false?

6.5   Summary

- `onClick` is for capturing mouse and trackpad clicks.
- The JSX syntax for event listeners is `<a onNAME={this.METHOD}>`.
- Bind event handlers with `bind()` in `constructor()` or in JSX if you want to use `this` in the event handler as the value of the component class instance.
- `componentDidMount()` is triggered only on the browser. `componentWillMount()` is triggered on both the browser and the server.
- React supports most of the standard HTML DOM events by providing and using synthetic event objects.
- `componentDidMount()` and `componentWillUnmount()` can be used to integrate React with other frameworks and events not supported by React.

6.6 *Quiz answers*

1 `onClick={this.doStuff}` is correct because only the function definition must be passed to `onClick`, not the result of the invocation (the result of the invocation, to be precise).

2 True. `componentDidMount()` is only executed for browser React (React in the browser), not for server-side React. That's why developers use `componentDidMount()` for AJAX/XHR requests. See chapter 5 for a refresher on component life-cycle events.

3 True. Moving data up the tree hierarchy of components lets you pass it to different child components.

4 False. This object is reused, so you can't use it in an asynchronous operation unless `persist()` is called on `SyntheticEvent`.

5 True. Component lifecycle events are one of the best places to do this, because they let you do the prep work before a component is active and before it's removed.

Watch this chapter's introduction video by scanning this QR code with your phone or going to http://reactquickly.co/videos/ch07.

7

Working with forms in React

This chapter covers

- Defining forms and form elements
- Capturing data changes
- Using references to access data
- Alternative approaches for capturing user-input data from form elements
- Setting default values for form elements

Thus far, you've learned about events, states, component composition, and other important React topics, features, and concepts. But aside from capturing user events, I haven't covered how to capture text input and input via other form elements like input, textarea, and option. Working with them is paramount to web development, because they allow your applications to receive data (such as text) and actions (such as clicks) from users.

This chapter refers to pretty much everything I've covered so far. You'll begin to see how everything fits together.

NOTE The source code for the examples in this chapter is at www.manning
.com/books/react-quickly and https://github.com/azat-co/react-quickly/
tree/master/ch07 (in the ch07 folder of the GitHub repository https://
github.com/azat-co/react-quickly). You can also find some demos at
http://reactquickly.co/demos.

7.1 *The recommended way to work with forms in React*

In regular HTML, when you're working with an input element, the page's DOM main-
tains that element's value in its DOM node. It's possible to access the value via methods
like `document.getElementById('email').value` or by using jQuery methods. In
essence, the DOM is your storage.

In React, when you're working with forms or any other user-input fields such as
standalone text fields or buttons, you have an interesting problem to solve. The React
documentation says, "React components must represent the state of the view at any
point in time and not only at initialization time." React is all about keeping things simple by using declarative style to describe UIs. React describes the UI: its end stage, how
it should look.

Can you spot a conflict? In traditional HTML form elements, the states of elements
change with user input. But React uses a declarative approach to describe UIs. Input
needs to be dynamic to reflect the state properly.

Thus, opting *not* to maintain the component state (in JavaScript) and not to sync it
with the view adds problems; there may be a situation when the internal state and view
are different. React won't know about the changed state. This can lead to all sorts of
trouble and bugs, and negates React's simple philosophy. The best practice is to keep
React's `render()` as close to the real DOM as possible—and that includes the data in
the form elements.

Consider the following example of a text-input field. React must include the new
value in its `render()` for that component. Consequently, you need to set the value for
the element to a new value using `value`. But if you implement an `<input>` field as in
HTML, React will always keep `render()` in sync with the real DOM. React won't allow
users to change the value. Try it yourself. It's peculiar, but that's the appropriate
behavior for React!

```
render() {
  return <input type="text" name="title" value="Mr." />
}
```

This code represents the view at any state, so the value will *always* be `Mr.`. On the other
hand, input fields must change in response to the user clicking or typing. Given these
points, let's make the value dynamic. This is a better implementation, because it'll be
updated from the state:

```
render() {
  return <input type="text" name="title" value={this.state.title} />
}
```

But what's the value of state? React can't know about users typing in the form elements. You need to implement an event handler to capture changes with onChange:

```
handleChange(event) {
  this.setState({title: event.target.value})
}
render() {
  return <input type="text" name="title" value={this.state.title}
  ➥ onChange={this.handleChange.bind(this)}/>
}
```

Given these points, the best practice is to implement these things to sync the internal state with the view (see figure 7.1):

1 Define elements in render() using values from state.
2 Capture changes to a form element as they happen, using onChange.
3 Update the internal state in the event handler.
4 New values are saved in state, and then the view is updated by a new render().

It may seem like a lot of work at first glance, but I hope that when you've used React more, you'll appreciate this approach. It's called *one-way binding* because the state changes views, and that's it. There's no trip back: only a one-way trip from state to view. With one-way binding, a library won't update the state (or the model) automatically. One of the main benefits of one-way binding is that it removes complexity when you're working with large apps where many views implicitly can update many states (data models) and vice versa (see figure 7.2).

Simple doesn't always mean writing less code. Sometimes, as in this case, you'll have to write extra code to manually set the data from event handlers to the state (which is rendered to the view); but this approach tends to be superior when it comes to complex UIs and single-page applications with myriads of views and states. Simple isn't always easy.

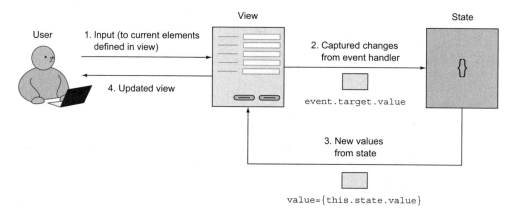

Figure 7.1 The *correct* way to work with form elements: from user input to events, then to the state and the view

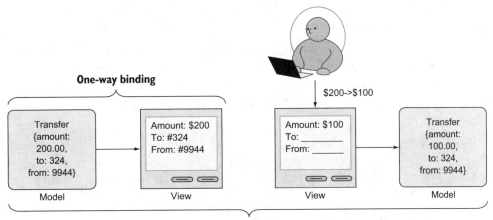

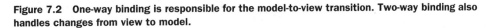

Figure 7.2 One-way binding is responsible for the model-to-view transition. Two-way binding also handles changes from view to model.

Conversely, two-way binding makes it possible for views to change states automatically without you explicitly implementing the process. Two-way binding is how Angular 1 works. Interestingly, Angular 2 borrowed the concept of one-way binding from React and made it the default (you can still have two-way binding explicitly).

For this reason, I'll first cover the recommended approach of working with forms. It's called using *controlled components*, and it ensures that the internal component state is always in sync with the view. Controlled form elements are called that because React controls or sets the values. The alternative approach is *uncontrolled components*, which I'll discuss in section 7.2.

You've learned the best practice of working with input fields in React: capturing the change and applying it to the state as shown in figure 7.1 (input to changed view). Next, let's look at how you define a form and its elements.

7.1.1 Defining a form and its events in React

Let's start with the `<form>` element. Typically, you don't want input elements hanging around randomly in the DOM. This situation can turn bad if you have many functionally different sets of inputs. Instead, you wrap input elements that share a common purpose in a `<form></form>` element.

Having a `<form>` wrapper isn't required. It's fine to use form elements by themselves in simple UIs. In more-complex UIs, where you may have multiple groups of elements on a single page, it's wise to use `<form>` for each such group. React's `<form>` is rendered like an HTML `<form>`, so whatever rules you have for the HTML form will apply to React's `<form>` element, too. For example, according to the HTML5 spec, you should *not* nest forms.[1]

---

[1] The specification says content must be flow content, but with no `<form>` element descendants. See www.w3.org/TR/html5/forms.html#the-form-element.

The <form> element can have events. React supports three events for forms in addition to the standard React DOM events (as outlined in table 6.1):

- onChange—Fires when there's a change in any of the form's input elements.
- onInput—Fires for each change in <textarea><input> element values. The React team doesn't recommend using it (see the accompanying sidebar).
- onSubmit—Fires when the form is submitted, usually by pressing Enter.

---

onChange vs. onInput

React's onChange fires on every change, in contrast to the DOM's change event (http://mng.bz/IJ37), which may not fire on each value change but fires on lost focus. For example, for <input type="text">, a user can be typing with no onChange; only after the user presses Tab or clicks away with their mouse to another element (lost focus) is onChange fired in HTML (regular browser event). As mentioned earlier, in React, onChange fires on each keystroke, not just on lost focus. On the other hand, onInput in React is a wrapper for the DOM's onInput, which fires on each change.

The bottom line is that React's onChange works differently than onChange in HTML: it's more consistent and more like HTML's onInput. The recommended approach is to use onChange in React and to use onInput only when you need to access native behavior for the onInput event. The reason is that React's onChange wrapper behavior provides consistency and thus sanity.

In addition to the three events already listed, <form> can have standard React events such as onKeyUp and onClick. Using form events may come in handy when you need to capture a specific event for the entire form (that is, a group of input elements).

For example, it helps provide a good UX if you allow users to submit data when they press Enter (assuming they're not in a textarea field, in which case Enter should create a new line). You can listen to the form-submit event by creating an event listener that triggers this.handleSubmit():

```
handleSubmit(event) {
  ...
}
render() {
  <form onSubmit={this.handleSubmit}>
    <input type="text" name="email" />
  </form>
}
```

NOTE You need to implement the handleSubmit() function outside of render(), just as you'd do with any other event. React doesn't require a naming convention, so you can name the event handler however you wish as long as the name is understandable and somewhat consistent. This book sticks with the most popular convention: prefixing event handlers with the word handle to distinguish them from regular class methods.

NOTE As a reminder, don't invoke a method (don't put parentheses) and don't use double quotes around curly braces (correct: EVENT={this .METHOD}) when setting the event handler. For some of you, this is basic JavaScript and straightforward, but you wouldn't believe how many times I've seen errors related to these two misunderstandings in React code: you pass the definition of the function, not its result; and you use curly braces as values of the JSX attributes.

Another way to implement form submission on Enter is to manually listen to the key-up event (onKeyUp) and check for the key code (13 for Enter):

```
handleKeyUp(event) {
  if (event.keyCode == 13) return this.sendData()
}
render() {
  return <form onKeyUp={this.handleKeyUp}>
  ...
  </form>
}
```

Note that the sendData() method is implemented somewhere else in the class/component. Also, for this.sendData() to work, you'll need to use bind(this) to bind the context to the event handler in constructor().

To summarize, you can have events on the form element, not just on individual elements in the form. Next, we'll look at how to define form elements.

7.1.2 *Defining form elements*

You implement almost all input fields in HTML with just four elements: <input>, <textarea>, <select>, and <option>. Do you remember that in React, properties are immutable? Well, form elements are special because users need to interact with the elements and change these properties. For all other elements, this is impossible.

React made these elements special by giving them the mutable properties value, checked, and selected. These special mutable properties are also called *interactive properties.*

NOTE React DOM also supports other elements related to building forms, such as <keygen>, <datalist>, <fieldset>, and <label>. These elements don't possess superpowers like a mutable value attribute/property. They're rendered as the corresponding HTML tags. For this reason, this book focuses only on the four main elements with superpowers.

Here's a list of the interactive properties/fields (ones that can change) you can read from events like onChange attached to form elements (covered in section 6.1.3):

- value—Applies to <input>, <textarea>, and <select>
- checked—Applies to <input> with type="checkbox" and type="radio"
- selected—Applies to <option> (used with <select>)

You can read the values and change them by working with these interactive (mutable) properties. Let's look at some examples of how to define each of the elements.

THE <INPUT> ELEMENT

The <input> element renders multiple fields by using different values for its type attribute:

- text—Plain text-input field.
- password—Text-input field with a masked display (for privacy).
- radio—Radio button. Use the same name to create a group of radio buttons.
- checkbox—Check box element. Use the same name to create a group.
- button—Button form element.

The main use case for all <input> type elements—except check boxes and radio buttons—is to use value as the element's interactive/changeable property. For example, an email input field can use the email state and onChange event handler:

```
<input
  type="text"
  name="email"
  value={this.state.email}
  onChange={this.handleEmailChange}/>
```

The two exceptions that don't have value as their primary mutable attribute are inputs with the types checkbox and radio. They use checked because these two types have one value per HTML element, and thus the value doesn't change, but the state of checked/selected does. For example, you can define three radio buttons in one group (radioGroup) by defining these three elements, as shown in figure 7.3.

Figure 7.3   Radio button group

As mentioned earlier, the values (value) are hardcoded because you don't need to change them. What changes with user actions is the element's checked attribute, as shown in the following listing (ch07/elements/jsx/content.jsx).

Listing 7.1   Rendering radio buttons and handling changes

```
class Content extends React.Component {
  constructor(props) {
    super(props)
    this.handleRadio = this.handleRadio.bind(this)
    ...
    this.state = {
      ...
      radioGroup: {
        angular: false,                    Sets the default checked
        react: true,                  ⊲─── radio button in the state
        polymer: false
      }
```

```
    }
  }
  handleRadio(event) {
    let obj = {}  // erase other radios
    obj[event.target.value] = event.target.checked // true
    this.setState({radioGroup: obj})
  }
  ...
  render() {
    return <form>
        <input type="radio"
          name="radioGroup"
          value='angular'
          checked={this.state.radioGroup['angular']}
          onChange={this.handleRadio}/>
      <input type="radio"
        name="radioGroup"
        value='react'
        checked={this.state.radioGroup['react']}
        onChange={this.handleRadio}/>
      <input type="radio"
        name="radioGroup"
        value='polymer'
        checked={this.state.radioGroup['polymer']}
        onChange={this.handleRadio}/>
      ...
    </form>
  }
}
```

> **Uses the target.checked attribute to get a Boolean that indicates whether this radio button is selected**

> **Uses an attribute from the state object or any state attribute**

> **Uses the same onChange event handler because you can get the radio button value from target.value**

For check boxes, you follow an approach similar to that for radio buttons: using the checked attribute and Boolean values for states. Those Booleans can be stored in a checkboxGroup state:

```
class Content extends React.Component {
  constructor(props) {
    super(props)
    this.handleCheckbox = this.handleCheckbox.bind(this)
    // ...
    this.state = {
      // ...
      checkboxGroup: {
        node: false,
        react: true,
        express: false,
        mongodb: false
      }
    }
  }
```

Then the event handler (which you bind in the constructor) grabs the current values, adds true or false from event.target.value, and sets the state:

```
handleCheckbox(event) {
  let obj = Object.assign(this.state.checkboxGroup)
  obj[event.target.value] = event.target.checked        ←—— True or false
  this.setState({checkboxGroup: obj})
}
```

There's no need for the assignment from the state in `radio`, because radio buttons can have only one selected value. Thus, you use an empty object. This isn't the case with check boxes: they can have multiple values selected, so you need a merge, not a replace.

In JavaScript, objects are passed and assigned by references. So in the statement `obj = this.state.checkboxGroup`, `obj` is really a state. As you'll recall, you aren't supposed to change the state directly. To avoid any potential conflicts, it's better to assign by value with `Object.assign()`. This technique is also called *cloning*. Another, less effective and more hacky way to assign by value is to use JSON:

```
clonedData = JSON.parse(JSON.stringify(originalData))
```

When you're using state arrays instead of objects and need to assign by value, use `clonedArray = Array.from(originArray)` or `clonedArray = originArray.slice()`.

You can use the `handleCheckbox()` event handler to get the value from `event.target.value`. The next listing shows `render()` (ch07/elements/jsx/content.jsx), which uses the state values for four check boxes, as shown in figure 7.4.

☐ **Node**
☑ **React**
☐ **Express**
☐ **MongoDB**

Figure 7.4 Rendering check boxes with React as the preselected option

Listing 7.2 Defining check boxes

```
<input type="checkbox"
  name="checkboxGroup"
  value='node'
  checked={this.state.checkboxGroup['node']}       ←┐  Uses state as a value. It can
  onChange={this.handleCheckbox}/>                    be an attribute of an object
<input type="checkbox"                                or just a state attribute.
  name="checkboxGroup"
  value='react'
  checked={this.state.checkboxGroup['react']}      ←┐  Uses onChange to
  onChange={this.handleCheckbox}/>                    capture actions
<input type="checkbox"
  name="checkboxGroup"
  value='express'
  checked={this.state.checkboxGroup.express}       ←┐  Uses dot notation when
  onChange={this.handleCheckbox}/>                    keys are valid JS names
<input type="checkbox"
  name="checkboxGroup"
  value='mongodb'
  checked={this.state.checkboxGroup['mongodb']}    ←┐  No need to bind in the element,
  onChange={this.handleCheckbox}/>                    due to binding in the constructor
                                                      (true for all check boxes)
```

In essence, when you're using check boxes or radio buttons, you can hardcode the value in each individual element and use `checked` as your mutable attribute. Let's see how to work with other input elements.

THE `<TEXTAREA>` ELEMENT

`<textarea>` elements are for capturing and displaying long text inputs such as notes, blog posts, code snippets, and so on. In regular HTML, `<textarea>` uses inner HTML (that is, children) for the value:

```
<textarea>
  With the right pattern, applications...
</textarea>
```

Figure 7.5 shows an example.

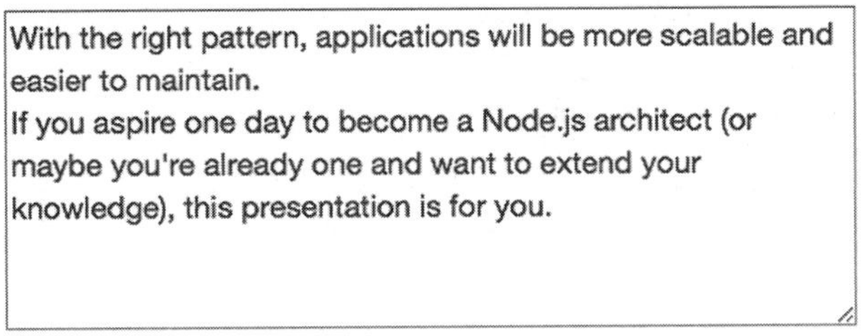

With the right pattern, applications will be more scalable and easier to maintain.
If you aspire one day to become a Node.js architect (or maybe you're already one and want to extend your knowledge), this presentation is for you.

Figure 7.5   Defining and rendering the `<textarea>` element

In contrast, React uses the value *attribute*. In view of this, setting a value as inner HTML/text is an antipattern. React will convert any children (if you use them) of `<textarea>` to the default value (more on default values in section 7.2.4):

```
<!-- Anti-pattern: AVOID doing this! -->
<textarea name="description">{this.state.description}</textarea>
```

Instead, it's recommended that you use the `value` attribute (or property) for `<textarea>`:

```
render() {
  return <textarea name="description" value={this.state.description}/>
}
```

To listen for the changes, use `onChange` as you would for `<input>` elements.

THE `<SELECT>` AND `<OPTION>` ELEMENTS

Select and option fields are great UX-wise for allowing users to select a single value or multiple values from a prepopulated list of values. The list of values is compactly hidden behind the element until users expand it (in the case of a single select), as shown in figure 7.6.

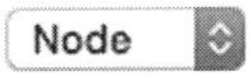

Node

`<select>` is another element whose behavior is different in React compared to regular HTML. For instance, in regular HTML, you might use `selectDOMNode.selectedIndex` to get the index

Figure 7.6   Rendering and preselecting the value of a drop-down

of the selected element, or `selectDOMNode.selectedOptions`. In React, you use `value` for `<select>`, as in the following example (ch07/elements/jsx/content.jsx).

Listing 7.3   Rendering form elements

```
...
constructor(props) {
  super(props)
  this.state = {selectedValue: 'node'}
}
handleSelectChange(event) {
  this.setState({selectedValue: event.target.value})
}
...
render() {
  return <form>
    <select
      value={this.state.selectedValue}
      onChange={this.handleSelectChange}>
        <option value="ruby">Ruby</option>
        <option value="node">Node</option>
        <option value="python">Python</option>
    </select>
  </form>
}
...
```

This code renders a drop-down menu and preselects the `node` value (which must be set in `constructor()`, as shown in figure 7.6). Yay for Node!

Sometimes you need to use a multiselect element. You can do so in JSX/React by providing the `multiple` attribute without any value (React defaults to true) or with the value `{true}`.

> **TIP** Remember that for consistency, and to avoid confusion, I recommend wrapping all Boolean values in curly braces {} and not "". Sure, `"true"` and `{true}` produce the same result. But `"false"` will also produce true. This is because the string `"false"` is treated as true in JavaScript (truthy).

To preselect multiple items, you can pass an array of options to `<select>` via its value attribute. For example, this code preselects Meteor and React:

```
<select multiple={true} value={['meteor', 'react']}>
  <option value="meteor">Meteor</option>
  <option value="react">React</option>
  <option value="jQuery">jQuery</option>
</select>
```

Figure 7.7   Rendering and preselecting multiselect elements

`multiple={true}` renders the multiselect element, and the Meteor and React values are preselected as shown in figure 7.7.

Overall, defining form elements in React isn't much different than doing so in regular HTML, except that you use `value` more often. I like this consistency. But defining is half the work; the other half is capturing the values. You did a little of that in the previous examples. Let's zoom in on event captures.

7.1.3 *Capturing form changes*

As mentioned earlier, to capture changes to a form element, you set up an `onChange` event listener. This event supersedes the normal DOM's `onInput`. In other words, if you need the regular HTML DOM behavior of `onInput`, you can use React's `onInput`. On the other hand, React's `onChange` isn't exactly the same as the regular DOM `onChange`. The regular DOM `onChange` may be fired only when the element loses focus, whereas React's `onChange` fires on all new input. What triggers `onChange` varies for each element:

- `<input>`, `<textarea>`, *and* `<select>`—`onChange` is triggered by a change in `value`.
- `<input>` *with type* `checkbox` *or* `radio`—`onChange` is triggered by a change in `checked`.

Based on this mapping, the approach to reading the value varies. As an argument of the event handler, you're getting a `SyntheticEvent`. It has a `target` property of `value`, `checked`, or `selected`, depending on the element.

To listen for changes, you define the event handler somewhere in your component (you can define it inline too, meaning in the JSX's `{}`) and create the `onChange` attribute pointing to your event handler. For example, this code captures changes from an email field (ch07/elements/jsx/content.jsx).

> **Listing 7.4 Rendering form elements and capturing changes**

```
handleChange(event) {
  console.log(event.target.value)
}
render() {
  return <input
    type="text"
    onChange={this.handleChange}
    defaultValue="hi@azat.co"/>
}
```

Interestingly, if you don't define `onChange` but provide `value`, React will issue a warning and make the element read-only. If your intention is to have a read-only field, it's better to define it explicitly by providing `readOnly`. This will not only remove the warning, but also ensure that other programmers who read this code know this is a read-only field by design. To set the value explicitly, set the `readOnly` value to `{true}`—that is, `readOnly={true}`—or add the `readOnly` attribute by itself without the value, and React by default will add the value of `true` to the attribute.

Once you capture changes in elements, you can store them in the component's state:

```
handleChange(event) {
  this.setState({emailValue: event.target.value})
}
```

Sooner or later, you'll need to send this information to a server or another component. In this case, you'll have the values neatly organized in the state.

For example, suppose you want to create a loan application form that includes the user's name, address, telephone number, and Social Security number. Each input field handles its own changes. At the bottom of this form, you'll put a Submit button to send the state to the server. The following listing shows the name field with onChange, which keeps all input in the state (ch07/elements/jsx/content.jsx).

Listing 7.5   Rendering form elements

```
constructor(props) {
  super(props)
  this.handleInput = this.handleInput.bind(this)
  this.handleSubmit = this.handleSubmit.bind(this)
  ...
}
handleFirstNameChange(event) {
  this.setState({firstName: event.target.value})
}
...
handleSubmit() {
    fetch(this.props['data-url'], {method: 'POST', body:
    JSON.stringify(this.state)})
      .then((response)=>{return response.json()})
      .then((data)=>{console.log('Submitted: ', data)})
}
render() {
  return <form>
    <input name="firstName"
      onChange={this.handleFirstNameChange}
      type="text"/>
        ...
    <input
      type="button"
      onClick={this.handleSubmit}
      value="Submit"/>
  </form>
}
```

Captures changes to the firstName field by saving them to the state (annotation pointing to `this.setState({firstName: event.target.value})`)

Sends data to a URL from the data-url property with the Fetch promise-based browser API (experimental as of this writing, but supported by most modern browsers) (annotation pointing to the fetch block)

Defines an event handler to handle the Submit button (annotation pointing to the input button)

NOTE   Fetch is an experimental native browser method to perform promise-based AJAX/XHR requests. You can read about its usage and support (it's supported by most modern browsers as of this writing) at http://mng.bz/mbMe.

You've learned how to define elements, capture changes with events, and update the state (which you use to display values). The next section walks through an example.

7.1.4 *Account field example*

Continuing with the loan application scenario, once the loan is approved, users need to be able to type in the number of the account to which they want their loan money transferred. Let's implement an account field component using your new skills. This is a controlled element, which is the best practice when it comes to working with forms in React.

In the component shown in listing 7.6 (ch07/account/jsx/content.jsx), you have an account number input field that needs to accept numbers only (see figure 7.8). To limit the input to a number (0–9), you can use a controlled component to weed out all non-numeric values. The event handler sets state only after filtering the input.

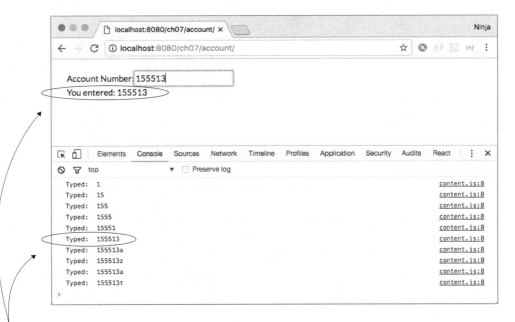

Only digits are allowed because React controls the element's value.

Figure 7.8   You can type anything you want, as shown in the console. But only digits are allowed as the value and in the view, because this element is controlled.

Listing 7.6   Implementing a controlled component

```
class Content extends React.Component {
  constructor(props) {
    super(props)
    this.handleChange = this.handleChange.bind(this)
    this.state = {accountNumber: ''}
  }
}
```

Sets the initial value of the account number to an empty string

```
handleChange(event) {                              ┐  Outputs the unfiltered
  console.log('Typed: ', event.target.value)   ◄─┘  value as it was typed
  this.setState({accountNumber: event.target.value.replace(/[^0-9]/ig,
  ➥ '')})                         ◄─┐ Filters the value and
}                                    └ updates the state
render() {
  return <div>
    Account Number:
    <input
      type="text"
      onChange={this.handleChange}
      placeholder="123456"                 ┐ Controls the element by
      value={this.state.accountNumber}/> ◄─┘ assigning value to state
    <br/>
    <span>{this.state.accountNumber.length > 0 ? 'You entered: ' +
    ➥ this.state.accountNumber: ''}</span>                        ◄─┐
  </div>
}
})              Prints the account number if it's not empty. "length"
                   is a string property that returns the number of
                 characters. If the value is empty, you print nothing.
```

Captures changes (annotation pointing to onChange={this.handleChange})

You use a regular expression (http://mng.bz/r7sq), /[^0-9]/ig, and the string function replace (http://mng.bz/2Qon) to remove all non-digits. replace(/[^0-9]/ig, '') is an uncomplicated regular expression function that replaces anything but numbers with an empty space. ig stands for case insensitive and global (in other words, find all matches).

render() has the input field, which is a controlled component because value={this.state.accountNumber}. When you try this example, you'll be able to type in only numbers because React sets the new state to the filtered number-only value (see figure 7.9).

By following React's best practice for working with input elements and forms, you can implement validation and enforce that the representation is what the app wants it to be.

> **NOTE** Obviously, in the account component, you're implementing a front-end validation, which won't prevent a hacker from inputting malicious data into your XHR request sent to the server. Therefore, make sure you have proper validation on the back-end/server and/or business layer, such as ORM/ODM (https://en.wikipedia.org/wiki/Object-relational_mapping).

So far, you've learned about the best practice for working with forms: creating controlled components. Let's cover some alternatives.

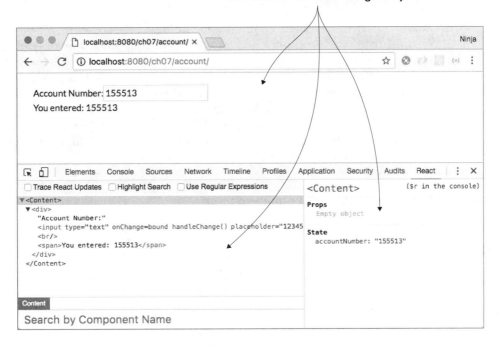

React DevTools shows element structure, props, and state, which in this case is restricted to digits only.

Figure 7.9   **The controlled element filters input by setting `state` to digits only.**

7.2   *Alternative ways to work with forms*

Using controlled form elements is best practice. But as you've seen, this approach requires additional work, because you need to manually capture changes and update states. In essence, if you define the value of the attributes `value`, `checked`, and `selected` using strings, properties, or states, then an element is controlled (by React).

At the same time, form elements can be uncontrolled when the `value` attributes aren't set (neither to a state nor to a static value). Even though this is discouraged for the reasons listed at the beginning of this chapter (the view's DOM state may be different than React's internal state), uncontrolled elements can be useful when you're building a simple form that will be submitted to the server. In other words, consider using the uncontrolled pattern when you're not building a complex UI element with a lot of mutations and user actions; it's a hack that you should avoid most of the time.

Typically, to use uncontrolled components, you define a form-submit event, which is typically `onClick` on a button and/or `onSubmit` on a form. Once you have this event handler, you have two options:

- Capture changes as you do with controlled elements, and use state for submission but not for values (it's an uncontrolled approach, after all!).
- Don't capture changes.

The first approach is straightforward. It's about having the same event listeners and updating the states. That's too much coding if you're using the state only at the final stage (for form submission).

> **WARNING** React is still relatively new, and the best practices are still being formed through real-life experiences of not just writing but also maintaining apps. Recommendations may change based on a few years of maintaining a large React app. The topic of uncontrolled components is a grey area for which there's no clear consensus. You may hear that this is an antipattern and should be avoided completely. I don't take sides but present you with enough information to make your own judgment. I do so because I believe you should have all the available knowledge and are smart enough to act on it. The bottom line is this: consider the rest of the chapter optional reading—a tool you may or may not use.

7.2.1 Uncontrolled elements with change capturing

As you've seen, in React, an *uncontrolled component* means the value property isn't set by the React library. When this happens, the component's internal value (or state) may differ from the value in the component's representation (or view). Basically, there's a dissonance between internal state and representation. The component state can have some logic (such as validation); and with an uncontrolled component pattern, your view will accept any user input in a form element, thus creating the disparity between view and state.

For example, this text-input field is uncontrolled because React doesn't set the value:

```
render() {
  return <input type="text" />
}
```

Any user input will be immediately rendered in the view. Is this good or bad? Bear with me; I'll walk you through this scenario.

To capture changes in an uncontrolled component, you use onChange. For example, the input field in figure 7.10 has an onChange event handler (this.handleChange), a reference (textbook), and a placeholder, which yields a grey text box when the field is empty.

Here's the handleChange() method that prints the values in the console and updates the state using event.target.value (ch07/uncontrolled/jsx/content.jsx).

Listing 7.7 Uncontrolled element that captures changes

```
class Content extends React.Component {
  constructor(props) {
    super(props)
    this.state = {textbook: ''}          Sets the initial value
                                         to an empty string
```

```
  }
  handleChange(event) {                              Updates the state
    console.log(event.target.value)                  on each change in
    this.setState({textbook: event.target.value})    the input field
  }
  render() {
    return <div>
      <input
        type="text"                                  Doesn't set the value for
        onChange={this.handleChange}                 input, only the event listener
        placeholder="Eloquent TypeScript: Myth or Reality" />
      <br/>
      <span>{this.state.textbook}</span>             Uses <span> to output the
    </div>                                           state variable, which you'll set
  }                                                  in the handleChange() method
}
```

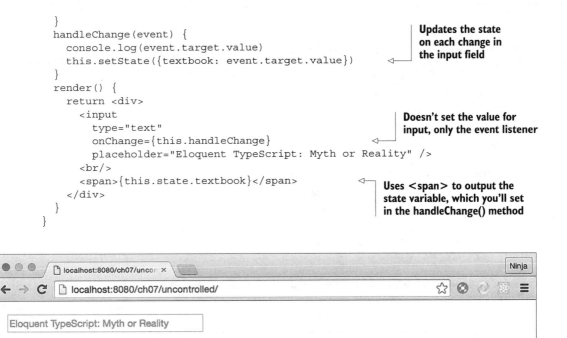

Figure 7.10 **This uncontrolled component has no value set by the application.**

The idea is that users can enter whatever they want because React has no control over the value of the input field. All React is doing is capturing new values (onChange) and setting the state. The change in state will, in turn, update <span> (see figure 7.11).

In this approach, you implement an event handler for the input field. Can you skip capturing events completely?

Figure 7.11   Typing updates the state due to capturing changes, but the value of the DOM text-input element isn't controlled.

7.2.2   *Uncontrolled elements without capturing changes*

Let's look at a second approach. There's a problem with having all the values ready when you want to use them (on form submit, for example). In the approach with change capturing, you have all the data in states. When you opt to not capture changes with uncontrolled elements, the data is still in the DOM. To get the data into a JavaScript object, the solution is to use references, as shown in figure 7.12. Contrast how uncontrolled elements work in figure 7.12 with the controlled elements flow in figure 7.1, which shows how controlled elements function.

> **NOTE**   When you're working with controlled components or with uncontrolled components that capture data, the data is in the state all the time. This isn't the case with the approach discussed in this subsection.

To sum up, in order for the approach of using uncontrolled elements without capturing changes to work, you need a way to access other elements to get data from them.

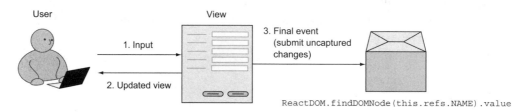
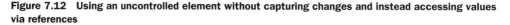

Figure 7.12   Using an uncontrolled element without capturing changes and instead accessing values via references

7.2.3 Using references to access values

You use references to access values when working with uncontrolled components that don't capture events, such as `onChange`, but the references aren't exclusive to this particular pattern. You can use references in any other scenario you see fit, although using references is frowned on as an antipattern. The reason is that when React elements are defined properly, with each element using internal state in sync with the view's state (DOM), the need for references is almost nonexistent. But you need to understand references, so I'll cover them here.

With references, you can get the DOM element (or a node) of a React.js component. This comes in handy when you need to get form element values, but you don't capture changes in the elements.

To use a reference, you need to do two things:

- Make sure the element in the render's return has the `ref` attribute with a camel-Case name (for example, email: `<input ref="userEmail" />`).
- Access the DOM instance with the named reference in some other method. For example, in the event handler, `this.refs.NAME` becomes `this.refs.userEmail`.

`this.refs.NAME` will give you an instance of a React component, but how do you get the value? It's more useful to have the DOM node! You can access the component's DOM node by calling `ReactDOM.findDOMNode(this.refs.NAME)`:

```
let emailNode = ReactDOM.findDOMNode(this.refs.email)
let email = emailNode.value
```

I find this method a bit clunky to write (too lengthy), so with this in mind you can use an alias:

```
let fD = ReactDOM.findDOMNode
let email = fD(this.refs.email).value
```

Consider the example shown in figure 7.13, which captures user email addresses and comments. The values are output to the browser console.

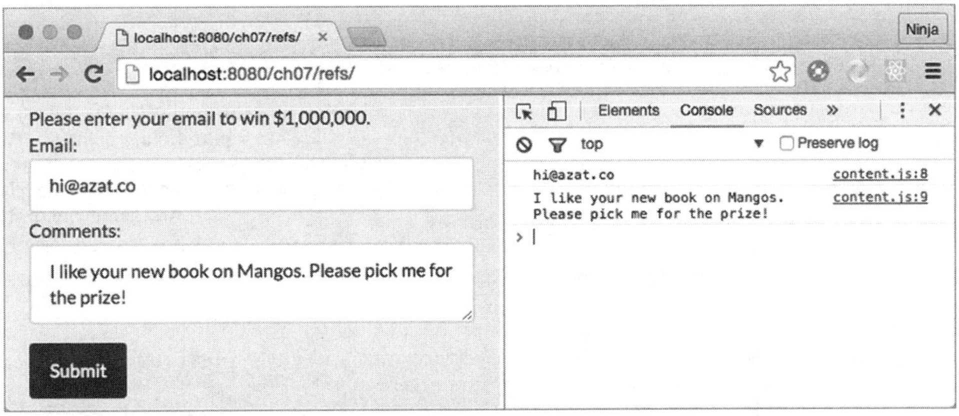

Figure 7.13   Uncontrolled form that gets data from two fields and prints it in logs

The project structure is very different from other project structures. It looks like this:

```
/email
  /css
    bootstrap.css
  /js
    content.js
    react.js
    react-dom.js
    script.js
  /jsx
    content.jsx
    script.jsx
  index.html
```

Compiled script with
the main component

ReactDOM.render()
statement in JSX

When the Submit button is clicked, you can access the `emailAddress` and `comments` references and output the values to two logs, as shown next (ch07/email/jsx/content.jsx).

Listing 7.8   Beginning of the email form

```
class Content extends React.Component {
  constructor(props) {
    super(props)
    this.submit = this.submit.bind(this)
    this.prompt = 'Please enter your email to win $1,000,000.'
  }
  submit(event) {
    let emailAddress = this.refs.emailAddress
    let comments = this.refs.comments
    console.log(ReactDOM.findDOMNode(emailAddress).value)
    console.log(ReactDOM.findDOMNode(comments).value)
  }
```

Defines a class
attribute

Accesses and prints
the value for the
email address
using a reference

Next, you have the mandatory `render()` function, which uses the Twitter Bootstrap classes to style the intake form (ch07/email/jsx/content.jsx). Remember to use `className` for the `class` attribute!

Listing 7.9   `render()` method of the email form

Implements the input field for the email, which
has a placeholder element attribute. A
placeholder property is a visual aid to show an
example of what to enter. Uses the className
and ref element attributes.

```
render: function() {
  return (
    <div className="well">
      <p>{this.prompt}</p>
      <div className="form-group">
        Email: <input ref="emailAddress" className="form-control"
        ⟹ type="text" placeholder="hi@azat.co"/>
      </div>
      <div className="form-group">
        Comments: <textarea ref="comments" className="form-control"
        ⟹ placeholder="I like your website!"/>
      </div>
      <div className="form-group">
```

Prints the
value of the
prompt
attribute of
the Content
component

```
          <a className="btn btn-primary" value="Submit"
      ➥ onClick={this.submit}>Submit</a>   ⟵
        </div>
      </div>
    )
  }
})
```

> **Code the Submit button with the onClick event that calls this.submit.**

A regular HTML DOM node for `<textarea>` uses `innerHTML` as its value. As mentioned earlier, in React you can use `value` for this element:

```
ReactDOM.findDOMNode(comments).value
```

This is because React implements the `value` property. It's just one of the nice features you get with a more consistent API for form elements. At the same time, because the `ReactDOM.findDOMNode()` method returns a DOM node, you have access to other regular HTML attributes (like `innerHTML`) and methods (like `getAttribute()`).

   Now you know how to access elements and their values from pretty much any component method, not just from an event handler for that particular element. Again, references are only for the rare cases when you use uncontrolled elements. The overuse of references is frowned on as a bad practice. Most of the time, you won't need to use references with controlled elements, because you can use component states instead.

   It's also possible to assign a function to the `ref` attribute in JSX. This function is called just once, on the mounting of the element. In the function, you can save the DOM node in an instance attribute `this.emailInput`:

```
<input ref={(input) => { this.emailInput = input }}
  className="form-control"
  type="text"
  placeholder="hi@azat.co"/>
```

Uncontrolled components require less coding (state updates and capturing changes are optional), but they raise another issue: you can't set values to states or hardcoded values because then you'll have controlled elements (for example, you can't use `value={this.state.email}`). How do you set the initial value? Let's say the loan application has been partly filled out and saved, and the user resumes the session. You need to show the information that has already been filled in, but you can't use the `value` attribute. Let's look at how you set default values.

7.2.4 *Default values*

Suppose you want the example loan application to prepopulate certain fields with existing data. In normal HTML, you define a form field with `value`, and users can modify the element on a page. But React uses `value`, `checked`, and `selected` to maintain consistency between the view and the internal state of elements. In React, if you hardcode the value like

```
<input type="text" name="new-book-title" value="Node: The Best Parts"/>
```

it'll be a read-only input field. That isn't what you need in most cases. Therefore, in React, the special attribute `defaultValue` sets the value and lets users modify form elements.

For example, assume the form was saved earlier, and you want to fill in the `<input>` field for the user. In this case, you need to use the `defaultValue` property for the form elements. You can set the initial value of the input field like this:

```
<input type="text" name="new-book-
     title" defaultValue="Node: The Best Parts"/>
```

If you use the `value` attribute (`value="JSX"`) instead of `defaultValue`, this element becomes read-only. Not only will it be controlled, but the value won't change when the user types in the `<input>` element, as shown in figure 7.14. This is because the value is hardcoded, and React will maintain that value. Probably not what you want. Obviously, in real-life applications, you get values programmatically, which in React means using properties (`this.props.name`)

JSX

Figure 7.14 The value of an `<input>` element appears frozen (unchangeable) on a web page when you set the value to a string.

```
<input type="text" name="new-book-title" defaultValue={this.props.title}/>
```

or states:

```
<input type="text" name="new-book-title" defaultValue={this.state.title}/>
```

The `defaultValue` React feature is most often used with uncontrolled components; but, as with references, default values can be used with controlled components or in any other scenario. You don't need default values as much in controlled components because you can define those values in the state in the constructor; for example, `this.state = { defaultName: 'Abe Lincoln'}`.

As you've seen, most UI work is done in handy form elements. You need to make them beautiful, yet easy to understand and use. And you must also have user-friendly error messages, front-end validation, and other nontrivial things like tooltips, scalable radio buttons, default values, and placeholders. Building a UI can be complicated and can quickly spiral out of control! Fortunately, React makes your job easier by letting you use a cross-browser API for form elements.

7.3 *Quiz*

1 An uncontrolled component sets a value, and a controlled component doesn't. True or false?

2 The correct syntax for default values is which of the following? `default-value`, `defaultValue`, or `defVal`

3 The React team recommends using `onChange` over `onInput`. True or false?

4 You set a value for the text area with which of the following? Children, inner HTML, or value

5 In a form, selected applies to which of the following? <input>, <textarea>, or <option>

6 Which of the following is the best way to extract the DOM node by reference? React.findDomNode(this.refs.email), this.refs.email, this.refs.email .getDOMNode, ReactDOM.findDOMNode(this.refs.email), or this.refs.email .getDomNode

7.4   Summary

- The preferred approach for forms is to use controlled components with event listeners capturing and storing data in the state.
- Using uncontrolled components with or without capturing changes is a hack and should be avoided.
- References and default values can be used with any elements but usually aren't needed when components are controlled.
- React's <textarea> uses a value attribute, not inner content.
- this.refs.NAME is a way to access class references.
- defaultValue allows you to set the initial view (DOM) value for an element.
- ref="NAME" is how you define references.

7.5   Quiz answers

6 Use ReactDOM.findDOMNode (reference) or a callback (not listed as an answer).

5 <option>.

4 In React, you set a value with value for consistency. But in vanilla HTML, you use inner HTML.

3 True. In regular HTML, onchange might not fire on every change, but in React it always does.

2 defaultValue. The other options are invalid names.

1 False. The definition of a controlled component/element is that it sets the value.

Watch this chapter's introduction video by scanning this QR code with your phone or going to http://reactquickly.co/videos/ch08.

8
Scaling
React components

Thus far, we've covered how to create components and make them interactive, and work with user input (events and input elements). Using this knowledge will take you a long way in building sites with React components, but you'll notice that certain annoyances keep cropping up. This is especially true for large projects when you rely on components created by other software engineers (open source contributors or your teammates).

For example, when you consume a component someone else wrote, how do you know whether you're providing the right properties for it? Also, how can you use an existing component with a little added functionality (which is also applied to other components)? These are *developmental scalability issues*: how to scale your code, meaning how to work with your code when the code base grows larger. Certain features and patterns in React can help with that.

These topics are important if you'd like to learn how to effectively build a complex React application. For example, higher-order components allow you to enhance the functionality of a component, and property types provide the security of type checking and no small measure of sanity.

By the end of this chapter, you'll be familiar with most features of React. You'll become adept at making your code more developer friendly (using property types) and your work more efficient (using component names and higher-order components). Your teammates may even marvel at your elegant solutions. These features will help you use React effectively, so let's dive in without further ado.

> **NOTE** The source code for the examples in this chapter is at www.manning
> .com/books/react-quickly and https://github.com/azat-co/react-quickly/
> tree/master/ch08 (in the ch08 folder of the GitHub repository
> https://github.com/azat-co/react-quickly). You can also find some demos at
> http://reactquickly.co/demos.

8.1   *Default properties in components*

Imagine that you're building a `Datepicker` component that takes a few required properties such as number of rows, locale, and current date:

```
<Datepicker currentDate={Date()} locale="US" rows={4}/>
```

What will happen if a new team member tries to use your component but forgets to pass the essential `currentDate` property? Then, what if another coworker passes a `"4"` string instead of a 4 number? Your component will do nothing (values `undefined`) or worse: it may crash, and they may blame you (`ReferenceError` anyone?). Oops.

Sadly, this isn't an uncommon situation in web development, because JavaScript is a loosely typed language. Fortunately, React provides a feature that lets you set default values for properties: the `defaultProps` static attribute. We'll return to flagging issues with property types in the next section.

The key benefit of `defaultProps` is that *if a property is missing, a default value is rendered.* To set a default property value on the component class, you define `defaultProps`. For example, in the aforementioned `Datepicker` component definition, you can add a static class attribute (not an instance attribute, because that won't work—instance attributes are set in `constructor()`):

```
class Datepicker extends React.Component {
  ...
}
Datepicker.defaultProps = {
  currentDate: Date(),
  rows: 4,
  locale: 'US'
}
```

To illustrate `defaultProps` further, let's say you have a component that renders a button. Typically, buttons have labels, but those labels need to be customizable. In case the custom value is omitted, it's good to have a default value.

The button's label is the `buttonLabel` property, which you use in `render()`'s return attribute. You want this property to always include `Submit`, even if the value isn't set from above. To do this, you implement the `defaultProps` static class attribute, which is an object containing the property `buttonLabel` with a default value:

```
class Button extends React.Component {
  render() {
    return <button className="btn" >{this.props.buttonLabel}</button>
  }
}
Button.defaultProps = {buttonLabel: 'Submit'}
```

The parent component `Content` renders four buttons. But three of these four button components are missing properties:

```
class Content extends React.Component {
  render() {
    return (
      <div>
        <Button buttonLabel="Start"/>
        <Button />
        <Button />
        <Button />
      </div>
    )
  }
}
```

Can you guess the result? The first button will have the label Start, and the rest of the buttons will have the label Submit (see figure 8.1).

Setting default property values is almost always a good idea, because doing so makes your components more fault tolerant. In other words, your components become smarter because they have a baseline look and behavior even when nothing is supplied.

Figure 8.1   The first button has a label that's set on creation. The other elements don't and thus fall back to the default property value.

Looking at it another way, having a default value means you can skip declaring the same old value over and over again. If you use a single property value most of the time but still want to provide a way to modify this value (override the default), the defaultProps feature is the way to go. Overriding a default value doesn't cause any issues, as you saw with the first button element in the example.

8.2 React property types and validation

Going back to the earlier example with the Datepicker component and coworkers who aren't aware of property types ("5" versus 5), you can set property types to use with React.js component classes. You do so via the propTypes static attribute. This feature of property types doesn't enforce data types on property values and instead gives you a warning. That is, if you're in development mode, and a type doesn't match, you'll get a warning message in the console and in production; nothing will be done to prevent the wrong type from being used. In essence, React.js suppresses this warning in production mode. Thus, propTypes is mostly a convenience feature to warn you about mismatches in data types at a developmental stage.

> **Production vs. development React**
> The React.js team defines *development mode* as using the unminified (uncompressed) version of React and *production mode* as using the minified version. From the React authors:
>
>> *We provide two versions of React: an uncompressed version for development and a minified version for production. The development version includes extra warnings about common mistakes, whereas the production version includes extra performance optimizations and strips all error messages.*

For React 15.5 and later versions (most of the examples in this book use React v15.5), type definitions come from a separate package called prop-types (www.npmjs.com/package/prop-types). You need to include prop-types in your HTML file. The package will become a global object (window.PropTypes):

```
<!-- development version -->
<script src="https://unpkg.com/prop-types/prop-types.js"></script>

<!-- production version -->
<script src="https://unpkg.com/prop-types/prop-types.min.js"></script>
```

If you're using React 15.4 and earlier, there's no need to include prop-types, because the types are in React: React.propTypes.

Here's a basic example of defining a static propTypes attribute on a Datepicker class with types string, number, and enumerator. The example uses React v15.5 and includes prop-types in HTML (not shown here):

```
class Datepicker extends React.Component {
  ...
}
Datepicker.propTypes = {
  currentDate: PropTypes.string,
  rows: PropTypes.number,
  locale: PropTypes.oneOf(['US', 'CA', 'MX', 'EU'])
}
```

window.PropTypes because the script includes prop-types.js

> **WARNING** Never rely on front-end user-input validation, because it can be easily bypassed. Use it only for a better UX, and check everything on the server side.

To validate property types, use the `propTypes` property with the object containing the properties as keys and types as values. React.js types are in the `PropTypes` object:

- `PropTypes.string`
- `PropTypes.string`
- `PropTypes.number`
- `PropTypes.bool`
- `PropTypes.object`
- `PropTypes.array`
- `PropTypes.func`
- `PropTypes.shape`

- `PropTypes.any.isRequired`
- `PropTypes.objectOf(PropTypes.number)`
- `PropTypes.arrayOf(PropTypes.number)`
- `PropTypes.node`
- `PropTypes.instanceOf(Message)`
- `PropTypes.element`
- `PropTypes.oneOfType([PropTypes.number, ...])`

To demonstrate, let's enhance the `defaultProps` example by adding some property types in addition to default property values. The structure of this project is similar: content.jsx, button.jsx, and script.jsx. The index.html file has a reference to prop-types.js:

```
<!DOCTYPE html>
<html>

  <head>
    <script src="js/react.js"></script>
    <script src="js/prop-types.js"></script>
    <script src="js/react-dom.js"></script>
    <link href="css/bootstrap.css" type="text/css" rel="stylesheet"/>
    <link href="css/style.css" type="text/css" rel="stylesheet"/>

  </head>

  <body>
    <div id="content" class="container"></div>
    <script src="js/button.js"></script>
    <script src="js/content.js"></script>
    <script src="js/script.js"></script>
  </body>

</html>
```

Let's define a `Button` class with an optional `title` with a `string` type. To implement it, you define a static class attribute (a property of that class) `propTypes` with key `title` and `PropTypes.string` as a value of that key. This code goes into button.js:

```
Button.propTypes = {
  title: PropTypes.string
}
```

You can also require properties. To do so, add `isRequired` to the type. For example, the `title` property is mandatory and of type `string`:

```
Button.propTypes = {
  title: PropTypes.string.isRequired
}
```

This button also requires a `handler` property, which must have a function as a value. (Last time I checked, buttons without actions were useless.)

```
Button.propTypes = {
  handler: PropTypes.func.isRequired
}
```

What's also nice is that you can define your own *custom validation*. To implement custom validation, all you need to do is create an expression that returns an instance of `Error`. Then, you use that expression in `propTypes: {..}` as the value of the property. For example, the following code validates the `email` property with the regex from `emailRegularExpression` (which I copied from the internet—that means it has to be correct, right?):[1]

```
...
propTypes = {
    email: function(props, propName, componentName) {
      var emailRegularExpression =
/^([\w-]+(?:\.[\w-]+)*)@((?:[\w-]+\.)*\w[\w-]{0,66})\.([a-z]{2,6}(?:\.
➥ [a-z]{2})?)$/i
      if (!emailRegularExpression.test(props[propName])) {
        return new Error('Email validation failed!')
      }
    }
}
...
```

Now let's put everything together. The `Button` component will be called with and without a property title (string) and a handler (required function). The following listing

---

[1] There are many versions of the email regex, depending on strictness, domain zones, and other criteria. See "Email Address Regular Expression That 99.99% Works," http://emailregex.com; "Validate email address in JavaScript?" (question on Stack Overflow), http://mng.bz/zm37; and *Regular Expression Library*, http://regexlib.com/Search.aspx?k=email.

(ch08/prop-types) uses property types to ensure that `handler` is a function, `title` is a string, and `email` adheres to the provided regular expression.

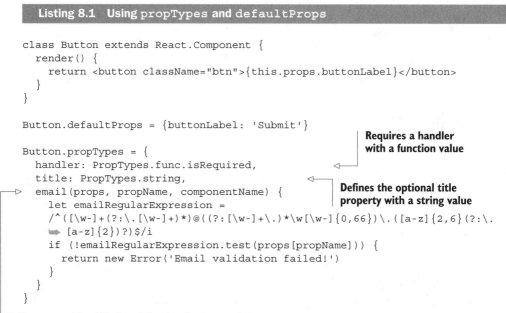

Listing 8.1   Using `propTypes` and `defaultProps`

```
class Button extends React.Component {
  render() {
    return <button className="btn">{this.props.buttonLabel}</button>
  }
}

Button.defaultProps = {buttonLabel: 'Submit'}

Button.propTypes = {
  handler: PropTypes.func.isRequired,
  title: PropTypes.string,
  email(props, propName, componentName) {
    let emailRegularExpression =
    /^([\w-]+(?:\.[\w-]+)*)@((?:[\w-]+\.)*\w[\w-]{0,66})\.([a-z]{2,6}(?:\.
    [a-z]{2})?)?$/i
    if (!emailRegularExpression.test(props[propName])) {
      return new Error('Email validation failed!')
    }
  }
}
```

Requires a handler with a function value

Defines the optional title property with a string value

Defines an email validation with a regular expression

Next, let's implement the parent component `Content`, which renders six buttons to test the warning messages produced from property types (ch08/prop-types/jsx/content.jsx).

Listing 8.2   Rendering six buttons

```
class Content extends React.Component {
  render() {
    let number = 1
    return (
      <div>
        <Button buttonLabel="Start"/>
        <Button />
        <Button title={number}/>
        <Button />
        <Button email="not-a-valid-email"/>
        <Button email="hi@azat.co"/>
      </div>
    )
  }
}
```

Triggers a warning that title must be a string

Triggers a warning that there's no handler

Triggers a warning about the wrong email format

Running this code results in three warning messages being displayed on your console (don't forget to open it); mine are shown here and in figure 8.2. The first

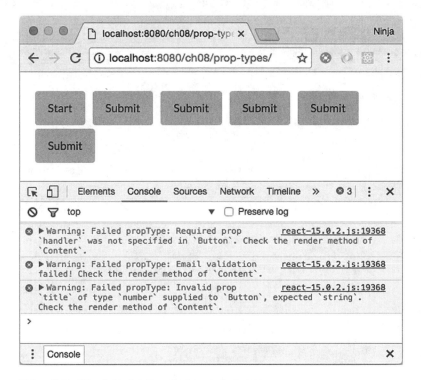

Figure 8.2 Warnings due to wrong property types

warning is about the `handler` function that must be specified, which I omitted in a few buttons:

```
Warning: Failed propType: Required prop `handler` was not specified in
`Button`. Check the render method of `Content`.
```

The second warning is about the wrong email format for the fourth button:

```
Warning: Failed propType: Email validation failed! Check the render method
of `Content`.
```

The third warning is about the wrong type for the title, which should be a string (I provided a number for one button):

```
Warning: Failed propType: Invalid prop `title` of type `number` supplied to
`Button`, expected `string`. Check the render method of `Content`.
```

The interesting thing is that more than one button is missing `handler`, but you see only one warning. React warns about each property only once per single `render()` of `Content`.

What I love about React is that it tells you what parent component to check. It's `Content` in the example. Imagine if you had hundreds of components. This is useful!

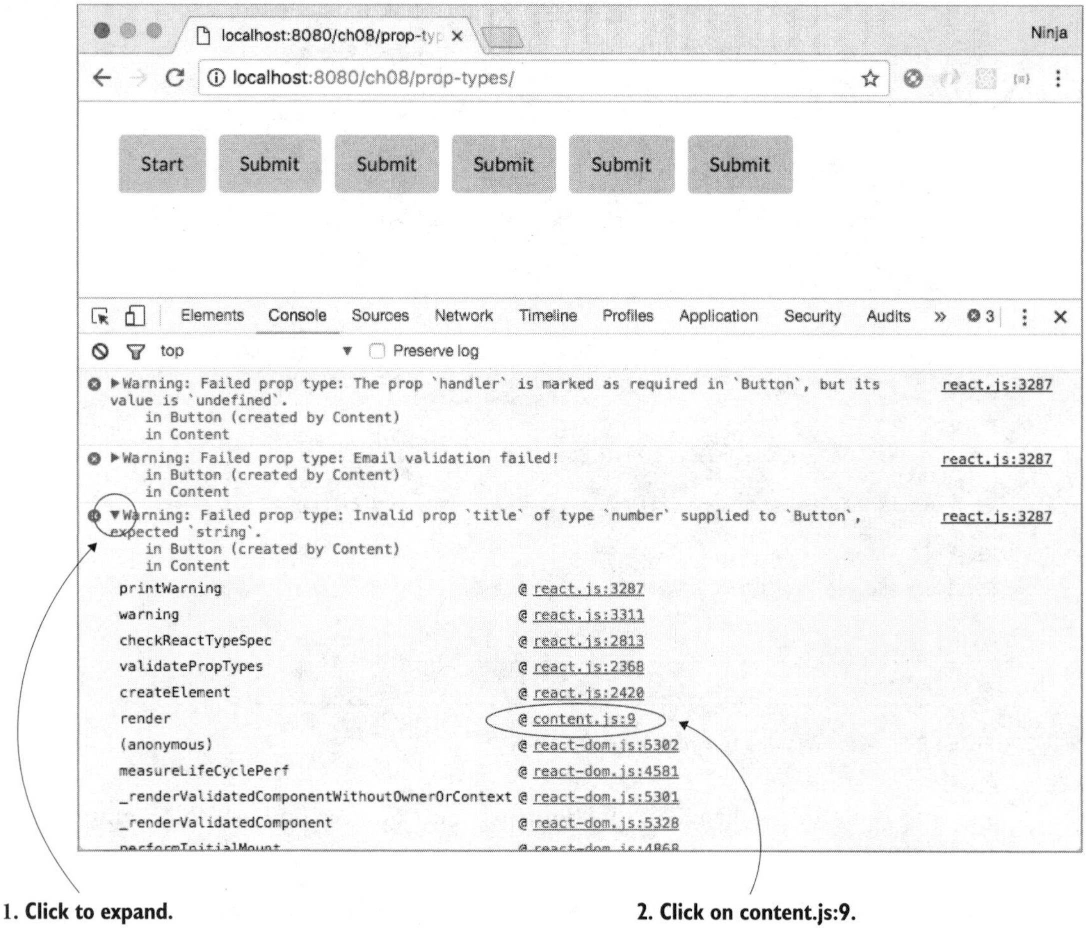

1. **Click to expand.**   2. **Click on content.js:9.**

Figure 8.3   Expanding a warning revealed the problematic line number: 9.

Conveniently, if you expand the message in DevTools, you can spot a line number for the Button element that's causing trouble and that resulted in the warning. In figure 8.3, I first expanded the message and then located my file (content.js). The message said that the issue was on line 9.

By clicking content.js:9 in the console, you can open the Source tab at that line, as shown in figure 8.4. It clearly shows what's to blame:

```
React.createElement(Button, { title: number }),
```

You don't need source maps (although you'll set them up and use them in part 2 of the book) to know that the third button is causing the problem.

NOTE   I'll repeat it again: only the unminified or uncompressed version (that is, development mode) of React shows these warnings.

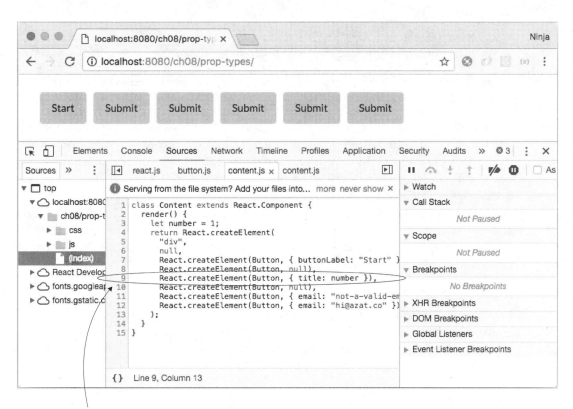

The message identified line 9
as the problem in content.js.

Figure 8.4   Inspecting the compiled source code is often enough to understand the problem.

Try playing with the property types and validation. It's a neat feature. Consider that this code uses the same `Button` component as before:

```
<Button title={number}/>
```

Can you spot the problem? How many warnings do you think you'll get? (Hint: `handler` and `title` properties.)

Source maps

I got the warnings shown in figure 8.2 because of the poorly written `Content` (I wrote it that way on purpose, to show how `defaultProps` and `propTypes` work). The warning messages identify the component and where in the component the problem is happening.

But the line numbers won't match your source code, because they refer to compiled JavaScript, not JSX. To get the correct line numbers, you'll need to use a source-map plugin like `source-map-support` (https://github.com/evanw/node-source-map-support) or Webpack. Chapter 12 discusses Webpack.

(continued)
You can get support for source maps with pure non-Webpack Babel by adding `--sourceMaps=true` to the command and/or the package.json build script. For more Babel options, see https://babeljs.io/docs/usage/options/#options.

It's important to know and use `propTypes` (property types and custom validation) in large projects or open source components. Of course, property types don't have strict enforcement or error exceptions, but the benefit is that when you use someone else's component, you can verify that the supplied properties are of the right type. Same applies when other software engineers use your components. They'll appreciate that you provided correct property types. That leads to a better developer experience for everyone!

Finally, there are many additional types and helper methods. To see the full reference, please refer to the documentation at http://mng.bz/4Lep.

8.3 *Rendering children*

Let's continue with the fictional React project; but instead of a `Datepicker` (which is now robust and warns you about any missing or incorrect properties), you're tasked with creating a component that's universal enough to use with any children you pass to it. It's a blog post `Content` component that may consist of a heading and a paragraph of text:

```
<Content>
  <h1>React.js</h1>
  <p>Rocks</p>
</Content>
```

Another blog post may consist of an image (think Instagram or Tumblr):

```
<Content>
  <img src="images/azat.jpg" width="100"/>
</Content>
```

Both posts use `Content`, but they pass different children to it. Wouldn't it be great to have a special way to render any children (`<p>` or `<img>`)? Meet `children`.

The `children` property is an easy way to render all children with `{this.props.children}`. You can also do more than rendering. For example, add a `<div>` and pass along child elements:

```
class Content extends React.Component {
  render() {
    return (
      <div className="content">
        {this.props.children}
      </div>
    )
  }
}
```

The parent of `Content` has the children `<h1>` and `<p>`:

```
ReactDOM.render(
  <div>
    <Content>
      <h1>React</h1>
      <p>Rocks</p>
    </Content>
  </div>,
  document.getElementById('content')
)
```

The end result is that `<h1>` and `<p>` are wrapped in the `<div>` container with a `content` class, as shown in figure 8.5. Remember, for class attributes, you use `className` in React.

Obviously, you can add many more things to a component like `Content`; for example, more classes for styling, layouts, and even access properties and interactivity with events and states. With `this.props.children`, you can create pass-through components that are flexible, powerful, and universal.

Figure 8.5 Rendering a single `Content` component with a heading and paragraph using `this.props`
`.children`, which shows two items

Let's say you need to display a link or a button in addition to text and images, as shown in the previous example. The `Content` component will still be the wrapper `<div>` with the CSS class `content` (`className` property), but now there will be more different children. The benefit is that `Content` can be children-agnostic.[2] You don't need to change the `Content` class.

Put the children in `Content` when you instantiate the class (ch08/children/jsx/script.jsx).

Listing 8.3   Rendering elements using `Content`

```
ReactDOM.render(
  <div>
    <Content>
      <h1>React</h1>
      <p>Rocks</p>
    </Content>
    <Content>
      <img src="images/azat.jpg" width="100"/>
    </Content>
    <Content>
      <a href="http://react.rocks">http://react.rocks</a>
    </Content>
    <Content>
      <a className="btn btn-danger"
      ➥ href="http://react.rocks">http://react.rocks</a>
    </Content>
  </div>,
  document.getElementById('content')
)
```

The resulting HTML will have two `<div>` elements with `content` CSS classes. Your layouts! One will have `<h1>` and `<p>` and the other will have `<span>`, as shown in DevTools in figure 8.6.

What's interesting about the `children` property is that it can be an array if there's more than one child element (as seen in figure 8.5). You can access individual elements like this:

```
{this.props.children[0]}
{this.props.children[1]}
```

Be careful when validating children. When there's only one child element, `this.props.children` isn't an array. If you use `this.props.children.length` and the single child node is a string, this can lead to bugs because `length` is a valid string property. Instead, use `React.Children.count(this.props.children)` to get an accurate count of child elements.

---

[2] "Agnostic, in an information technology (IT) context, refers to something that is generalized so that it is interoperable among various systems." From http://whatis.techtarget.com/definition/agnostic.

Figure 8.6   Rendering four elements with different content using a single component class

React has other helpers like `React.Children.count`. The most interesting (in my opinion) are these:

- `React.Children.map()`
- `React.Children.forEach()`
- `React.Children.toArray()`

There's no reason to duplicate the ever-changing list; you can find the official documentation at http://mng.bz/Oi2W.

8.4   *Creating React higher-order components for code reuse*

We'll continue to suppose that you work on a large team and create components that other developers use in their projects. Let's say you're working on a piece of an interface. Three of your teammates ask you to implement a way to load a resource (the React.js website), but each of them wants to use their own visual representation for the button, image, and link. Perhaps you could implement a method and call it from an event handler, but there's a more elegant solution: *higher-order components.*

A higher-order component (HOC) lets you enhance a component with additional logic (see figure 8.7). You can think of this pattern as components inheriting functionality when used with HOCs. In other words, *HOCs let you reuse code.* This allows you and your team to share functionality among React.js components. By doing so, you can avoid repeating yourselves (DRY, http://mng.bz/1K5k).

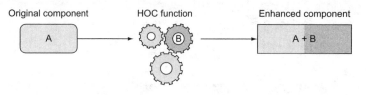

Original component   HOC function   Enhanced component

Figure 8.7   Simplified representation of the higher-order component pattern, where an enhanced component has properties not just of A but of A and B

In essence, HOCs are React component classes that render the original classes while adding extra functionality along the way. Defining an HOC is straightforward, because it's only a function. You declare it with a fat arrow:

```
const LoadWebsite = (Component) => {
  . . .
}
```

The name `LoadWebsite` is arbitrary; you can name the HOC anything, as long as you use the same name when you enhance a component. The same is true for the argument to the function (`LoadWebsite`); it's the original (not yet enhanced) component.

   To demonstrate, let's set up a project for your three coworkers. The project structure is as follows, with three stateless components, `Button`, `Link`, and `Logo` in elements.jsx, and the HOC function in load-website.jsx:

```
/hi-order
  /css
    bootstrap.css
    style.css
  /js
    content.js
    elements.js
    load-website.js
    react.js
    react-dom.js
    script.js
  /jsx
    content.jsx
    elements.jsx
    load-website.jsx
    script.jsx
  index.html
  logo.png
```

Your coworkers need a label and a click event handler. Let's set the label and define the `handleClick()` method. The mounting events demonstrate the component lifecycle (ch08/hi-order/jsx/load-website.jsx).

Listing 8.4 Implementing a higher-order component

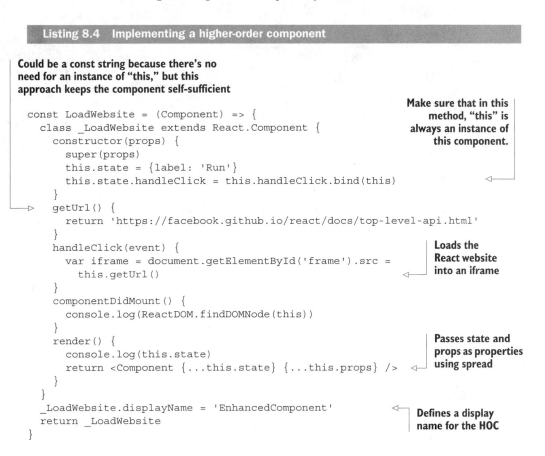

Could be a const string because there's no
need for an instance of "this," but this
approach keeps the component self-sufficient

Make sure that in this
method, "this" is
always an instance of
this component.

```
const LoadWebsite = (Component) => {
  class _LoadWebsite extends React.Component {
    constructor(props) {
      super(props)
      this.state = {label: 'Run'}
      this.state.handleClick = this.handleClick.bind(this)
    }
    getUrl() {
      return 'https://facebook.github.io/react/docs/top-level-api.html'
    }
    handleClick(event) {
      var iframe = document.getElementById('frame').src =
        this.getUrl()
    }
    componentDidMount() {
      console.log(ReactDOM.findDOMNode(this))
    }
    render() {
      console.log(this.state)
      return <Component {...this.state} {...this.props} />
    }
  }
  _LoadWebsite.displayName = 'EnhancedComponent'
  return _LoadWebsite
}
```

Loads the
React website
into an iframe

Passes state and
props as properties
using spread

Defines a display
name for the HOC

Nothing complex, right? There are two new techniques not covered previously in this book: displayName and the spread operator .... Let's quickly (as the title of this book suggests) examine them now.

8.4.1 *Using displayName: distinguishing child components from their parent*

By default, JSX uses the class name as the name of the instance (element). Thus elements created with an HOC in the example have _LoadWebsite names.

> **Underscore in JavaScript**
>
> In JavaScript, an underscore (_) is a valid character for a name (the Lodash and Underscore libraries use it). In addition, an underscore as the start of a name of a variable or method typically means it's a private attribute, variable, or method that isn't intended for use as a public interface (for example, by another module, class, object, function, and so on). Using private APIs is highly discouraged because they're likely to change more often and contain undocumented behavior.

> **(continued)**
> An underscore at the beginning of a name is a *convention*, meaning it's not enforced by the engine or platform. It's solely a common pattern used and recognized by JavaScript software engineers. In other words, methods and variables don't become private *automatically* when _ is used in their names. To make a variable/method private, use a closure. See http://developer.mozilla.org/en/docs/Web/JavaScript/Closures and http://javascript.crockford.com/private.html.

When you want to change this name, there's the `displayName` static attribute. As you may know, static class attributes in ES6 must be defined outside of the class definition. (As of this writing, the standard for static attributes hasn't been finalized.)

To sum up, `displayName` is necessary to set React element names when they need to be different from the component class name, as shown in figure 8.8. You can see how useful it is to use `displayName` in the load-website.jsx HOC to augment the name, because by default the component name is the function name (which may not always be the name you want).

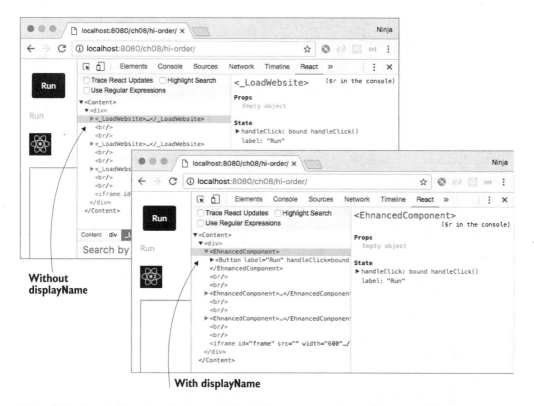

Figure 8.8   By using the `displayName` static attribute, you can change the name of the component from `_LoadWebsite` to `EnhancedComponent`.

8.4.2 *Using the spread operator: passing all of your attributes*

Next, let's look at the spread operator (...). It's part of ES6+/ES2015+ for arrays (http://mng.bz/8fjN); as of the time of this writing, there's a proposal to use spreads for objects (https://github.com/sebmarkbage/ecmascript-rest-spread). It's only natural that the React team added support for spreads to JSX.

The idea isn't complicated. The spread operator lets you pass all the attributes of an object (`obj`) as properties when used in the element:

```
<Component {...obj}/>
```

You used spread in load-website.jsx to pass state and property variables to the original component when you were rendering it. You needed it because you didn't know ahead of time all the properties the function would take as arguments; thus, the spread operator is a blanket statement to pass all of your data (in that variable or an object).

In React and JSX, you can have more than one spread operator or mix them with traditional `key=value` property declarations. For example, you can pass all states and all properties from a current class as well as `className` to a new element `Component`:

```
<Component {...this.state} {...this.props} className="main" />
```

Let's consider an example with children. In this scenario, using the spread operator with `this.props` will pass all the properties of `DoneLink` to the anchor element `<a>`:

```
class DoneLink extends React.Component {
  render() {
    return <a {...this.props}>                         ⟵ Takes any properties
                                                         passed to DoneLink and
                                                         copies them to <a>
      <span class="glyphicons glyphicons-check"></span>  ⟵
      {this.props.children}                                Uses Glyphicons
      </a>                                                 (http://glyphicons.com)
  }                                                        to render a check icon
}

ReactDOM.render(
  <DoneLink href="/checked.html">        ⟵
    Click here!                             Passes the
  </DoneLink>,                              value for href
  document.getElementById('done-link')
)
```

In the HOC, you pass all properties and states to the original component when you render it. By doing so, you don't have to manually add properties to or remove them from `render()` each time you want to pass something new or stop passing existing data from `Content`, where you instantiate `LoadWebsite`/`EnhancedComponent` for each original element.

8.4.3 *Using higher-order components*

You've learned more about `displayName` and ... in JSX and React. Now we can look at how to use HOCs.

Let's go back to Content and content.jsx, where you're using LoadWebsite. After defining the HOC, you need to create components using it in content.jsx:

```
const EnhancedButton = LoadWebsite(Button)
const EnhancedLink = LoadWebsite(Link)
const EnhancedLogo = LoadWebsite(Logo)
```

Now, you'll implement three components—Button, Link, and Logo—to reuse the code with the HOC pattern. The Button component is created via LoadWebsite and as a result magically inherits its properties (this.props.handleClick and this.props.label):

```
class Button extends React.Component {
  render() {
    return <button
      className="btn btn-primary"
      onClick={this.props.handleClick}>
      {this.props.label}
    </button>
  }
}
```

The Link component is created by the HOC, which is why you can also use handle-Click and label properties:

```
class Link extends React.Component {
  render() {
    return <a onClick={this.props.handleClick} href="#">
    {this.props.label}</a>
  }
}
```

And finally, the Logo component also uses the same properties. You guessed it: they're magically there because you used a spread operator when you created Logo in content.jsx:

```
class Logo extends React.Component {
  render() {
    return <img onClick={this.props.handleClick} width="40" src="logo.png"
    href="#"/>
  }
}
```

The three components have different renderings, but they all get this.props.handleClick and this.props.label from LoadWebsite. The parent component Content renders the elements as shown in the following listing (ch08/hi-order/jsx/content.jsx).

Listing 8.5 HOCs sharing an event handler

```
const EnhancedButton = LoadWebsite(Button)
const EnhancedLink = LoadWebsite(Link)
const EnhancedLogo = LoadWebsite(Logo)
```

```
class Content extends React.Component {
  render() {
    return (
      <div>
        <EnhancedButton />
        <br />
        <br />
        <EnhancedLink />
        <br />
        <br />
        <EnhancedLogo />
        <br />
        <br />
        <iframe id="frame" src="" width="600" height="500"/>
      </div>
    )
  }
}
```

Declares the iframe in which the click method loads the React site

Finally, let's not forget to render `Content` on the last lines of script.jsx:

```
ReactDOM.render(
  <Content />,
  document.getElementById('content')
)
```

When you open the page, it has the three elements (`Button`, `Link`, and `Logo`). The elements have the same functionality: they load the IFrame when a click happens, as shown in figure 8.9.

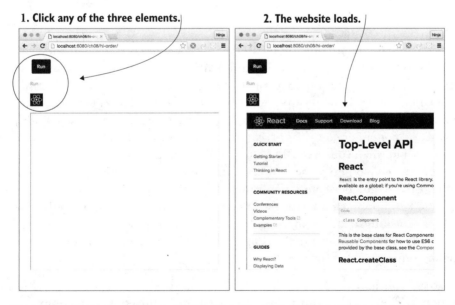

1. Click any of the three elements.

2. The website loads.

Figure 8.9   All three components load the React website, thanks to the function that provides the code to load it.

As you've seen, HOCs are great for abstracting code. You can use them to write your own mini-modules, which are reusable React components. HOCs, along with property types, are excellent tools for creating developer-friendly components that others will love to use.

8.5   *Best practices: presentational vs. container components*

There's a distinction that lets you scale your React code in terms of code and team size: *presentational* versus *container* components. We've touched on them in previous chapters, but now, because you know about passing children and HOCs, it'll be easier to reason about container components.

Generally speaking, splitting your code into two types makes it simpler and more maintainable. Presentational components typically only add structure to DOM and styling. They take properties but often don't have their own states. Most of the time, you can use functions for stateless presentational components. For example, Logo is a good illustration of a presentational component in a class style

```
class Logo extends React.Component {
  render() {
    return <img onClick={this.props.handleClick} width="40" src="logo.png"
    ➥ href="#"/>
  }
}
```

or in a functional style:

```
const Logo = (props)=>{
    return <img onClick={props.handleClick} width="40" src="logo.png"
    ➥ href="#"/>
}
```

Presentational components often use this.props.children when they act as wrappers to style child components. Examples are Button, Content, Layout, Post, and so on. But they rarely deal with data or states; that's the job of container components.

Container components are often generated by HOCs to inject data sources. They have states. Examples are SaveButton, ImagePostContent, and so on. Both presentational and container components can contain other presentational or container components; but when you're starting out, you'll generally use presentational components containing *only* other presentational components. Container components contain either other container components or presentational ones.

The best approach is to start with components that solve your needs. If you begin to see repeating patterns or properties that you're passing over multiple layers of nested components but aren't using in the interim components, introduce a container component or two.

> **NOTE** You may hear terms such as *dumb* or *skinny* and *smart* or *fat* components. These are synonyms for presentational and container components, with the latter being more recent additions to React terminology.

8.6   Quiz

1 React provides robust validation, which eliminates the necessity to check input on the server side. True or false?

2 In addition to setting properties with `defaultProps`, you can set them in `constructor` using `this.prop.NAME = VALUE`. True or false?

3 The `children` property can be an array or a node. True or false?

4 A higher-order component pattern is implemented via a function. True or false?

5 The main difference between the minified development and unminified production versions of the React library file is that the minified version has warnings and the unminified version has optimized code. True or false?

8.7   Summary

- You can define a default value for any component property by setting the component's `defaultProps` attribute.
- You can enforce validation checks on component property values while working with the uncompressed, development version of the React library.
- You can check the type of a property, set it to `isRequired` so it's mandatory, or define your own custom validation, as required.
- If a property value fails validation, a warning appears in your browser's console.
- The minified, production version of the React library doesn't include these validation checks.
- React allows you to encapsulate and reuse common properties, methods, and events among your components by creating higher-order components.
- Higher-order components are defined as functions that take another component as an argument. This argument is the component inheriting from the HOC.
- Any HTML or React components nested within a JSX element can be accessed through the `props.children` property of the parent component.

8.8   Quiz answers

5 True. The minified version doesn't show warnings.

4 True. The HOC pattern is implemented as a function that takes a component and creates another component class with enhanced functionality. This new class renders the original component while passing properties and states to it.

3 True. If there's only one child, then `this.props.children` is a single node.

2 False. React needs `defaultProps` as a static class field/attribute when an element is created, but `this.props` is an instance attribute.

1 False. Front-end validation isn't a substitute for back-end validation. Front-end code is exposed to anyone, and anyone can bypass it by reverse-engineering how the front-end app communicates with the server and send any data directly to the server.

Watch this chapter's introduction video by scanning this QR code with your phone or going to http://reactquickly.co/videos/ch09.

Project: Menu component

9

This chapter covers

- Understanding the project structure and scaffolding
- Building the `Menu` component without JSX
- Building the `Menu` component in JSX

The next three chapters will walk you through several projects, gradually building on the concepts you've learned in chapters 1–8. These projects will also reinforce the material by repeating some of the techniques and ideas that are most important in React. The first project is minimal, but don't skip it.

Imagine that you're working on a unified visual framework that will be used in all of your company's apps. Having the same look and feel in various apps is important. Think about how Twitter Bootstrap for many Twitter apps and Google's Material UI[1] are used across many properties that belong to Google: AdWords, Analytics, Search, Drive, Docs, and so on.

---

[1] Twitter Bootstrap: http://getbootstrap.com. React components that implement Twitter Bootstrap: https://react-bootstrap.github.io. Google Material Design: https://material.io. React Components that implement Material Design: www.material-ui.com.

Your first task is to implement a menu like the one shown in figure 9.1. It will be used in the layout's header across many pages in various applications. The menu items need to change based on the user role and what part of the application is currently being viewed. For example, admins and managers should see a Manage Users menu option. At the same time, this layout

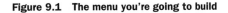

Figure 9.1   The menu you're going to build

will be used in a customer-relationship app that needs its own unique set of menu options. You get the idea. The menu needs to be generated dynamically, meaning you'll have some React code that generates menu options.

For simplicity, the menu items will just be `<a>` tags. You'll create two custom React components, `Menu` and `Link`, in a way that's similar to the way you created the `Hello-World` component in chapter 1—or how you create any component, for that matter.

This project will show you how to render programmatically nested elements. Manually hardcoding menu items isn't a great idea; what happens when you need to change an item? It's not dynamic! You'll use the `map()` function to do this.

NOTE   To follow along with the project, you'll need to download the *unminified* version of React (so that you can take advantage of the helpful warnings it returns if something goes wrong). You can also download and install Node.js and npm. They aren't strictly necessary for this project, but they're useful for compiling JSX later in this chapter. Appendix A covers the installation of both tools.

NOTE   The source code for the examples in this chapter is at www.manning .com/books/react-quickly and https://github.com/azat-co/react-quickly/ tree/master/ch09 (in the ch09 folder of the GitHub repository https:// github.com/azat-co/react-quickly). You can also find some demos at http:// reactquickly.co/demos.

9.1   Project structure and scaffolding

Let's start with an overview of the project structure. It's flat, to keep it simple:

```
/menu
    index.html          ⟵── Main HTML file
    package.json
    react-dom.js
    react.js
    script.js           ⟵── Main script
```

Keep in mind that this is what you'll have by the end of this walk-through. You should begin with an empty folder. So, let's create a new folder and start implementing the project:

```
$ mkdir menu
$ cd menu
```

Download react.js and react-dom.js version 15, and drop them into the folder.
Next is the HTML file:

```
<!DOCTYPE html>
<html>
  <head>
    <script src="react.js"></script>
    <script src="react-dom.js"></script>
  </head>
```

The HTML for this project is very basic. It includes the react.js and react-dom.js files, which, for simplicity, are in the same folder as the HTML file. Of course, later you'll want to have your *.js files in some other folder, like js or src.

The body has just two elements. One element is a `<div>` container with the ID menu; this is where the menu will be rendered. The second element is a `<script>` tag with your React application code:

```
<body>
    <div id="menu"></div>
    <script src="script.js"></script>
  </body>
</html>
```

You're finished with the scaffolding. This is the foundation on which you'll build the menu—first, without JSX.

9.2   *Building the menu without JSX*

script.js is your main application file. It contains `ReactDOM.render()` as well as two components (ch09/menu/script.js).

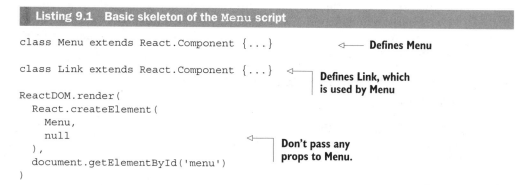

Listing 9.1   Basic skeleton of the `Menu` script

```
class Menu extends React.Component {...}        ◁——— Defines Menu

class Link extends React.Component {...}    ◁─┐
                                              │ Defines Link, which
                                              │ is used by Menu
ReactDOM.render(
  React.createElement(
    Menu,
    null                                    ◁─┐
  ),                                          │ Don't pass any
  document.getElementById('menu')             │ props to Menu.
)
```

Of course, it's possible to make `Menu` dependent on an external list of menu items, provided in a property such as `menuOptions` that's defined elsewhere:

```
const menuOptions = [...]
//...
ReactDOM.render(
  React.createElement(
```

```
    Menu,
      {menus: menuOptions}
    ),
    document.getElementById('menu')
)
```

These two approaches are both valid, and you'll need to choose one depending on your answer to this question: do you want Menu to be just about structure and styling or also about getting information? We'll continue with the latter approach in this chapter and make Menu self-sustained.

9.2.1 The Menu component

Now to create the Menu component. Let's step through the code. To create it, you extend React.Component():

```
class Menu extends React.Component {...}
```

The Menu component will render the individual menu items, which are link tags. Before you can render them, you need to define the menu items. They're hardcoded in the menus array as follows (you could get them from a data model, store, or server in a more complex scenario):

```
render() {
  let menus = ['Home',          ⟵—— Mock data store
    'About',
    'Services',
    'Portfolio',
    'Contact us']
    //...
```

Next, you'll return the menu Link elements (four of them). Recall that return can have only one element. For this reason, you wrap <div> around the four links. This is the start of the wrapper <div> element with no attributes:

```
return React.createElement('div',
  null,
  //... we will render links later
```

It's worth mentioning that {} can output not just a variable or an expression, but an array as well. This comes in handy when you have a list of items. Basically, to render every element of an array, you can pass that array to {}. Although JSX and React can output arrays, they don't output objects. So, the objects must be converted to an array.

Knowing that you can output an array, you can proceed to generate an array of React elements. The map() function is a good method to use because it returns an array. You can implement map() so that each element is the result of the expression React.createElement(Link, {label: v}) wrapped in <div>. In this expression, v is a value of the menus array item (Home, About, Services, and so on), and i is its index number (0, 1, 2, 3, and so on):

```
      menus.map((v, i) => {
        return React.createElement('div',
          {key: i},
          React.createElement(Link, {label: v})
        )
      }
    )
  )
}})
```

Did you notice that the key property is set to the index i? This is needed so React can access each <div> element in a list more quickly. If you don't set key, you'll see the following warning (at least, in React 15, 0.14 and 0.13):

```
Warning: Each child in an array or iterator should have a unique "key" prop.
Check the render method of `Menu`. See https://fb.me/react-warning-keys for
more information.
    in div (created by Menu)
    in Menu
```

Again, kudos to React for good error and warning messages.

So each element of a list must have a unique value for a key attribute. They don't have to be unique across the entire app and other components, just within this list. Interestingly, since React v15, you won't see the key attributes in HTML (and that's a good thing—let's not pollute HTML). But React DevTools shows the keys, as you can see in figure 9.2.

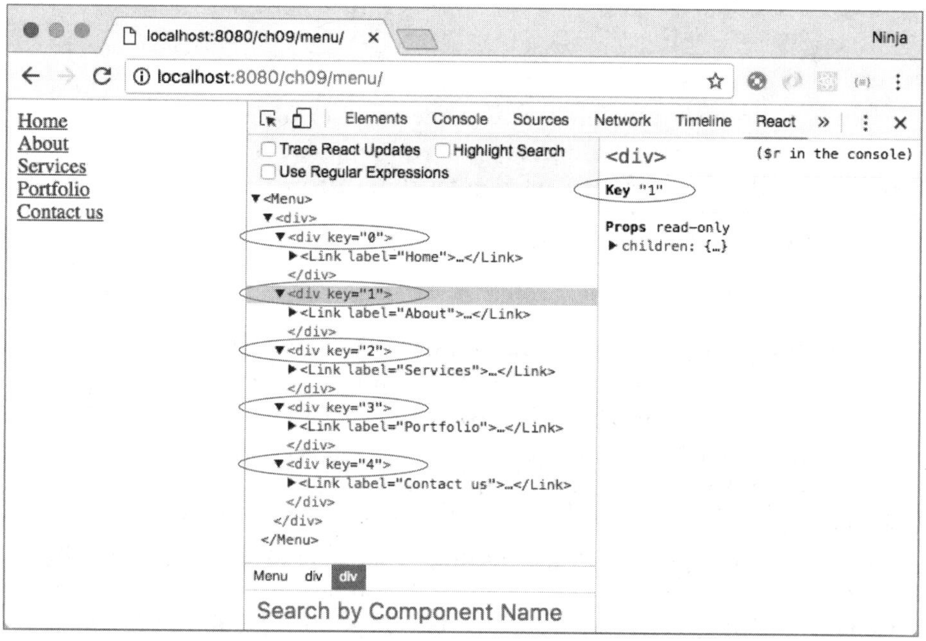

Figure 9.2   React DevTools show you the keys of the list elements.

The Array.map() function

The mapping function from the `Array` class is used frequently in React components to represent lists of data. This is because when you create UIs, you do so from data represented as an array. The UI is also an array, but with slightly different elements (React elements!).

`map()` is invoked on an array, and it returns new array elements that are transformed from the original array by the function. At a minimum, when working with `map()`, you need to pass this function:

```
[1, 2, 3].map( value => <p>value</p>)
   // <p>1</p><p>2</p><p>3</p>
```

You can use two more arguments in addition to the value of the item (`value`)—`index` and `list`:

```
[1, 2, 3].map( (value, index, list) => {
  return <p id={index}>{list[index]}</p>
}) // <p id="0">1</p><p id="1">2</p><p id="2">3</p>
```

The `<div>` has a `key` attribute, which is important. It allows React to optimize rendering of lists by converting them to hashes, and access time for hashes is better than that for lists or arrays. Basically, you create numerous `Link` components in an array, and each of them takes the property `label` with a value from the `menus` array.

Here's the full code for `Menu` (ch09/menu/script.js); it's simple and straightforward.

Listing 9.2 `Menu` component that uses `map()` to render links

```
class Menu extends React.Component {
  render() {
    let menus = ['Home',
      'About',
      'Services',
      'Portfolio',
      'Contact us']
    return React.createElement('div',
      null,
      menus.map((v, i) => {
        return React.createElement('div',
          {key: i},
          React.createElement(Link, {label: v})
        )
      })
    )
}}
```

Now let's move on to the `Link` implementation.

9.2.2   *The Link component*

The call to map() creates a Link component for each item in the menus array. Let's look at the code for Link and see what happens when each Link component is rendered.

In the Link component's render code, you write an expression to create a URL. That URL will be used in the href attribute of the <a> tag. The this.props.label value is passed to Link from Menu when Link is created. In the render() function of the Menu component, Link elements are created in the map's closure/iterator function using React.createElement(Link, {label: v}).

The label property is used to construct the URL slug (must be lowercase and should not include spaces):

```
class Link extends React.Component {
  render() {
    const url='/'
      + this.props.label
        .toLowerCase()
        .trim()
        .replace(' ', '-')
```

The methods toLowerCase(), trim(), and replace() are standard JavaScript string functions. They perform conversion to lowercase, trim white space at edges, and replace white spaces with dashes, respectively.

The URL expression produces the following URLs:

- /home for Home
- /about for About
- /services for Services
- /portfolio for Portfolio
- /contact-us for Contact us

Now you can implement Link's UI: the render() return value. In the render function's return of the Link component, you pass this.props.label as a third argument to createElement(). It becomes part of the <a> tag content (link text). Link could render this element:

```
    //...
    return React.createElement(
      'a',
      {href: url},
      this.props.label
    )
  }
}
```

But it's better to separate each link with a line-break element (<br>). And because the component must return only *one* element, you'd have to wrap the anchor element

(<a>) and line break (<br>) in a div container (<div>). Therefore, you start the return in the Link component's render() with div, without attributes:

```
//...
return React.createElement('div',
  null,
  //...
```

Each argument after the second to createElement() (for example, the third, fourth, and fifth) will be used as content (children). To create the link element, you pass it as the second argument. And to create a break element after each link, you pass the line-break element <br> as the fourth argument:

```
//...
return React.createElement('div',
  null,
  React.createElement(
    'a',
    {href: url},
    this.props.label
  ),
  React.createElement('br')
)
}
})
```

Here's the code for the full Link component for your reference (ch09/menu/ script.js). The url function can be created as a class method or as a method outside of the component.

Listing 9.3 Link component

```
class Link extends React.Component {
  render() {
    const url='/'                          Defines a function that
      + this.props.label                   creates URL fragments
        .toLowerCase()                     out of the menu names
        .trim()
        .replace(' ', '-')
    return React.createElement('div',
      null,
      React.createElement(
        'a',                               Passes the URL fragment
        {href: url},                       to set the href attribute
        this.props.label
      ),
      React.createElement('br')            Adds a line-break element
    )                                      to separate menu items
  }
}
```

Let's get this menu running.

9.2.3   *Getting it running*

To view the page, shown in figure 9.3, open it as a file in Chrome, Firefox, Safari, or (maybe) Internet Explorer. That's it. *No compilation is needed for this project.*

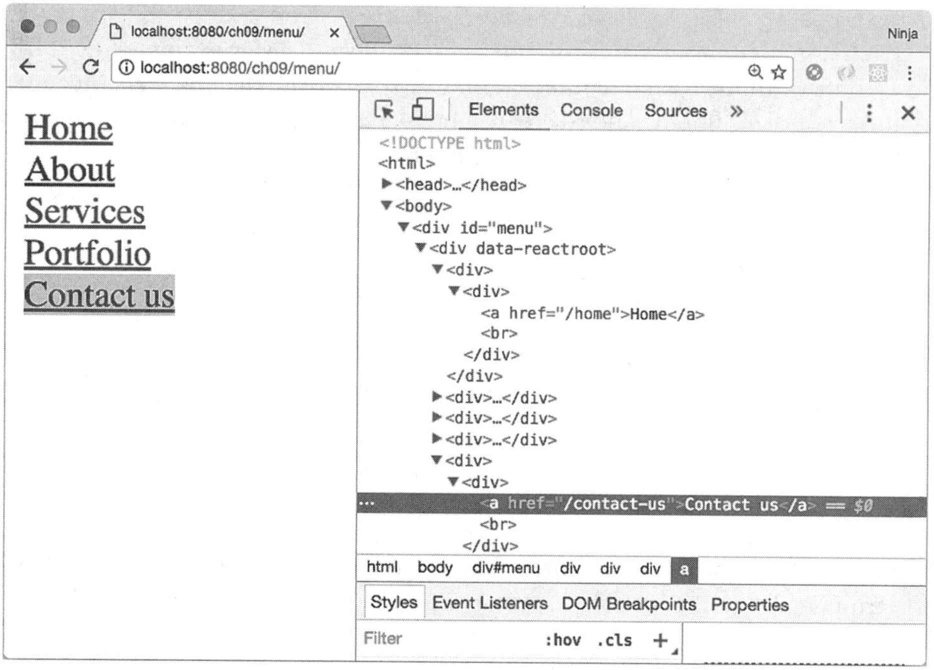

Figure 9.3   **React menu showing rendering of nested components**

> #### Using a local web server
>
> When you open the example page, the protocol in the address bar will be file://....
> This isn't ideal but will do for this project. For real development, you'll need a web
> server; with a web server, the protocol is http://... or https://..., as in figure 9.3.
>
> Yes, even for a simple web page like this one, I prefer to use a local web server. It
> makes the running code more closely resemble how it would be in production. Plus,
> you can use AJAX/XHR, which you can't use if you're opening an HTML file in a browser.
>
> The easiest way to run a local web server is to use node-static
> (www.npmjs.com/package/node-static) or a similar Node.js tool like http-server
> (www.npmjs.com/package/http-server). This is true even for Windows, although I
> stopped using that OS many years ago. If you're hell-bent on not using Node.js, then
> alternatives include IIS, Apache HTTP Server, NGINX, MAMP, LAMP, and other varia-
> tions of web servers. Needless to say, Node.js tools are highly recommended for their
> minimalist, lightweight approach.

> **(continued)**
> To install node-static, use npm:
>
> ```
> $ npm install -g node-static@0.7.6
> ```
>
> Once it's installed, run this command from your project's root folder (or from a parent folder) to make the file available on http://localhost:8080. This isn't an external link—run the following command before clicking the link:
>
> ```
> $ static
> ```
>
> If you run `static` in react-quickly/ch09/menu, then the URL will be http://localhost:8080. Conversely, if you run `static` from react-quickly, then the URL needs to be http://localhost:8080/ch09/menu.
>
> To stop the server on macOS or Unix/Linux (POSIX systems), press Ctrl-C. As for Windows, I don't know!

No thrills here, but the page should display five links (or more, if you add items to the menus array), as shown earlier in figure 9.1. This is much better than copying and pasting five <a> elements and then ending up with multiple places to modify the labels and URLs. And the project can be even better with JSX.

9.3 Building the menu in JSX

This project is more extensive, containing node_modules, package.json, and JSX:

```
/menu-jsx                              Babel dev dependency for
  /node_modules          ⊲──────┐     JSX-to-JS transpilation
  index.html
  package.json
  react-dom.js
  react.js
  script.js
  script.jsx             ⊲─────── Main JSX script
```

As you can see, there's a node_modules folder for developer dependencies such as Babel, which is used for JSX-to-JS transpilation.

> **NOTE** Although it's possible to install `react` and `react-dom` as npm modules instead of having them as files, doing so leads to additional complexity if you decide to deploy. Right now, to deploy this app, you can just copy the files in the project folder without node_modules. If you install React and ReactDOM with npm, then you have to include that folder as well, use a bundler, or copy the JS files from dist into root (where you already have them). So, for this example, we'll use the files in root. I cover bundlers in part 2 of this book, but for now let's keep things simple.

Create a new folder:

```
$ mkdir menu-jsx
$ cd menu-jsx
```

Then, create the package.json file in it using `npm init -y`. Add the following code to package.json to install and configure Babel (ch09/menu-jsx/package.json).

Listing 9.4   package.json for `Menu` in JSX

```
{
  "name": "menu-jsx",
  "version": "1.0.0",
  "description": "",
  "main": "script.js",
  "scripts": {
    "build": "./node_modules/.bin/babel script.jsx -o script.js -w"
  },
  "author": "Azat Mardan",
  "license": "MIT",
  "babel": {
    "presets": ["react"]
  },
  "devDependencies": {
    "babel-cli": "6.9.0",
    "babel-preset-react": "6.5.0"
  }
}
```

> **Defines a build script with the watch flag**

> **Configures Babel to transpile React's JSX**

> **Includes the Babel CLI as well as a React/JSX preset**

Install the developer dependencies packages with `npm i` or `npm install`. Your setup should be ready now.

Let's look at script.jsx. At a higher level, it has these parts:

```
class Menu extends React.Component {
  render() {
    //...
  }
}

class Link extends React.Component {
  render() {
    //...
  }
}

ReactDOM.render(<Menu />, document.getElementById('menu'))
```

Looks familiar, right? It's the same structure as in `Menu` without JSX. The primary change in this high-level listing is replacing `createElement()` for the `Menu` component in `ReactDOM.render()` with this line:

```
ReactDOM.render(<Menu />, document.getElementById('menu'))
```

Next, you'll refactor the components.

9.3.1 *Refactoring the Menu component*

The beginning of Menu is the same:

```
class Menu extends React.Component {
  render() {
    let menus = ['Home',
      'About',
      'Services',
      'Portfolio',
      'Contact us']
    return //...
  }
}
```

In the refactoring example for the Menu component, you need to output the value v as a label's attribute value (that is, label={v}). In other words, you assign the value v as a property for label. So the line to create the Link element changes from

```
React.createElement(Link, {label: v})
```

to this JSX code:

```
<Link label={v}/>
```

The label property of the second argument ({label: v}) becomes the attribute label={v}. The attribute's value v is declared with {} to make it dynamic (versus a hardcoded value).

> **NOTE** When you use curly braces to assign property values, you don't need double quotes ("").

React also needs the key={i} attribute to access the list more efficiently. Therefore, the final Menu component is restructured as this JSX code (ch09/menu-jsx/script.jsx).

Listing 9.5 Menu with JSX

```
class Menu extends React.Component {
  render() {
    let menus = ['Home',
      'About',
      'Services',
      'Portfolio',
      'Contact us']
    return <div>
      {menus.map((v, i) => {
        return <div key={i}><Link label={v}/></div>
      })}
    </div>
}}
```

Do you see the increase in readability? I do!

In Menu's render(), if you prefer to start the <div> on a new line, you can do so by putting () around it. For example, this code is identical to listing 9.5, but <div> starts on a new line, which may be more visually appealing:

```
//...
   return (
     <div>
       {menus.map((v, i) => {
         return <div key={i}><Link label={v}/></div>
       })}
     </div>
   )
}})
```

9.3.2 *Refactoring the Link component*

The <a> and <br> tags in the Link component also need to be refactored from this

```
//...
   return React.createElement('div',
     null,
     React.createElement(
       'a',
       {href: url},
       this.props.label),
     React.createElement('br')
     )
   //...
```

to this JSX code:

```
//...
   return <div>
     <a href={url}>
     {this.props.label}
     </a>
     <br/>
   </div>
   //...
```

The entire JSX version of the Link component should look something like this (ch09/menu-jsx/script.jsx).

Listing 9.6   JSX version of Link

```
class Link extends React.Component {
  render() {
    const url='/'
      + this.props.label
        .toLowerCase()
```

```
        .trim()
        .replace(' ', '-')
    return <div>
      <a href={url}>
      {this.props.label}
      </a>
      <br/>
    </div>
  }
}
```

Phew. You're finished! Let's run the JSX project.

9.3.3 *Running the JSX project*

Open your Terminal, iTerm, or Command Prompt app. In the project's folder (ch09/menu-jsx or whatever you named it when you downloaded the source code), install dependencies with npm i (short for npm install) following the entries in package.json.

Then, run the npm build script with npm run build. The npm script will launch the Babel command with a watch flag (-w), which will keep Webpack running so it can watch for any file changes and recompile code from JSX to JS if there are changes to the JSX source code.

Needless to say, watch mode is a time-saver because it eliminates the need to recompile each time there's a change to the source code. Hot module replacement is even better for development (so good that it could easily be the only reason to use React); I'll cover it in chapter 12.

The actual command in the build script is as follows (but who wants to type it? It's too long!):

```
./node_modules/.bin/babel script.jsx -o script.js -w
```

If you need a refresher on the Babel CLI, refer to chapter 3. You'll find all the details there.

On my computer, I got this message from the Babel CLI (on yours, the path will differ):

```
> menu-jsx@1.0.0 build /Users/azat/Documents/Code/react-quickly/ch09/menu-jsx
> babel script.jsx -o script.js -w
```

You're good to go. With script.js generated, you can use static (node-static on npm: npm i -g node-static) to serve the files over HTTP on localhost. The application should look and work exactly like its regular JavaScript brethren, as shown in figure 9.4.

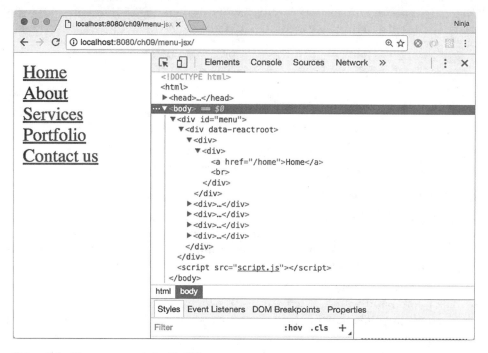

Figure 9.4   The menu created with JSX

9.4   Homework

For bonus points, do the following:

- Load `menu` from menus.json via the Fetch API. See chapter 5 for inspiration about how to load data.
- Create an npm script that will grab react.js from the `react` npm package installed in node_modules and copy it into the project folder to be used by index.html. This will replace the need to manually download react.js for future versions; instead, you can use `npm i react` and then run your script.

Submit your code in *a new folder under ch09* as a pull request to this book's GitHub repository: https://github.com/azat-co/react-quickly.

9.5   Summary

- `key` is your friend. Set this attribute when you're generating lists.
- `map()` is an elegant way to create a new array based on the original array. Its iterator arguments are `value`, `index`, and `list`.
- For JSX to work, at a bare minimum, you need the Babel CLI and React presets.

Project: Tooltip component

10

This chapter covers

- Understanding the project structure and scaffolding
- Building the `Tooltip` component

When you're working on websites that have a lot of text, such as Wikipedia, it's a great idea to allow users to get additional information without losing their position and context. For example, you can give them an extra hint in a box when they hover the cursor (see figure 10.1). This hint hover box is called a *tooltip*.

React is all about UIs and a better UX, so it's a good fit for a tooltip implementation. Let's build a component to display helpful text on a mouse-over event.

There are a few out-of-the-box tooltip solutions, including `react-tooltip` (www.npmjs.com/package/react-tooltip), but the goal here is to learn about React. Building a tooltip from scratch is a *really* good exercise. Maybe you'll use this example in your daily work by making it a part of *your* app, or extend it into a new open source React component!

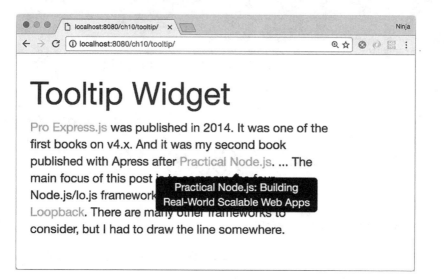

Figure 10.1   A tooltip appears when a user hovers their cursor over the marked text.

The key to creating the `Tooltip` component is to be able to take any text, hide it with CSS, and make it visible again on mouse-over. You'll use `if/else` conditions, JSX, and other programming elements for this project. For the CSS part, you'll use Twitter Bootstrap classes and a special Twitter Bootstrap theme to make the tooltip look nice in a short amount of time.

> **NOTE**   To follow along with this project, you'll need to download the unminified version of React and install node.js and npm for compiling JSX. In this example, I also use a theme called Flatly from Bootswatch (https://bootswatch.com/flatly). This theme depends on Twitter Bootstrap. Appendix A covers how to install everything.

> **NOTE**   The source code for the example in this chapter is at www.manning .com/books/react-quickly and https://github.com/azat-co/react-quickly/ tree/master/ch10 (in the ch10 folder of the GitHub repository https:// github.com/azat-co/react-quickly). You can also find some demos at http:// reactquickly.co/demos.

10.1   *Project structure and scaffolding*

The project structure for the `Tooltip` component is as follows:

```
/tooltip
  /node_modules
  bootstrap.css              ◁———  Babel dev dependency for
  index.html                       JSX-to-JS transpilation
  package.json
  react-dom.js
  react.js
  script.js
  script.jsx                 ◁———  Main JSX script
```

As in chapter 9, there's a node_modules folder for developer dependencies such as Babel, which is used for JSX-to-JS transpilation. The structure is flat, with styles and scripts in the same folder. I did this to keep everything simple. Of course, in a real app, you'll put styles and scripts in separate folders.

The key parts in package.json are the npm script to build, the Babel configuration, dependencies, and other metadata.

Listing 10.1   Tooltip project package.json file

```
{
  "name": "tooltip",
  "version": "1.0.0",
  "description": "",
  "main": "script.js",
  "scripts": {
    "build": "./node_modules/.bin/babel script.jsx -o script.js -w"
  },
  "author": "Azat Mardan",
  "license": "MIT",
  "babel": {
    "presets": ["react"]
  },
  "devDependencies": {
    "babel-cli": "6.9.0",
    "babel-preset-react": "6.5.0"
  }
}
```

After you've created package.json, be sure to run `npm i` or `npm install`.

Next, you'll start on the HTML. Create index.html, as shown in the following listing (ch10/tooltip/index.html).

Listing 10.2   Tooltip project index.html file

```
<!DOCTYPE html>
<html>

  <head>
    <script src="react.js"></script>
    <script src="react-dom.js"></script>
    <link href="bootstrap.css"                    ⟵── Applies styles
      rel="stylesheet"
      type="text/css"/>
  </head>

  <body class="container">                        Defines the render element
    <h1>Tooltip Widget</h1>                        for React and Tooltip
    <div id="tooltip"></div>              ⟵──┘
    <script src="script.js" type="text/javascript"></script>
  </body>

</html>
```

In <head>, you include React, React DOM files, and Twitter Bootstrap styles. body is minimal: it contains a <div> with ID tooltip and the application's script.js file.

Next, you'll create script.jsx. That's right—this isn't a typo. The source code is in script.jsx, but you include the script.js file in your HTML. That's because you'll be using the command-line Babel tool.

10.2   *The Tooltip component*

Let's look at script.jsx (ch10/tooltip/script.jsx). It's pretty much just the code for the component and the tooltip text you want to render. The tooltip text is a property that you set when you create Tooltip in ReactDOM.render().

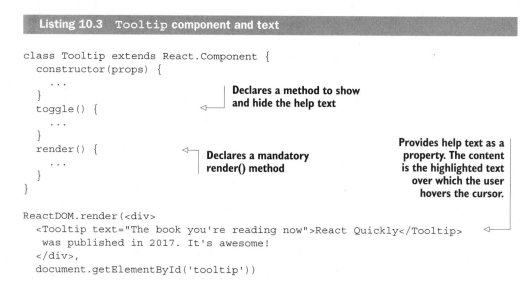

Listing 10.3   Tooltip component and text

Let's implement Tooltip and declare the component with an initial state of opacity: false. This state commands the help text to be hidden or shown. (Chapter 4 covered states in more detail.) Here's the constructor() method in action:

```
class Tooltip extends React.Component {
  constructor(props) {
    super(props)
    this.state = {opacity: false}
    this.toggle = this.toggle.bind(this)
  }
  ...
}
```

The initial state hides the help text. Toggling changes this state and the visibility of the tooltip—that is, whether the help text is shown. Let's implement toggle().

10.2.1 *The toggle() function*

Now you'll define the `toggle()` function that switches the visibility of the tooltip by changing the `opacity` state to the opposite of what it was before (true to false, or false to true):

```
toggle() {
    const tooltipNode = ReactDOM.findDOMNode(this)
    this.setState({
      opacity: !this.state.opacity,
      ...
    })
  }
```

To change `opacity`, you use the `this.setState()` method, which you learned about in chapter 4.

A tricky thing about tooltip help text is that you must place the help text close to the element the mouse is hovering over. To do so, you need to get the position of the component using `tooltipNode`. You position the tooltip text using `offsetTop` and `offsetLeft` on the DOM node. These are DOM Node properties from the HTML standard (https://developer.mozilla.org/en-US/docs/Web/API/Node), not a React thing:

```
      top: tooltipNode.offsetTop,
      left: tooltipNode.offsetLeft
    })
  },
```

Here's the full code for `toggle()` (ch10/tooltip/script.jsx).

Listing 10.4 `toggle()` **function**

```
toggle() {
  const tooltipNode = ReactDOM.findDOMNode(this)
  this.setState({
    opacity: !this.state.opacity,
    top: tooltipNode.offsetTop,
    left: tooltipNode.offsetLeft
  })
}
```

Here it is using ES destructuring:

```
toggle() {
  const {offsetTop: top, offsetLeft: left} = ReactDOM.findDOMNode(this)

  this.setState({
   opacity: !this.state.opacity,
    top,
    left
  })
}
```

Looking at the code, you can see that it changes the state and position. Do you need to rerender the view now? No, because React will update the view for you. `setState()` will invoke a rerender automatically. It may or may not result in DOM changes, depending on whether the state was used in `render()`—which you'll implement next.

10.2.2 *The render() function*

The `render()` function holds the CSS `style` object for the help text and also holds Twitter Bootstrap styles. First, you need to define the `style` object. You'll set the `opacity` and `z-index` CSS styles depending on the value of `this.state.opacity`. You need `z-index` to float the help text above any other elements, so set the value reasonably high—1000 when the text is visible and -1000 when it's not:

```
zIndex: (this.state.opacity) ? 1000 : -1000,
```

For `z-index`, you need to use `zIndex` (note the camelCase). Figure 10.2 shows how the styles are applied at mouse-over (`opacity` is true).

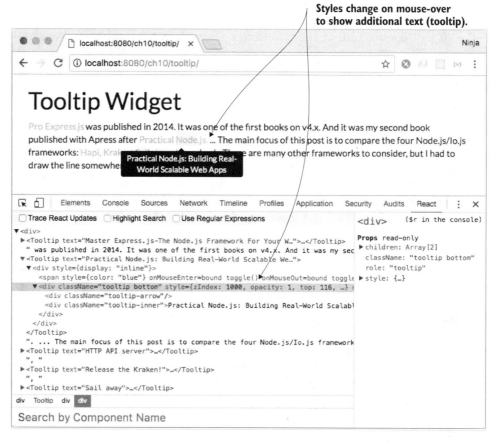

Figure 10.2   The help text is shown on mouse-over by using an `opacity` value of `1` and `zIndex` value of `1000`.

> **TIP** Remember to use camelCase with React instead of dash syntax. The CSS property z-index becomes the React style property zIndex; background-color becomes backgroundColor; font-family becomes fontFamily, and so on. When you use valid JavaScript names, React can update the real DOM from the virtual one more quickly.

State opacity this.state.opacity is a Boolean true or false, but CSS opacity is a binary 0 or 1. If state opacity is false, CSS opacity is 0; and if state opacity is true, CSS opacity is 1. You need to convert, using a binary operator (+):

```
opacity: +this.state.opacity,
```

As far as the position of the tooltip goes, you want to place the help text near the text over which the mouse is hovering by adding 20 pixels to top (the distance from the top edge of the window to the element) and subtracting 30 pixels from left (the distance from the left edge of the window to the element). The values were chosen visually; feel free to adjust the logic as you see fit:

```
render() {
  const style = {
    zIndex: (this.state.opacity) ? 1000 : -1000,
    opacity: +this.state.opacity,
    top: (this.state.top || 0) + 20,
    left: (this.state.left || 0) -30
  }
```

Next is return. The component will render both the text over which to hover and the help text. I'm using Twitter Bootstrap classes along with my style object to hide the help text and to show it later.

The text over which users can hover to see a tooltip is colored blue, so they can tell it apart visually from other text. It has two mouse events for when the cursor enters and leaves the span:

```
return (
  <div style={{display: 'inline'}}>
    <span style={{color: 'blue'}}
      onMouseEnter={this.toggle}
      onMouseOut={this.toggle}>
      {this.props.children}
    </span>
```
Outputs whatever inner HTML will pass to Tooltip later

Next is the code for the help text. It's static-like, except for {style}. React will change the state, and that will trigger the change in the UI:

Uses the arrow class for a pointy arrow

Applies the style object to the style attribute

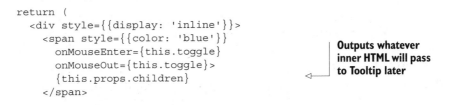

```
<div className="tooltip bottom" style={style} role="tooltip">
    <div className="tooltip-arrow"></div>
    <div className="tooltip-inner">
```

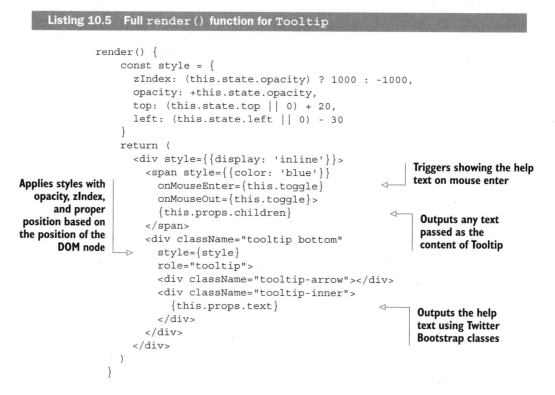

```
                         {this.props.text}          ◁──┐  Outputs the text of the
                    </div>                               │  tooltip from the text
                  </div>                                 │  property {this.props.text}
                </div>
              )
            }
          }
```

The next listing shows the `Tooltip` component's full `render()` method.

Listing 10.5   Full `render()` function for `Tooltip`

```
        render() {
          const style = {
            zIndex: (this.state.opacity) ? 1000 : -1000,
            opacity: +this.state.opacity,
            top: (this.state.top || 0) + 20,
            left: (this.state.left || 0) - 30
          }
          return (
            <div style={{display: 'inline'}}>
              <span style={{color: 'blue'}}
                onMouseEnter={this.toggle}
                onMouseOut={this.toggle}>
                {this.props.children}
              </span>
              <div className="tooltip bottom"
                style={style}
                role="tooltip">
                <div className="tooltip-arrow"></div>
                <div className="tooltip-inner">
                  {this.props.text}
                </div>
              </div>
            </div>
          )
        }
```

That's it. You're finished with the `Tooltip` component!

10.3   *Getting it running*

Try this component or use it in your projects by compiling the JSX with npm:

```
$ npm run build
```

This `Tooltip` component is pretty cool, thanks to Twitter Bootstrap styles. Maybe it's not as versatile as some other modules out there, but you built it yourself from scratch. That's what I'm talking about! With the help of Twitter Bootstrap classes and React, you were able to create a good tooltip (see figure 10.3) in almost no time. It's even responsive: it adapts to various screen sizes, thanks to dynamic positioning!

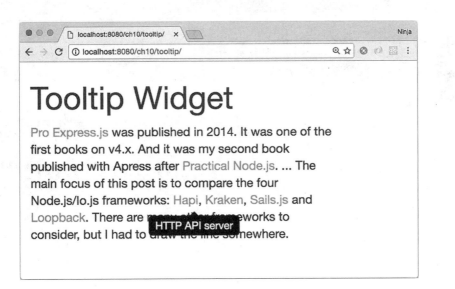

Figure 10.3 When the user hovers over blue text, a black container with text and a pointy arrow appears, offering additional information.

10.4 Homework

For bonus points, do the following:

- Create a variation that works in response to a mouse click—that is, shows the tooltip when you click the highlighted text and hides it when you click the text again.
- Enhance `Tooltip` by making it take a property that determines whether it's on-mouse-over or on-click behavior.
- Enhance `Tooltip` by making it take a property that positions the help text above the text instead of in the default position below the text (hint: change the TB class, and change `top` and `left`).

Submit your code in *a new folder under ch10* as a pull request to this book's GitHub repository: https://github.com/azat-co/react-quickly.

10.5 Summary

- React style properties are camelCase, unlike CSS style properties.
- `this.props.children` has the component's content.
- There's no need to manually rerender, because React automatically rerenders after `setState()`.

Watch this chapter's introduction video by scanning this QR code with your phone or going to http://reactquickly.co/videos/ch11.

11

Project:
Timer component

This chapter covers

- Understanding the project structure and scaffolding
- Building the app's architecture

Studies have shown that meditation is great for health (calming) and productivity (focus).[1] Who doesn't want to be healthier and more productive, especially with minimal monetary investment?

Gurus recommend starting with as little as 5 minutes of meditation and progressing to 10 minutes and then 15 minutes over the span of a few weeks. The target is 30–60 minutes of meditation per day, but some people notice improvements with as little as 10 minutes per day. I can attest to that: after meditating 10 minutes per day every day for 3 years, I am more focused, and it has also helped me in other areas.

---

[1] See "Research on Meditation," *Wikipedia*, https://en.wikipedia.org/wiki/Research_on_meditation; "Meditation: In Depth," *National Institutes of Health*, http://mng.bz/01om; "Harvard Neuroscientist: Meditation Not Only Reduces Stress, Here's How It Changes Your Brain," *The Washington Post*, May 26, 2015, http://mng.bz/1ljZ; and "Benefits of Meditation," *Yoga Journal*, http://mng.bz/7Hp7.

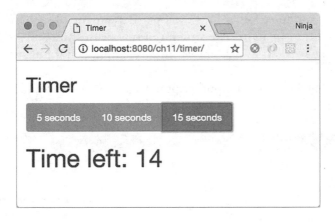

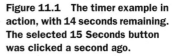

Figure 11.1 **The timer example in action, with 14 seconds remaining. The selected 15 Seconds button was clicked a second ago.**

But how do you know when you've reached your daily meditation goal? You need a timer! So in this chapter, you'll put your React and HTML5 skills to the test and create a web timer (see figure 11.1). To make it easy for testing purposes, this timer will only run for 5, 10, or 15 seconds.

The idea is to have three controls that set a countdown timer (n to 0). Think of a typical kitchen timer, but instead of minutes, it will count seconds. Click a button, and the timer starts. Click it again, or click another button, and the timer starts over.

> **NOTE** To follow along with this project, you'll need to download the unminified version of React and install node.js and npm for compiling JSX. In this example, I also use a theme called Flatly from Bootswatch (https://bootswatch .com/flatly). This theme depends on Twitter Bootstrap. Appendix A covers how to install everything.

> **NOTE** The source code for the example in this chapter is at www.manning .com/books/react-quickly and https://github.com/azat-co/react-quickly/ tree/master/ch11 (in the ch11 folder of the GitHub repository https:// github.com/azat-co/react-quickly). You can also find some demos at http:// reactquickly.co/demos.

11.1 Project structure and scaffolding

The project structure for the `Timer` component, not unlike `Tooltip` and `Menu`, is as follows:

```
/timer
  /node_modules
  bootstrap.css
  flute_c_long_01.wav
  index.html
  package.json
  react-dom.js
  react.js
  timer.js
  timer.jsx
```

Babel dev dependency for JSX-to-JS transpilation ⟵

Sound file to signal the end of the time ⟵

Main JSX script ⟵

As before, there's a node_modules folder for developer dependencies such as Babel, which is used for JSX-to-JS transpilation. The structure is flat, with styles and scripts in the same folder. I did this to keep things simple; in a real app, you'll put styles and scripts in separate folders.

The key parts of package.json are the npm script to build, the Babel configuration, dependencies, and other metadata.

Listing 11.1   Timer project package.json file

```
{
  "name": "timer",
  "version": "1.0.0",
  "description": "",
  "main": "script.js",
  "scripts": {
    "build": "./node_modules/.bin/babel timer.jsx -o timer.js -w"
  },
  "author": "Azat Mardan",
  "license": "MIT",
  "babel": {
    "presets": ["react"]
  },
  "devDependencies": {
    "babel-cli": "6.9.0",
    "babel-preset-react": "6.5.0"
  }
}
```

Creates an npm script to transpile JSX into JS ⟵

After you've created package.json, either by copying and pasting or by typing, be sure to run npm i or npm install.

The HTML for this project is very basic (ch11/timer/index.html). It includes the react.js and react-dom.js files, which, for the sake of simplicity, are in the same folder as the HTML file.

Listing 11.2   Timer project index.html file

```
<!DOCTYPE html>
<html>
  <head>
    <meta charset="utf-8">
    <title>Timer</title>
    <script src="react.js" type="text/javascript"></script>
    <script src="react-dom.js" type="text/javascript"></script>
    <link href="bootstrap.css" rel="stylesheet" type="text/css"/>
  </head>
  <body class="container-fluid">
    <div id="timer-app"/>
  </body>
  <script src="timer.js" type="text/javascript"></script>
</html>
```

This file only includes the library and points to timer.js, which you'll create from timer.jsx. To do so, you'll need the Babel CLI (see chapter 3).

11.2 App architecture

The timer.jsx file will have three components:

- `TimerWrapper`—Primary component that will do most of the work and render other components
- `Timer`—Component to display the number of seconds remaining
- `Button`—Component to render three buttons and trigger (reset) the timer

Figure 11.2 shows how they'll look on the page. You can see the `Timer` and `Button` components; `TimerWrapper` has all three buttons and `Timer` inside it. `TimerWrapper` is a container (smart) component, whereas the other two are representational (dumb).

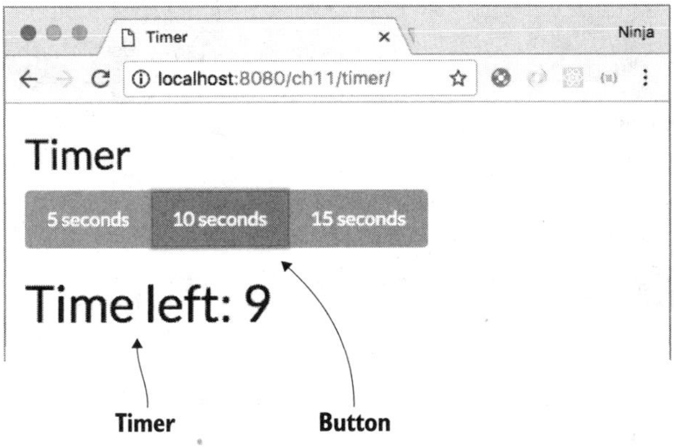

Figure 11.2 `Timer` and `Button` components

We're breaking the app into three pieces because in software engineering, things tend to change quickly with each new release. By separating the presentation (`Button` and `Timer`) and logic (`TimerWrapper`), you can make the app more adaptable. Moreover, you'll be able to reuse elements like buttons in other apps. The bottom line is that keeping representation and business logic separate is a best practice when working with React.

You need `TimerWrapper` to communicate between `Timer` and `Buttons`. The interaction between these three components and a user is shown in figure 11.3:

1 `TimerWrapper` renders `Timer` and the `Buttons` by passing `TimerWrapper`'s states as properties.
2 The user interacts with a button, which triggers an event in the button.
3 The event in the button calls the function in `TimerWrapper` with the time value in seconds.
4 `TimerWrapper` sets the interval and updates `Timer`.
5 Updates continue until there are 0 seconds left.

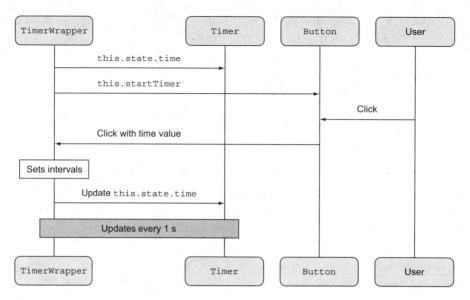

Figure 11.3   Timer app execution, starting at the top

For simplicity, you'll keep all three components in the timer.jsx file.

Listing 11.3   Outline of timer.jsx

```
class TimerWrapper extends React.Component {
  constructor(props) {                          Sets initial
    // ...                                       states
  }
  startTimer(timeLeft) {          Triggers the new
    // ...                        timer (reset)
  }
  render() {
    // ...
  }
}

class Timer extends React.Component {
  render() {
    // ...
  }
}

class Button extends React.Component {
  startTimer(event) {                   Triggers the new timer
    // ...                              (reset) from a user click. Calls
  }                                     startTimer from TimerWrapper.
  render() {
    // ...
  }
}
```

```
ReactDOM.render(                              Renders
  <TimerWrapper/>,                       ◄──┘ TimerWrapper
  document.getElementById('timer-app')
)
```

Let's start from the bottom of the timer.jsx file and render the main component (TimerWrapper) into the <div> with ID timer-app:

```
ReactDOM.render(
  <TimerWrapper/>,
  document.getElementById('timer-app')
)
```

ReactDOM.render() will be the last call in the file. It uses TimerWrapper, so let's define this component next.

11.3 The TimerWrapper component

TimerWrapper is where all the fun happens! This is the high-level overview of the component:

```
class TimerWrapper extends React.Component {
  constructor(props) {
    // ...
  }
  startTimer(timeLeft) {
    // ...
  }
  render() {
    // ...
  }
}
```

First, you need to be able to save the time left (using timeLeft) and reset the timer (using timer). Therefore, you'll use two states: timeLeft and timer.

On the first app load, the timer shouldn't be running; so, in the constructor of TimerWrapper, you need to set the time (timeLeft) state to null. This will come in handy in Timer, because you'll be able to tell the difference between the first load (timeLeft is null) and when the time is up (timeLeft is 0).

You also set the timer state property to null. This property holds a reference to the setInterval() function that will do the countdown. But right now there's no running timer—thus, the null value.

Finally, bind the startTimer() method, because you'll be using it as an event handler (for buttons):

```
class TimerWrapper extends React.Component {
  constructor(props) {
    super(props)
    this.state =  {timeLeft: null, timer: null}
```

```
    this.startTimer = this.startTimer.bind(this)
  }
  ...
```

Next is the startTimer event handler. It's called each time a user clicks a button. If a user clicks a button when the timer is already running, then you need to clear the previous interval and start anew. You definitely don't want multiple timers running at the same time. For this reason, the first thing the startTimer() method does is stop the previous countdown by clearing the result of setInterval(). The current timer's setInterval object is stored in the this.state.timer variable.

To remove the result of setInterval(), there's a clearInterval() method. Both clearInterval() (http://mng.bz/7104) and setInterval() (http://mng.bz/P2d6) are browser API methods; that is, they're available from a window object without additional libraries or even prefixes. (window.clearInterval() will also work for browser code, but it will break in Node.js.) Call clearInterval() on the first line of the event handler for the buttons:

```
class TimerWrapper extends React.Component {
  constructor(props) {
    // ...
  }
  startTimer(timeLeft) {
    clearInterval(this.state.timer)
    // ...
  }
}
```

After you clear the previous timer, you can set a new one with setInterval(). The code passed to setInterval() will be called every second. For this code, let's use a fat-arrow function to bind the this context. This will allow you to use TimerWrapper state, properties, and methods in this function (closure/callback) of setInterval():

```
class TimerWrapper extends React.Component {
  constructor(props) {
    // ...
  }
  startTimer(timeLeft) {
    clearInterval(this.state.timer)
    let timer = setInterval(() => {
      // ...
    }, 1000)
    // ...
  }
  render() {
    // ...
  }
}
```

Now, you'll implement the function. The timeLeft variable stands for the amount of time left on the timer. You use it to save the current value minus 1 and check whether it reached 0. If it did, then you remove the timer by invoking `clearInterval()` with a reference to the `timer` object (created by `setInterval()`), which is stored in the `timer` variable. The reference to `timer` is saved in `setInterval()`'s closure even for future function calls (each second that passes). This is the way JavaScript scoping works. So, there's no need to pull the value of the `timer` object from the state (although you could).

Next, save `timeLeft` during every interval cycle. And finally, save `timeLeft` and the `timer` object when the button is clicked:

```
//...
startTimer(timeLeft) {
  clearInterval(this.state.timer)
  let timer = setInterval(() => {
    var timeLeft = this.state.timeLeft - 1
    if (timeLeft == 0) clearInterval(timer)
    this.setState({timeLeft: timeLeft})
  }, 1000)
  return this.setState({timeLeft: timeLeft, timer: timer})
}
//...
```

You set the states to the new values using `setState()`, which is asynchronous. The `setInterval()` interval length is 1,000 ms, or 1 second. You need to set the state to the new values of `timeLeft` and `timer` because the app needs to update those values, and you can't use simple variables or properties for that.

`setInterval()` is scheduled to be executed asynchronously in the JavaScript event loop. The returned `setState()` will fire before the first `setInterval()` callback. You can easily test it by putting console logs in your code. For example, the following code will print 1 and then 2, not 2 and then 1:

```
...
startTimer(timeLeft) {
  clearInterval(this.state.timer)
  let timer = setInterval(() => {
    console.log('2: Inside of setInterval')
    var timeLeft = this.state.timeLeft - 1
    if (timeLeft == 0) clearInterval(timer)
    this.setState({timeLeft: timeLeft})
  }, 1000)
  console.log('1: After setInterval')
  return this.setState({timeLeft: timeLeft, timer: timer})
}
...
```

Last is the mandatory `render()` function for `TimerWrapper`. It returns `<h2>`, three buttons, and the `Timer` component. `row-fluid` and `btn-group` are Twitter Bootstrap classes—they make buttons look better and aren't essential to React:

```
render() {
  return (
    <div className="row-fluid">
      <h2>Timer</h2>
      <div className="btn-group" role="group" >
        <Button time="5" startTimer={this.startTimer}/>
        <Button time="10" startTimer={this.startTimer}/>
        <Button time="15" startTimer={this.startTimer}/>
      </div>
```

This code shows how you can reuse the Button component by providing different values for the time property. These time property values allow buttons to display different times in their labels and to set different timers. The startTimer property of Button has the same value for *all three* buttons. The value is this.startTimer from TimerWrapper, which starts/resets the timer, as you know.

Next, you display the text "Time left: ...," which is rendered by the Timer component. To do so, you pass the time state as a property to Timer. To adhere to the best React practice, Timer is stateless. React updates the text on the page (Timer) automatically when the property (Timer) is updated by the change of the state (TimerWrapper). You'll implement Timer later. For now, use it like this:

```
<Timer time={this.state.timeLeft}/>
```

In addition, the <audio> tag (an HTML5 tag that points to a file) alerts you when the time is up:

```
        <audio id="end-of-time" src="flute_c_long_01.wav" preload="auto">
        ➥ </audio>
      </div>
    )
  }
}
```

For your reference and better understanding (sometimes it's nice to see the entire component), here's the meat—or tofu, for my vegetarian readers—of the timer app: the full code for TimerWrapper (ch11/timer/timer.jsx).

Listing 11.4   TimerWrapper component

```
class TimerWrapper extends React.Component {
  constructor(props) {
    super(props)
    this.state = {timeLeft: null, timer: null}
    this.startTimer = this.startTimer.bind(this)
  }
  startTimer(timeLeft) {
    clearInterval(this.state.timer)        ◁── Clears the timer to reset
    let timer = setInterval(() => {               it, in case any other
      console.log('2: Inside of setInterval')     timers were running
```

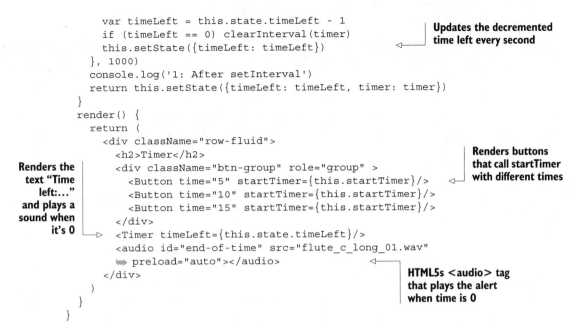

```
      var timeLeft = this.state.timeLeft - 1
      if (timeLeft == 0) clearInterval(timer)          Updates the decremented
      this.setState({timeLeft: timeLeft})              time left every second
    }, 1000)
    console.log('1: After setInterval')
    return this.setState({timeLeft: timeLeft, timer: timer})
  }
  render() {
    return (
      <div className="row-fluid">
        <h2>Timer</h2>                                         Renders buttons
        <div className="btn-group" role="group" >             that call startTimer
          <Button time="5" startTimer={this.startTimer}/>     with different times
          <Button time="10" startTimer={this.startTimer}/>
          <Button time="15" startTimer={this.startTimer}/>
        </div>
        <Timer timeLeft={this.state.timeLeft}/>
        <audio id="end-of-time" src="flute_c_long_01.wav"
          preload="auto"></audio>
      </div>                                          HTML5s <audio> tag
    )                                                 that plays the alert
  }                                                   when time is 0
}
```

Renders the text "Time left:..." and plays a sound when it's 0

`TimerWrapper` has a lot of logic. Other components are stateless and basically clueless. Nevertheless, you need to implement the other two components. Remember the `<audio>` tag in `TimerWrapper`, which will play sounds when the time remaining reaches 0? Let's implement the `Timer` component next.

11.4 The Timer component

The goal of the `Timer` component is to show the time left and to play a sound when the time is up. It's a stateless component. Implement the class, and check whether the `timeLeft` property equals 0:

```
class Timer extends React.Component {
  render() {
    if (this.props.timeLeft == 0) {
      // ...
    }
    // ...
  }
}
```

To play the sound (file flute_c_long_01.wav), this project uses the special HTML5 `<audio>` element; you defined it in `TimerWrapper`, with src pointing to the WAV file and id set to end-of-time. All you need to do is get the DOM node (the vanilla JavaScript `getElementById()` will work fine) and invoke `play()` (also vanilla JavaScript from HTML5). This again shows how well React plays with other JavaScripty things like HTML5, jQuery 3,[2] and even Angular 4, if you're brave enough:

---

[2] For examples of integration with browser events and jQuery, see chapter 6.

```
class Timer extends React.Component {
  render() {
    if (this.props.timeLeft == 0) {
      document.getElementById('end-of-time').play()
    }
    // ...
```

As explained earlier, you don't want the timer's text to say "0" at first, because the timer has never run. So, in `TimerWrapper` (listing 11.4), you set the `timeLeft` value to `null` initially. If `timeLeft` is `null` or `0`, then the `Timer` component renders an empty `<div>`. In other words, the app won't display 0:

```
if (this.props.timeLeft == null || this.props.timeLeft == 0)
  return <div/>
```

Otherwise, when `timeLeft` is greater than 0, an `<h1>` element shows the time remaining. In other words, now you need to show the time left when the timer is running:

```
return <h1>Time left: {this.props.timeLeft}</h1>
```

For your reference, the following listing shows the `Timer` component in full (ch11/timer/timer.jsx).

Listing 11.5 `Timer` component, showing time remaining

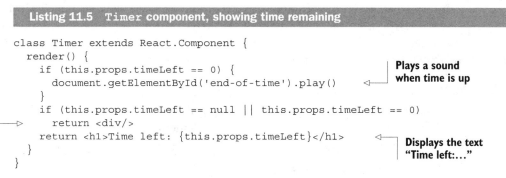

```
class Timer extends React.Component {
  render() {
    if (this.props.timeLeft == 0) {                          Plays a sound
      document.getElementById('end-of-time').play()    ◁───  when time is up
    }
    if (this.props.timeLeft == null || this.props.timeLeft == 0)
      return <div/>
      return <h1>Time left: {this.props.timeLeft}</h1>   ◁──  Displays the text
  }                                                           "Time left:..."
}
```
Displays nothing initially

For `Timer` to show a number of seconds, you need to start the timer first. This happens when you click the buttons. Onward to those cute little buttons!

11.5   *The Button component*

To follow the DRY (don't repeat yourself) principle,[3] you'll create *one* `Button` component and use it three times to show three different buttons. `Button` is another stateless (and very simple) component, as it should be in accordance with a Reactive mindset, but `Button` is not as straightforward as `Timer`, because `Button` has an event handler.

---

[3] The DRY principle is as follows: "Every piece of knowledge must have a single, unambiguous, authoritative representation within a system"; see "Don't Repeat Yourself," *Wikipedia*, http://mng.bz/1K5k; and *The Pragmatic Programmer: From Journeyman to Master* by Andrew Hunt (Addison-Wesley Professional, 1999), http://amzn.to/2ojjXoY.

Buttons must have an `onClick` event handler to capture users' button clicks. Those clicks trigger the timer countdown. The function to start the timer isn't implemented in `Button`: it's implemented in `TimerWrapper` and is passed down to the `Button` component from its parent, `TimerWrapper`, in `this.props.startTimer`. But how do you pass `time` (5, 10, or 15) to `TimerWrapper`'s `startTimer`? Look at this code from `TimerWrapper`, which passes time-period values as properties:

```
<Button time="5" startTimer={this.startTimer}/>
<Button time="10" startTimer={this.startTimer}/>
<Button time="15" startTimer={this.startTimer}/>
```

The idea is to render three buttons using this component (code reuse—yay!). To know what time the user selected, though, you need the value in `this.props.time`, which you pass as an argument to `this.props.startTimer`.

If you write the following code, it won't work:

```
// Won't work. Must be a definition.
<button type="button" className='btn-default btn'
  onClick={this.props.startTimer(this.props.time)}>
  {this.props.time} seconds
</button>
```

The function passed to `onClick` must be a definition, not an invocation. How about this?

```
// Yep. You are on the right path young man.
<button type="button" className='btn-default btn'
  onClick={()=>{this.props.startTimer(this.props.time)}}>
  {this.props.time} seconds
</button>
```

Yes. This snippet has the right code to pass the value. This is the correct approach: a middle step (function) passes the different time values. You can make it more elegant by creating a class method. Another way would be to use a currying `bind()` instead of an interim function:

```
onClick = {this.props.startTimer.bind(null, this.props.time)}
```

Recall that `bind()` returns a function definition. As long as you pass a function definition to `onClick` (or any other event handler), you're good.

Let's get back to the `Button` component. The event handler `onClick` calls the class method `this.startTimer`, which in turn calls a function from the property `this.props.startTimer`. You can use the `this` object (`this.props.startTimer`) in `this.startTimer` because you applied `bind(this)`.

The `Button` component is stateless, which you can confirm by looking at the full code (ch11/timer/timer.jsx). What does that mean? It means you can refactor it into a function instead of it being a class.

Listing 11.6   `Button` component that triggers the countdown

Renders the
Button UI

Kick-starts or resets
the timer with the
proper time value

Captures onClick

```
class Button extends React.Component {
  startTimer(event) {
    return this.props.startTimer(this.props.time)
  }
  render() {
    return <button type="button" className='btn-default btn'
      onClick={this.startTimer.bind(this)}>
        {this.props.time} seconds
    </button>
  }
}
```

Obviously, you don't need to use the same names for methods (such as `startTimer()`) in `Button` and `TimerWrapper`. A lot of people get confused during my React workshops when I use the same names; others find it easier to trace the chain of calls when they use the same names. Just know that you can name `Button`'s method something like `handleStartTimer()`, for example. Personally, I find that using the same name helps me to mentally link properties, methods, and states from different components.

Note that `Timer` could also be named `TimerLabel`, if not for the audio `play()` method. Is there room for improvement and refactoring? Absolutely! Check the "Homework" section of this chapter.

Congrats—you're officially finished coding. Now, to get this thing running so you can begin using this timer for work[4] or hobbies.

11.6   *Getting it running*

Compile the JSX into JavaScript with the following Babel 6.9.5 command, assuming you have the Babel CLI and its presets installed (hint: package.json!):

```
$ ./node_modules/.bin/babel timer.jsx -o timer.js -w
```

If you copied my build npm script from package.json at the beginning of this chapter, then you can run `npm run build`.

If you've done everything correctly, enjoy your beautiful timer application, shown in figure 11.4! Turn off your music to hear the alarm when the time is up.

Make sure the app works *properly*: you should see a time-remaining number that changes every second. When you click the button, a new countdown should begin; that is, the timer is interrupted and starts over on each click of a button.

---

[4] Try the Pomodoro technique (https://cirillocompany.de/pages/pomodoro-technique) for increasing your productivity.

Figure 11.4   Clicking 15 Seconds launched the timer. Now it says that 14 seconds remain.

11.7   Homework

For bonus points, do the following:

- Convert `Timer` to a stateless component implemented by a fat-arrow function.
- Implement a Pause/Resume button that stops/resumes the timer.
- Implement a Cancel button that stops the countdown and hides the time remaining.
- Implement a Reset button that resets the time remaining to the original value (5, 10, or 15 seconds).
- Modify the final version of this project to use 5, 10, and 15 minutes, rather than seconds.
- Decouple the `<audio>` tag in `TimerWrapper` from `play()` in `Timer`.
- Refactor the project to have four files—timer.jsx, timer-label.jsx, timer-button.jsx, and timer-sound.jsx—with as much loose coupling as possible.
- Implement a slider button that changes with every time interval (chapter 6 discusses slider integration).

Submit your code in *a new folder under ch11* as a pull request to this book's GitHub repository: https://github.com/azat-co/react-quickly.

11.8   Summary

- Keep components simple and as close to representational as possible.
- Pass functions as values of properties, not just data.
- Two components can exchange data between each other via a parent.

Part 2

React architecture

Welcome to part 2. Now that you know the most important concepts, features, and patterns of React, you're ready to embark on your own React journey. Part 1 prepared you to build simple UI elements; and the bottom line is, if you're building web UIs, core React is sufficient. But to build full-blown, front-end apps, React developers rely on open source modules written by the React community. Most of these modules are hosted on GitHub and npm, so they're within easy reach—you can grab them and go.

These chapters cover the most-popular, most-used, mature libraries that, together with core React, form the *React stack* (or *React and friends*, as some developers jokingly call this ensemble). To get started, in chapters 12–17, you'll learn about using Webpack for asset pipelines, React Router for URL routing, Redux and GraphQL for data flow, Jest for testing, and Express and Node for Universal React. Then, as in part 1, chapters 18–20 present real-world projects.

This may seem like a lot, but my experience with reading and writing books has shown me that baby steps and textbook examples don't provide good value for readers and don't show how things work in real life. So, in this part of the book, you'll both learn about and work with the React stack. Interesting, complex projects await you. When you've finished, you'll be knowledgeable about data flow, skilled in setting up the monstrosity called Webpack, and able to talk like a know-it-all at local meetups.

Read on.

The Webpack build tool

12

This chapter covers

- Adding Webpack to a project
- Modularizing your code
- Running Webpack and testing the build
- Performing hot module replacement

Before we go any further with the React stack (a.k.a. React and friends), let's look at a tool that's essential to most modern web development: a *build tool* (or *bundler*). You'll use this tool in subsequent chapters to bundle your many code files into the minimum number of files needed to run your applications and prepare them for easy deployment. The build tool you'll be using is Webpack (https://webpack.js.org).

If you've not come across a build tool before, or if you've used another one such as Grunt, Gulp, or Bower, this chapter is for you. You'll learn how to set up Webpack, configure it, and get it running against a project.

This chapter also covers hot module replacement (HMR), a feature of Webpack that enables you to hot-swap updated modules for those running on a live server. First, though, we'll look at what Webpack can do for you.

NOTE Code generators such as `create-react-app` (https://github.com/facebookincubator/create-react-app) create boilerplate/scaffolding code and help you start projects quickly. `create-react-app` also uses Webpack and Babel, along with other modules. But this book primarily teaches fundamentals, so you won't use a code generator; instead, you'll do the setup yourself to make sure you understand each part. If you're interested, you can learn how to use a code generator for yourself—it just takes a few commands.

NOTE The source code for the examples in this chapter is at www.manning .com/books/react-quickly and https://github.com/azat-co/react-quickly/ tree/master/ch12 (in the ch12 folder of the GitHub repository https:// github.com/azat-co/react-quickly). You can also find some demos at http:// reactquickly.co/demos.

12.1 What does Webpack do?

Have you ever wondered why (in web development) everyone and their mother are talking about Webpack? Webpack's core focus is optimizing the JavaScript you write so that it's contained in as few files as possible for a client to request. This reduces the strain on the servers for popular sites and also reduces the client's page-load time. Of course, it's not as simple as that. JavaScript is often written in modules that are easy to reuse. But they often depend on other modules that may depend on other modules, and so on; and keeping track of what needs to be loaded when so that all the dependencies resolve quickly can be a headache.

Let's say you have a utility module `myUtil`, and you use it in many React components—accounts.jsx, transactions.jsx, and so on. Without a tool like Webpack, you'd have to manually keep track of the fact that each time you use one of those components, you need to include `myUtil` as a dependency. Additionally, you might be loading `myUtil` unnecessarily for a second or third time, because another component that depends on `myUtil` has already loaded it. Of course, this is a simplified example; real projects have dozens or even hundreds of dependencies that are used in other dependencies. Webpack can help.

Webpack knows how to deal with all three types of JavaScript module—CommonJS (www.commonjs.org), AMD (https://github.com/amdjs/amdjs-api/wiki/AMD), and ES6 (http://mng.bz/VjyO)—so you don't need to worry if you're working with a hodgepodge of module types. Webpack will analyze the dependencies for all the JavaScript in your project and do the following:

- Ensure that all dependencies are loaded in the correct order
- Ensure that all dependencies are loaded only once
- Ensure that your JavaScript is bundled into as few files as possible (called *static assets*)

Webpack also supports *code splitting* and *asset hashing*, which let you identify blocks of code that are required only under certain circumstances. These blocks are split out to be loaded on demand rather than bundled in with everything else. You must opt in to use these features and further optimize your JavaScript and its deployment.

> **NOTE** Code splitting and asset hashing are outside the scope of this book. Check out the Webpack website for more information: https://webpack .github.io/docs/code-splitting.html.

Webpack isn't just about JavaScript, though. It supports the preprocessing of other static files through the use of *loaders*. For example, you can do the following before any bundling takes place:

- Precompile your JSX, Jade, or CoffeeScript files into plain JavaScript
- Precompile ES6+ code into ES5 for browsers that don't yet support ES6
- Precompile Sass and Compass files into CSS
- Optimize sprites into a single PNG or JPG file or inline data assets

Many loaders are available for all sorts of file types. In addition, plug-ins that modify Webpack's behavior are catalogued on the Webpack homepage. If you can't find what you're looking for, there's documentation about how to write your own plug-in.

For the rest of this book, you'll be using Webpack to do the following:

- Manage and bundle dependencies from npm modules, so you don't have to manually download files from the internet, and include them with `<script>` tags in HTML
- Transpile JSX into regular JavaScript while providing source maps for easier debugging
- Manage styles
- Perform hot module reloading
- Build a development web server

As you'll see, you can configure the order in which Webpack loads, precompiles, and bundles your files using its webpack.config.js file. But first, let's look at how to install Webpack and get it working with a project.

12.2 Adding Webpack to a project

To illustrate how you can get starting working with Webpack, let's slightly modify the project from chapter 7 shown in figure 12.1. It has email and comment input fields, two style sheets, and one `Content` component.

Figure 12.1   Original email project before using Webpack

Here's the new project structure. I've pointed out where it differs from the project in chapter 7:

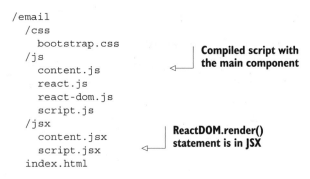

Contrast that with the non-Webpack setup from chapter 7:

```
/email
  /css
    bootstrap.css
  /js
    content.js
    react.js
    react-dom.js
    script.js
  /jsx
    content.jsx
    script.jsx
  index.html
```

Compiled script with
the main component

ReactDOM.render()
statement is in JSX

NOTE   Do you have Node.js and npm? This is the best time to install them—you'll need them, in order to proceed. Appendix A covers installation.

This section walks you through the following steps:

1 Installing `webpack`
2 Installing dependencies and saving them to package.json
3 Configuring Webpack's webpack.config.js
4 Configuring the dev server and hot module replacement

Let's get started.

12.2.1 *Installing Webpack and its dependencies*

To use Webpack, you'll need a few additional dependencies, as noted in package.json:

- *Webpack*—The bundler tool (npm name: `webpack`); use v2.4.1
- *Loaders*—Style, CSS, hot module replacement (HMR), and Babel/JSX preprocessors (npm names: `style-loader`, `css-loader`, `react-hot-loader` and `babel-loader`, `babel-core`, and `babel-preset-react`); use the versions specified in package.json
- *The webpack-dev-server*—An Express development server that lets you use HMR (npm name: `webpack-dev-server`); use v2.4.2

You can install each module manually, but I recommend copying the package.json file shown in listing 12.1 (ch12/email-webpack/package.json) from the GitHub repository to your project root (see the project structure shown in section 12.2). Then, run `npm i` or `npm install` from the project root (where you have package.json) to install the dependencies. This will ensure that you don't forget any of the 10 modules (a synonym for *package* in Node). It also ensures that your versions are close to the ones I used. Using wildly different versions is a *fantastic* way to break the app!

Listing 12.1   Setting up the dev environment

```
{
  "name": "email-webpack",
  "version": "1.0.0",
  "description": "",
  "main": "index.js",
  "scripts": {
    "build": "./node_modules/.bin/webpack -w"          ⊲
    "wds-cli": "./node_modules/.bin/webpack-dev-server --inline --hot
    ➥ --module-bind 'css=style-loader!css-loader'
    ➥ --module-bind 'jsx=react-hot-loader!babel-loader'
    ➥ --config webpack.dev-cli.config.js",
    "wds": "./node_modules/.bin/webpack-dev-server --config
    ➥ webpack.dev.config.js"
  },
  "author": "Azat Mardan",
  "license": "MIT",
```

Saves the Webpack build script as an npm script for convenience

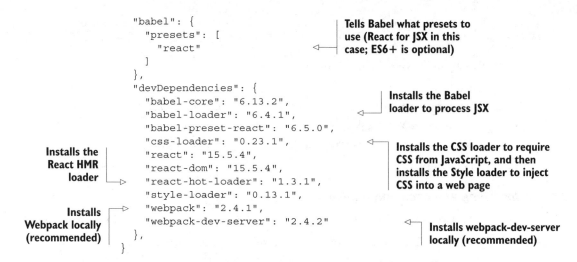

The `babel` property in package.json should be familiar to you from part 1 of this book, so I won't spend time repeating myself. As a reminder, you need this property to configure Babel to convert JSX to JS. If you need to support browsers that can't work with ES6, you can add the `es2015` preset to `presets`:

```
"babel": {
  "presets": [
    "react",
    "es2015"
  ]
},
```

Also add `babel-preset-es2015` to `devDependencies`:

```
"devDependencies": {
  "babel-preset-es2015": "6.18.0",
  ...
}
```

In addition to new dependencies, there are new npm scripts. The commands in `scripts` in package.json are optional but highly recommended, because using npm scripts for launching and building is a best practice when working with React and Node. Of course, you can run all the builds manually without using npm scripts, but why type extra characters?

You can either run Webpack with `npm run build` or run it directly with `./node_modules/.bin/webpack -w`. The `-w` flag means *watch*—that is, continue to monitor for any source code changes, and rebuild bundles if there are any. In other words, Webpack will keep running to automatically make changes. Of course, you must have all the necessary modules installed with `npm i`.

The `webpack -w` command looks for webpack.config.js by default. You can't run Webpack with this configuration file. Let's create it next.

NOTE The `wds` and `wds-cli` npm scripts in package.json are explained in section 12.5.

12.2.2 Configuring Webpack

Webpack needs to know what to process (the source code) and how to do it (with the loaders). That's why there's webpack.config.js in the root of the project structure. In a nutshell, in this project, you're using Webpack to do the following:

- Transform your JSX files into JS files: `babel-loader`, `babel-core`, and `babel-preset-react`
- Load CSS via `require` and resolve `url` and `imports` in the process with `css-loader` (https://github.com/webpack/css-loader)
- Add CSS by injecting the `<style>` element with `style-loader` (https://github.com/webpack/style-loader)
- Bundle all the resulting JS files into one file called bundle.js
- Provide the proper source code–line mapping in DevTools via source maps

Webpack needs its own configuration file: email-webpack/webpack.config.js.

Listing 12.2 Webpack configuration file

Defines a path for the bundled files

Defines the file to start bundling (typically, the main file that loads other files)

Defines a filename for the bundled file you'll be using in index.html

Specifies that you need proper mapping of compiled source code lines to the JSX source code lines. This is useful for debugging and appears in DevTools.

Specifies the loader to import, and then injects CSS into the web page from JavaScript

Specifies the loader that will perform the JSX transformation (and ES6+ if needed)

```
module.exports = {
    entry: './jsx/app.jsx',
    output: {
        path: __dirname + '/js/',
        filename: 'bundle.js'
    },
    devtool: '#sourcemap',
    module: {
        loaders: [
            { test: /\.css$/, loader: 'style-loader!css-loader' },
            {
                test: /\.jsx?$/,
                exclude: /(node_modules)/,
                loaders: ['babel-loader']
            }
        ]
    }
}
```

The `devtool` property is useful during development because it provides source maps that show you the line numbers in source—not compiled—code. You're now ready to run Webpack for this project and also bootstrap any Webpack-based projects in the future.

> **Configuration files**
>
> If you wish, you can have more than one configuration file. These files can come in handy for development, production, testing, and other builds. In the example's project structure, I created these files:
>
> ```
> webpack.dev-cli.config.js
> webpack.dev.config.js
> ```
>
> Naming doesn't matter as long as you and your teammates can understand the meaning of each file. The name is passed to Webpack with `--config`. You'll learn more about these configuration files in section 12.4.

Webpack has a lot of features, and we've only covered the basics; but they're enough to compile JSX, provide source maps, inject and import CSS, and bundle JavaScript. When you need more Webpack functionality, you can consult the documentation or a book like *SurviveJS* by Juho Vepsäläinen (https://survivejs.com).

Now you're ready to use some of Webpack's power in JSX.

12.3   *Modularizing your code*

As you'll recall, in chapter 7, the email app used global objects and `<script>`. That's fine for this book or a small app. But in large apps, using globals is frowned on because you may run into trouble with name collisions or managing multiple `<script>` tags with duplicate inclusions. You can let Webpack do all the dependency management by using CommonJS syntax. Webpack will include only needed dependencies and package them into a single bundle.js file (based on the configs in webpack.config.js).

Organizing your code by modularizing it is a best practice not only for React but also for software engineering in general. You can use Browserify, SystemJS, or another bundler/module loader and still use CommonJS/Node.js syntax (`require` and `module.exports`). Thus, the code in this section is transferable to other systems, once you refactor it away from primitive globals.

As of this writing, `import` (http://mng.bz/VjyO) is supported by only one browser—Edge—and isn't supported by Node.js. ES6 modules with `import` syntax will need more work in the Webpack setup. It isn't an exact replacement for CommonJS `require`/`module.exports` syntax, because those commands work differently. For this reason, the following listing (ch12/email-webpack/app.jsx) refactors app.jsx to use `require()` and `module.exports` instead of global objects and HTML `<script>`. Due to the use of `style-loader`, you can require CSS files as well. And because of the Babel loader, you can require JSX files.

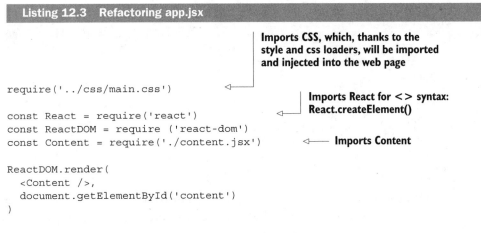

Listing 12.3 Refactoring app.jsx

```
require('../css/main.css')

const React = require('react')
const ReactDOM = require ('react-dom')
const Content = require('./content.jsx')

ReactDOM.render(
  <Content />,
  document.getElementById('content')
)
```

Imports CSS, which, thanks to the style and css loaders, will be imported and injected into the web page

Imports React for < > syntax: **React.createElement()**

◁── **Imports Content**

In contrast, ch07/email/jsx/script.jsx looks like this:

```
ReactDOM.render(
  <Content />,
  document.getElementById('content')
)
```

The old file is smaller, but this is one of the rare cases in which less isn't more. It relies on the global `Content`, `ReactDOM`, and `React` objects, which, as I just explained, is a bad practice.

In content.jsx, you can use `require()` in a similar way. The code for `constructor()`, `submit()`, and `render()` doesn't change:

```
const React = require('react')          ◁── Imports React
const ReactDOM = require('react-dom')   ◁
                                           Imports ReactDOM
class Content extends React.Component {
  constructor(props) {
      // ...
  }
  submit(event) {
    // ...
  }
  render() {
      // ...
  }
}

module.exports = Content          ◁── Exports Content
```

The index.html file needs to point to the bundle that Webpack creates for you: the js/bundle.js file. Its name is specified in webpack.config.js, and now you need to add it. It will be created after you run `npm run build`. Here's the new index.html code:

```
<!DOCTYPE html>
<html>

  <head>
    <link href="css/bootstrap.css" type="text/css" rel="stylesheet"/>
  </head>

  <body>
    <div id="content" class="container"></div>
    <script src="js/bundle.js"></script>
  </body>

</html>
```

Note that you also remove the reference to the stylesheet main.css from index.html. Webpack will inject a <style> element with a reference to main.css into index.html for you, because of require('main.css') in app.jsx. You can use require() for bootstrap.css as well.

That's the last step in refactoring your project.

12.4   *Running Webpack and testing the build*

This is the moment of truth. Run $ npm run build, and compare your output with the following:

```
> email-webpack@1.0.0 build
  /Users/azat/Documents/Code/react-quickly/ch12/email-webpack
> webpack -w

Hash: 2ffe09fff88a4467788a
Version: webpack 1.12.9
Time: 2545ms
        Asset      Size  Chunks              Chunk Names
    bundle.js    752 kB       0  [emitted]  main
bundle.js.map    879 kB       0  [emitted]  main
    + 177 hidden modules
```

If there are no errors and you can see newly created bundle.js and bundle.js.map files in the js folder, bingo! Now spin up your favorite web server (perhaps node-static or http-server), and check the web app. You'll see that it's logging emails and comments in the console.

As you can see, incorporating Webpack into a project is straightforward and yields great results.

> **177 hidden modules—or, the Webpack bundle under the hood**
>
> There are 177 modules in ch12/email-webpack/js/bundle.js! You can open the file and search for webpack_require(1), webpack_require(2), and so on, through webpack_require(176), which is the Content component. The followed compiled code from app.jsx imports Content (lines 49–53 in bundle.js):

(continued)

```
const React = __webpack_require__(5);
const ReactDOM = __webpack_require__(38);
const Content = __webpack_require__(176);

ReactDOM.render(React.createElement(Content, null),
  document.getElementById('content'));
```

At a bare minimum, you're ready to use Webpack for the rest of this book. But I strongly recommend that you set up one more thing: hot module replacement (HMR), which can speed up development dramatically. Before we proceed with React development, let's look at this great Webpack feature.

ESLint and Flow

I want to mention two other useful development tools. Obviously, they're optional, but they're a pretty big deal.

ESLint (http://eslint.org, npm name `eslint`) can take predefined rules or sets of rules and make sure your code (JS or JSX) adheres to the same standards. For example, how many spaces is an indent—four or two? Or, what if you accidentally put a semicolon in your code? (Semicolons are optional in JavaScript, and I prefer not to use them.) ESLint will even give you a warning about unused variables. It can prevent bugs from sneaking into your code! (Not all of them, of course.)

Check out "Getting Started with ESLint" (http://eslint.org/docs/user-guide/getting-started). You'll also need `eslint-plugin-react` (https://github.com/yannickcr/eslint-plugin-react). Make sure you add the React rules to .eslintrc.json (the full code is in the ch12/email-webpack-eslint-flow folder):

```
"rules": {
    "react/jsx-uses-react": "error",
    "react/jsx-uses-vars": "error",
}
```

Here's an example of some warnings from running ESLint React on ch12/email-webpack-lint-flow/jsx/content.jsx:

```
/Users/azat/Documents/Code/react-quickly/ch12/
  email-webpack-lint-flow/jsx/content.jsx
   9:10   error   'event' is defined but never used   no-unused-vars
  12:5    error   Unexpected console statement         no-console
  12:17   error   Do not use findDOMNode               react/no-find-dom-node
  13:5    error   Unexpected console statement         no-console
  13:17   error   Do not use findDOMNode               react/no-find-dom-node
```

(continued)

Next, Flow (https://flowtype.org, npm name `flow-bin`) is a static type-checking tool you can use to add a special comment (`// @flow`) to your scripts and types. Yes! Types in JavaScript! Rejoice, if you're a software engineer with a preference for strongly typed languages like Java, Python, and C. Once you've added the comment, you can run a Flow check to see whether there are any issues. Again, this tool can prevent some pesky bugs:

```
// @flow

var bookName: string = 13
console.log(bookName) // number. This type is incompatible with string
```

Flow has extensive documentation: see "Getting started with Flow" (https://flowtype .org/docs/getting-started.html) and "Flow for React" (https://flowtype.org/docs/ react.html).

You can configure Atom or any other modern code editor to work with ESLint and Flow to catch problems on the fly.

The Atom code editor supports Flow, which shows issues in the bottom pane and marks on the code line during development.

You can find the email project code with ESLint v3.8.1 and Flow v0.33.0 in the ch12/email-webpack-eslint-flow folder.

12.5 *Hot module replacement*

Hot module replacement (HMR) is one of the coolest features of Webpack and React. It lets you write code and test it more quickly by updating the browser with changes while preserving the app's state.

Say you're working on a complex single-page web application, and getting to the current page you're working on takes 12 clicks. If you upload new code to the site, then to get it running, you have to click Reload/Refresh in your browser and repeat those 12 clicks. If you're using HMR, on the other hand, there are no page reloads, and your changes are reflected on the page.

HMR's primary benefit is that you can iterate (write, test, write, test, and so on) more quickly, because your app will save state when you make changes. Some developers consider HMR so groundbreaking that if React didn't have any other features, they would still use it just for HMR!

For the nitty-gritty details of how the HMR process works, see the documentation at http://mng.bz/L9d5. This section covers the practical application of this technology as it pertains to the example email form.

The process of hot-updating code requires multiple steps, shown in a simplified form in figure 12.2. Webpack HMR and the dev server use WebSockets to monitor update notifications from the server. If there are any, the front end gets chunks (JavaScript code) and an update manifest (JSON), which are basically the delta of the changes. The front-end app preserves its state (such as data in an input field or a screen position), but the UI and code change. Magic.

To see HMR in an example, you'll use a new configuration file and webpack-dev-server (WDS). It's possible to use HMR with your own server, built with Express/Node; WDS is

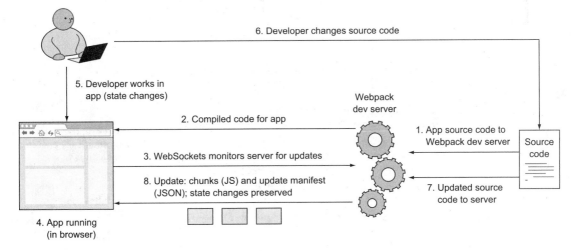

Figure 12.2 Webpack listens for code changes and sends update notifications along with updates to the running app in the browser.

optional, but it's provided by Webpack as a separate `webpack-dev-server` module, so I'll cover it here.

Once everything is configured, you'll enter an email in the form and make a few changes in the code. Thanks to HMR, you'll see that the entered email remains on the form and your changes are propagated to the web app.

12.5.1 Configuring HMR

First, duplicate webpack.config.js by creating a copy named webpack.dev.config.js:

```
$ cp webpack.config.js webpack.dev.config.js
```

Next, open the newly created webpack.dev.config.js file. You need to add a few things such as new entry points, a public path, and the HMR plug-in, and set the dev-server flag to true. The following listing shows the final file (ch12/email-webpack/webpack.dev.config.js).

Listing 12.4 `webpack-dev-server` and HMR configuration

```
const webpack = require('webpack')                    ⟵  Imports the
                                                          webpack module
module.exports = {
  entry: [
    'webpack-dev-server/client/?http://localhost:8080',   ⟵── Includes WDS
    './jsx/app.jsx'                                   ⟵
  ],                                                      Includes the main app
  output: {
    publicPath: 'js/',                               ⟵
    path: __dirname + '/js/',                            Sets the path for WDS to
    filename: 'bundle.js'                               make bundle.js available
  },                                                     (it won't write to disk)
  devtool: '#sourcemap',
  module: {
    loaders: [
      { test: /\.css$/, loader: 'style-loader!css-loader' },
      {
        test: /\.jsx?$/,
        exclude: /(node_modules)/,
        loaders: ['react-hot-loader', 'babel-loader']   ⟵
      }                                                    Includes react-hot-loader
    ]                                                      to automatically enable
  },                                                       HMR on all JSX files
  devServer: {                          Sets WDS to
    hot: true                       ⟵  HMR mode
  },                                                       Includes the
  plugins: [new webpack.HotModuleReplacementPlugin()]  ⟵  HMR plug-in
}
```

You need to tell WDS to use this new configuration file by providing the `--config` option:

```
./node_modules/.bin/webpack-dev-server --config webpack.dev.config.js
```

Save this in package.json for convenience, if you don't have it there already. As you'll recall, `react-hot-loader` is in the dependencies. This module enables HMR for all JSX files (which are in turn converted to JS).

I prefer to enable HMR for all files with `react-hot-loader`. But if you want to have HMR only for certain modules, not all of them, don't use `react-hot-loader`; instead, opt in manually by adding the `module.hot.accept()` statement to the JSX/JS modules you want to cherry-pick for HMR. This `module.hot` magic comes from Webpack. It's recommended that you check whether `module.hot` is available:

```
if(module.hot) {
  module.hot.accept()
}
```

That's a lot of configurations! But there's another way to use and configure Webpack: you can use command-line options and pack some configs in the commands.

If you prefer to use the command line, be my guest. Your config file will be smaller, but the commands will be bigger. For example, this webpack.dev-cli.config.js file has fewer configs:

```
module.exports = {
  entry: './jsx/app.jsx',
  output: {
    publicPath: 'js/',
    path: __dirname + '/js/',
    filename: 'bundle.js'
  },
  devtool: '#sourcemap',
  module: {
    loaders: [
      {
        test: /\.jsx?$/,
        exclude: /(node_modules)/,
        loaders: []
      }
    ]
  }
}
```

But it uses more CLI options:

```
./node_modules/.bin/webpack-dev-server --inline --hot
  --module-bind 'css=style-loader!css-loader'
  --module-bind 'jsx=react-hot-loader!babel-loader'
  --config webpack.dev-cli.config.js
```

Several things are happening here. First, `--inline` and `--hot` include the entries enabling WDS and HMR mode. Then, you pass your loaders with `--module-bind` using the following syntax:

```
fileExtension=loader1!loader2!...
```

Make sure `react-hot` is before `babel`; otherwise, you'll get an error.

When it comes to using the CLI or a full config file, the choice is yours. I find the CLI approach better for simpler builds. To avoid crying later when you discover that you mistyped this monstrosity of a command, you should save the command as an npm script in package.json. And no, batch/shell scripts/Make scripts aren't cool anymore. Use npm scripts, like all the cool kids do! (Disclaimer: This is a joke. I'm not advocating fashion-driven development.)

> ### npm scripts
> npm scripts offer certain advantages, and they're commonly used in Node and React projects. They've become a de facto standard, and you'll generally find them when you first learn about a project. When I start working on a new project or library, the npm scripts are the first place I look, after readme.md—and sometimes instead of readme.md, which may be out of date.
>
> npm scripts offer a flexible way to save essential scripts for testing, building, seeding with data, and running in development or other environments. In other words, any work that's performed via the CLI and related to the app but that isn't the app itself can be saved to npm scripts. They function as documentation, as well, to show others how building and testing work. You can call other npm scripts from npm scripts, thus simplifying your project further. The following example includes different versions of builds:
>
> ```
> "scripts": {
>   "test": "echo \"Error: no test specified\" && exit 1",
>   "build": "./node_modules/.bin/babel -w",
>   "build:method": " npm run build -- method/jsx/script.jsx -o
>   method/js/script.js",
>   "build:hello-js-world-jsx": "npm run build --
>   hello-js-world-jsx/jsx/script.jsx -o
>   hello-js-world-jsx/js/script.js",
>   "build:hello-world-jsx": "npm run build --
>   hello-world-jsx/jsx/script.jsx -o
>   hello-world-jsx/js/script.js",
>   "build:hello-world-class-jsx": "npm run build --
>   hello-world-class-jsx/jsx/script.jsx -o
>   hello-world-class-jsx/js/script.js"
> },
> ```

(continued)

npm scripts also support `pre` and `post` hooks, which makes them even more versatile. In general, a *hook* is a pattern in which some code is triggered when another event happens. For example, you can create a `learn-react` task along with two tasks that have `pre` and `post` hooks: `prelearn-react` and `postlearn-react`. As you may guess, the `pre` hook will be executed before `learn-react`, and the `post` hook will be executed after `learn-react`. For example, these bash scripts

```
"scripts": {
    "prelearn-react": "echo \"Purchasing React Quickly\"",
    "learn-react": "echo \"Reading React Quickly\" ",
    "postlearn-react": "echo \"Creating my own React app\""
},
```

print the following output, based on the `pre` / `post` order:

```
...
Purchasing React Quickly
...
Reading React Quickly
...
Creating my own React app
```

With `pre` and `post` hooks, npm can easily replace some build steps performed by Webpack, Gulp, or Grunt.

See the documentation at https://docs.npmjs.com/misc/scripts and Keith Cirkel's article "How to Use npm as a Build Tool" (www.keithcirkel.co.uk/how-to-use-npm-as-a-build-tool) for more npm tips, including parameters and arguments. Any functionality that's missing with npm scripts can be implemented from scratch as a Node script. The advantage is that you'll have fewer dependencies on plug-ins for your project.

12.5.2 *Hot module replacement in action*

Go ahead and start WDS with `npm run wds` or `npm run wds-cli`. Then, go to http://localhost:8080 and open the DevTools console. You'll see messages from HMR and WDS, as follows:

```
[HMR] Waiting for update signal from WDS...
[WDS] Hot Module Replacement enabled.
```

Enter some text in the email or comment field, and then change content.jsx. You can modify something in `render()`—for example, change the form text from `Email` to `Your Email`:

```
Your Email: <input ref="emailAddress" className="form-control" type="text"
➥ placeholder="hi@azat.co"/>
```

You'll see some logging:

```
[WDS] App updated. Recompiling...
...
[HMR] App is up to date.
```

Then your changes will appear on the web page, as shown in figure 12.3, along with the text you entered previously. Great—you no longer need to waste time entering test data or navigating deep inside nested UIs! You can spend more time doing important things instead of typing and clicking around the front-end app. Development is faster with HMR!

> **NOTE**   HMR isn't bulletproof. It won't update or fail in some situations. WDS will reload the page (live reload) when that happens. This behavior is controlled by `webpack/hot/dev-server`; another option is to reload manually using `webpack/hot/only-dev-server`.

Webpack is a nice tool to use with React to streamline and enhance your bundling. It's great not only for optimizing code, images, styles, and other assets when you deploy, but also for development, thanks to WDS and HMR.

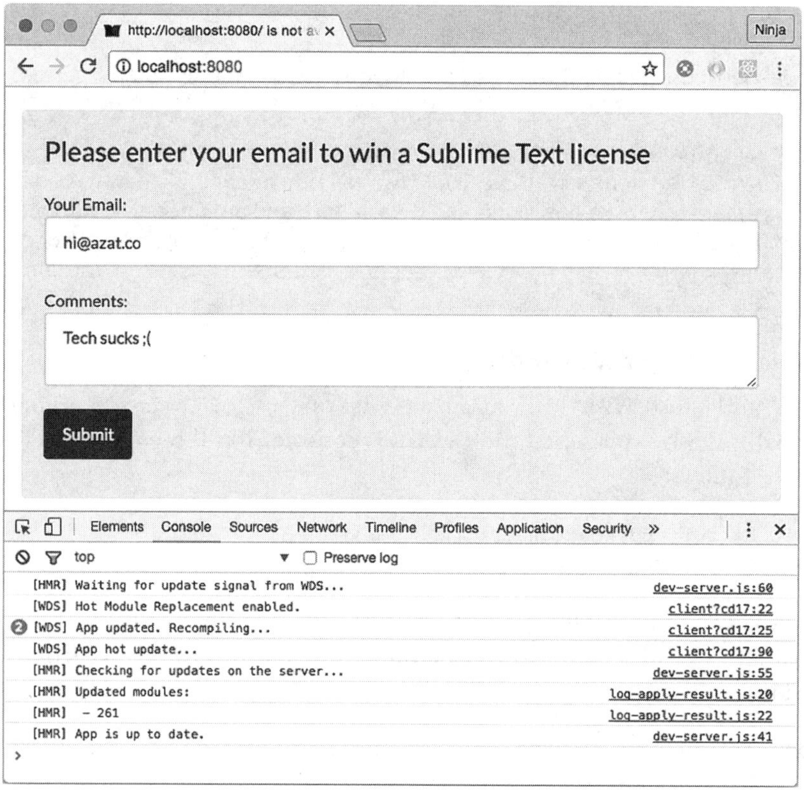

Figure 12.3   HMR updated the view from "Email" to "Your Email" without erasing the data in the fields, as shown in the log.

12.6 Quiz

1 What is the command to run the dev npm script (`"dev": "./node_modules/ .bin/webpack-dev-server --config webpack.dev.config.js"`)? npm dev, npm run dev, NODE_ENV=dev npm run, or npm run development

2 HMR is just a React term for live reloading. True or false?

3 WDS will write compiled files to disk, just like the `webpack` command. True or false?

4 webpack.config.js must be a valid JSON file, just like package.json. True or false?

5 What loaders do you need to use in order to import and then inject CSS into a web page using Webpack?

12.7 Summary

- To make hot module replacement work, you need `webpack-dev-server` and `react-hot-loader` in your config or `module.hot.accept()` in files.

- You can use `require()` to load CSS with `style-loader` and `css-loader`.

- The `--inline --hot` options with CLI commands launch WDS in hot inline mode.

- `devtool: '#sourcemap'` enables proper line numbers for compiled code.

- `publicPath` is a WDS setting that tells WDS where to put the bundle.

12.8 Quiz answers

5 The style loader imports, and the CSS loader injects.

4 False. webpack.config.js is a default Webpack configuration file. It must be a Node.js/JavaScript file with the CommonJS/Node.js module exporting the object literal for configurations (the object can have double quotes, akin to JSON).

3 False. WDS only serves files without writing them to disk.

2 False. HMR can replace live reloading and fall back to it when HMR fails; but HMR is more advanced and offers more benefits, such as updating only parts of your app and preserving the app's state.

1 npm run dev. Only start and test npm scripts can be run without run. All other scripts follow npm run NAME syntax.

Watch this chapter's introduction video by scanning this QR code with your phone or going to http://reactquickly.co/videos/ch13.

React routing

13

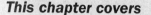

This chapter covers

- Implementing a router from scratch
- Working with React Router
- Routing with Backbone

In the past, in many single-page applications, the URL rarely, if ever, changed as you progressed through the app. There was no reason to go to the server, thanks to browser rendering! Only the content on part of the page changed. This approach had some unfortunate consequences:

- Refreshing your browser took you back to the original form of the page you were reading.
- Clicking the Back button in your browser might take you to a completely different site, because the browser's history function only recorded a single URL for the site you were on. There were no URL changes reflecting your navigation between content.
- You couldn't share a precise page on the site with your friends.
- Search engines couldn't index the site because there were no distinct URLs to index.

Fortunately, today we have *browser URL routing*. URL routing lets you configure an application to accept request URLs that don't map to physical files. Instead, you can define URLs that are semantically meaningful to users, that can help with search-engine optimization (SEO), and that can reflect your application's state. For example, a URL for a page that displays product information might be

```
https://www.manning.com/books/react-quickly
```

This is neatly mapped behind the scenes to a single page that displays the product with ID `react-quickly`. As you browse various products, the URL can change, and both the browser and search engines will be able to interact with the product pages as you'd expect. If you want to avoid complete page reloads, you can use a hash (#) in your URLs, as these well-known sites do:

```
https://mail.google.com/mail/u/0/#inbox
https://en.todoist.com/app?v=816#agenda%2Foverdue%2C%20today
https://calendar.google.com/calendar/render?tab=mc#main_7
```

URL routing is a requirement for a user-friendly, well-designed web app. Without specific URLs, users can't save or share links without losing the state of the application, be it a single-page application (SPA) or a traditional web app with server rendering.

In this chapter, you'll build a simple React website and learn about a couple of different options for implementing routing within it. I'll introduce the React Router library later in the chapter; first, let's build some simple routing from scratch.

> **NOTE** The source code for the examples in this chapter is at www.manning
> .com/books/react-quickly and https://github.com/azat-co/react-quickly/
> tree/master/ch13 (in the ch13 folder of the GitHub repository https://
> github.com/azat-co/react-quickly). You can also find some demos at http://
> reactquickly.co/demos.

13.1 *Implementing a router from scratch*

Although there are existing libraries that implement routing for React, let's start by implementing a simple router to see how easy it is. This project will also help you understand how other routers work under the hood.

The end goal of this project is to have three pages that change along with the URL when you navigate around. You'll use hash URLs (#) to keep things simple; non-hash URLs require a special server configuration. These are the pages you'll create:

- *Home*—/ (empty URL path)
- *Accounts*—/#accounts
- *Profile*—/#profile

Figure 13.1 shows the navigation from the home page to the Profile page.

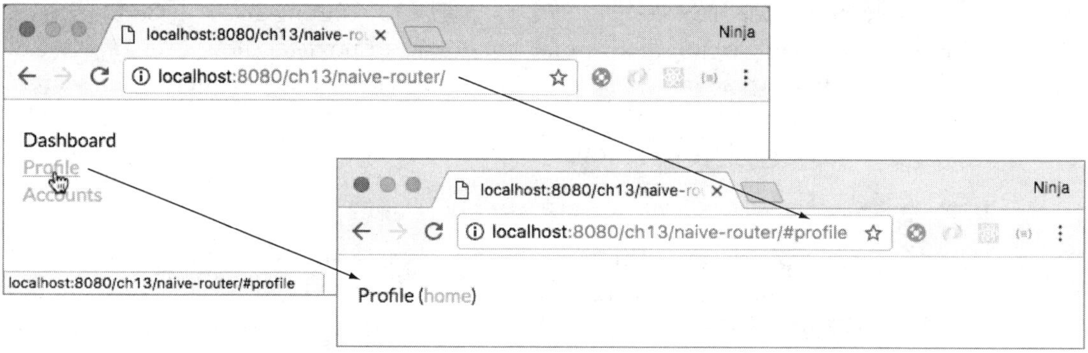

Figure 13.1   Navigating from the home page to the Profile page and changing the URL by clicking a link

To implement this project, which will demonstrate and use a URL router, you'll create a router component (router.jsx), a mapping, and an HTML page. The router component will take information from the URL and update the web page accordingly. The implementation of the project breaks down into these steps:

1. Write the *mapping* between the URL entered and the resource to be shown (React elements or components). Mapping is app-specific, and a *different* mapping will be needed for each new project.

2. Write the *router* library from scratch. It will access the requested URL and check the URL against the mapping (step 1). The router library will be a single `Router` component in router.jsx. This `Router` can be reused without modifications in various projects.

3. Write the *example app*, which will use the `Router` component from step 2 and the mapping from step 1.

You'll use JSX to create React elements for the markup. Obviously, `Router` doesn't have to be a React component; it can be a regular function or a class. But using a React component reinforces concepts you've learned about in this book, such as event lifecycles and taking advantage of React's rendering and handling of the DOM. In addition, your implementation will be closer to the React Router implementation, which will help you understand React Router better when we discuss it later.

13.1.1 *Setting up the project*

The structure of the project (which you can call a *simple* or *naive* router) is as follows:

```
/naive-router
  /css
    bootstrap.css
    main.css
  /js
    bundle.js
  /jsx
    app.jsx
```

```
   router.jsx
/node_modules
index.html
package.json
webpack.config.js
```

You'll begin by installing dependencies. I put them in package.json; you can copy the dependencies as well as the `babel` config and `scripts`, and run `npm install` (ch13/naive-router/package.json).

Listing 13.1 Setting up the dev environment

```
{
  "name": "naive-router",
  "version": "1.0.0",
  "description": "",
  "main": "index.js",
  "scripts": {
    "test": "echo \"Error: no test specified\" && exit 1",
    "build": "./node_modules/.bin/webpack -w"
  },
  "author": "Azat Mardan",
  "license": "MIT",
  "babel": {
    "presets": [
      "react"
    ]
  },
  "devDependencies": {
    "babel-core": "6.18.2",
    "babel-loader": "6.2.4",
    "babel-preset-react": "6.5.0",
    "webpack": "2.4.1"
    "react": "15.5.4",
    "react-dom": "15.5.4"
  },
  "dependencies": {
  }
}
```

Saves the Webpack build script as an npm script for convenience

Tells Babel what presets to use (React for JSX in this case; ES6+ is optional)

Installs Webpack v2.4.1 locally (recommended)

This isn't all. Webpack needs its own configuration file, webpack.config.js (as explained in chapter 9). The key is to configure the source (`entry`) and the desired destination (`output`). You also need to provide the loader.

Listing 13.2 webpack.config.js

Defines a filename for the bundled file that you'll use in index.html

Defines the file to start bundling (typically the main file that loads other files)

```
module.exports = {
  entry: './jsx/app.jsx',
  output: {
    path: __dirname + '/js/',
    filename: 'bundle.js'
  },
```

Defines a path for the bundled files

```
        module: {
          loaders: [
            {
              test: /\.jsx?$/,
              exclude: /(node_modules)/,
              loader: 'babel-loader'
            }
          ]
        }
      }
```

Specifies the loader that will perform JSX transformation (and ES6+ if needed)

13.1.2 Creating the route mapping in app.jsx

First, you'll create a mapping with a mapping object, where the keys are URL fragments and the values are the content of the individual pages. A *mapping* takes a value and ties/connects it to another value. In this case, the key (URL fragment) will map to JSX. You could create a separate file for each page, but for now let's keep them all in app.jsx.

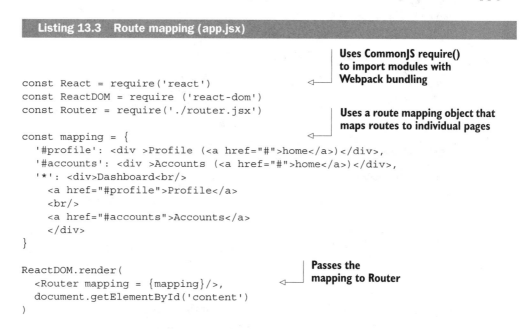

Listing 13.3   Route mapping (app.jsx)

```
const React = require('react')
const ReactDOM = require ('react-dom')
const Router = require('./router.jsx')

const mapping = {
  '#profile': <div >Profile (<a href="#">home</a>)</div>,
  '#accounts': <div >Accounts (<a href="#">home</a>)</div>,
  '*': <div>Dashboard<br/>
    <a href="#profile">Profile</a>
    <br/>
    <a href="#accounts">Accounts</a>
    </div>
}

ReactDOM.render(
  <Router mapping = {mapping}/>,
  document.getElementById('content')
)
```

Uses CommonJS require() to import modules with Webpack bundling

Uses a route mapping object that maps routes to individual pages

Passes the mapping to Router

Next, you'll implement Router in router.jsx.

13.1.3 Creating the Router component in router.jsx

In a nutshell, Router needs to take information from the URL (#profile) and map it to JSX using the mapping property provided to it. You can access the URL from the window.location.hash of the browser API:

```
const React = require('react')
module.exports = class Router extends React.Component {
  constructor(props) {
```

```
      super(props)
      this.state = {hash: window.location.hash}
      this.updateHash = this.updateHash.bind(this)
   }
   render() {
      ...
   }
}
```

Next, you need to listen for any URL changes with hashchange. If you don't implement listening to new URLs, then your router will work only once: when the entire page reloads and the Router element is created. The best places to attach and remove listeners for hashchange are the componentDidMount() and componentWillUnmount() lifecycle event listeners:

```
updateHash(event) {
   this.setState({hash: window.location.hash})
}
componentDidMount() {
   window.addEventListener('hashchange', this.updateHash, false)
}
componentWillUnmount() {
   window.removeEventListener('hashchange', this.updateHash, false)
}
```

> ### componentDidMount() and componentWillUnmount()
>
> Chapter 5 discusses lifecycle events, but here's a refresher. componentDidMount() is fired when an element is mounted and appears in the real DOM node (you can say that an element has a real DOM node). For this reason, this is the safest place to attach events that integrate with other DOM objects, and also to make AJAX/XHR calls (not used here).
>
> On the other hand, componentWillUnmount() is the best place to remove event listeners; your element will be unmounted, and you need to remove whatever you created outside of this element (such as an event listener on window). Leaving a lot of event listeners hanging around without the elements that created and used them is a bad practice: it leads to performance issues such as memory leaks.

In render(), you use if/else to see whether there's a match with the current URL value (this.state.hash) and the keys/attributes/properties in the mapping property. If so, you access mapping again to get the content of the individual page (JSX). If not, you fall back to * for all other URLs, including the empty value (home page). Here's the complete code (ch13/naive-router/jsx/router.jsx).

Listing 13.4   Implementing a URL router

```
const React = require('react')
module.exports = class Router extends React.Component {
   constructor(props) {
```

```
    super(props)
    this.state = {hash: window.location.hash}          Assigns an initial
    this.updateHash = this.updateHash.bind(this)       URL hash value
  }
  updateHash(event) {
    this.setState({hash: window.location.hash})
  }
  componentDidMount() {                                 Feeds new URL hash values
    window.addEventListener('hashchange', this.updateHash, false)
  }
  componentWillUnmount() {
    window.removeEventListener('hashchange', this.updateHash, false)
  }
  render() {
    if (this.props.mapping[this.state.hash])
      return this.props.mapping[this.state.hash]        Renders the content
    else                                                corresponding to the
      return this.props.mapping['*']                    URL hash
  }
}
```

Finally, in index.html, you include the CSS file and bundle.js that Webpack will produce when you run npm run build (which in turn runs ./node_modules/.bin/webpack -w):

```
<!DOCTYPE html>
<html>

  <head>
    <link href="css/bootstrap.css" type="text/css" rel="stylesheet"/>
    <link href="css/main.css" type="text/css" rel="stylesheet"/>
  </head>

  <body>
    <div id="content" class="container"></div>
    <script src="js/bundle.js"></script>
  </body>

</html>
```

Run the bundler to get bundle.js, and open the web page in a browser. Clicking the links changes the URL as well as the content of the page, as shown earlier in figure 13.1.

As you can see, building your own router with React is straightforward; you can use lifecycle methods to listen for changes in the hash and render the appropriate content. But although this is a viable option, things become more complex if you need nested routes, use route parsing (extracting URL parameters), or use "nice" URLs without #. You could use a router from Backbone or another front-end, MVC-like framework, but there's a solution designed for React specifically (hint: it uses JSX).

13.2 React Router

React is amazing at building UIs. If I haven't convinced you yet, go back and reread the previous chapters! It can also be used to implement simple URL routing from scratch, as you've seen with router.jsx.

But for more-sophisticated SPAs, you'll need more features. For instance, passing a URL parameter is a common feature to signify an individual item rather than a list of items: for example, `/posts/57b0ed12fa81dea5362e5e98`, where `57b0ed12-fa81dea5362e5e98` is a unique post ID. You could extract this URL parameter using a regular expression; but sooner or later, if your application grows in complexity, you may find yourself reinventing existing implementations for front-end URL routing.

Semantic URLs

Semantic or *nice* URLS (https://en.wikipedia.org/wiki/Semantic_URL) are aimed at improving the usability and accessibility of a website or web app by decoupling the internal implementation from the UI. A non-semantic approach might use query strings and/or script filenames. On the other hand, the semantic way embraces using the path only in a manner that helps users interpret the structure and manipulate the URLs. Here are some examples:

Non-semantic (okay)	Semantic (better)
http://webapplog.com/show?post=es6	http://webapplog.com/es6
https://www.manning.com/books/react-quickly?a_aid=a&a_bid=5064a2d3	https://www.manning.com/books/react-quickly/a/5064a2d3
http://en.wikipedia.org/w/index.php?title=Semantic_URL	https://en.wikipedia.org/wiki/Semantic_URL

Major frameworks such as Ember, Backbone, and Angular have routing built in to them. When it comes to routing and React, React Router (`react-router`; https://github.com/reactjs/react-router) is a ready-to-go, off-the-shelf solution. Section 13.4 covers a Backbone implementation and illustrates how nicely React plays with this MVC-like framework that many people use for SPAs. Right now, let's focus on React Router.

React Router isn't part of the official React core library. It came from the community, but it's mature and popular enough that a third of React projects use it.[1] It's a default option for most React engineers I've talked to.

The syntax of React Router uses JSX, which is another plus because it allows you to create more-readable hierarchical definitions than you can with a mapping object (as you saw in the previous project). Like the naive Router implementation, React Router has a `Router` React component (React Router inspired my implementation!). Here are the steps you'll follow:

1 Create a mapping in which URLs will translate into React components (which turn into markup on a web page). In React Router, this is achieved by passing the `path` and `component` properties as well as nesting `Route`. The mapping is done in JSX by declaring and nesting `Route` components. You must implement this part for each new project.

---

[1] React.js Conf 2015, "React Router Increases Your Productivity," https://youtube.com/watch?v=XZfvW1a8Xac.

2   Use the React Router's `Router` and `Route` components, which perform the magic of changing views according to changes in URLs. Obviously, you won't implement this part, but you'll need to install the library.

3   Render `Router` on a web page by mounting it with `ReactDOM.render()` like a regular React element. Needless to say, this part must be implemented for each new project.

You'll use JSX to create a `Route` for each page, and nest them either in another `Route` or in `Router`. The `Router` object goes in the `ReactDOM.render()` function, like any other React element:

```
ReactDOM.render((
  <Router ...>
    <Route ...>
      <Route ../>
      ...
    </Route>
    <Route .../>
  </Router>
), document.getElementById('content'))
```

Each `Route` has at least two properties: `path`, which is the URL pattern to match to trigger this route; and `component`, which fetches and renders the necessary component. You can have more properties for a `Route`, such as event handlers and data. They'll be accessible in `props.route` in that `Route` component. This is how you pass data to route components.

To illustrate, let's consider an example of an SPA with routing to a few pages: About, Posts (like a blog), an individual Post, Contact Us, and Login. They have different paths and render from different components:

- *About*—/about
- *Posts*—/posts
- *Post*—/post
- *Contact*—/contact

The About, Posts, Post, and Contact Us pages will use the same layout (`Content` component) and render inside it. Here's the initial React Router code (not the complete, final version):

```
<Router>
  <Route path="/" component={Content} >
    <Route path="/about" component={About} />
      <Route path="/about/company" .../>
      <Route path="/about/author" .../>
    <Route path="/posts" component={Posts} />
    <Route path="/posts/:id" component={Post}/>
    <Route path="/contact" component={Contact} />
  </Route>
</Router>
```

Interestingly, you can nest routes to reuse layouts from parents, and their URLs can be independent of nesting. For instance, it's possible to have a nested About component with the /about URL, even though the "parent" layout route Content uses /app. About will still have the Content layout (implemented by this.props.children in Content):

```
<Router>
  <Route path="/app" component={Content} >
    <Route path="/about" component={About} />
    . . .
```

In other words, About doesn't need the nested URL /app/about unless you want it to be this way. This gives you more flexibility in terms of paths and layouts.

To navigate, you'll implement a menu as shown in figure 13.2. The menu and the header will be rendered from Content and reused on the About, Posts, Post, and Contact Us pages. In the figure, several things are happening: the About page is rendered,

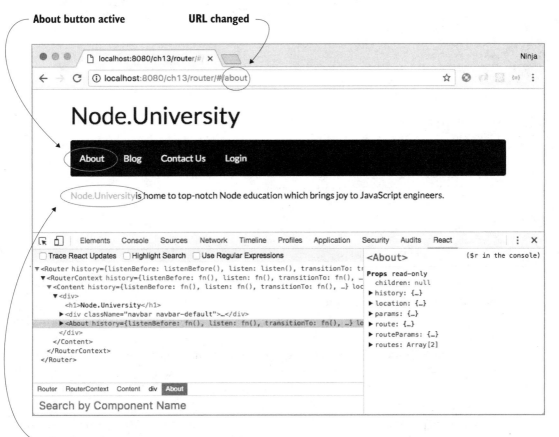

Figure 13.2   Navigating to /about renders the About text in the Content component, changes the URL, and makes the button active.

the menu button is active, the URL reflects that you're on the About page by showing you /#/about, and the text Node.University reflects what's in the About component (you'll see it later).

13.2.1 *React Router's JSX style*

As I mentioned earlier, you'll use JSX to create the Router element and Route elements nested within it (and each other). Each element (Router or Route) has at least two properties, path and component, that tell the router the URL path and the React component class to create and render. It's possible to have additional custom properties/ attributes to pass data; you'll use that approach to pass a posts array.

Let's put your knowledge to work by importing the React Router objects and using them in ReactDOM.render() to define the routing behavior (ch13/router/jsx/app.jsx). In addition to About, Posts, Post, and Contact Us, you'll create a Login page.

> **Listing 13.5 Defining Router**

```
const ReactRouter = require('react-router')
let { Router,
  Route,
  Link
} = ReactRouter

ReactDOM.render((
  <Router history={hashHistory}>
    <Route path="/" component={Content} >
      <Route path="/about" component={About} />
      <Route path="/posts" component={Posts} posts={posts}/>
      <Route path="/posts/:id" component={Post}  posts={posts}/>
      <Route path="/contact" component={Contact} />
    </Route>
    <Route path="/login" component={Login}/>
  </Router>
), document.getElementById('content'))
```

This last route, Login (/login, shown in figure 13.3), lives outside of the Content route and doesn't have the menu (which is in Content). Anything that doesn't need the common interface provided in Content can be left out of the Content route. This behavior is determined by the hierarchy of the nested routes.

The Post component renders blog post information based on the post *slug* (part of the URL—think ID), which it gets from the URL (for example, /posts/http2) via the props.params.id variable. By using a special syntax with a colon in the path, you tell the router to parse that value and populate it into props.params.

Router is passed to the ReactDOM.render() method. Notice that you pass history to Router. Starting with version 2 of React Router, you must supply a history implementation. You have two choices: bundling with the React Router history or using a standalone history implementation.

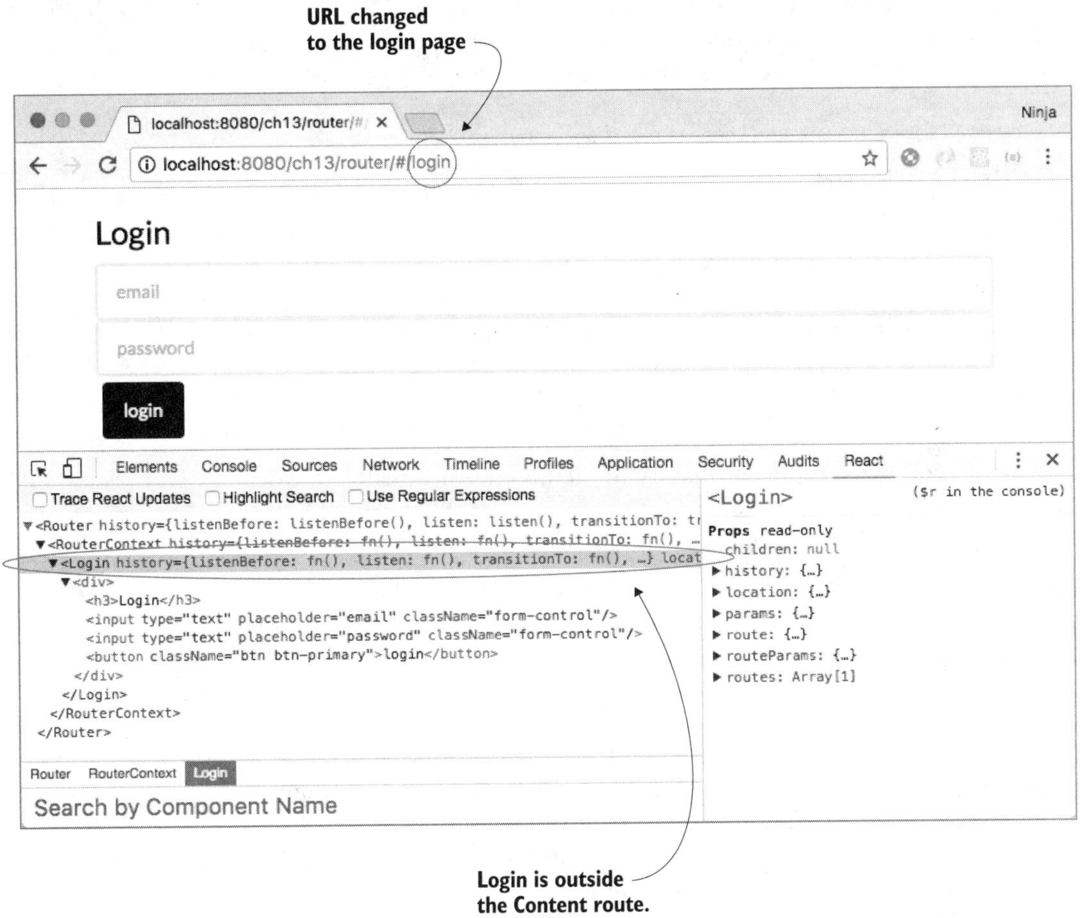

Figure 13.3 The Login page (/#/login) doesn't use the common layout (`Content`) that includes a menu. There's only a Login element.

13.2.2 Hash history

The hash history, as you can probably guess, relies on the hash symbol #, which is how you navigate on the page without reloading it; for example, router/#/posts/http2. Most SPAs use hashes because they need to reflect changes in context within the app without causing a complete refresh (request to the server). You did this when you implemented a router from scratch.

> **NOTE** The proper term for a hash is *fragment identifier* (https://en.wikipedia .org/wiki/Fragment_identifier).

In this example, you'll also uses hashes, which come standalone from the `history` library (http://npmjs.org/history). You'll import the library, initialize it, and pass it to React Router.

You need to set `queryKey` to `false` when you initialize `history`, because you want to disable the pesky query string (for example, `?_k=vl8reh`) that's there by default to support older browsers and transfer states when navigating:

```
const ReactRouter = require('react-router')
const History = require('history')
let hashHistory = ReactRouter.useRouterHistory(History.createHashHistory)({
  queryKey: false
})
<Router history={hashHistory}/>
```

To use a bundled hash history, import it from React Router like this:

```
const { hashHistory } = require('react-router')
<Router history={hashHistory} />
```

You can use a different history implementation with React Router if you prefer. Old browsers love hash history, but that means you'll see the # hashtag. If you need URLs without hash signs, you can do that, too. You just need to switch to the browser history and implement some server modifications, which are simple if you use Node as your HTTP server back end. To keep this project simple, you'll use hash history, but we'll go over the browser history briefly.

13.2.3   *Browser history*

An alternative to hash history is the browser HTML5 `pushState` history. For example, a browser history URL might be router/posts/http2 rather than router/#/posts/http2. Browser history URLs are also called *real URLs*.

Browser history uses regular, unfragmented URLs, so each request triggers a server request. That's why this approach requires some server-side configuration that I won't cover here. Typically, SPAs should use fragmented/hash URLs, especially if you need to support older browsers, because browser history requires a more complex implementation.

You can use browser history in a way similar to hash history. You import the module, plug it in, and finally configure the server to serve the same file (not the file from your SPA's routing).

Browser implementations come from a standalone custom package (like `history`) or from the implementation in React Router (`ReactRouter.browserHistory`). After you import the browser history library, apply it to `Router`:

```
const { browserHistory } = require('react-router')
<Router history={browserHistory} />
```

Next, you need to modify the server to respond with the same file no matter what the URL is. This example is just one possible implementation; it uses Node.js and Express:

```
const express = require('express')
const path = require('path')
const port = process.env.PORT || 8080
const app = express()


app.use(express.static(__dirname + '/public'))

app.get('*', function (request, response){
  response.sendFile(path.resolve(__dirname, 'public', 'index.html'))
})

app.listen(port)
console.log("server started on port " + port)
```

The reason for the required server-side behavior of the HTTP server is that once you switch to real URLs without the hash sign, they'll start hitting the HTTP server. The server needs to serve the same SPA JavaScript code to every request. For example, requests to /posts/57b0ed12fa81dea5362e5e98 and /about should resolve in index.html, not posts/57b0ed12fa81dea5362e5e98.html or about.html (which will probably result in 404: Not Found).

Because hash history is the preferred way to implement URL routing when support for older browsers is needed, and to keep this example simple without having to implement the back-end server, we'll use hash history in this chapter.

13.2.4 *React Router development setup with Webpack*

When you're working with React Router, there are libraries you need to use and import as well as the JSX compilation to run. Let's look at the development setup for React Router using Webpack, which will perform these tasks.

The following listing shows devDependencies from package.json (ch13/router/package.json). Most of this should be familiar to you already. New packages include history and react-router. As always, make sure you're using the exact versions shown; otherwise, you can't be sure the code will run.

> **Listing 13.6 Dependencies to use Webpack v1, React Router v2.6, React v15.2, and JSX**

```
{
  ...
  "devDependencies": {
    "babel-core": "6.11.4",
    "babel-loader": "6.2.4",
    "babel-preset-react": "6.5.0",
    "history": "2.1.2",
    "react": "15.2.1",
    "react-dom": "15.2.1",
    "react-router": "2.6.0",
    "webpack": "1.12.9"
  }
}
```

In addition to devDependencies, package.json must have a babel configuration. I also recommend adding npm scripts:

```
{
  ...
  "scripts": {
    "test": "echo \"Error: no test specified\" && exit 1",
    "build": "./node_modules/.bin/webpack -w",
    "i": "rm -rf ./node_modules && npm cache clean && npm install"
  },
  "babel": {
    "presets": [
      "react"
    ]
  },
  ...
}
```

Note that because the JSX will be converted to React.createClass(), you'll need to import and define React in files that use JSX even when they don't use React. To illustrate, in listing 13.7, it looks as though the About component (which is stateless—that is, a function) doesn't use React. But when this code is transpiled, it will use React in the form of React.createElement() calls. In chapters 1 and 2, React was defined as a global window.React; but with a modular, nonglobal approach, it isn't. Hence, you need to define React explicitly (ch13/router/jsx/about.jsx).

Listing 13.7   Defining React explicitly

```
const React = require('react')

module.exports = function About() {
  return <div>
    <a href="http://Node.University" target="_blank">Node.University</a>
      is home to top-notch Node education which brings joy to JavaScript
      ➥ engineers.
  </div>
}
```

The rest of the files and the project as whole will use this structure:

```
/router
  /css
    bootstrap.css
    main.css                     Bundled (concatenated)
  /js                            file and its source map,
    bundle.js            ◁────┘  for better debugging
    bundle.js.map
  /jsx
    about.jsx
    app.jsx
    contact.jsx
    content.jsx
```

```
        login.jsx
        post.jsx
        posts.jsx
  /node_modules
        index.html
        package.json                    Data for blog posts, such
        posts.js                        as URLs, titles, and text
        webpack.config.js
```

The index.html file is bare-bones because it includes only the bundled file.

Listing 13.8   index.html

```html
<!DOCTYPE html>
<html>

  <head>
    <link href="css/bootstrap.css" type="text/css" rel="stylesheet"/>
    <link href="css/main.css" type="text/css" rel="stylesheet"/>
  </head>

  <body>
    <div id="content" class="container"></div>
    <script src="js/bundle.js"></script>
  </body>

</html>
```

webpack.config.js needs to have at least an entry-point app.jsx, babel-loader, and source maps (ch13/router/webpack.config.js).

Listing 13.9   Configuring Webpack

```js
module.exports = {
  entry: './jsx/app.jsx',
  output: {
    path: __dirname + '/js/',              Sets the devtool value to see the
    filename: 'bundle.js'                  proper mapping to your JSX source
  },                                       code, not the transpiled one
  devtool: '#sourcemap',
  stats: {
   colors: true,
   reasons: true
  },
  module: {
    loaders: [
      {
        test: /\.jsx?$/,
        exclude: /(node_modules)/,
        loader: 'babel-loader'
      }
    ]
  }
}
```

Next, let's implement the Content layout component.

13.2.5 *Creating a layout component*

The Content component, which is defined as a parent Route, will serve as a layout for the About, Posts, Post, and Contact components. Figure 13.4 shows how it's implemented.

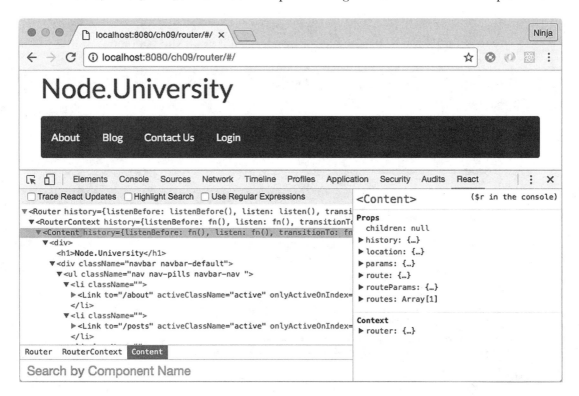

Figure 13.4   The Content component as the Home page (no children)

First, you'll import React and Link from React Router. The latter is a special component to render navigation links. Link is a special wrapper for <a>; it has some magic attributes that the normal anchor tag doesn't, such as activeClassName="active", which adds the active class when this route is active.

The Content component's structure looks something like this, with the omission of a few pieces (the complete code is shown later):

```
const React = require('react')
const {Link} = require('react-router')

class Content extends React.Component {
  render() {
    return (
      <div>
```

```
        ...
      </div>
    )
  }
}
...
module.exports = Content
```

In `render()`, you use the amazing Twitter Bootstrap UI library (http://getbootstrap
.com) to declare the menu with the proper classes. The menu can be created using
ready-made CSS classes, such as these:

```
<div className="navbar navbar-default">
  <ul className="nav nav-pills navbar-nav ">
    <li ...>
      <Link to="/about" activeClassName="active">
        About
      </Link>
    </li>
    <li ...>
      <Link to="/posts" activeClassName="active">
        Blog
      </Link>
    </li>
    ...
  </ul>
</div>
```

You'll access the `isActive()` method, which returns true or false. This way, an active
menu link will be visually different from other links:

```
<li className={(this.context.router.isActive('/about'))? 'active': ''}>
  <Link to="/about" activeClassName="active">
    About
  </Link>
</li>
```

Notice the `activeClassName` attribute of `Link`. When you set this attribute to a value,
`Link` will apply the class to an active element (the selected link). But you need to set
the style on `<li>`, not just on `Link`. That's why you also access `router.isActive()`.

After you're finished with the `Content` class definition (full implementation shown
shortly), you define a static field/attribute `contextTypes` that enables the use of
`this.context.router`. If you're using ES2017+/ES8+,[2] you may have support for static
fields, but that's not the case in ES2015/ES6 or ES2016/ES7. They don't have this feature. The ES2017/ES8 standard isn't final yet, but as of this writing it doesn't have this

---

[2] Learn more about ES2016/ES7 and ES2017/ES8 features at https://node.university/blog/498412/es7-es8
and https://node.university/p/es7-es8.

feature either. Be sure to check the current list of finished proposals/features,[3] or consider using ES Next (collection of stage 0 proposals).

This static attribute will be used by React Router such that if it's required, React Router populates `this.context` (from which you can access `router.isActive()` and other methods):

```
Content.contextTypes = {
  router: React.PropTypes.object.isRequired
}
```

Having `contextType` and `router` set to required gives you access to `this.context .router.isActive('/about')`, which in turn will tell you when this particular route is active.

Phew! Here's the full implementation of the `Content` layout.

Listing 13.10   Complete `Content` component

```
const React = require('react')
const {Link} = require('react-router')

class Content extends React.Component {
  render() {
    return (
      <div>
        <h1>Node.University</h1>
        <div className="navbar navbar-default">
          <ul className="nav nav-pills navbar-nav ">
            <li className={(this.context.router.isActive('/about'))?
            ➥ 'active': ''}>                                            ⟵─┐  Accesses Router and
              <Link to="/about" activeClassName="active">                     its method to check
                About                                                         the active route
              </Link>
            </li>
            <li className={(this.context.router.isActive('/posts'))?
            ➥ 'active': ''}>
              <Link to="/posts" activeClassName="active">
                Blog
              </Link>
            </li>
            <li className={(this.context.router.isActive('/contact'))?
            ➥ 'active': ''}>
              <Link to="/contact" activeClassName="active">
                Contact Us
              </Link>
            </li>
            <li>                                                       Uses Link to create
              <Link to="/login" activeClassName="active">         ⟵─┘  a navigation link
```

---

[3] For the current list of stage 0–3 and finished proposals, see the TC39 documents on GitHub: https://github.com/tc39/proposals/blob/master/README.md and https://github.com/tc39/proposals/blob/master/finished-proposals.md.

```
          Login
        </Link>
      </li>
    </ul>
  </div>
  {this.props.children}
  </div>
 )
 }
}
Content.contextTypes = {
  router: React.PropTypes.object.isRequired
}
module.exports = Content
```

Renders child routes (defined in app.jsx)

Defines that this component needs a router object in the context

The `children` statement enables you to reuse the menu on every subroute (route nested in the / route), such as /posts, /post, /about, and /contact:

```
{this.props.children}
```

Let's look at another way to access a router in an individual route, other than using `contextTypes`.

13.3 React Router features

To learn more about React Router's features and patterns, let's look at another way to access a router from child components and how to navigate programmatically within those components. And, of course, the chapter wouldn't be complete if I didn't cover how to parse URL parameters and pass data.

13.3.1 Accessing router with the withRouter higher-order component

Using `router` allows you to navigate programmatically and access the current route, among other things. It's good to include access to `router` in your components.

You've seen how to access `router` from `this.context.router` by setting the static class attribute `contextTypes`:

```
Content.contextTypes = {
  router: React.PropTypes.object.isRequired
}
```

In a way, you're using the validation mechanism to define the API; that is, the component must have the router. The `Content` component used this approach.

But `context` depends on React's context, which is an experimental approach; its use is discouraged by the React team. Fortunately, there's another way (some might argue it's simpler and better; see http://mng.bz/Xhb9): `withRouter`.

`withRouter` is a higher-order component (HOC; more about these in chapter 8) that takes a component as an argument, injects `router`, and returns another HOC. For example, you can inject `router` into `Contact` like this:

```
const {withRouter} = require('react-router')
...
<Router ...>
  ...
  <Route path="/contact" component={withRouter(Contact)} />
</Router>
```

When you look at the Contact component implementation (a function), the router object is accessible from the properties (argument object to the function):

```
const React = require('react')

module.exports = function Contact(props) {
  // props.router - GOOD!
  return <div>
    ...
  </div>
}
```

The advantage of withRouter is that it works with regular, stateful React classes as well as with stateless functions.

> **NOTE** Even though there's no direct (visible) use of React, you must require React because this code will be converted to code with React.create-Element() statements that depend on the React object. For more information, see chapter 3.

13.3.2 *Navigating programmatically*

A popular use of router is to navigate programmatically: changing the URL (location) from within your code based on logic, not user actions. To demonstrate, suppose you have an app in which the user types a message on a contact form and then submits the form. Based on the server response, the app navigates to an Error page, a Thank-you page, or an About page.

Once you have router, you can navigate programmatically if you need to by calling router.push(URL), where URL must be a defined route path. For instance, you can navigate to About from Contact after 1 second.

Listing 13.11 Calling `router.push()` to navigate

```
const React = require('react')

module.exports = function Contact(props) {                    Navigates away
  setTimeout(()=>{props.router.push('about')}, 1000)    ◄──   after 1 second
  return <div>
    <h3>Contact Us</h3>
    <input type="text" placeholder="your email" className="form-control"
    ➥ ></input>
    <textarea type="text" placeholder="your message" className="form-control">
    ➥ </textarea>
    <button className="btn btn-primary">send</button>
  </div>
}
```

Navigating programmatically is an important feature because it lets you change the state of the application. Let's see how you access URL parameters such as a post ID.

13.3.3 URL parameters and other route data

As you've seen, having contextTypes and router will give you the this.context .router object. It's an instance of <Router/> defined in app.jsx, and it can be used to navigate, get the active path, and so on. On the other hand, there's other interesting information in this.props, and you don't need a static attribute to access it:

- history (deprecated in v2.x; you can use context.router)
- location
- params
- route
- routeParams
- routes

The this.props.location and this.props.params objects contain data about the current route, such as path name, URL parameters (names defined with a colon [:]), and so on.

Let's use params.id in post.jsx for the Post component in Array.find() to find the post corresponding to a URL path such as router/#/posts/http2 (ch13/router/ jsx/post.jsx).

Listing 13.12 Rendering post data

```
const React = require('react')

module.exports = function Product(props) {
  let post = props.route.posts.find(element=>element.slug ==
  props.params.id)                          Finds a post by
  return (                                  its slug property
    <div>
      <h3>{post.title}</h3>
      <p>{post.text}</p>
      <p><a href={post.link} target="_blank">Continue reading...</a></p>
    </div>
  )
}
```

When you navigate to the Posts page (see figure 13.5), there's a list of posts. As a reminder, the route definition is as follows:

```
<Route path="/posts" component={Posts} posts={posts}/>
```

Clicking a post navigates to #/posts/ID. That page reuses the layout of the Content component.

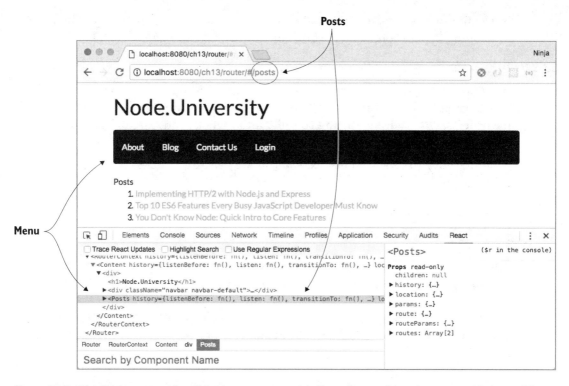

Figure 13.5   The Posts page renders the `Posts` component in the `Content` (menu) component because it's defined as a child route of `Content` in app.jsx.

Now, let's move on and work with data.

13.3.4 Passing properties in React Router

You often need to pass data to nested routes, and it's easy to do. In the example, `Posts` needs to get data about posts. In listing 13.13, `Posts` accesses a property passed to you in `<Route/>` in app.jsx: posts, from the posts.js file. It's possible to pass any data to a route as an attribute; for example, `<Route path="/posts" component={Posts} posts={posts}/>`. You can then access the data in props.route; for example, props.route.posts is a list of posts.

Listing 13.13   `Posts` implementation with data from `props.route`

```
const {Link} = require('react-router')
const React = require('react')

module.exports = function Posts(props) {
  return <div>Posts
    <ol>
    {props.route.posts.map((post, index)=>
      <li key={post.slug}><Link
```

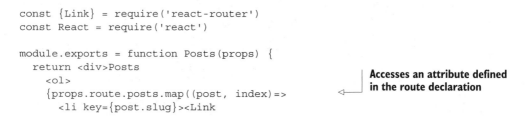

Accesses an attribute defined
in the route declaration

```
      ⮕ to={`/posts/${post.slug}`} >{post.title}</Link></li>
    )}
    </ol>
  </div>
}
```

Of course, the value of this data can be a function. That way, you can pass event handlers to stateless components and implement them only in the main component, such as app.jsx.

You're finished with all the major parts and ready to launch this project! You can do so by running an npm script (`npm run build`) or using `./node_modules/.bin/webpack -w` directly. Wait for the build to finish, and you'll see something like this:

```
> router@1.0.0 build /Users/azat/Documents/Code/react-quickly/ch13/router
> webpack -w

Hash: 07dc6eca0c3210dec8aa
Version: webpack 1.12.9
Time: 2596ms
        Asset      Size  Chunks            Chunk Names
    bundle.js    976 kB       0  [emitted]  main
bundle.js.map   1.14 MB       0  [emitted]  main
    + 264 hidden modules
```

In a new window, open your favorite static server (I use node-static, but you can create your own using Express), and navigate to the location in your browser. Try going to / and /#/about; the exact URL will depend on whether you're running your static server from the same folder or a parent folder.

> **NOTE** The full source code for this example isn't included here, for space reasons. If you want to play with it or use it as boilerplate, or if you found the preceding snippets confusing when taken out of context, you can find the complete code at www.manning.com/books/react-quickly or https://github .com/azat-co/react-quickly/tree/master/ch13/router.

13.4 *Routing with Backbone*

When you need routing for a single-page application, it's straightforward to use React with other routing or MVC-like libraries. For example, Backbone is one of the most popular front-end frameworks that has front-end URL routing built in. Let's look at how you can easily use the Backbone router to render React components by doing the following:

- Defining a router class with the routes object as a mapping from URL fragments to functions
- Rendering React elements in the methods/functions of the Backbone Router class
- Instantiating and starting the Backbone the Router object

This is the project structure:

```
/backbone-router
  /css
    bootstrap.css
    main.css
  /js
    bundle.js
    bundle.map.js
  /jsx
    about.jsx
    app.jsx
    contact.jsx
    content.jsx
    login.jsx
    post.jsx
    posts.jsx
  /node_modules
    ...
  index.html
  package.json
  posts.js
  webpack.config.js
```

package.json includes Backbone v1.3.3 in addition to the usual suspects, such as Webpack v2.4.1, React v15.5.4, and Babel v6.11:

```
{
  "name": "backbone-router",
  "version": "1.0.0",
  "description": "",
  "main": "index.js",
  "scripts": {
    "test": "echo \"Error: no test specified\" && exit 1",
    "build": "./node_modules/.bin/webpack -w",
    "i": "rm -rf ./node_modules && npm cache clean && npm install"
  },
  "author": "Azat Mardan",
  "license": "MIT",
  "babel": {
    "presets": [
      "react"
    ]
  },
  "devDependencies": {
    "babel-core": "6.11.4",
    "babel-loader": "6.4.1",
    "babel-preset-react": "6.5.0",
    "backbone": "1.3.3",
    "jquery": "3.1.0",
    "react": "15.5.4",
    "react-dom": "15.5.4",
    "webpack": "2.4.1"
  }
}
```

The main logic's source is in app.jsx, where you perform all three of the aforementioned tasks:

```
const Backbone = require ('backbone')
// Include other libraries
const Router = Backbone.Router.extend({
  routes: {
    ''      : 'index',
    'about' : 'about',
    'posts' : 'posts',
    'posts/:id' : 'post',
    'contact' : 'contact',
    'login': 'login'
  },
  ...
})
```

Once the routes object is defined, you can define the methods. The values in routes must be used as method names:

```
// Include libraries
const Router = Backbone.Router.extend({
  routes: {
    ''      : 'index',
    'about' : 'about',
    'posts' : 'posts',
    'posts/:id' : 'post',
    'contact' : 'contact',
    'login': 'login'
  },
  index: function() {
    ...
  },
  about: function() {
    ...
  }
  ...
})
```

Each URL fragment maps to a function. For example, #/about will trigger about. Thus, you can define these functions and render your React components in them. The data will be passed as a property (router or posts):

```
const {render} = require ('react-dom')
// ...
const Router = Backbone.Router.extend({
  routes: {
    ...
  },
  index: function() {
    render(<Content router={router}/>, content)
  },
```

◁─── **Uses destructuring to import and define render() from ReactDOM.render()**

```
   about: function() {
     render(<Content router={router}>
       <About/>
     </Content>, content)
   },
   posts: function() {
     render(<Content>
       <Posts posts={posts}/>
     </Content>, content)
   },
   post: function(id) {
     render(<Content>
       <Post id={id} posts={posts}/>
     </Content>, content)
   },
   contact: function() {
     render(<Content>
       <Contact />
     </Content>, content)
   },
   login: function() {
     render(<Login />, content)
   }
})

let router = new Router()

Backbone.history.start()
```

Creates Content, with About inside it. You can pass the router as a property.

Passes necessary data to Post, such as a URL parameter (id), and posts data

Renders Login without Content

Instantiates Router, and starts browser history

The content variable is a DOM node (which you declare before the router):

```
let content = document.getElementById('content')
```

Compared to the React Router example, nested components such as Post get their data not in props.params or props.route.posts, but in props.id and props.posts. In my opinion, that means less magic—which is always good. On the other hand, you don't get to use declarative JSX syntax and must use a more imperative style.

The complete code for this project is available at www.manning.com/books/react-quickly and https://github.com/azat-co/react-quickly/tree/master/ch13/backbone-router. This example will give you a head start if you have a Backbone system or are planning to use Backbone. And even if you're not planning to use Backbone, it's shown you yet again that React is amazing at working with other libraries.

13.5   *Quiz*

1   You must provide a history implementation for React Router v2.x (the one covered in this chapter) because by default it doesn't use one. True or false?

2   What history implementation is better supported by older browsers: hash history or browser HTML5 pushState history?

3 What do you need to implement to have access to the `router` object in a route component when using React Router v2.x ?

4 How would you access URL parameters in a route component (stateless or stateful) when using React Router v2.x?

5 React Router requires the use of Babel and Webpack. True or false?

13.6   Summary

- You can implement routing with React in a naive way by listening to hashchange.
- React Router provides the JSX syntax for defining a routing hierarchy: `<Router><Route/></Router>`.
- Nested routes don't have to have nested URLs relative to their parent routes; path and nestedness are independent.
- You can use hash history without tokens by setting `queryKey` to `false`.
- You must include React (`require('react')`) when using JSX even if there's no visible use of React, because JSX converts to `React.createElement()`, which needs React.

13.7   Quiz answers

1 True. Version 1.x of React Router loaded a history implementation by default; but in version 2.x, you must provide a library, either from a standalone package or one bundled with the router library.

2 Hash history is better supported by older browsers.

3 The static class attribute `contextTypes`, with `router` as a required object.

4 From `props.params` or `props.routeParams`.

5 False. You can use it plain and/or with other build tools such as Gulp and Browserify.

Watch this chapter's introduction video by scanning this QR code with your phone or going to http://reactquickly.co/videos/ch14.

Working with data using Redux

This chapter covers

- Understanding unidirectional data flow in React
- Understanding the Flux data architecture
- Working with the Redux data library

So far, you've been using React to create user interfaces. This is the most common use case for React. But most UIs need to work with data. This data comes from either a server (back end) or another browser component.

When it comes to working with data, React offers many options:

- *Integrating with MVC-like frameworks*—This option is ideal if you're already using or are planning to use an MVC-like framework for a single-page application: for example, using Backbone and Backbone models.
- *Writing your own data method or a library*—This option is well suited for small UI components: for example, fetching a list of accounts for a List of Accounts grid.
- *Using the React stack (a.k.a. React and friends)*—This option offers the most compatibility (your code will integrate with less friction) and the most adherence to the React philosophy.

This chapter covers one of the most popular options for the third approach: Redux. Let's start by outlining how data flows in React components.

NOTE There's the *Flux architecture*, and then there's the `flux` library from Facebook. I'll be showing you Redux rather than the `flux` library, because Redux is more actively used in projects. `flux` serves as more of a proof of concept for the Flux architecture that Redux adheres to and implements. Think of Redux and `flux` (the library) as the two implementations of the Flux architecture. (I'll cover the Flux architecture but not the library.)

NOTE The source code for the examples in this chapter is at www.manning .com/books/react-quickly and https://github.com/azat-co/react-quickly/ tree/master/ch14 (in the ch14 folder of the GitHub repository https:// github.com/azat-co/react-quickly). You can also find some demos at http:// reactquickly.co/demos.

14.1 React support for unidirectional data flow

React is a view layer that's designed to work with *unidirectional data flow* (see figure 14.1). A unidirectional data pattern (a.k.a. *one-way binding*) exists when there are no mutable (or two-way) references between concerns. *Concerns* are parts with different functionality. For example, a view and a model can't have two-way references. I'll talk about bidirectional flow again in a few moments.

To illustrate, if you have an account model and an account view, then data can flow only from the account model to the account view and not vice versa. In other words, changes in the model will cause changes in the view (see figure 14.2). The key to understanding this is that views can't modify models directly.

Unidirectional data flow ensures that for any given input into your components, you'll get the same predictable result: a `render()` expression. This React pattern is in

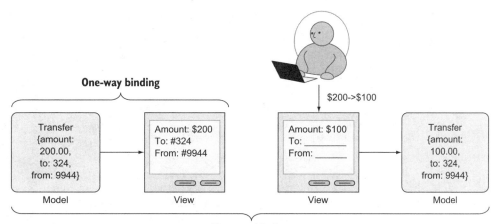

Figure 14.1   Unidirectional vs. bidirectional data flow

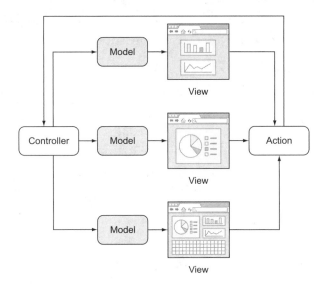
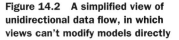

Figure 14.2   A simplified view of unidirectional data flow, in which views can't modify models directly

stark contrast to the bidirectional, two-way binding pattern of Angular.js and some other frameworks.

For example, in bidirectional data flow, changes in models cause changes in views *and* changes in views (user input) cause changes in models. For this reason, with bidirectional data flow, the state of a view is less predictable, making it harder to understand, debug, and maintain (see figure 14.3). The key to remember is that views *can* modify models directly. This is in stark contrast to unidirectional flow.

Interestingly enough, bidirectional data flow (*two-way binding*) is considered a benefit by some Angular developers. Without getting into a debate, it's true that with bidirectional flow, you can write less code.

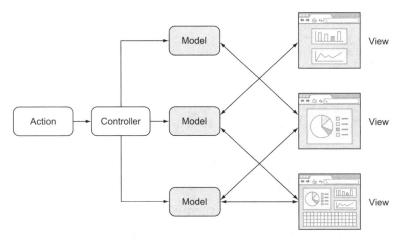

Figure 14.3   A simplified view of the bidirectional data flow typical for an MVC-like architecture

For example, let's say you have an input field like the one shown in figure 14.1. All you need to do is define a variable in the template, and the value will be updated in the model when the user types in the field. At the same time, the value on the web page will be updated if there's a change in the model (as a result of an XHR GET request, for example). Therefore, changes are possible in two directions: from view to model and from model to view. This is great for prototyping, but not so great for complex UIs when it comes to performance, debugging, development scaling, and so on. This may sound controversial—please bear with me.

I've built a lot of complex UI applications with MVC and MVW frameworks that have bidirectional flows, and they'll do the job. In a nutshell, problems arise because various views can manipulate various models, and vice versa. That's fine when you have one or two models and views in isolation; but the bigger the application, the more models and views are updating each other. It becomes harder and harder to figure out why one model or view is in a given state, because you can't easily determine which models/views updated it and in which order. Traceability becomes a huge issue, as does finding bugs. That's why the bidirectional data flow in MVC frameworks (such as Angular) isn't favored by many developers: they find this antipattern difficult to debug and scale.

On the other hand, with unidirectional flow, the model updates the view, and that's that. As an added bonus, unidirectional data flow allows for server-side rendering, because views are an immutable function of state (that is, isomorphic/universal JavaScript).

For now, keep in mind that unidirectional data flow is a major selling point of React:

- Code readability and reasoning due to one source of truth (state/model → view).
- Debuggable code with time travel;[1] for example, it's trivial to send a dump with history to the server on exceptions and bugs.
- Server-side rendering without a headless browser: isomorphic,[2] or universal,[3] JavaScript, as some call it.

Here's my personal experience with Angular, in case you're curious. I worked only a little bit with Angular 1 because I thought it was lacking, but then I took a course on Angular 2—and then I realized how wrong I was. I corrected my mistake. Now I completely avoid any Angular code.

---

[1] Dan Abramov, "Live React: Hot Reloading with Time Travel" (presentation, ReactEurope 2015), http://mng.bz/uSxq.
[2] Spike Brehm, "Isomorphic JavaScript: The Future of WebAir Apps," *Airbnb Engineering & Data Science*, November 11, 2013, http://mng.bz/i34M.
[3] Michael Jackson, "Universal JavaScript," June 8, 2015, http://mng.bz/7GXE.

14.2   *Understanding the Flux data architecture*

Flux (https://facebook.github.io/flux) is an architecture pattern for data flow developed by Facebook to be used in React apps. The gist of Flux is unidirectional data flow and elimination of the complexity of MVC-like patterns.

Let's consider a typical MVC-like pattern, shown in figure 14.4. Actions trigger events in the controller, which handles models. Then, according to the models, the app renders the views, and the madness begins. Each view updates the models—not just its own model, but the other models too—and the models update the views (bidirectional data flow). It's easy to get lost in this architecture. The architecture is difficult to understand and debug.

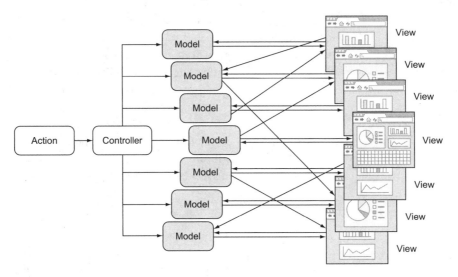

Figure 14.4   An MVC-like architecture introduces complexity by allowing views to trigger changes on any model, and vice versa.

Conversely, Flux suggests using a unidirectional data flow, as shown in figure 14.5. In this case, you have actions from views going through a dispatcher, which in turn calls the data store. (Flux is a replacement for MVC. This isn't just new terminology.) The store is responsible for the data and the representation in the views. Views don't modify the data but have actions that go through the dispatcher again.

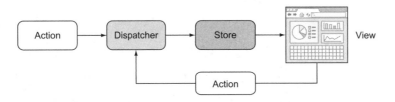

Figure 14.5   The Flux architecture simplifies the data flow by having it go in one direction (from store to view).

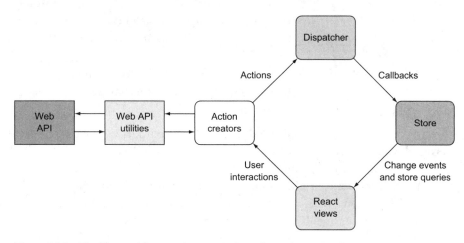

Figure 14.6   The Flux architecture in a nutshell: actions trigger the dispatcher, which triggers the store, which renders views.

The unidirectional data flow enables better testing and debugging. A more detailed diagram of the Flux architecture is shown in figure 14.6.

Historically, Flux was an architecture. Only later did the Facebook team release the flux module (www.npmjs.com/package/flux, https://github.com/facebook/flux) that can be used with React to implement Flux. The flux module is more or less a proof of concept for the Flux architecture, and React developers rarely use it.

> **TIP** There's no reason for me to duplicate the great minds who have already spoken about Flux. I suggest that you watch the video "Hacker Way: Rethinking Web App Development at Facebook," from the official Flux website: http://mng.bz/wygf.

Personally, I find Flux confusing—and I'm not alone. There are many implementations of Flux, including Redux, Reflux, and other libraries. Early Manning Access Program readers of this book know that Reflux was included in the first version of the book, but I omitted it from this version. My anecdotal evidence, David Waller's "React.js architecture - Flux vs. Reflux" at http://mng.bz/5GHx, and the hard data from numbers of npm downloads all indicate that Redux is more popular than Flux or Reflux. In this book, I use Redux, which some argue is a better alternative to Flux.

14.3   Using the Redux data library

Redux (redux, www.npmjs.com/package/redux) is one of the most popular implementations of the Flux architecture. Redux has these qualities:

- *Rich ecosystem*—See, for example, Awesome Redux (https://github.com/xgrommx/awesome-redux).
- *Simplicity*—No dispatcher or store registration is required, and the minimal version has only 99 lines of code (http://mng.bz/00Ap).

- *Good developer experience (DX)*—For example, you can do hot reloading with time travel (see the video "Live React: Hot Reloading with Time Travel," http://mng.bz/uSxq).
- *Reducer composition*—For example, the undo/redo higher-order component requires minimal code (https://github.com/omnidan/redux-undo).
- Support for server-side rendering.

I won't take time to go over all the details of why Redux is better than Flux. If you're interested, you can read some thoughts by the author of Redux: "Why Use Redux over Facebook Flux?" at http://mng.bz/z9ok.

Redux is a standalone library that implements a state container. It's like a huge variable that contains all the data your application works with, stores, and changes in the runtime. You can use Redux alone or on the server. As already mentioned, Redux is also popular in combination with React; this combination is implemented in another library, react-redux (https://github.com/reactjs/react-redux).

A few moving parts are involved when you use Redux in your React apps:

- A store that stores all the data and provides methods to manipulate this data. The store is created with the createStore() function.
- A Provider component that makes it possible for any components to take data from the store.
- A connect() function that wraps any component and lets you *map* certain parts of your application state from the store to the component's properties.

Look back at the Flux architecture diagram in figure 14.5: you can see why there's a store. The only way to mutate the internal state is to dispatch an action, and actions are in the store.

Every change in the store is performed via *actions*. Each action tells your application what happened and what part of the store should be changed. Actions can also provide data; you'll find this useful because, well, every app works with data that changes.

The way the data in the store changes is specified by *reducers* that are pure functions. They have a (state, action) ⇒ state signature. In other words, by applying an action to the current state, you get a new state. This allows for predictability and the ability to rewind actions (via undo and debugging) to previous states.

Here's the reducer file for a Todo list app in which SET_VISIBILITY_FILTER and ADD_TODO are actions:

```
                       function todoApp(state = initialState, action) {
Defines                   switch (action.type) {
an action                   case 'SET_VISIBILITY_FILTER':
                              return Object.assign({}, state, {
                                visibilityFilter: action.filter
                              })
```

Applies a reducer to create a new state by copying[4] the current state and the visibilityFilter values

---

[4] Object.assign(), http://mng.bz/O6pl.

Defines the ADD_TODO action

```
case 'ADD_TODO':
    return Object.assign({}, state, {
        todos: [
            ...state.todos,
            {
                text: action.text,
                completed: false
            }
        ]
    })
default:
    return state
    }
}
```

Applies a reducer to create a new state by copying the current state and the new TODO values "text" and "completed" as the last item of the todos array

Defines a default fallback that, in this case, returns the current state

You may have one or many reducers (or none) in your Redux application. Every time you call an action, every reducer is called. Reducers are responsible for changing the data in the store; this is why you need to be careful about what they do during certain types of actions.

Typically, a reducer is a function with state and an action as arguments. For example, an action can be "to fetch a movie" (FETCH_MOVIE), which you get by using a reducer. The action code describes how an action transforms the state into the next state (adds a movie to the state). This reducer function contains a huge switch/case statement to process actions. But there's a handy library that makes reducers more functional and—surprise!—easier to read. The library is called redux-actions, and you'll see how to use it instead of switch/case.

> **TIP** Redux creator Dan Abramov (https://github.com/gaearon) suggests the following before-bed reading about Redux: "Why Use Redux Over Facebook Flux?" (http://mng.bz/9syg) and "What Could Be the Downsides of Using Redux Instead of Flux" (http://mng.bz/Ux9l).

14.3.1 Redux Netflix clone

We all like good old Hollywood movies, right? Let's make an app that shows a list of classic movies: that is, a Netflix clone (but only the home page—no streaming or anything like that). The app will display a grid of movies (see figure 14.7); and when you click a movie's image, you'll see a detailed view (figure 14.8).

The goal of this tutorial is to learn how to use Redux in a real-life scenario to feed data to React components. This data will come from a JSON file to keep things simple. Each individual movie's detail view will be facilitated with React Router, which you learned about in the previous chapter.

The project will have three components: App, Movies, and Movie. Each component will have a CSS file and live in its own folder for better code organization (that's the

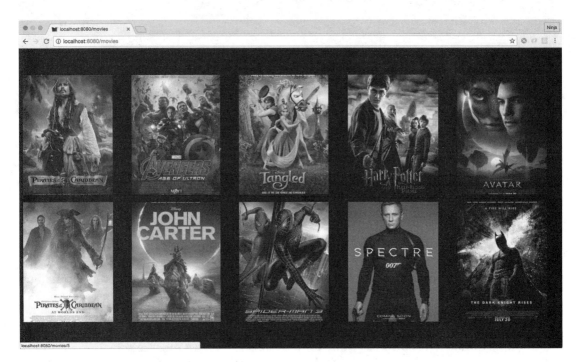

Figure 14.7   The Netflix clone will show a grid of movies on the home page.

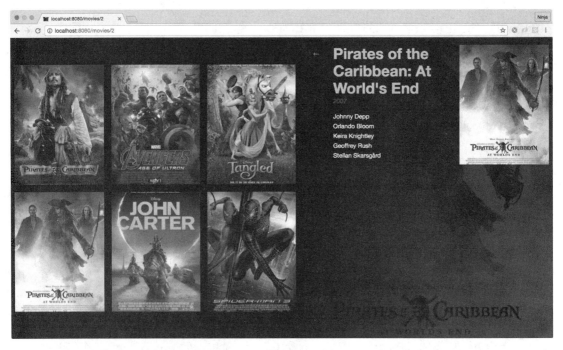

Figure 14.8   Details of a movie are shown when you click its poster.

best practice to encapsulate React components together with styles). The project structure is as follows:

```
. /redux-netfix
    /build                          Build folder where Webpack
       index.js                     will write bundles
       styles.css
    /node_modules
       ...
    /src
       /components                   App folder for the
        /app                         layout component
          app.css
          app.js
        /movie
          movie.css
          movie.js
        /movies                      Movies folder for
          movies.css                 the grid of movies
          movies.js
       /modules
         index.js                    Redux reducers to fetch movies
         movies.js                   and a single movie's data
       index.js
       movies.json                   Movie data
       routes.js
     index.html                      React Router routes
     package.json
     webpack.config.json
```

Movie folder for individual movie view components →

File that will combine reducers and expose them →

Entry point of the project that defines a Redux provider with reducers

Now that the project's folder structure is ready, let's look at the dependencies and build configuration.

14.3.2 Dependencies and configs

You need to set up a number of dependencies for this project. You'll use Webpack (https://github.com/webpack/webpack) to bundle all the files for live use and an additional plug-in called extract-text-webpack-plugin to bundle styles from multiple <style> includes (inline) into one style.css. Webpack loaders are also used in the project:

- json-loader
- style-loader
- css-loader
- babel-loader

Other project development dependencies modules include the following:

- Babel (https://github.com/babel/babel) and its presets transpile ECMAScript 6 into browser-friendly, old-school JavaScript (a.k.a. ECMAScript 5): babel-polyfill emulates a full ES2015 environment, babel-preset-es2015 is for ES6/ES2015, babel-preset-stage-0 provides cutting-edge new ES7+ features, and babel-preset-react is for JSX.

- react-router (https://github.com/reactjs/react-router) shows a hierarchy of components based on their current location. It also helps arrange components into a hierarchy based on URL location.
- redux-actions (https://github.com/acdlite/redux-actions) organizes the reducers.
- ESLint (http://eslint.org) and its plug-ins maintain proper JavaScript/JSX style.
- concurrently (www.npmjs.com/package/concurrently) is a Node tool to make processes such as Webpack builds run concurrently (at the same time).

The package.json file lists all dependencies, Babel configs, and npm scripts and should contain at least the data shown in the following listing (ch14/redux-netflix/package.json). As always, you can install modules manually with npm i NAME, type package.json, and run npm i, or copy package.json and run npm i. Make sure you use the exact versions of the libraries from package.json; otherwise, your code might break.

Listing 14.1 Dependences for the Netflix clone

```
{
  "name": "redux-netflix",
  "version": "0.0.1",
  "description": "A sample project in React and Redux that copies Netflix's
   features and workflow",
  "main": "./build/index.js",
  "scripts": {
    "test": "echo \"Error: no test specified\" && exit 1",
    "start": "concurrently \"webpack --watch --config webpack.config.js\"
     \"webpack-dev-server\""
  },
  "repository": {
    "type": "git",
    "url": "git+https://github.com/azat-co/react-quickly.git"
  },
  "author": "Azat Mardan (http://azat.co)",
  "license": "MIT",
  "bugs": {
    "url": "https://github.com/azat-co/react-quickly/issues"
  },
  "homepage": "https://github.com/azat-co/react-quickly#readme",
  "devDependencies": {
    "babel-core": "6.11.4",
    "babel-eslint": "6.1.2",
    "babel-loader": "6.2.4",
    "babel-polyfill": "6.9.1",
    "babel-preset-es2015": "6.9.0",
    "babel-preset-react": "6.11.1",
    "babel-preset-stage-0": "6.5.0",
    "concurrently": "2.2.0",
    "css-loader": "0.23.1",
    "eslint": "3.1.1",
    "eslint-plugin-babel": "3.3.0",
```

Defines the script to build and run Webpack Dev Server using the concurrently tool

Installs various Babel plug-ins, loaders, and modules

Installs concurrently to run npm scripts more quickly

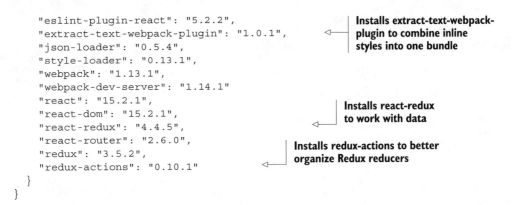

```
"eslint-plugin-react": "5.2.2",
"extract-text-webpack-plugin": "1.0.1",       ◄─── Installs extract-text-webpack-
"json-loader": "0.5.4",                             plugin to combine inline
"style-loader": "0.13.1",                           styles into one bundle
"webpack": "1.13.1",
"webpack-dev-server": "1.14.1"
"react": "15.2.1",
"react-dom": "15.2.1",                         Installs react-redux
"react-redux": "4.4.5",            ◄───        to work with data
"react-router": "2.6.0",
"redux": "3.5.2",                     Installs redux-actions to better
"redux-actions": "0.10.1"             organize Redux reducers
  }                                 ◄───
}
```

Because you use Webpack to bundle the dependencies, all of the necessary packages are in bundle.js. For this reason, you put all the dependencies in devDependencies. (I'm picky about what's deployed—I don't want any unused modules in my deployment environment just sitting idly and causing security vulnerabilities.) npm ignores devDependencies when the --production flag is used, as in npm i --production.

Next, let's define the build process by creating webpack.config.js (ch14/redux-netflix/webpack.config.js).

Listing 14.2 Netflix clone Webpack configuration file

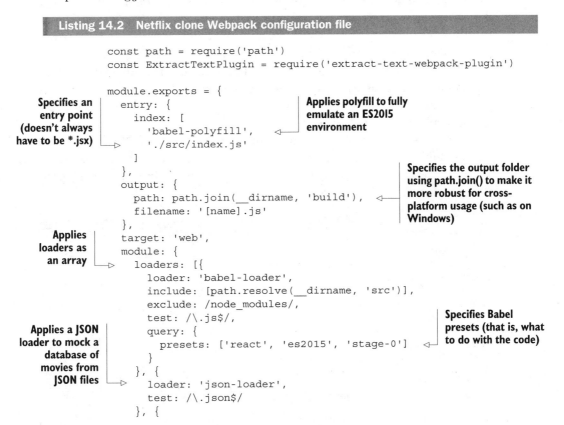

```
const path = require('path')
const ExtractTextPlugin = require('extract-text-webpack-plugin')

module.exports = {
  entry: {
    index: [
      'babel-polyfill',
      './src/index.js'
    ]
  },
  output: {
    path: path.join(__dirname, 'build'),
    filename: '[name].js'
  },
  target: 'web',
  module: {
    loaders: [{
      loader: 'babel-loader',
      include: [path.resolve(__dirname, 'src')],
      exclude: /node_modules/,
      test: /\.js$/,
      query: {
        presets: ['react', 'es2015', 'stage-0']
      }
    }, {
      loader: 'json-loader',
      test: /\.json$/
    }, {
```

Specifies an entry point (doesn't always have to be *.jsx)

Applies polyfill to fully emulate an ES2015 environment

Specifies the output folder using path.join() to make it more robust for cross-platform usage (such as on Windows)

Applies loaders as an array

Applies a JSON loader to mock a database of movies from JSON files

Specifies Babel presets (that is, what to do with the code)

```
        loader: ExtractTextPlugin.extract('style',
          'css?modules&localIdentName=[local]__[hash:base64:5]'),
        test: /\.css$/,
        exclude: /node_modules/
      }]
    },
    resolve: {
      modulesDirectories: [
        './node_modules',
        './src'
      ]
    },
    plugins: [
      new ExtractTextPlugin('styles.css')
    ]
  }
}
```

Applies a loader from a plug-in to extract styles and combine them into one file (instead of many files)

Provides a plug-in for text extraction

Enough with configurations. In the next section, you'll start working with Redux.

14.3.3 *Enabling Redux*

To make Redux work in your React application, the hierarchy of components needs the `Provider` component at the top level. This component comes from the `react-redux` package and injects data from the store into components. That's right: using `Provider` as the top-level component means all children will have the store. Neat.

To make `Provider` work, you need to provide the store to its `store` property. The `Store` is an object that represents the application state. Redux (`react-redux`) comes with a `createStore()` function that takes reducer(s) from ch14/redux-netflix/scr/modules/index.js and returns the `Store` object.

To render the `Provider` component and its entire subtree of components, you use `react-dom`'s `render()`. It takes the first argument (`<Provider>`) and mounts it into the element you pass as the second argument (`document.getElementById('app')`).

Combining all of this, the entry point of your application should now look like the following listing (ch14/redux-netflix/index.js). You define `Provider` by passing a `Store` instance (with reducers) in a JSX format.

Listing 14.3 Main app entry point

```
const React = require('react')
const { render } = require('react-dom')
const { Provider } = require('react-redux')
const { createStore } = require('react-redux')
const reducers = require('./modules')
const routes = require('./routes')

module.exports = render((
  <Provider store={createStore(reducers)}>
    {routes}
  </Provider>
), document.getElementById('app'))
```

For the entire application to be able to use Redux features, you need to implement some code in child components, such as connecting the store. The connect() function from the same react-redux package accepts a few arguments. It returns a function that then wraps your component so it can receive certain parts of the store into its properties. You'll see it in a bit.

You're finished with index.js. The Provider component takes care of delivering data from the store to all the connected components, so there's no need to pass properties directly. But a few parts are missing, such as routes, reducers, and actions. Let's look at them one by one.

14.3.4 Routes

With react-router, you can declare a hierarchy of components per browser location. I covered React Router in chapter 13, so it should be familiar; you used it for client-side routing. React routing is not strictly connected with server-side routes, but sometimes you may want to use it for that, especially in conjunction with techniques discussed in chapter 16.

The gist of React Router is that every route can be declared by a couple of nested Route components, each of which takes two properties:

- path—URL path or location that can contain URL parameters: for example, /movies:/id for localhost:8080/movies/1021. Using / can define a path regardless of the parent route path: for example, /:id for localhost:8080/1012.
- component—Reference to the component that will be rendered when a user goes to a path/location. All the parent components up to Provider will be rendered as well. For example, going to localhost:8080/movies/1021 in listing 14.4 will render Movie, Movies, and App.

You need to show a collection of movie covers at both the root and /movies locations. In addition, you need to show the details of a given movie at the /movies/:id location. The route configuration uses IndexRoute, as shown next (ch14/redux-netflix/src/routes.js).

Listing 14.4　Defining URL routing with React Router

```
const React = require('react')
const {
  Router,
  Route,
  IndexRoute,
  browserHistory
} = require('react-router')
const App = require('components/app/app.js')
const Movies = require('components/movies/movies.js')
const Movie = require('components/movie/movie.js')

module.exports = (
  <Router history={browserHistory}>
    <Route path="/" component={App}>
      <IndexRoute component={Movies} />
```

Defines the index route: the route for the empty URL /

Provides either browser or hash history to the router

```
    <Route path="movies" component={Movies}>
      <Route path=":id" component={Movie} />
    </Route>
  </Route>
</Router>
)
```

> Defines the movie ID
> URL parameter with
> a colon—:id

Both `IndexRoute` and `Route` are nested into the topmost route. This makes the `Movies` component render for both the root and /movies locations. The individual movie view needs a movie ID to fetch info about that particular movie from the Redux store, so you define the path with a URL parameter. To do so, use the colon syntax: `path=":id"`. Figure 14.9 shows how the individual view and its URL look on a small screen, thanks to responsive CSS. Notice that the URL is movies/8, where 8 is a movie ID. Next, you'll see how to fetch the data with Redux reducers.

Figure 14.9   Individual movie
view on a small screen. The URL
includes the movie ID.

14.3.5 *Combining reducers*

Let's look at the modules the createStore() function in src/index.js is applied to:

```
...
const reducers = require('./modules')          ◁──── Imports (combined)
...                                                   reducers from ./modules
                                                      (./modules/index.js)

module.exports = render((
  <Provider store={createStore(reducers)}>      ◁──── Applies reducers
    {routes}
  </Provider>
), document.getElementById('app'))
```

What does this do? You need to store movie data in the store. Perhaps in the future you'll implement additional parts of the store, such as user accounts or other entities. So let's use Redux's feature that allows you to create as many distinct parts of the store as you need, although you need only one at the moment. In a way, you're creating a better architecture by performing this middle step of combining reducers so that later, you can extend your app effortlessly by adding more reducers to ./modules/ index.js (or ./modules), using the plug-in Node pattern.[5] This approach is also called *splitting reducers* (http://mng.bz/Wprj).

Each reducer can change data in the store; but to make this operation safe, you may need to divide the application state into separate parts and then combine them into a single store. This divide-and-conquer approach is recommended for larger apps in which you'll have increasing numbers of reducers and actions. You can easily combine multiple reducers with the combineReducers() function from redux (ch14/redux-netflix/src/modules/index.js).

Listing 14.5   Combining reducers

```
const { combineReducers } = require('redux')    ◁──── Imports combineReducers
const {                                                from the combineReducers
  reducer: movies                   ◁────               property in redux
} = require('./movies')

module.exports = combineReducers({
  movies
  // more reducers go here
})
```

Exports the combined reducer movies (label pointing to `module.exports = combineReducers({`)

Applies ES6/ES2015 destructuring assignment to create a reducer object called movies from the reducer property of ./movies.js

You can pass as many reducers as you like and create independent branches in the store. You can name them as you like. In this case, the movies reducer is imported and then passed into the combineReducers() function as a property of a plain object with the key "movies".

This way, you declare a separate part of the store and call it "movies." Every action that the reducer from ./movies is responsible for will touch only this part and nothing else.

---

5   Azat Mardan, "Node Patterns: From Callbacks to Observer," webapplog, http://mng.bz/p9vd.

14.3.6 *Reducer for movies*

Next, let's implement the "movies" reducer. A *reducer*, in Redux, is a function that runs *every time* any action is dispatched. It's executed with two arguments:

- The first argument, `state`, is a reference to the part of the state that this reducer manages.
- The second argument, `action`, is an object that represents the action that has just been dispatched.

In other words, the reducer inputs are results of previous actions: the current state (`state`) and a current action (`action`). The reducer takes the current state and applies the action. The result of a reducer is a new state. If your reducers are pure functions without side effects (which they should be), you get all the benefits of using Redux with React, such as hot reloading and time travel.

Reducers in JavaScript

The term *reducers* comes from functional programming. JavaScript has a somewhat functional nature, so it has `Array.reduce()`.

In a nutshell, a *reduce method* is an operation that summarizes a list of items so that the input has multiple values and the output has a single value. The list on which a reducer works can be an array, as is the case with JavaScript, or it can be another data structure like a list, as is the case outside of JavaScript.

For example, you can return the number of occurrences of a name in a list of names. The list of names is the input, and the number of occurrences is the output.

To use a reducer, you call a method and pass a reducing function that accepts the following:

- *Accumulator value*—What is passed to the next iteration and what will eventually become the output
- *Current value*—Item from the list

With each iteration over the items in the list (or array in JS), the reducer function gets the accumulator value. In JavaScript, the method is `Array.reduce()`. For example, to get a name frequency, you can run the following reducer code, which uses a ternary if the current value (`curr`) is "azat" and then adds 1 to the accumulator (`acc`):[6]

```
const users = ['azat', 'peter', 'wiliam','azat','azat']
console.log(users
  .reduce((acc, curr)=>(
    (curr == 'azat') ? ++acc : acc
  ), 0)
)
```

In Redux reducers, the accumulator value is the state object, and the current value is the current action. The function result is the new state.

---

[6] For detailed documentation of `Array.prototype.reduce()`, see the Mozilla Developer Network, http://mng.bz/Z55j.

TIP Avoid putting API calls into reducers. Remember, reducers are supposed to be pure functions with no side effects. They're state machines; they shouldn't do asynchronous operations such as HTTP calls to an API. The best place to put these types of async calls is in middleware (http://redux .js.org/docs/advanced/Middleware.html) or the dispatch() action creator (http://mng.bz/S31I; an *action creator* is a function that creates actions). You'll see dispatch() in a component later in this chapter.

A typical reducer is a function containing a huge switch/case statement:

```
const FETCH_MOVIES = 'movies/FETCH_MOVIES'
const FETCH_MOVIE = 'movies/FETCH_MOVIE'

const initialState = {
  movies: [],
  movie: {}
}

function reducer(state = initialState, action) {
  switch(action.type) {
    case FETCH_MOVIES:
      return {
        ...state,                        ⟵  ES6 spread operator
        all: action.movies                   that passes the state
      }                                       object key by key
    case FETCH_MOVIE:
      return {
        ...state,
        current: action.movie            ⟵  Saves or changes a certain
      }                                      movie in the store
    }
}

module.exports = {
  reducer                                ⟵  Exports an object with the reducer
}                                            method using ES6 syntax
```

Saves or changes the list of all movies in the store (annotation pointing to the `case FETCH_MOVIES` block)

But using switch/case is considered a bad practice by the luminary Douglas Crockford in his classic *JavaScript: The Good Parts* (O'Reilly Media, 2008). There's a handy redux-actions library (https://github.com/acdlite/redux-actions) that can bring this reducer function into a cleaner, more functional form. Instead of a huge switch/case statement, you can use a more robust object.

Let's use handleActions from redux-actions. It takes a map-like plain object, where keys are action types and values are functions. This way, only a single function is called per action type; in other words, this function is cherry-picked by action type.

The function from the previous snippet can be rewritten with redux-actions and handleActions as shown next (ch14/redux-netflix/src/modules/movies.js).

Listing 14.6   Using the `redux-actions` library

```
const { handleActions } = require('redux-actions')

const FETCH_MOVIES = 'movies/FETCH_MOVIES'
const FETCH_MOVIE = 'movies/FETCH_MOVIE'

const initialState = {
  movies: [],
  movie: {}
}

module.exports = {
  fetchMoviesActionCreator: (movies) => ({
    type: FETCH_MOVIES,
    movies
  }),
  fetchMovieActionCreator: (index) => ({
    type: FETCH_MOVIE,
    index
  }),
  reducer: handleActions({
    [FETCH_MOVIES]: (state, action) => ({
      ...state,
      all: action.movies
    }),
    [FETCH_MOVIE]: (state, action) => ({
      ...state,
      current: state.all[action.index - 1]
    })
  }, initialState)
}
```

Defines the **FETCH_MOVIES** action creator that returns an action object

Defines the **FETCH_MOVIE** action creator that returns an action object

Gets all movies in the Movies component

Gets the current movie in the Movie component by using index (URL param for movie ID)

This code looks similar to `switch/case`, but it's more about mapping functions to actions than selecting them in a potentially huge conditional statement.

14.3.7 *Actions*

To change data in the store, you use actions. To clarify, an action can be anything, not just user input in a browser. For example, it could be the result of an async operation. Basically, any code can become an action. Actions are the only sources of information for the store; this data is sent from an app to the store. Actions are executed via `store.dispatch()`, which I mentioned earlier, or via a `connect()` helper. But before we look at how to call an action, let's cover its `type`.

Every action is represented by a plain object that has at least one property: `type`. It can have as many other properties as you want, usually to pass data into the store. So, every action has a type, like this:

```
{
  type: 'movies/I_AM_A_VALID_ACTION'
}
```

Here, the action type is a string.

> **NOTE** It's common to name actions using uppercase letters preceded by the module name in lowercase letters. You can omit the module name if you're sure duplicates will never occur.

In modern Redux development, action types are declared as constant strings:

```
const FETCH_MOVIES = 'movies/FETCH_MOVIES'
const FETCH_MOVIE = 'movies/FETCH_MOVIE'
```

Here, two action types are declared. Both are strings that consist of two parts: the name of the Redux module and the name of the action type. This practice may be useful when you have different reducers with similarly named actions.

Every time you want to change the application state, you need to dispatch a corresponding action. An appropriate reducer function is executed, and you end up with the updated application state. Think about data that you receive from an API or a form a user fills in: it all can be placed or updated in the store. Here's an example:

```
this.props.dispatch({
  type: FETCH_MOVIE,
  movie: {}
})
```

This is the series of steps:

1 Invoke `dispatch()` with an action object that has a `type` property and has data, if needed, in a component.
2 Execute the corresponding reducer in the reducer module.
3 Update the new state in the store, which is available in components.

More on dispatching later. Let's see how you can avoid passing/using action types in your components.

14.3.8 Action creators

To change anything in the store, you need to run an action through all the reducers. A reducer then changes the application state based on the action type. For this reason, *you always need to know the action type.* But a shortcut lets you conceal action types under action creators. Overall, the steps are as follows:

1 Invoke the action creator with data (if needed). The action creator can be defined in the reducer module.
2 Dispatch the action in a component. *No action type is needed.*
3 Execute the corresponding reducer in the reducer module.
4 Update the new state in the store.

Check this out:

```
this.props.dispatch(fetchMoviesActionCreator({movie: {}}))
```

Simply put, an *action creator* is a function that returns an action. It's as straightforward as this:

```
function fetchMoviesActionCreator(movies) {
  return {
    type: FETCH_MOVIES,
    movies
  }
}
```

With action creators, you can hide complex logic in a single function call. In this case, though, there's no logic. The only operation this function performs is returning an action: a plain object with a `type` property that defines this action and also a `movies` property that has the value of an array of movies. If you were to extend the Netflix clone so it could add a movie, you'd need an `addMovie()` action creator:

```
function addMovie(movie) {
  return {
    type: ADD_MOVIE,
    movie
  }
}
```

Or how about `watchMovie()`?

```
function watchMovie(movie, watchMovieIndex, rating) {
  return {
    type: WATCH_MOVIE,
    movie,
    index: watchMovieIndex,
    rating: rating,
    receivedAt: Date.now()
  }
}
```

Remember, an action *must* have the `type` property!

To be able to dispatch actions, you must connect components to the store. This is getting more interesting, because you're close to state updates.

14.3.9 *Connecting components to the store*

Now that you've learned how to put data into the store, let's see how you can access store data from components. Luckily, the `Provider` component has a feature to bring the data into your components in properties. But to access the data, you'll need to *connect* your component to the store explicitly.

By default, a component isn't connected to a data store; and having it somewhere in the hierarchy of the topmost `Provider` component isn't enough. Why? Well, think of connecting as an explicit opt-in for certain components.

If you remember, there are two types of components, according to React best practices: presentational (dumb) and container (smart), as discussed in chapter 8. Presentational components should *not* need the store; they should just consume properties. At the same time, container components need the store and the dispatcher. Even the definition of container components in the Redux documentation specifies that they subscribe to the store (http://mng.bz/p4f9). All `Provider` is doing is providing a store for all components automatically so that some of them can subscribe/connect to it. Thus, for container components, you need both `Provider` and the store.

To sum up, a connected component can access any data from the store in its properties. How do you connect components to the store? With the `connect()` method, of course! Confused? Let's look at an example. Think about your root component, `App`. It will use `Movies`, which at minimum should have this code to display the list of movies (the actual `Movies` component has a bit more code):

```
class Movies extends React.Component {
  render() {
    const {
      movies = []
    } = this.props

    return (
      <div className={styles.movies}>
        {movies.map((movie, index) => (
          <div key={index}>
            {movie.title}
          </div>
        ))}
      </div>
    )
  }
}
```

Currently, the `Movies` component isn't connected to the store despite having `Provider` as a parent. Let's connect it by adding the following snippet. The `connect()` function comes with the `react-redux` package and accepts up to four arguments, but you'll use just one at the moment:

```
const { connect } = require('react-redux')
class Movies extends React.Component {
  ...
}
module.exports = connect()(Movies)
```

The `connect()` function returns a function that's then applied to the `Movies` component. As a result not of exporting `Movies` but of calling `connect()` with `Movies`, and having `Provider` as a parent, the `Movies` component becomes connected to the store.

Now the `Movies` component can receive any data from the store and dispatch actions (you didn't see this coming, did you?). But to receive the data in the format you need, you must *map the state to component properties* by creating a simple mapper function (*expression* is a more precise term, because you need to return the result).

In some tutorials, you may see a function called `mapStateToProps()`, although it doesn't have to be an explicitly declared function. Using an anonymous arrow function is just as clean and straightforward. This mapper function goes into a special method, `connect()`, from your favorite `react-redux`. Remember, state is the first argument of `connect()`:

```
module.exports = connect(function(state) {
  return state
})(Movies)
```

Or, here's the fancy, hipster, ESNext React-friendly implicit return style:

```
module.exports = connect(state => state)(Movies)
```

With this setup, you take the *entire* application state from the store and put it into the properties of the `Movies` component. You'll find that, usually, you need only a limited subset of the state. In the example, `Movies` only needs `movies.all`:

```
class Movies extends React.Component {
  render() {
    const {
      children,
      movies = [],
      params = {}
    } = this.props
    ...

module.exports = connect(({movies}) => ({
  movies: movies.all
}), {
  fetchMoviesActionCreator
})(Movies)
```

And this is the `Movie` snippet, which only maps `movies.current` from the state:

```
class Movie extends React.Component {
  render() {
    const {
      movie = {
        starring: []
      }
    } = this.props
    ...

module.exports = connect(({movies}) => ({
  movie: movies.current
}), {
  fetchMovieActionCreator
})(Movie)
```

You'll also see that if the store is empty, the component won't receive any extra properties, because, well, there aren't any.

Some Redux magic happens next: every time part of the store is updated, all components that depend on that part receive new properties and therefore are rerendered. This happens when you dispatch an action, which means your components are now loosely interdependent and update only when the store is updated. Any component can cause this update by dispatching a proper action. There's no need to use classic callback functions passed as properties and stream them from the topmost component down to the most deeply nested; just connect your components to the store.

14.3.10 Dispatching an action

To apply changes to data in the store, you need to dispatch an action. Once you've connected the component to the store, you can receive properties mapped to certain properties of the application state, and you also receive the `dispatch` property.

The `dispatch()` method is a function that takes an action as an argument and dispatches (sends) it into the store. Hence, you can dispatch an action by invoking `this.props.dispatch()` with an action:

```
componentWillMount() {
  this.props.dispatch({
    type: FETCH_MOVIE,
    movie: {}
  })
}
```

`type` is a string value that the Redux library applies to all reducers matching this type. After the action has been dispatched, which usually means you've changed the store, all components that are connected to the store and that have properties mapped from the updated part of the application state are rerendered. There's no need to check whether components should update or do anything at all. You can rely on new properties in components' `render()` function:

```
class Movie extends React.Component {
  render() {
    const {
      movie = {
        starring: []
      }
    } = this.props
  ...
```

You can replace a bare action (an object with `type`) with an action creator (the `fetchMovieActionCreator()` function):

```
const fetchMovieActionCreator = (response) => {
  type: FETCH_MOVIE,
  movie: response.data.data.movie
}
```

```
...
  componentWillMount() {
    ... // Make AJAX/XHR request
    this.props.dispatch(fetchMovieActionCreator(response))
  }
```

Because `fetchMovieActionCreator()` returns a plain object that's identical to the object in the previous example (type and `movie` keys), you can call this action-creator `fetchMovieActionCreator()` function and pass the result to `dispatch()`:

1 Fetch data asynchronously (response).
2 Create an action (`fetchMovieActionCreator()`).
3 Dispatch the action (`this.props.dispatch()`).
4 Execute the reducer.
5 Update the new state in properties (`this.props.movie`).

14.3.11 *Passing action creators into component properties*

You can define action creators as functions right in the component file, but there's another way to use action creators: you can define them in a module, import them, and put them into component properties. To do that, you can use the second argument of the `connect()` function and pass your action creator as a method:

```
const {
  fetchMoviesActionCreator                  Imports the action creator
} = require('modules/movies.js')            from client/modules/movies.js
class Movies extends Component {
  ...
}
module.exports = connect(state => ({
  movies: state.movies.all                  Maps the data to populate
}),{                                         the movies property
  fetchMoviesActionCreator
})(Movies)
```

Now you can refer to `fetchMovieActionCreator()` via properties and pass an action without using `dispatch()`, like this:

```
class Movies extends Component {                      Calls the action
  componentWillMount() {                              creator directly to
    this.props.fetchMoviesActionCreator()             dispatch the action
  }
  render() {
    const {
      movies = []                                     Assigns movies to
    } = this.props                                    this.props.movies or
                                                      to an empty array
    return (                                          (ES6 destructuring)
      <div className={styles.movies}>
        {movies.map((movie, index) => (
          <div key={index}>
```

```
          {movie.title}
        </div>
      ))}
    </div>
  )
 }
}
```

This new action creator is automatically wrapped in a valid dispatch() call. You don't need to worry about doing it yourself. Awesome! This is how the Movies component is implemented in ch14/redux-netflix/src/components/movies/movies.js.

For clarity, you can rename fetchMoviesActionCreator() as fetchMovies() or do this:

```
const {
  fetchMoviesActionCreator
} = require('modules/movies.js')
class Movies extends Component {
  componentWillMount() {                      Dispatches with
    this.props.fetchMovies()          ◁──┘    fetchMovies()
  }
  ...
module.exports = connect(state => ({
  movies: state.movies.all
}), {                                         Renames the
  fetchMovies: fetchMoviesActionCreator   ◁──┘ action method
}) (Movies)
```

The first argument to connect(), which is a function that maps state to component properties, takes the entire state (state) as the only argument and returns a plain object with a single property, movies:

```
...
module.exports = connect(state => ({
  movies: state.movies.all
}), {
  fetchMoviesActionCreator
}) (Movies)
```

You can make the code more eloquent by destructuring state.movies:

```
module.exports = connect(({movies}) => ({
  movies: movies.all
}), {
  fetchMoviesActionCreator
}) (Movies)
```

In the render() function of the Movies component, the value of movies is obtained from properties and is rendered into a collection of sibling DOM elements. Each is a div element with its inner text set to movie.title. This is a typical approach to rendering an array into a fragment of sibling DOM elements.

Wonder what the final `Movies` component looks like? Here's the code (ch14/redux-netflix/src/components/movies/movies.js).

```
const React = require('react')
const { connect } = require('react-redux')
const { Link } = require('react-router')
const movies = require('../../movies.json')
const {
  fetchMoviesActionCreator
} = require('modules/movies.js')
const styles = require('./movies.css')

class Movies extends React.Component {
  componentWillMount() {
    this.props.fetchMovies(movies)
  }

  render() {
    const {
      children,
      movies = [],
      params = {}
    } = this.props

    return (
      <div className={styles.movies}>
        <div className={params.id ? styles.listHidden : styles.list}>
          {movies.map((movie, index) => (
            <Link
              key={index}
              to={`/movies/${index + 1}`}>
              <div
                className={styles.movie}
                style={{backgroundImage: `url(${movie.cover})`}} />
            </Link>
          ))}
        </div>
        {children}
      </div>
    )
  }
}

module.exports = connect((({movies}) => ({
  movies: movies.all
}), {
  fetchMovies: fetchMoviesActionCreator
})(Movies)
```

Loads a mock database from a JSON file (thanks to json-loader) into movies

Dispatches an action using fetchMoviesActionCreator() (FETCH_MOVIES) with the data from the JSON object movies, which could be substituted for an AJAX/XHR call to an API server

Passes children as defined in the React Router hierarchy

Connects the component to a store that provides access to store data and the fetchMoviesActionCreator() action creator from properties

As you can see, swapping for async data is straightforward: make an async call (using the `fetch()` API, axios, and so on), and then dispatch an action in `componentWillMount()`.

Or even better, let's use `componentDidMount()`, which is recommended by the React team for AJAX/XHR calls:

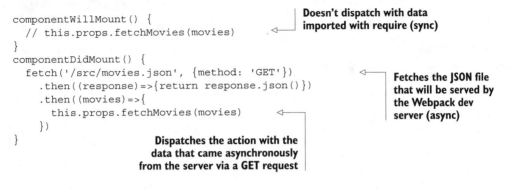

```
componentWillMount() {
  // this.props.fetchMovies(movies)
}
componentDidMount() {
  fetch('/src/movies.json', {method: 'GET'})
    .then((response)=>{return response.json()})
    .then((movies)=>{
      this.props.fetchMovies(movies)
    })
}
```

Doesn't dispatch with data imported with require (sync)

Fetches the JSON file that will be served by the Webpack dev server (async)

Dispatches the action with the data that came asynchronously from the server via a GET request

And you can do the same thing with POST, PUT, and other HTTP calls that you did with GET. You'll be making some of these calls in the next chapter.

We're finished with `Movies`. Next, we'll cover the `Movie` component—but only briefly, because much of the Redux wiring is similar to that in `Movies`. What's different is that `Movie` will get the URL parameter's movie ID. React Router puts it in `this.props.params.id`. This ID will be sent via action dispatch and used in the reducer to filter out only a single movie. As a reminder, these are the reducers from src/modules/movies.js:

```
...
  reducer: handleActions({
    [FETCH_MOVIES]: (state, action) => ({
      ...state,
      all: action.movies
    }),
    [FETCH_MOVIE]: (state, action) => ({
      ...state,
      current: state.all[action.index - 1]
    })
  },
...
```

Uses the movie index to return a single movie

Now, let's look at the implementation of `Movie`, which uses a different state-to-properties mapping by taking a movie ID from a React Router's URL parameter and using it as an index (src/components/movie/movie.js).

Listing 14.8   `Movie` implementation

```
const React = require('react')
const { connect } = require('react-redux')
const { Link } = require('react-router')
const {
  fetchMovieActionCreator
```

```
} = require('modules/movies.js')
const styles = require('./movie.css')                    ⟵——— Imports a CSS file

class Movie extends React.Component {
  componentWillMount() {
    this.props.fetchMovie(this.props.params.id)
  }                                                           ┌ Dispatches only
  componentWillUpdate(next) {                                 │ when the URL
    if (this.props.params.id !== next.params.id) {   ⟵——┘ param changes
      this.props.fetchMovie(next.params.id)
    }
  }
}
render() {
  const {
    movie = {
      starring: []
    }
  } = this.props

  return (                                         ┌ Applies styles to
    <div                                           │ elements inline
      className={styles.movie}              ⟵——┘
      style={{backgroundImage: `linear-gradient(90deg, rgba(0, 0, 0, 1) 0%,
      ➡ rgba(0, 0, 0, 0.625) 100%), url(${movie.cover})`}}>
      <div
        className={styles.cover}
        style={{backgroundImage: `url(${movie.cover})`}} />
      <div className={styles.description}>
        <div className={styles.title}>{movie.title}</div>
        <div className={styles.year}>{movie.year}</div>
        <div className={styles.starring}>
          {movie.starring.map((actor = {}, index) => (
            <div
              key={index}
              className={styles.actor}>
              {actor.name}
            </div>
          ))}
        </div>
      </div>
      <Link
        className={styles.closeButton}
        to="/movies">
        ←
      </Link>
    </div>
  )
}
}
                                                      ┌ Maps the data
module.exports = connect((({movies}) => ({             │ from the reducer
  movie: movies.current                        ⟵——┘ to the property
}), {
  fetchMovie: fetchMovieActionCreator
})(Movie)
```

14.3.12 *Running the Netflix clone*

It's time to run the project. Of course, you could have done it in the beginning, because the start script is in package.json. This script uses an npm library concurrently to run two processes at the same time: Webpack build in watch mode and Webpack development server (port 8080):

```
"start": "concurrently \"webpack --watch --config webpack.config.js\"
➥ \"webpack-dev-server\""
```

Navigate to the project root (ch14/redux-netflix). Install the dependencies with npm i, and run the project from the project folder: npm start. Open your favorite browser at http://localhost:8080.

Click around to see that the routing is working and the images are loading regardless of whether you used mock data (require()) or loaded it via the GET request. Notice that if you're at http://localhost:8080/movies/1 and refresh the page, you don't see anything. You'll take care of that in the next chapter, where you'll implement Node and Express server to support hash-less URLs. Now it's time to wrap up this chapter.

14.3.13 *Redux wrap-up*

Redux provides a single place to store an entire application's data; the only way to change the data is through actions. This makes Redux universal—you can use it anywhere, not only in React apps. But with the react-redux library, you can use the connect() function to connect any component to the store and make it react to any change there.

This is the basic idea of reactive programming: an entity A that observes changes in entity B reacts to those changes as they occur, but the opposite is not true. Here, A is any of your components, and B is the store.

As you connect (connect()) the component and map properties of the store to a component's properties (this.props), you can refer to the latter in the render() function. Usually, you need to first update the store with data to refer to that data. This is why you call an action in a component's componentWillMount() function. By the time the component is mounted for the first time and render() is called, the part of the store that the component refers to may be empty. But once the store data is updated, it's preserved. This is why in the Netflix clone example, the list of movies remains intact even after you navigate across the app's locations (pages or views). Yes. Data doesn't disappear from the store after a component is unmounted, unlike when you use the component's state (remember this.state() and this.setState()?). Thus, your Redux store can serve different parts of your application that require the same data without the data having to be reloaded.

It's also safe to update component properties in the render() function via the store by dispatching an action, because this operation is deferred. On the other hand, *without* Redux, you can't use setState() at any point when the component may be updated: render(), componentWillMount(), or componentWillUpdate(). This feature of Redux adds to its flexibility.

14.4   Quiz

1 Name the two main arguments of a reducing function (callback) to the `Array.reduce()` method in JavaScript.

2 Redux offers simplicity, a larger ecosystem, and a better developer experience than Facebook Flux (`flux`). True or false?

3 Which of the following would you use to create a store and provider? `new Provider (createStore(reducers))`, `<Provider store={createStore(reducers)}>`, or `provider(createStore(reducers))`

4 Redux needs a dispatcher because that's what Flux defines. True or false?

5 In this project, `movies.all` fetches all movies, and `movies.current` fetches the current movie. They're used in the `Movies` and `Movie` components, respectively, in the `connect` call. Where do you define the logic of `movies.all` and `movies.current`?

14.5   Summary

- Unidirectional data flow provides predictability and ease of maintenance for React apps.
- Flux is the recommended architecture when working with React and unidirectional data flow.
- Redux is one of the most popular implementations of the Flux architecture.
- With Redux, you can dispatch an action or put in into the properties object.
- Redux's `connect()` lets you access store data and dispatch actions—necessary features for container (smart) components.
- The Redux `Provider` component provides access to the store to children so you don't have to pass the store in properties manually.
- A reducer is a file with a reducing function that uses (typically) a `switch/case` statement or `handleActions` to apply actions to a new state: that is, the current state and actions are input, and the new state is output.
- Redux `combineReducers` conveniently merges multiple reducers, letting you split the code for those reducers into various modules/files.

14.6   Quiz answers

5 In src/modules/movies.js, in reducers.

4 False. Redux adheres to Flux but doesn't require a dispatcher, so Redux is simpler to implement.

3 `<Provider store={createStore(reducers)}>`

2 True. See the introduction to this chapter and Dan Abramov's post "Why Use Redux over Facebook Flux?" on Stack Overflow (http://mng.bz/z9oك).

1 The accumulator value and the current value are the two primary arguments. Without them, you can't summarize a list.

Working with data using GraphQL

This chapter covers

- Requesting data from the server with GraphQL and Axios
- Supplying data to a Redux store
- Implementing a GraphQL back end with Node/Express
- Supporting hash-less URL routing

In chapter 14, you implemented a Netflix clone with Redux. The data came from a JSON file, but you could instead have used a RESTful API call using `axios` or `fetch()`. This chapter covers one of the most popular options for providing data to a front-end app: GraphQL.

Thus far, you've been importing a JSON file as your back-end data store or making RESTful calls to fetch the same file to emulate a `GET` RESTful endpoint. Ah, mocking APIs. This approach is good for prototyping, because you have the front end ready; when you need persistent storage, you can replace mocks with a back-end server, which is typically a REST API (or, if you *really* have to, SOAP[1]).

---

[1] SOAP is a mostly outdated protocol that relied heavily on XML and has now been replaced by REST.

Imagine that the Netflix clone API has to be developed by another team. You agree on the JSON (or XML) data format over the course of a few meetings. They deliver. The handshake is working, and your front-end app gets all the data. Then, the product owners talk to the clients and decide they want a new field to show stars and ratings for movies. What happens when you need an extra field? You must implement a new `movies/:id/ratings` endpoint, or the back-end team needs to bump up the version of the old endpoint and add an extra field.

Maybe the app is still in the prototyping phase. If so, the field could probably be added to the existing `movies/:id`. It's easy to see that over time, you'll get more requests to change formats and structure. What if ratings must appear in `movies` as well? Or, what if you need new nested fields from other collections, such as friend recommendations? In the age of rapid agile development and lean startup methodology, flexibility is an advantage. The faster these fields and data can be adapted to the end product, the better. An elegant solution called GraphQL clears many of these hurdles.

> **NOTE** The source code for the examples in this chapter is at www.manning
> .com/books/react-quickly and https://github.com/azat-co/react-quickly/
> tree/master/ch15. You can also find some demos at http://
> reactquickly.co/demos.

15.1   GraphQL

In this chapter, you'll continue developing the Netflix clone by adding a server to it. This server will provide a GraphQL API, a modern way of exposing data to React apps. GraphQL is often used with Relay; but as you'll see in this example, you can use it with Redux or any other browser data library. You'll use `axios` for the AJAX/XHR/HTTP requests.

When you work with GraphQL and Redux, the server (back end and web server) can be built using anything (Ruby, Python, Java, Go, Perl), not necessarily Node.js; but Node is what I recommend, and that's what you'll use in this section because it lets you use JavaScript across the entire development tech stack.

In a nutshell, GraphQL (https://github.com/graphql/graphql-js) uses query strings that are interpreted by a server (typically Node), which in turn returns data in a format specified by those queries. The queries are written in a JSON-like format:

```
{
  user(id: 734903) {
    id,
    name,
    isViewerFriend,
    profilePicture(size: 50)  {
      uri,
      width,
      height
    }
  }
}
```

And the response is good-old JSON:

```
{
  "user" : {
    "id": 734903,
    "name": "Michael Jackson",
    "isViewerFriend": true,
    "profilePicture": {
      "uri": "https://twitter.com/mjackson",
      "width": 50,
      "height": 50
    }
  }
}
```

The Netflix clone server could use REST or older SOAP standards. But with the newer GraphQL pattern, you can reverse control by letting clients (front-end or mobile apps) dictate what data they need instead of coding this logic into server endpoints/routes. Some of the advantages of this inverted approach are as follows:[2]

- *Client-specific queries*—Clients get exactly what they need.
- *Structure, arbitrary code*—The uniform API offers server-side flexibility.
- *Strong typing*—More robust validation and certainty in responses, plus easier data consumption by strongly typed languages such as TypeScript, Swift, Java, and Objective-C.
- *Hierarchical queries*—Queries follow the data they return, which is important because data is used by hierarchical views.
- *Faster prototyping*—There's no need for extensive back-end development or large, separate back-end and API teams, because the query has a single endpoint.
- *Fewer API calls*—The front-end app makes fewer server requests because the data structure is dictated by the front-end app and can contain what was previously obtainable only via several REST endpoints.

> **Relay and Relay Modern**
>
> You can also consume a GraphQL API in a React application using Relay (https://facebook.github.io/relay; `graphql-relay-js` and `react-relay` on npm). Some developers prefer to use Relay instead of Redux when working with a GraphQL back end. If you look at the examples provided in the documentation, you may see a similarity to how Redux connects components; and instead of a store, you have a remote GraphQL API.
>
> Whereas React allows you to define views as components (UI) by composing many simple components to build complex UIs and apps, Relay lets components specify what data they need so the data requirements become localized. React components don't care about the logic and rendering of other components.

---

[2] For more on the advantages of GraphQL, such as strong typing, see Nick Schrock, "GraphQL Introduction," *React*, May 1, 2015, http://mng.bz/DS65.

(continued)

The same is true with Relay: components keep their data closer to themselves, which allows for easier composition (building complex UIs and apps from simple components).

Relay Modern is the latest version of Relay. It's easier to use and more extensible.[3] If you or your team plan to use GraphQL seriously, then I highly recommend looking into Relay/Relay Modern as well.

15.2   *Adding a server to the Netflix clone*

To deliver data to your React app, you'll use a simple server made with Express (https://github.com/expressjs/express) and GraphQL. Express is great at organizing and exposing API endpoints, and GraphQL takes care of making your data accessible in a browser-friendly way, as JSON.

The project structure is as follows (you'll reuse a lot of code from `redux-netflix`):

```
/redux-graphql-netflix        ⊲───┐  Compiled files
  /build                          │
    /public                    ⊲──── Compiled front-end files
      index.js
      style.css
    server.js                  ⊲──── Compiled back-end file
  /client                      ⊲──┐
    /components                   │  React source code files
      /app                        │  for the front end
        app.css
        app.js
      /movie
        movie.css
        movie.js
      /movies
        movies.css
        movies.js
      /modules
        index.js
        movies.js
      index.js
      routes.js
    /node_modules
  /server                      ⊲──┐  Express source code
    index.js                      │  file for the back end
    movies.json
    schema.js                  ⊲──── GraphQL schema
  index.html
  package.json
  webpack.config.js
  webpack.server.config.js
```

---

[3] See https://facebook.github.io/relay/docs/relay-modern.html.

The data will still be taken from a JSON file, but this time it's a server file. You can easily replace the JSON file movies.json with database calls in server/schema.js. But before we discuss schemas, let's install all the dependencies, including Express.

The following listing shows the package.json file (ch15/redux-graphql-netflix/package.json). Do you know what to do? Copy it and run `npm i`, of course!

Listing 15.1 Netflix clone package.json

```json
{
  "name": "redux-graphql-netflix",
  "version": "1.0.0",
  "description": "A sample project in React, GraphQL, Express and Redux that
 copies Netflix's features and workflow",
  "main": "index.js",
  "scripts": {
    "start": "concurrently \"webpack --watch --config webpack.config.js\"
 \"webpack --watch --config
 webpack.server.config.js\" \"webpack-dev-server\" \"nodemon
 ./build/server.js\""
  },
  "repository": {
    "type": "git",
    "url": "git+https://github.com/azat-co/react-quickly.git"
  },
  "author": "Azat Mardan (http://azat.co)",
  "license": "MIT",
  "bugs": {
    "url": "https://github.com/azat-co/react-quickly/issues"
  },
  "homepage": "https://github.com/azat-co/react-quickly#readme",
  "devDependencies": {
    "babel-core": "6.11.4",
    "babel-eslint": "6.1.2",
    "babel-loader": "6.2.4",
    "babel-polyfill": "6.9.1",
    "babel-preset-es2015": "6.9.0",
    "babel-preset-react": "6.11.1",
    "babel-preset-stage-0": "6.5.0",
    "concurrently": "2.2.0",
    "css-loader": "0.23.1",
    "eslint": "3.1.1",
    "eslint-plugin-babel": "3.3.0",
    "eslint-plugin-react": "5.2.2",
    "extract-text-webpack-plugin": "1.0.1",
    "json-loader": "0.5.4",
    "nodemon": "1.10.0",
    "style-loader": "0.13.1",
    "webpack": "1.13.1",
    "webpack-dev-server": "1.14.1",
    "axios": "0.13.1",
    "clean-tagged-string": "0.0.1-b6",
    "react": "15.2.1",
    "react-dom": "15.2.1",
```

Adds the start script, which will compile the browser and server code and launch the server

Adds the nodemon dev tool to start and restart Express

Adds axios to make HTTP calls with promises (similar to fetch) to use on the front end

Adds a utility to remove spaces from ES6 string templates and do other cleanup

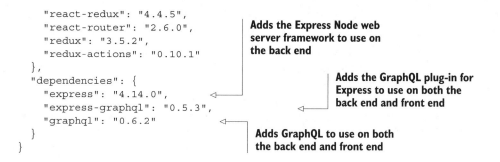

```
    "react-redux": "4.4.5",
    "react-router": "2.6.0",              Adds the Express Node web
    "redux": "3.5.2",                     server framework to use on
    "redux-actions": "0.10.1"            the back end
  },
  "dependencies": {                                 Adds the GraphQL plug-in for
    "express": "4.14.0",                            Express to use on both the
    "express-graphql": "0.5.3",                     back end and front end
    "graphql": "0.6.2"
  }                                        Adds GraphQL to use on both
}                                          the back end and front end
```

Next, you'll implement the main server file server/index.js.

15.2.1 Installing GraphQL on a server

The powerhouse of the web server implemented with Express and Node is its starting point (sometime referred to as an *entry point*): index.js. This file is in the server folder because it's used only on the back end and must not be exposed to clients, for security concerns (it can contain API keys and passwords). The file's high-level structure is as follows:

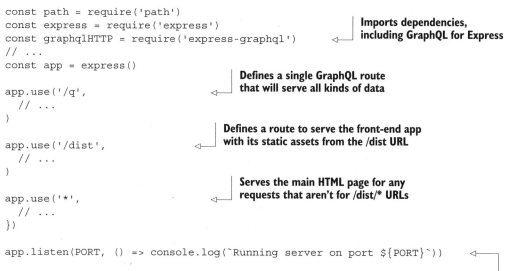

```
const path = require('path')
const express = require('express')
const graphqlHTTP = require('express-graphql')        Imports dependencies,
// ...                                                  including GraphQL for Express
const app = express()

app.use('/q',                      Defines a single GraphQL route
  // ...                           that will serve all kinds of data
)

app.use('/dist',                   Defines a route to serve the front-end app
  // ...                           with its static assets from the /dist URL
)

app.use('*',                       Serves the main HTML page for any
  // ...                           requests that aren't for /dist/* URLs
})

app.listen(PORT, () => console.log(`Running server on port ${PORT}`))

                                                    Boots up the server
```

Let's fill in the missing pieces. First, keep in mind that you need to deliver the same file, index.html, for *every* route except the API endpoint and bundle files. This is necessary because when you use the HTML5 History API and go to a location using a hash-less URL like /movies/8, refreshing the page will make the browser query that exact location.

You've probably noticed that in the previous Netflix clone version, when you refreshed/reloaded the page on an individual movie (such as /movies/8), it didn't show you anything. The reason is that you need to implement something additional for browser history to work. This code must be on the server, and it's responsible for sending out the main index.html file on all requests (even /movies/8/).

In Express, when you need to declare a single operation for every route, you can use * (asterisk):

```
app.use('*', (req, res) => {
  res.sendFile('index.html', {
    root: PWD
  })
})
```

Sending the HTML file per any location (* URL pattern) doesn't do the trick. You'll end up with 404 errors, because this HTML includes references to compiled CSS and JS files (/dist/styles.css and /dist/index.js). So, you need to catch those locations first:

```
app.use('/dist/:file', (req, res) => {
  res.sendFile(req.params.file, {
    root: path.resolve(PWD, 'build', 'public')
  })
})
```

As an alternative, I recommend that you use using a piece of Express middleware called express.static(), like this:

```
app.use('/dist',
  express.static(path.resolve(PWD, 'build', 'public'))
)
```

> **TIP** For more information about middleware and tips on Express, refer to appendix C and my books *Pro Express.js* (Apress, 2014) and *Express Deep API Reference* (Apress, 2014).

Static, public, and dist

The importance of having the public folder *inside* build *cannot* be overstated. If you don't restrict the act of serving resources (such as files) to a subfolder (such as dist or public), then all of your code will be exposed to anyone who visits the server. Even back-end code such as server.js can be exposed if you forego using a subfolder. For example, this

```
// Anti-pattern. Don't do this or you'll be fired
app.use('/dist',
  express.static(path.resolve(PWD, 'build'))
)
```

will expose server.js to attackers—and it might contain secrets, API keys, passwords, and the details of implementation over the /dist/server.js URL.

By using a subfolder such as dist or public, exposing *only* it to the world (over HTTP), and putting *only* the front-end files in this exposed subfolder, you can restrict unauthorized access to other files.

For the GraphQL API to work, you need to set up one more route (/q) in which you use the graphqlHTTP library along with a schema (server/schema.js) and session (req.session) to respond with data:

```
app.use('/q', graphqlHTTP(req => ({
  schema,
  context: req.session
}))))
```

And finally, to make the server work, you need to make it listen to incoming requests on a certain port:

```
app.listen(PORT, () => console.log(`Running server on port ${PORT}`))
```

Here, PORT is an *environment variable*. It's a variable that you can pass into the process from the command-line interface, like this:

```
PORT=3000 node ./build/server.js
```

> **nodemon vs. node**
>
> Recall that in package.json, you use nodemon:
>
> ```
> nodemon ./build/server.js
> ```
>
> Using nodemon is the same as running node, but nodemon will restart the code if you made changes to it.

WARNING   In chapter 14, you used port 8080, because that's the default value for the Webpack Development Server. There's nothing wrong with using 8080 for this example's Express server, but for some weird historical reason, the convention emerged that Express apps run on port 3000. Maybe we can blame Rails for that!

The server also uses another variable declared in uppercase: PWD. It's an environment variable, too, but it's set by Node to the project directory: that is, the path to the folder where the package.json file is located, which is the root folder of your project.

And finally, you use the graphqlHTTP and schema variables. You receive graphqlHTTP from the express-graphql package, and schema is your data schema built using GraphQL definitions.

The following listing shows the complete server setup (ch15/redux-graphql-netflix/server/index.js).

Listing 15.2   Express server to provide data and static assets

```
const path = require('path')
const express = require('express')
const graphqlHTTP = require('express-graphql')
```

```
const schema = require('./schema')
const {
  PORT = 3000,
  PWD = __dirname
} = process.env
const app = express()

app.use('/q', graphqlHTTP(req => ({
  schema,
  context: req.session
}))))

app.use('/dist', express.static(path.resolve(PWD, 'build', 'public')))

app.use('*', (req, res) => {
  res.sendFile('index.html', {
    root: PWD
  })
})

app.listen(PORT, () =>,
  console.log(`Running server on port ${PORT}`))
```

Saves the working directory of this file (PWD = "print working directory")

Boots up the server using 3000 as the port value (not 8080)

GraphQL is strongly typed, meaning it uses schemas as you saw in /q. The schema is defined in server/schema.js, as you saw in the project structure. Let's see what the data looks like: the structure of the data will determine the schema you'll use.

15.2.2 Data structure

The app is a UI that displays data about movies. Therefore, you need to have this data somewhere. The easiest option is to save it in a JSON file (server/movies.json). The file contains all the movies, and each movie can be represented by a plain object with a bunch of properties, so the entire file is an array of objects:

```
[{
  "title": "Pirates of the Caribbean: On Stranger Tides"
  ...
}, {
  "title": "Pirates of the Caribbean: At World's End"
  ...
}, {
  "title": "Avengers: Age of Ultron"
  ...
}, {
  "title": "John Carter"
  ...
}, {
  "title": "Tangled"
  ...
}, {
  "title": "Spider-Man 3"
  ...
}, {
```

```
    "title": "Harry Potter and the Half-Blood Prince"
    ...
}, {
    "title": "Spectre"
    ...
}, {
    "title": "Avatar"
    ...
}, {
    "title": "The Dark Knight Rises"
    ...
}]
```

NOTE The example uses data for 10 of the most expensive movies according to Wikipedia (https://en.wikipedia.org/wiki/List_of_most_expensive_films).

Each object contains information such as the movie's title, cover URL, year released, production cost in millions of dollars, and starring actors. For example, *Pirates of the Caribbean* has this data:

```
{
    "title": "Pirates of the Caribbean: On Stranger Tides",
    "cover": "/dist/images/On_Stranger_Tides_Poster.jpg",
    "year": "2011",
    "cost": 378.5,
    "starring": [{
        "name": "Johnny Depp"
    }, {
        "name": "Penélope Cruz"
    }, {
        "name": "Ian McShane"
    }, {
        "name": "Kevin R. McNally"
    }, {
        "name": "Geoffrey Rush"
    }]
}
```

Currently, each movie is an object that only has a title. Later, you can add as many properties as you want; but right now let's focus on the data schema.

15.2.3 *GraphQL schema*

You can use any data source with GraphQL: an SQL database, an object store, a bunch of files, or a remote API. Two things matter:

- Purity of the data—that is, identical requests should return identical responses (a.k.a. *idempotent*).
- It should be possible to represent the data with JSON.

You have the list of movies stored in a JSON file, so you can import it:

```
const movies = require('./movies.json')
```

A typical GraphQL schema defines a query with fields and arguments. The example data schema has only a list of objects, and each object has only a single property: title. The schema definition is shown next. This is a basic example—you'll see the full schema later:

```
const movies = require('./movies.json')
new graphql.GraphQLSchema({
  query: new graphql.GraphQLObjectType({
    name: 'Query',
    fields: {
      movies: {
        type: new graphql.GraphQLList(new graphql.GraphQLObjectType({
          name: 'Movie',
          fields: {
            title: {
              type: graphql.GraphQLString
            }
          }
        })),
        resolve: () => movies
      }
    }
  })
})
```

Imports movies from a file (mock database)

Defines the title field in the schema as a string

Defines the getter for this query, which will send data from the JSON file (could be a database call)

The core idea is that when the query is performed, the function assigned to the resolve key is executed. After that, only properties of objects that are requested are picked from the result of this function call. These properties will be in the resulting objects, and fields that aren't listed won't appear. Thus you need to specify what properties you want to receive every time you perform a query. This makes your API flexible and efficient: you can arrange parts of the data as you want them in the runtime.

The example has two types of queries and more fields. The following listing shows how you can implement them (ch15/redux-graphql-netflix/server/schema.js).

Listing 15.3 GraphQL schema

```
const {
  GraphQLSchema,
  GraphQLObjectType,
  GraphQLList,
  GraphQLString,
  GraphQLInt,
  GraphQLFloat
} = require('graphql')
const movies = require('./movies.json')

const movie = new GraphQLObjectType({
  name: 'Movie',
  fields: {
    title: {
```

Sets the name of the object to "movie" so you can use it in two queries

Defines all the fields with proper types

```
          type: GraphQLString
        },
        cover: {
          type: GraphQLString
        },
        year: {
          type: GraphQLString
        },
        cost: {                                          Uses float
          type: GraphQLFloat          <--------------    for the cost
        },
        starring: {
          type: new GraphQLList(new GraphQLObjectType({
            name: 'starring',
            fields: {
              name: {
                type: GraphQLString
              }
            }
          }))
        }
      }
    }
  })

module.exports = new GraphQLSchema({
  query: new GraphQLObjectType({
    name: 'Query',
    fields: {
      movies: {
        type: new GraphQLList(movie),                Sends back the entire
        resolve: () => movies          <--------     array of movies
      },
      movie: {
        type: movie,
        args: {                                      Sends back only a single
          index: {                                   movie using the index
            type: GraphQLInt                          (from the URL parameter)
          }
        },
        resolve: (r, {index}) => movies[index - 1]        <--------
      }
    }
  })
})
```

Phew! Now let's move to the front end and see how to query this neat little server.

15.2.4 Querying the API and saving the response into the store

To get the list of movies, you need to query the server. And after the response has been received, you must pass it to the store. This operation is asynchronous and involves an HTTP request, so it's time to unveil axios.

Promises and callbacks

The `axios` library implements promise-based HTTP requests. This means it returns a promise immediately after calling a function. Because an HTTP request isn't guaranteed to be performed immediately, you need to wait until this promise is *resolved*.

To get data from a promise once it's resolved, you use its `then` property. It accepts a function as a callback, which is called with a single argument; and this argument is the result of the initial operation—in this case, an HTTP call:

```
getPromise(options)
  .then((data)=>{
    console.log(data)
  })
```

Using a promise and a callback (in `then`) is an alternative to using just a callback, in the sense that the previous code can be rewritten without promises:

```
getResource(options,  (data)=>{
  console.log(data)
})
```

There's a controversy associated with promises. Although some people prefer promises and callbacks over plain callbacks due to the convenience of the promise `catch.all` syntax, others feel promises aren't worth the hassle (I'm in this camp), especially considering that promises can bury errors and fail silently. Nevertheless, promises are part of ES6/ES2015 and are here to stay. At the same time, new patterns such as generators and async/await are emerging as part of the next evolution of writing async code.[4]

Rest assured, you can do any asynchronous coding with plain callbacks. But most modern (especially front-end) code uses (or will use) promises or async/await. For this reason, this book uses promises with `fetch()` and `axios`.

For more information on the promise API, refer to the documentation at MDN (http://mng.bz/7DcO) and my article "Top 10 ES6 Features Every Busy JavaScript Developer Must Know" (https://webapplog.com/es6).

axios uses promise-based requests, not unlike `fetch()`. To perform a GET HTTP call, use the `get` property of `axios`:

```
axios.get('/q')
```

Because axios returns a promise, you can immediately access its `then` property:

```
axios.get('/q').then(response => response)
```

---

[4] See my courses on ES6 and ES7+ES8 at https://node.university/p/es6 and https://node.university/p/es7-es8.

The function you pass as the argument to then returns into the context of the promise and not the context of your component's method. You need to call an action creator to deliver new data into the store:

```
axios.get('/q').then(response => this.props.fetchMovie(response))
```

Now, let's build a proper query against your GraphQL API. To do that, you can use a multiline template string (notice that it uses backticks instead of single quotes):

```
axios.get(`/q?query={
  movie(index:1) {
    title,
    cover
  }
}`).then(response => this.props.fetchMovie(response))
```

Using a multiline template literal (the backticks) preserves line breaks, so the query string will have new lines. Not good. New lines in a query string might break the API endpoint URLs. For this reason, you need to remove unnecessary spaces and line breaks in the HTTP calls but keep them in the source code. The clean-tagged-string library (https://github.com/taxigy/clean-tagged-string) does only that: it transforms a huge, multiline template string into a smaller, single-line string resulting in this

```
clean`/q?query={
  movie(index:1) {
    title,
    cover
  }
}`
```

looking like this:

```
'/q?query={ movie(index:1) { title, cover } }'
```

Notice the syntax: there are no parentheses (round brackets) after clean, and it's attached to the template string. This is valid syntax and is called using *tagged strings* (http://mng.bz/9CqH).

Now, let's get the first movie, with an index of 1:

```
const clean = require('clean-tagged-string').default

axios.get(clean`/q?query={
  movie(index:1) {
    title,
    cover
  }
}`).then(response => this.props.fetchMovie(response))
```

Figure 15.1　Single-movie view server from Express server (port 3000) with browser history (no hash signs!)

Next, you need to implement code to get any movie based on its ID. You also want to request more fields, not just `title` and `cover`, so you can display the view shown in figure 15.1. It's good to know that the single-movie page won't be lost on reload, because you added the special server code to `sendFile()` for `*` to catch all routes that send index.html.

You can fetch the data for a single movie from the API in the lifecycle component using your favorite promise-based HTTP agent, `axios`:

```
componentWillMount() {
  const query = clean`{
    movie(index:${id}) {
      title,
      cover,
      year,
      starring {
        name
      }
    }
  }`
  axios.get(`/q?query=${query}`)
    .then(response =>
      this.props.fetchMovie(response)
    )
}
```

The list of requested properties for a movie entity is a little longer: not just `title` and `cover`, but also `year` and `starring`. Because `starring` is itself an array of objects, you also need to declare which properties of those objects you want to request. In this case, you only want `name`.

The response from the API goes to the `fetchMovie` action creator. After that, the store is updated with the movie the user wants to see.

Connect it:

```
const {
  fetchMovieActionCreator
} = require('modules/movies.js')
...
module.exports = connect(({movies}) => ({
  movie: movies.current
}), {
  fetchMovie: fetchMovieActionCreator
})(Movie)
```

And render it:

```
render() {
  const {
    movie = {
      starring: []
    }
  } = this.props;
  return (
    <div>
      <img src={`url(${movie.cover})`} alt={movie.title} />
      <div>
        <div>{movie.title}</div>
        <div>{movie.year}</div>
        {movie.starring.map((actor = {}, index) => (
          <div key={index}>
            {actor.name}
          </div>
        ))}
      </div>
      <Link to="/movies">
        ?
      </Link>
    </div>
  )
}
```

To better organize the code, let's add a `fetchMovie()` method to the `Movie` component that's already familiar to you from chapter 14 (ch14/redux-netflix/src/components/movie/movie.js). This new method will be used to make AJAX-y calls that will, in turn, dispatch actions. The method is in the `Movie` component (ch15/redux-graphql-netflix/client/components/movie/movie.js).

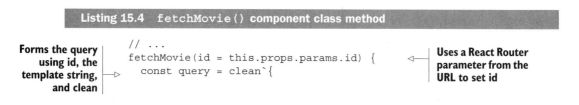

Listing 15.4   `fetchMovie()` component class method

Forms the query using id, the template string, and clean

```
// ...
fetchMovie(id = this.props.params.id) {
  const query = clean`{
```

Uses a React Router parameter from the URL to set id

```
        movie(index:${id}) {
          title,
          cover,
          year,
          starring {
            name
          }                          Makes the
        }                            request to /q
      }`

      axios.get (`/q?query=${query}`)                    Dispatches the
        .then(response => {              ◁                action with the data
          this.props.fetchMovie(response)  ◁              from the server
        }
      )
    }
    // ...
```

Next, let's move on to getting the list of movies.

15.2.5 *Showing the list of movies*

When you show a list of movies, the query to the API is different, and it's rendered in a different way than when you fetch a single movie. You fetched the data from the GraphQL server using a valid GraphQL query, via an asynchronous GET request performed with the axios library, and you put this data into the store via an action. The next thing to do is show this data to the user: time to *render* it.

You already know that, to take data from the store, a component needs to be connected: wrapped with a connect() function call that maps state and actions to properties. In the component's render() function, you use component properties. But these properties need values; that's why you make AJAX/XHR calls, usually after the component has been mounted for the first time (lifecycle events!).

Let's declare a component to pick the data from the store, take it from properties, and render it. First, connect the component to the store (this snippet is from ch15/redux-graphql-netflix/client/components/movies/movies.js):

```
const React = require('react')
const { connect } = require('react-redux')
const {
  fetchMoviesActionCreator
} = require('modules/movies')

class Movies extends Component {
  // ...
}

module.exports = connect(({movies}) => ({
  movies: movies.all
}), {
  fetchMovies: fetchMoviesActionCreator
}) (Movies)
```

The connect () function takes two arguments: the first maps the store to component properties, and the second maps action creators to component properties. After that, the component has two new properties: this.props.movies and this.props.fetchMovies ().

Next, let's fetch those movies and, as the data is received, place it in the store via the action creator (dispatch an action). Usually, data may be requested from a remote API when the component starts its lifecycle (componentWillMount () or component-DidMount ()):

```
const {
  fetchMoviesActionCreator              ⟵—— Imports an action creator
} = require('modules/movies.js')
. . .
class Movies extends React.Component {
  componentWillMount() {
    const query = clean`{
      movies {
        title,
        cover
      }
    }`

    axios.get(`/q?query=${query}`)                    Dispatches an action to
      .then(response => {                             update the store with the
        this.props.fetchMovies(response)     ⟵——     response from the server
      }
    )
  }
// . . .
}
module.exports = connect(({movies}) => ({           Lets you dispatch an
  movies: movies.all                                action provided by
}), {                                               the action creator
  fetchMovies: fetchMoviesActionCreator    ⟵——
})(Movies)
```

Finally, render the Movies component using data from properties, which comes from the Redux store:

```
// . . .
render() {
  const {
    movies = []
  } = this.props

  return (
    <div>
      {movies.map((movie, index) => (
        <Link
          key={index}
          to={`/movies/${index + 1}`}>
```

```
          <img src={`url(${movie.cover})`} alt={movie.title} />
        </Link>
      ))}
    </div>
  )
}
// ...
```

Every movie has `cover` and `title` properties. A link to a movie is basically a reference to its position in the array of movies. This setup isn't stable when you have thousands of elements in a collection, because, well, the order is never guaranteed, but for now it's okay. (A better way would be to use a unique ID, which is typically autogenerated by a database like MongoDB.)

The component now renders the list of movies, although it lacks styles. Check out this chapter's source code to see how it works with styles and a three-level hierarchy of components.

15.2.6 *GraphQL wrap-up*

Adding GraphQL support on a basic level is straightforward and transparent. GraphQL works differently than a typical RESTful API: you can query any property, at any nesting level, for any subset of entities the API provides. This makes GraphQL efficient for datasets of complex objects, whereas a REST design usually requires multiple requests to get the same data.

GraphQL is a promising pattern for implementing server-client handshakes. It allows for more control from the client, which can dictate the structure of the data to the REST API. This inversion of control allows front-end developers to request only the data they need and not have to modify back-end code (or ask a back-end team to do so).

15.3 *Quiz*

1 Which command creates a GraphQL schema? `new graphql.GraphQLSchema()`, `graphql.GraphQLSchema()`, or `graphql.getGraphQLSchema()`

2 It's okay to put API calls into reducers. True or false? (Hint: See a Tip in chapter 14.)

3 Where do you make the GraphQL call to fetch a movie? `componentDidUnmount()`, `componentWillMount()`, or `componentDidMount()`

4 You used this URL for GraphQL: `` `/q?query=${query}` `` . What does this syntax refer to? Inline Markdown, comments, template literal, string template, or string interpolation

5 `GraphQLString` is a special GraphQL schema type, and you can pull this class from the `graphql` package. True or false?

15.4   Summary

- GraphQL is a robust, reliable way to provide data to the front end. It also eliminates a lot of duplicate back-end code.
- To enable the browser history and hash-less URL with React Router, you can use `sendFile()` in the * Express route to serve index.html.
- To use Express not just as a data provider/API but as a static web server, use `express.static` with `app.use()`.
- GraphQL's URL structure is /q?query=... where query has the value of your data query.

15.5   Quiz answers

1   new graphql.GraphQLSchema()
2   False. Avoid putting API calls in reducers. It's better to put them in components (container/smart components, to be specific).
3   componentWillMount(), but componentDidMount() is also a good location. componentDidUnmount() isn't a valid method.
4   Template literal, string template, and string interpolation are all valid names to define the query with a variable.
5   True. This is valid code: const {GraphQLString} = require('graphql'). See listing 15.3.

Watch this chapter's introduction video by scanning this QR code with your phone or going to http://reactquickly.co/videos/ch16.

Unit testing
React with Jest
16

This chapter covers

- Reasons to use Jest
- Unit testing with Jest
- UI testing with Jest and TestUtils

In modern software engineering, testing is important. It's at least as important as using Agile methods, writing well-documented code, and having enough coffee on hand—sometimes even more so. Proper testing will save you from many hours of debugging later. The code isn't an asset, it's a liability, so your goal is to make it as easy to maintain as possible.

Code is a liability?

Googling the phrase "Code isn't an asset, it's a liability" gives 191 million results, which makes it hard to pinpoint its origins. Although I can't find an author, I can tell you the gist of the idea: when you write software, you're building apps/products/services that are assets, but your code is *not* one of them.

(continued)

Assets are things that generate income. Code does not generate any income by itself. Yes, code enables products, but the code is a tool to make the products (which are assets). The code itself isn't an asset—it's more of a necessary evil to get to the end goal of having a working application.

Thus, code is a liability, because you have to maintain it. More code does *not* automatically translate into more revenue or better product quality; but more code almost always increases complexity and the cost of maintenance. Some of the best ways to minimize the cost of maintaining code are to make it simple, robust, and flexible for future changes and enhancements. And testing—especially automated testing—helps when you're making changes, because you have more assurance that the changes didn't break your app.

Using test-driven/behavior-driven development (TDD/BDD) can make maintenance easier. It can also make your company more competitive by letting you iterate more quickly and make you more productive by giving you the confidence that your code works.

NOTE The source code for the examples in this chapter is at www.manning .com/books/react-quickly and https://github.com/azat-co/react-quickly/ tree/master/ch16. You can also find some demos at http:// reactquickly.co/demos.

16.1   *Types of testing*

There are multiple types of testing. Most commonly, they can be separated into three categories: unit, service, and UI testing, as shown in figure 16.1. Here's an overview of each category, from lowest to highest level:

- *Unit testing*—The system tests standalone methods and classes. There are no or few dependencies or interconnected parts. The code for the tested subject should be enough to verify that the method works as it should work. For example, a module that generates random passwords can be tested by invoking a method from a module and comparing the output against a regular-expression pattern. This category also includes tests that may involve a few parts or modules working together to produce one piece of functionality. For example, several components have to work together to provide the functionality for password input with a strength check. They can be tested by supplying the value to one component (input) and monitoring changes in the strength check (sufficient or not). These tests are durable; according to industry best practices, this category should make up roughly 70% of your tests (see figure 16.1) and should definitely outnumber any other types of tests.
- *Service (integration) testing*—Tests typically involve other dependencies and require a separate environment. Integration tests should be roughly 20% of all

your tests. Once you have a solid foundation of unit tests and the assurance of functional tests, you don't want to have too many integration tests, because maintaining them will slow development. Each time there's a UI change, your integration tests need to be updated. This often leads to flaky UI tests and no integration testing at all, which is even worse.

- *UI (acceptance)*—Tests often mimic Agile user stories and/or involve testing the entire system, which obviously has all the dependencies and complexities imaginable. UI tests are more fragile and difficult (expensive) to maintain, and thus they should be only about 10% of your overall tests.

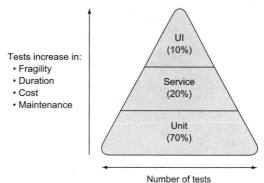

This chapter covers unit testing of React apps with a bit of UI testing of React components, using the mock DOM rendering of React and Jest. You'll also use the standard toolchain of Node, npm, Babel, and Webpack. To begin unit testing, let's investigate Jest.

Figure 16.1   Testing pyramid according to software engineering's best practices

16.2   Why Jest (vs. Mocha or others)?

Jest (https://facebook.github.io/jest) is a command-line tool based on Jasmine. It has a Jasmine-like interface. If you've worked with Mocha, you'll find that Jest looks similar to it and is easy to learn. Jest is developed by Facebook and is often used together with React; the API documentation is at https://facebook.github.io/jest/docs/api.html#content.

Jest offers these features:

- Powerful mocking (https://facebook.github.io/jest/docs/mock-functions.html) of JavaScript/Node modules makes it easier to isolate code in order to unit test it.
- Less setup is required to get started than with other test runners, such as Mocha, where you need to import Chai or standalone Expect. Jest also finds tests in the __tests__ folder.
- Tests can be sandboxed and executed in parallel to run them more quickly.[1]
- You can perform static analysis with the support of Facebook's Flow (https://flowtype.org), which is a static type checker for JS.
- Jest provides modularity, configurability, and adaptability (via the support of Jasmine assertions).

---

[1]   Christopher Poher, "JavaScript Unit Testing Performance," *Jest*, March 11, 2016, http://mng.bz/YfXz.

> ### Mocking, static analysis, and Jasmine
>
> The term *mocking* means faking a certain part of a dependency so you can test the current code. *Automocking* means mocking is done for you automatically. In Jest before v15,[2] every imported dependency is automocked, which can be useful if you frequently rely on mocking. Most developers don't need automocking, so in Jest v15+ it's off by default—but automocking can be turned on if necessary.
>
> *Static analysis* means the code can be analyzed before you run it, which typically involves type checking. Flow is a library that adds type checking to otherwise type-less (more or less) JavaScript.
>
> Jasmine is a feature-rich testing framework that comes with an assertion language. Jest extends and builds on Jasmine under the hood so you don't need to import or configure anything. Thus, you have the best of both worlds: you can tap into the common interface of Jasmine without needing extra dependencies or setup.

There are many opinions about what test framework is better for what job. Most projects use Mocha, which has a lot of features. Jasmine arose from front-end development but is interchangeable with Mocha and Jest. All of them use the same constructs to define test suites and tests:

- `describe`—Test suite
- `it`—Test case
- `before`—Preparation
- `beforeEach`—Preparation for every suite or case
- `after`—Cleanup
- `afterEach`—Cleanup for every suite or case

Without getting into a heated debate in this book about what framework is the best, I encourage you to keep an open mind and explore Jest because of the features I've listed and because it comes from the same community that develops React. This way, you can make a better judgment about which framework to use for your next React project.

Most modern frameworks like Mocha, Jasmine, and Jest are similar for most tasks. Any difference will depend on your preferred style (maybe you like automocking, or maybe you don't) and on the edge cases of your particular project (do you need all the features Mocha provides, or you need something lightweight like the Test Anything Protocol's [TAP, https://testanything.org] `node-tap` [www.node-tap.org]?). Jest is a good place to start, because once you learn how to use Jest with React utilities and methods, you can use other test runners and testing frameworks such as Mocha, Jasmine, and `node-tap`.

---

[2] See Christoph Pojer, "Jest 15.0: New Defaults for Jest," September 1, 2016, http://mng.bz/p20n.

16.3 *Unit testing with Jest*

If you've never worked with any of the testing frameworks I've been discussing, don't worry; Jest is straightforward to learn. The main statement is `describe`, which is a test suite that acts as a wrapper for tests; and `it`, which is an individual test called a *test case*. Test cases are nested within the test suite.

Other constructs such as `before`, `after`, and their `Each` brethren `beforeEach` and `afterEach` execute either before or after the test suite or test case. Adding `Each` executes a piece of code many times as compared to just one time.

Writing tests consists of creating test suites, cases, and assertions. *Assertions* are like true or false questions, but in a nice readable format (BDD).

Here's an example, without assertions for now:

Defines the done() callback

```
describe('Noun: method or a class/module name', () => {
  before((done) => {
    // This code will be called just once before all it statements
    done()
  })
  beforeEach((done) => {
    // This code will be called many times before all it statements
    done()
  })
  it('Verb describing the behavior', (done) => {
    // Assertions
      done()
  })
  it('Verb describing the behavior', (done) => {
    // Assertions
    done()
  })
  ...
  after((done) => {
    // This code will be called just once after all it statements
    done()
  })
  afterEach((done) => {
    // This code will be called many times after all it statements
    done()
  })
})
```

Invokes done() when the async test code is finished

You must have at least one `describe` and one `it`, but their number isn't limited. Everything else, such as `before` and `after`, is optional.

You won't be testing any React components yet. Before you can work with React components, you need to learn a little more about Jest by working on a Jest example that doesn't have a UI.

In this section, you'll create and unit-test a module that generates random passwords. Imagine you're working on a sign-up page for a cool new chat app. You need the ability to generate passwords, right? This module will automatically generate random passwords. To keep things simple, the format will be eight alphanumeric characters. The project (module) structure is as follows:

```
/generate-password
  /__test__
    generate-password.test.js
  /node_modules
    generate-password.js
    package.json
```

You'll use the CommonJS/Node module syntax, which is widely supported in Node (duh) and also in browser development via Browserify and Webpack. Here's the module in the ch16/generate-password.js file.

Listing 16.1   Module for generating passwords

```
module.exports = () => {
  return Math.random().toString(36).slice(-8)   ⟵  Uses slice with a negative number
}                                                    to reverse the order (right to left)
```

Just as a refresher, in this file you export the function via the `module.exports` global. This is Node.js and CommonJS notation. You can use it on the browser with extra tools like Webpack and Browserify (http://browserify.org).

The function uses `Math.random()` to generate a number and convert it to a string. The string length is eight characters, as specified by `slice(-8)`.

To test the module, you can run this eval Node command from the terminal. It imports the module, invokes its function, and prints the result:

```
node -e \"console.log(require('./generate-password.js')())\"
```

You could improve this module by making it work with different numbers of characters, not just eight.

16.3.1   Writing unit tests in Jest

To begin using Jest, you need to create a new project folder and `npm init` it to create package.json. If you don't have npm, this is the best time to install it; follow the instructions in appendix B.

Once you've created the package.json file in a new folder, install Jest:

```
$ npm install jest-cli@19.0.2 --save-dev --save-exact
```

I'm using `jest-cli` version 19.0.2; make sure your version is the same or compatible. `--save-dev` adds the entry to the package.json file. Open the file, and manually change the `test` entry to `jest` as shown next (ch16/jest/package.json). This will add the testing command. Also add the start script.

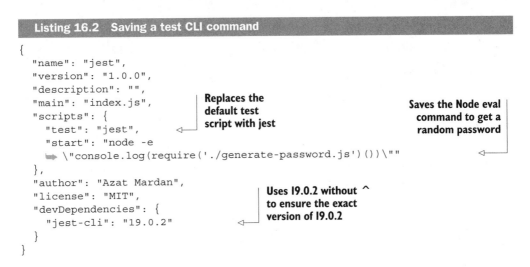

Listing 16.2   Saving a test CLI command

```
{
  "name": "jest",
  "version": "1.0.0",
  "description": "",
  "main": "index.js",
  "scripts": {
    "test": "jest",
    "start": "node -e
    \"console.log(require('./generate-password.js')())\""
  },
  "author": "Azat Mardan",
  "license": "MIT",
  "devDependencies": {
    "jest-cli": "19.0.2"
  }
}
```

Replaces the default test script with jest

Saves the Node eval command to get a random password

Uses 19.0.2 without ^ to ensure the exact version of 19.0.2

Now, create a folder named __tests__. The name is important because Jest will pick up tests from that folder. Then, create your first Jest test in __tests__/generate-password.js.

Typically, you only mock dependencies that you don't need to isolate the library you're currently unit testing. Jest prior to v15 automatically mocks every required file, so you need to use dontMock() or jest.autoMockOff() to avoid this for the main module you test (generate-password.js). This is one way to do it:

```
jest.dontMock('../generate-password.js')         ◁─── Only for Jest prior to v15
```

Luckily, for the version of Jest used in this chapter (v19), you *don't need to disable auto-mock*, because it's disabled by default. So, you can skip this dontMock() line of code or leave it commented out.

The test file has a single suite (only one describe), which expects the value to match the /^[a-z0-9]{8}$/ regular-expression pattern—only alphanumerics and exactly eight characters—to satisfy your condition for a strong password (ch16/generate-password/__tests__/generate-password.test.js). You don't want your chat users to be hacked by brute force!

Listing 16.3   Test file for the password-generating module

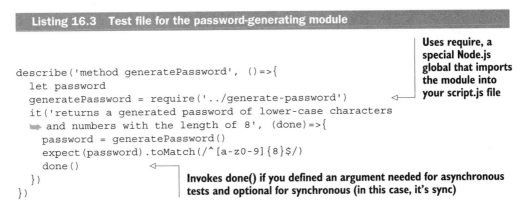

```
describe('method generatePassword', ()=>{
  let password
  generatePassword = require('../generate-password')
  it('returns a generated password of lower-case characters
  and numbers with the length of 8', (done)=>{
    password = generatePassword()
    expect(password).toMatch(/^[a-z0-9]{8}$/)
    done()
  })
})
```

Uses require, a special Node.js global that imports the module into your script.js file

Invokes done() if you defined an argument needed for asynchronous tests and optional for synchronous (in this case, it's sync)

You can run the test with $ npm test. You'll see something like this as the terminal output:

```
Using Jest CLI v13.2.3, jasmine2
 PASS  __tests__/generate-password.test.js (0.031s)
1 test passed (1 total in 1 test suite, run time 1.339s)
```

> **How many tests passed and how many you have in total**

16.3.2 *Jest assertions*

By default, Jest uses BDD syntax (https://en.wikipedia.org/wiki/Behavior-driven _development) powered by Expect syntax (https://facebook.github.io/jest/docs/ api.html). Expect is a popular language that's a replacement for TDD assertions. It has many flavors, and Jest uses a somewhat simplified version (in my opinion). Unlike other frameworks, such as Mocha, where you need to install additional modules for syntax support, in Jest it's automatic.

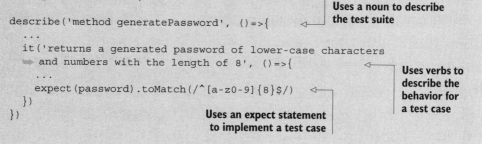

TDD and BDD

TDD can mean test-driven development or TDD syntax with assertions. Briefly, during test-driven development you write a test, then run it (failing), then make it work (passing), and then make it right (refactor).

You most certainly can perform test-driven development with BDD. The main benefit of BDD style is that it's intended for communicating with *every member of a cross- functional team*, not just software engineers. TDD is more of a techie language. BDD format makes it easier to read tests—ideally the spec title should tell you what you're testing, as in this example:

```
describe('method generatePassword', ()=>{
  ...
  it('returns a generated password of lower-case characters
    and numbers with the length of 8', ()=>{
    ...
    expect(password).toMatch(/^[a-z0-9]{8}$/)
  })
})
```

> **Uses a noun to describe the test suite**
>
> **Uses verbs to describe the behavior for a test case**
>
> **Uses an expect statement to implement a test case**

Here's a list of the main Expect methods that Jest supports (there are many more). You pass the actual values—returned by the program—to expect() and use the following methods to compare those values with expected values that are hardcoded in the tests:

- .not—Inverses the next comparison in the chain
- expect(OBJECT).toBe(value)—Expects the value to be equal with JavaScript's triple equal sign === (checks for value and type, not just value)[3]

---

[3] See "Equality Comparisons and Sameness," Mozilla Developer Network, http://mng.bz/kliO.

- `expect(OBJECT).toEqual(value)`—Expects the value to be deep-equal[4]
- `expect(OBJECT).toBeFalsy()`—Expects the value to be falsy (see the following sidebar)
- `expect(OBJECT).toBeTruthy()`—Expects the value to be truthy
- `expect(OBJECT).toBeNull()`—Expects the value to be `null`
- `expect(OBJECT).toBeUndefined()`—Expects the value to be undefined
- `expect(OBJECT).toBeDefined()`—Expects the value to be defined
- `expect(OBJECT).toMatch(regexp)`—Expects the value to match the regular expression

Truthy and falsy

In JavaScript/Node, a *truthy* value translates to `true` when evaluated as a Boolean in an `if/else` statement. A *falsy* value, on the other hand, evaluates to `else` in an `if/else`.

The official definition is that a value is truthy if it's not falsy, and there are only six falsy values:

- `false`
- `0`
- `""` (empty string)
- `null`
- `undefined`
- `NaN` (not a number)

Everything not listed here is truthy.

To summarize, Jest can be used for unit tests, which should be the most numerous of your tests. They're lower level, and for this reason they're more solid and less brittle, which makes them less costly to maintain.

Thus far, you've created a module and tested its method with Jest. This is a typical unit test. There are no dependencies involved—only the tested module itself. This skill should prepare you to continue with testing React components. Next, let's look at more-complicated UI testing. The following section deals with the React testing utility, which enables you to perform UI testing.

16.4   *UI testing React with Jest and TestUtils*

Generally speaking, in UI testing (recommended to make up only 10% of your tests), you test entire components, their behavior, and even entire DOM trees. You can test components manually, which is a terrible idea! Humans make mistakes and take a long time to perform tests. Manual UI testing should be minimal or nonexistent.

---

[4] *Deep equality* compares objects, including all their properties and values, to the last level of nestedness (going deep). There's no standard API for it in JavaScript, but there are implementations like Node's core `assert` module (http://mng.bz/rhoX) and `deep-equal` (www.npmjs.com/package/deep-equal).

What about automated UI testing? You can test automatically using *headless browsers* (https://en.wikipedia.org/wiki/Headless_browser), which are like real browsers but without a GUI. That's how most Angular 1 apps are tested. It's possible to use this process with React, but it isn't easy, it's often slow, and it requires a lot of processing power.

Another automated UI testing approach uses React's virtual DOM, which is accessible via a browser-like testing JavaScript environment implemented by jsdom (https://github.com/tmpvar/jsdom). To use React's virtual DOM, you'll need a utility that's closely related to the React Core library but not part of it: TestUtils, which is a React utility to test its components. Simply put, TestUtils allows you to create components and render them into the fake DOM. Then you can poke around, looking at the elements by tags or classes. It's all done from the command line, without the need for browsers (headless or not).

> **NOTE** There are other React add-ons, listed at https://facebook.github.io/react/docs/addons.html. Most of them are no longer in development or are still in the experimental stage, which in practice means the React team may change their interface or stop supporting them. All of them follow the naming convention react-addons-NAME. TestUtils is an add-on, and, like other React add-ons, it's installed via npm. (You can't use TestUtils without npm; if you haven't already, you can get npm by following the instructions in appendix A.)

For versions of React before v15.5.4, TestUtils was in an npm package `react-addons-test-utils` (https://facebook.github.io/react/docs/test-utils.html). For example, if you're using React version 15.2.1, you can install `react-addons-test-utils` v15.2.1 with npm using the following command:

```
$ npm install react-addons-test-utils@15.2.1 --save-dev --save-exact
```

And this goes in your test source code (React prior to v15.5.4):

```
const TestUtils = require('react-addons-test-utils')
```

In React v15.5.4, things are somewhat easier, because TestUtils is in ReactDOM (`react-dom` on npm). You don't have to install a separate package for this example, because you're using the newer v15.5.4:

```
const TestUtils = require('react-dom/test-utils')
```

TestUtils has a few primary methods for rendering components; simulating events such as `click`, `mouseOver`, and so on; and finding elements in a rendered component. You'll begin by rendering a component and learn about other methods as you need them.

To illustrate the TestUtils `render()` method, the following listing renders an element into a `div` variable without using a headless (or real, for that matter) browser (ch16/testutils/__tests__/render-props.js).

Listing 16.4   Rendering a React element in Jest

```
describe('HelloWorld', ()=>{
  const TestUtils = require('react-dom/test-utils')
  const React = require('react')

  it('has props', (done)=>{

    class HelloWorld extends React.Component {
      render() {
        return <div>{this.props.children}</div>
      }
    }
    let hello = TestUtils.renderIntoDocument(<HelloWorld>Hello Node!
    ➥ </HelloWorld>)
    expect(hello.props).toBeDefined()
    console.log('my hello props:', hello.props) // my div: Hello Node!

    done()
  })
})
```

And package.json for ch16/testutils example looks like this with Babel, Jest CLI, React, and React DOM:

```
{
  "name": "password",
  "version": "2.0.0",
  "description": "",
  "main": "index.html",
  "scripts": {
    "test": "jest",
    "test-watch": "jest --watch",
    "build-watch": "./node_modules/.bin/webpack -w",
    "build": "./node_modules/.bin/webpack"
  },
  "author": "Azat Mardan",
  "license": "MIT",
  "babel": {
    "presets": [
      "react"
    ]
  },
  "devDependencies": {
    "babel-jest": "19.0.0",
    "babel-preset-react": "6.24.1",
    "jest-cli": "19.0.2",
    "react": "15.5.4",
    "react-dom": "15.5.4"
  }
}
```

WARNING renderIntoDocument() only works on custom components, not standard DOM components like <p>, <div>, <section>, and so on. So if you see an error like Error: Invariant Violation: findAllInRenderedTree(...): instance must be a composite component, make sure you're rendering a custom (your own) component class and not a standard class. See the commit at http://mng.bz/8AOc and the https://github.com/facebook/react/issues/4692 thread on GitHub for more information.

Once you have hello, which has the value of the React component tree (includes all child components), you can look inside it with one of the find-element methods. For example, you can get the <div> from within the <HelloWorld/> element, as shown next (ch16/testutils/__tests__/scry-div.js).

> **Listing 16.5   Finding a React element's child element <div>**

```
describe('HelloWorld', ()=>{
  const TestUtils = require('react-dom/test-utils')
  const React = require('react')

  it('has a div', (done)=>{

    class HelloWorld extends React.Component {
      render() {
        return <div>{this.props.children}</div>
      }
    }
    let hello = TestUtils.renderIntoDocument(
      <HelloWorld>Hello Node!</HelloWorld>
    )
    expect(TestUtils.scryRenderedDOMComponentsWithTag(
      hello, 'div'
    ).length).toBe(1)
    console.log('found this many divs: ',
      TestUtils.scryRenderedDOMComponentsWithTag(hello, 'div').length)

    done()
  })
})
...
```

scryRenderedDOMComponentsWithTag() allows you to get an array of elements by their tag names (such as div). Are there any other ways to get elements? Yes!

16.4.1 Finding elements with TestUtils

In addition to scryRenderedDOMComponentsWithTag(), there are a few other ways to get either a list of elements (prefixed with scry, plural Components) or a single element (prefixed with find, singular Component). Both use an element class, not a component class, which is a different thing. For example, btn, main, and so on.

In addition to tag names, you can get elements by type (component class) or by their CSS classes. For example, HelloWorld is a type, whereas div is a tag name (you used it to pull the list of criteria).

You can mix and match `scry` and `find` with Class, Type, and Tag to get six methods, depending on your needs. Here's what each method returns:

- `scryRenderedDOMComponentsWithTag()`—Many elements; you know their tag name.
- `findRenderedDOMComponentWithTag()`—A single element; you know its unique tag name. That is, no other elements in the component have a similar tag name.
- `scryRenderedDOMComponentsWithClass()`—Many elements; you know their class name.
- `findRenderedDOMComponentWithClass()`—A single element; you know its unique class name.
- `scryRenderedComponentsWithType()`—Many elements; you know their type.
- `findRenderedComponentWithType()`—A single element; you know its type.

As you can see, there's no shortage of methods when it comes to pulling the necessary element(s) from your components. If you need some guidance, I suggest using classes or types (component classes), because they let you target elements more robustly. For instance, suppose you use tag names now because there's just one <div>. If you decide to add elements with the same tag names to your code (more than one <div>), you'll need to rewrite your test. If you use an HTML class to test a <div>, your test will work fine after you add more <div> element to the tested component.

The only case when using tag names might be appropriate is when you need to test all the elements with a specific tag name (`scryRenderedDOMComponentsWithTag()`) or your component is so small that there are no other elements with the same tag name (`findRenderedDOMComponentWithTag()`). For example, if you have a stateless component that wraps an anchor tag <a> and you add a few HTML classes to it, there will be no additional anchor tags.

16.4.2 *UI-testing the password widget*

Consider a UI widget that can be used on a sign-up page to automatically generate passwords of a certain strength. As shown in figure 16.2, it has an input field, a Generate button, and a list of criteria.

The following section walks through the entire project. For now, we're focusing on using TestUtils and its interface. Once TestUtils and other dependencies (such as Jest) are installed, you can create the Jest test file to UI-test your widget; let's call it password/__tests__/password.test.js, because you're testing a password component. The structure of this test is as follows:

```
describe('Password', function() {
  it('changes after clicking the Generate button', (done)=>{
    // Importations
    // Perform rendering
    // Perform assertions on content and behavior
    done()
  })
})
```

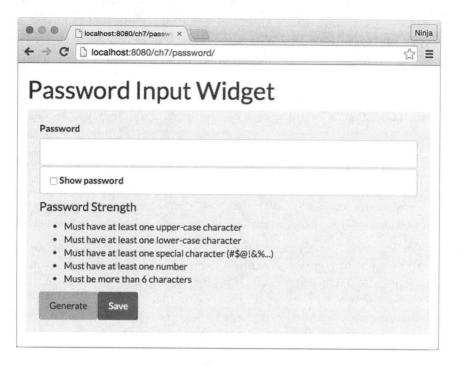

Figure 16.2 Password widget that autogenerates a password according to the given strength criteria

Let's define the dependencies in `describe`. Note that I've created the shortcut `fD` for `ReactDOM.findDOMNode()` because you'll use it a lot:

```
const TestUtils = require('react-dom/test-utils')
    const React = require('react')
    const ReactDOM = require('react-dom')
    const Password = require('../jsx/password.jsx')
    const fD = ReactDOM.findDOMNode
```

To render a component, you need to use `renderIntoDocument()`. For example, this is how you can render a `Password` component and save a reference to the object in the password variable. The properties you're passing will be the keys of the rules for the password strength. For example, `upperCase` requires at least one uppercase character:

```
let password = TestUtils.renderIntoDocument(<Password
    upperCase={true}
    lowerCase={true}
    special={true}
    number={true}
    over6={true}
    />
    )
```

This example is in JSX because Jest automatically uses `babel-jest` when you have installed this module (`npm i babel-jest --save-dev`) and sets the Babel configuration to use `"presets": ["react"]`. You cannot use JSX in Jest if you don't want to include `babel-jest`. In this case, call `createElement()`:

```
let password = TestUtils.renderIntoDocument(
    React.createElement(Password, {
        upperCase: true,
        lowerCase: true,
        special: true,
        number: true,
        over6: true
    })
)
```

Once you've rendered the component with `renderIntoDocument()`, it's straightforward to extract the needed elements—children of `Password`—and execute assertions to see how your widget is working. Think of the extraction calls as your jQuery; you can use tags or classes. At the bare minimum, your test should check for these things:

1 There's a `Password` element with a list of items (`<li>`) that are the strength criteria.
2 The first item in the strength list has specific text.
3 The second item isn't fulfilled (strikethrough).
4 There's a Generate button (class `generate-btn`)—click it!
5 After you click Generate, the second list item become fulfilled (visible).

Clicking Generate fulfills all criteria and makes the password visible (so users can memorize it), but you won't see the test code for that feature in this book. That's your homework for next week.

Let's start with item 1. `TestUtils.scryRenderedDOMComponentsWithTag()` gets all elements from a particular class. In this case, the class is `li` for the `<li>` elements because that's what the criteria list will use: `<ul><li>`. `toBe()`, which works like the triple equal (`===`), can be used to validate the list length as 5:

```
let rules = TestUtils.scryRenderedDOMComponentsWithTag(password, 'li')
    expect(rules.length).toBe(5)
```

For item 2, which checks that the first list item has specific text, you use `toEqual()`. You expect the first item to say that an uppercase character is required. This will be one of the rules for password strength:

```
expect(fD(rules[0]).textContent).toEqual('Must have
➥ at least one uppercase character')
```

To check items 3, 4, and 5, you find a button, click it, and compare the values of the second criteria (it must change from text to strikethrough).

toBe() vs. toEqual()

toBe() and toEqual() aren't the same in Jest. They behave differently. The easiest way to remember is that toBe() is === (strict equal), whereas toEqual() checks that two *objects* have the same value. Thus both assertions will be correct:

```
const copy1 = {
  name: 'React Quickly',
  chapters: 19,
}
const copy2 = {
  name: 'React Quickly',
  chapters: 19,
}

describe('Two copies of my books', () => {
  it('have all the same properties', () => {
    expect(copy1).toEqual(copy2) // correct
  })
  it('are not the same object', () => {
    expect(copy1).not.toBe(copy2) // correct
  })
})
```

But when you're comparing literals such as the number 5 and the string "Must have at least one uppercase character," toBe() and toEqual() will produce the same results:

```
expect(rules.length).toBe(5) // correct
expect(rules.length).toEqual(5) // correct
expect(fD(rules[0]).textContent).toEqual('Must have
➥ at least one upper-case character') // correct
expect(fD(rules[0]).textContent).toBe('Must have
➥ at least one upper-case character') // correct
```

There's a `TestUtils.findRenderedDOMComponentWithClass()` method that's similar to `TestUtils.scryRenderedDOMComponentsWithTag()` but returns only one element; it'll throw an error if you have more than one element. And to simulate user actions, there's a `TestUtils.Simulate` object that has methods with the names of events in camelCase: for example, `Simulate.click`, `Simulate.keyDown`, and `Simulate.change`.

Let's use `findRenderedDOMComponentWithClass()` to get the button and then use `Simulate.click` to click it. All this is done in the code without a browser:

```
let generateButton =
➥ TestUtils.findRenderedDOMComponentWithClass(password, 'generate-btn')
  expect(fD(rules[1]).firstChild.nodeName.toLowerCase()).toBe('#text')
  TestUtils.Simulate.click(fD(generateButton))
  expect(fD(rules[1]).firstChild.nodeName.toLowerCase()).toBe('strike')
```

This test checks that the `<li>` component has a `<strike>` element (to make the text strikethrough) when the button is clicked. The button generates a random password that satisfies the second (rules[1]) criterion (as well as others), which is to have at least one lowercase character. You're finished here; let's move on to the next tests.

You've seen TestUtils.Simulate in action. It can trigger not just clicks, but other interactions as well, such as a change of value in an input field or an Enter keystroke (keyCode 13):

```
ReactTestUtils.Simulate.change(node)
ReactTestUtils.Simulate.keyDown(node, {
  key: "Enter",
  keyCode: 13,
  which: 13})
```

> **NOTE** You must manually pass data that will be used in the component, such as key or keyCode, because TestUtils won't autogenerate it. There are methods in TestUtils for every user action supported by React.

For your reference, following is the project manifest file, package.json. It also includes the shallow-rendering library we'll cover next. To run the examples from ch16/password, install dependencies with npm i and then execute npm test:

```json
{
  "name": "password",
  "version": "2.0.0",
  "description": "",
  "main": "index.html",
  "scripts": {
    "test": "jest",
    "test-watch": "jest --watch",
    "build-watch": "./node_modules/.bin/webpack -w",
    "build": "./node_modules/.bin/webpack"
  },
  "author": "Azat Mardan",
  "license": "MIT",
  "babel": {
    "presets": [
      "react"
    ]
  },
  "devDependencies": {
    "babel-core": "6.10.4",
    "babel-jest": "13.2.2",
    "babel-loader": "6.4.1",
    "babel-preset-react": "6.5.0",
    "jest-cli": "19.0.2",
    "react": "15.5.4",
    "react-dom": "15.5.4",
    "react-test-renderer": "15.5.4",
    "webpack": "2.4.1"
  }
}
```

Next, let's look at another way to render React elements.

16.4.3 *Shallow rendering*

In some cases, you may want to test a single level of rendering: that is, the result of `render()` in a component *without rendering its children* (if any). This simplifies testing because it doesn't require having a DOM—the system creates an element, and you can assert facts about it. First, you must have a package called `react-test-renderer` v15.5.4 (for older versions of React, this class was part of TestUtils, but it's not as of v15.5.4):

```
npm i react-test-renderer -SE
```

To illustrate, here's the same password element being tested with the shallow-rendering approach. This code can go in the same test file ch16/password/__tests__/password .test.js. In this case, you create a renderer and then pass a component to it to get its shallow rendering:

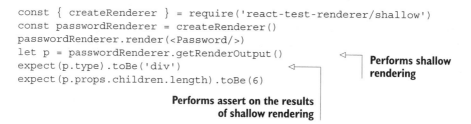

```
const { createRenderer } = require('react-test-renderer/shallow')
const passwordRenderer = createRenderer()
passwordRenderer.render(<Password/>)
let p = passwordRenderer.getRenderOutput()                    Performs shallow
expect(p.type).toBe('div')                                    rendering
expect(p.props.children.length).toBe(6)
```

**Performs assert on the results
of shallow rendering**

Now, if you log p as in `console.log(p)`, the result contains the children but object p isn't a React instance. Look at this result of shallow rendering:

```
{ '$$typeof': Symbol(react.element),
  type: 'div',
  key: null,
  ref: null,
  props:
   { className: 'well form-group col-md-6',
     children: [ [Object], [Object], [Object], [Object],
     [Object], [Object] ] },
  _owner: null,
  _store: {} }
```

Contrast that with the logs of the results of `renderIntoDocument(<Password/>)`, which produces an instance of the `Password` React element with state. Look at this full rendering (not shallow):

```
Password {
  props: {},
  context: {},
  refs: {},
  updater:
   {...
      },
  state: { strength: {}, password: '',
    visible: false, ok: false },
```

**You get state, which
you don't get with
shallow rendering.**

```
generate: [Function: bound generate],
checkStrength: [Function: bound checkStrength],
toggleVisibility: [Function: bound toggleVisibility],
_reactInternalInstance:
  { _currentElement:
    { '$$typeof': Symbol(react.element),
      type: [Function: Password],
      key: null,
      ref: null,
      props: {},
      _owner: null,
      _store: {} },
      ...
    }
  }
}
```

> **You get an element that looks like the result of shallow rendering.**

Needless to say, you can't test user behavior and nested elements with shallow rendering. But shallow rendering can be used to test the first level of children in a component as well as the component's type. You can use this feature for custom (composable) component classes.

In the real world, you'd use shallow rendering for highly targeted (almost unit-like) testing of a single component and its rendering. You can use it when there's no need to test children, user behavior, or changing states of a component—in other words, when you only need to test the render() function of a single element. As a rule of thumb, start with shallow rendering and then, if that's not enough, continue with regular rendering.

Standard HTML classes can inspect and assert el.props, so there's no need for a shallow renderer. For example, this is how you can create an anchor element and test that it has the expected class name and tag name:

```
let el = <a className='btn'/>
expect(el.props.className).toBe('btn')
expect(el.type).toBe('a')
```

16.5 *TestUtils wrap-up*

You've learned a lot about TestUtils and Jest—enough to begin using them in your projects. That's exactly what you'll be doing in the projects in part 2 of this book: using Jest and TestUtils for behavior-driven development (BDD) of React components. (chapters 18–20). The password widget is in chapter 19, if you want to look at the Webpack setup and all the dependencies used in the real world.

For more information on TestUtils, refer to the official documentation at https://facebook.github.io/react/docs/test-utils.html. Jest is an extensive topic, and full coverage is outside the scope of this book. Feel free to consult the official API documentation to learn more: https://facebook.github.io/jest/docs/api.html#content.

Finally, the Enzyme library (https://github.com/airbnb/enzyme, http://mng.bz/Uy4H) provides a few more features and methods than TestUtils as well as more-compact names for methods. It's developed by AirBnb and requires TestUtils as well as jsdom (which comes with Jest, so you'll need jsdom only if you're not using Jest).

Testing is a beast. It's so frightful that some developers skip it—but not you. You stuck it out to the end. Congratulations! Your code will be better quality, and you'll develop more quickly and live a happier life. You won't have to wake up in the middle of the night to fix a broken server—or at least, not as frequently as someone without tests.

16.6   *Quiz*

1   Jest tests must be in a folder named which of the following? tests, __test__, or __tests__

2   TestUtils is installed with npm from `react-addons-test-utils`. True or false?

3   What TestUtils method allows you to find a single component by its HTML class?

4   What is the `expect` expression to compare objects (deep comparison)?

5   How do you test the behavior when the user hovers with a mouse? `TestUtils.Simulate.mouseOver(node)`, `TestUtils.Simulate.onMouseOver(node)`, or `TestUtils.Simulate.mouseDown(node)`

16.7   *Summary*

- To install Jest, use `npm i jest-cli --save-dev`.
- To test a module, turn off automocking for it with `jest.dontMock()`.
- Use `expect.toBe()` and other Expect functions.
- To install TestUtils, use `npm i react-addons-test-utils --save-dev`.
- Use `TestUtils.Simulate.eventName(node)`, where `eventName` is a React event (without the on prefix) to test trigger DOM events.
- Use `scry...` methods to fetch multiple elements.
- Use `find...` methods to fetch a single element (you'll get an error if you have more than one element: `Did not find exactly one match (found: 2+)`).

16.8   *Quiz answers*

1   __tests__. This is the convention Jest follows.

2   True. TestUtils is a separate npm module.

3   `findRenderedDOMComponentWithClass()`

4   `expect(OBJECT).toEqual(value)` compares objects on sameness without comparing that they're the same objects (which is done with `===` or `toBe()`).

5   `TestUtils.Simulate.mouseOver(node)`. The `mouseOver` event is triggered by hovering the cursor.

Watch this chapter's introduction video by scanning this QR code with your phone or going to http://reactquickly.co/videos/ch17.

React on Node and Universal JavaScript

17

This chapter covers

- Using React on the server
- Understanding Universal JavaScript
- Using React on Node
- Working with React and Express
- Using Universal JavaScript with Express and React

React is primarily a front-end library to build full-blown, single-page applications or simple UIs on *the browser.* So why should we concern ourselves with using it on the server? Isn't rendering HTML on the server the old way to do things? Well, yes and no. It turns out that when you build web apps that *always* render on the browser, they miss out on a few key goodies. In fact, they miss out to the point of not being able to rank high in Google search results and maybe even losing millions of dollars in revenue. Arghhh.

Read on to find out why. You can skip this chapter in only one case: if you're oblivious to the performance of your apps (that is, if you're a newbie developer). All others, please proceed. You'll gain precious knowledge that you can use to build amazing apps and that will make you look smart during developers' happy hour when you use the term *Universal JavaScript*. You'll also learn how to use React with Node and build Node servers, and by the end of the chapter you'll understand how to build Universal JavaScript apps with React.js and Express.js (the most popular Node.js framework).

> **TIP** If you haven't come across Express before, check out my book *Pro Express.js* (Apress, 2014), which covers the current v4; it's comprehensive and still very relevant. See also *Express in Action*, by Evan Hahn (Manning, 2015). You can also check out my online course Express Foundation: https://node.university/p/express-foundation. If you're familiar with Express but need a refresher, you can find an Express.js cheatsheet in appendix C, and Express installation is covered in appendix A.

> **NOTE** The source code for the examples in this chapter is at www.manning.com/books/react-quickly and https://github.com/azat-co/react-quickly/tree/master/ch17. You can also find some demos at http://reactquickly.co/demos.

17.1 Why React on the server? And what is Universal JavaScript?

You may have heard about Universal JavaScript in relation to web development. It's become such a buzzword that it seems as though every web tech conference in 2016 had not one but several presentations about it. There are even a few synonyms for *Universal JavaScript*, such as *isomorphic JavaScript* and *full stack JavaScript*. For simplicity, I'll stick with *Universal* for this chapter. This section will help you understand what isomorphic/Universal JavaScript is about.

But before I define Universal JavaScript, let's discuss some of the issues you face when building SPAs. The three main problems are these:

- *No search engine optimization (SEO)*—Single-page apps (SPAs) generate HTML entirely on the browser, and search crawlers don't like that.
- *Poor performance*—Huge bundled files and AJAX calls slow performance (especially on the first page load, when it's critical).
- *Poor maintainability*—Often, SPAs lead to duplication of code on the browser and server.

Let's take a closer look at each of these problems.

17.1.1 Proper page indexing

SPAs built with frameworks like Backbone.js, Angular.js, Ember.js, and others are widely used for protected apps—that is, apps that require the user to enter a username and password in order to gain access (for example, see figure 17.1). Most SPAs serve protected resources and don't need indexing, but the vast majority of websites aren't protected behind logins.

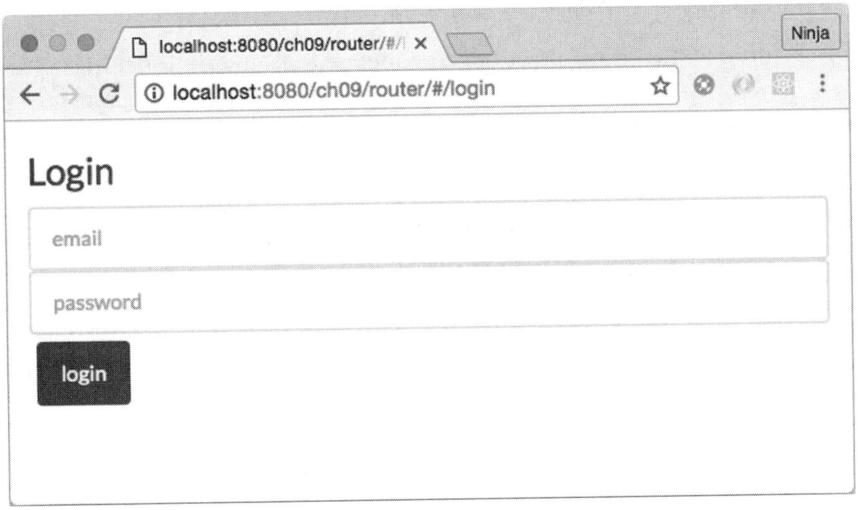

Figure 17.1   SPA that doesn't need SEO support because it's behind a login screen

For such public apps, SEO is important and mandatory, because their business depends heavily on search indexing and organic traffic. The majority of websites fall in this category.

Unfortunately, when you try to use SPA architecture for public-facing websites, which should have good search engine indexing, it's not straightforward. SPAs rely on browser rendering, so you need to either reimplement the templates on the server or pre-generate static HTML pages using headless browsers just for the search engine crawlers.

Google support for browser rendering

Recently, Google added a JavaScript rendering capability to its crawlers. You may think this means that browser-rendered HTML will be indexed correctly now. You may think that by using Angular with a REST API server, you don't need server-side rendering. Unfortunately, this may not be the case.

The following comes from the *Google Webmaster Central Blog* post "Understanding Web Pages Better" (http://mng.bz/Yv3B): "Sometimes things don't go perfectly during rendering, which may negatively impact search results for your site." The gist is that Google doesn't advocate that we rely on its indexing of SPAs. Google can't guarantee that what's in its cache, index, and search results is exactly what your SPA rendered. So, to be on the safe side, you need to render without JavaScript as closely as possible to the JavaScript-enabled rendering.

With Universal JavaScript and React, in particular, you can generate HTML on the server for crawlers from the same components that browsers use to generate HTML for users. No need for bulky headless browsers to generate HTML on the server. Win-win!

17.1.2 Better performance with faster loading times

Although some applications must have proper search engine indexing, others thrive on faster performance. Websites like http://mobile.walmart.com[1] and http://twitter .com[2] have done research that showed that they needed to render the first page (first load) on the server to improve performance. Companies lose millions of dollars because users will leave if the first page doesn't load quickly enough.

Being a web developer, and working and living with good internet connection speeds, you might forget that your website may be accessed via a slow connection. What loads in a split second for you might take half a minute in other cases. Suddenly, a bundle that's more than 1 MB is too large. And loading the bundled file is just half the story: the SPA needs to make AJAX requests to the server to load the data, while your users patiently stare at the Loading… spinner. Yeah, right. Some of them already left, and others are frustrated.

You want to show users a functional web page as fast as you possibly can, not just some skeleton HTML and Loading…. Other code can be loaded later while the user browses the web page.

With Universal JavaScript, it's easy to generate HTML to show the first page *on the server.* As a result, when users load the first page, they won't see the obstructing Loading… message. The data is in the HTML for users to enjoy. They see a functional page and thus have a better user experience.

The performance boost comes from the fact that users don't have to wait for AJAX calls to resolve. There are other opportunities to optimize performance as well, such as preloading data and caching it on the server before AJAX calls come to the server (that's exactly what we did at DocuSign by implementing a data router).[3]

17.1.3 Better code maintainability

Code is a liability. The more code you have, the more you and your team will need to support it. For these reasons, you want to avoid having different templates and logic for the same pages. Avoid duplication. Don't repeat yourself (DRY).

Fortunately, Node.js, which is an essential part of Universal JavaScript, makes it effortless to use front-end/browser modules on the server. Many template engines, such as Handlebars.js, Mustache, Dust.js, and others, can be used on the server.

Given these problems, and knowing that Universal JavaScript can solve them, what's a practical application?

17.1.4 Universal JavaScript with React and Node

Universal, in regard to web development, means using the same code (typically written in JavaScript) on both the server side and the client side. A narrow use case for Universal

---

[1] Kevin Decker, "Mobile Server Side Rendering," *GitHub Gist,* 2014, http://mng.bz/2B6P.

[2] Dan Webb, "Improving Performance on twitter.com," *Twitter,* May 29, 2012, http://mng.bz/2st9.

[3] Ben Buckman, "The New DocuSign Experience, All in Javascript," *DocuSign Dev,* March 30, 2014, http://mng.bz/4773.

JavaScript is rendering on the server and client from the same source. Universal JavaScript often implies the use of JavaScript and Node.js, because this language and platform combination allows for the reuse of the libraries.

Browser JavaScript code can be run in the Node.js environment with few modifications. As a consequence of this interchangeability, the Node.js and JavaScript ecosystem has a wide variety of isomorphic frameworks, such as React.js (http://facebook.github.io/react), Next.js (https://github.com/zeit/next.js), Catberry (http://catberry.org/), LazoJS (https://github.com/lazojs/lazo), Rendr (https://github.com/rendrjs/rendr), Meteor (https://meteor.com), and others. Figure 17.2 shows how an universal/isomorphic stack works: isomorphic code is shared between server and client.

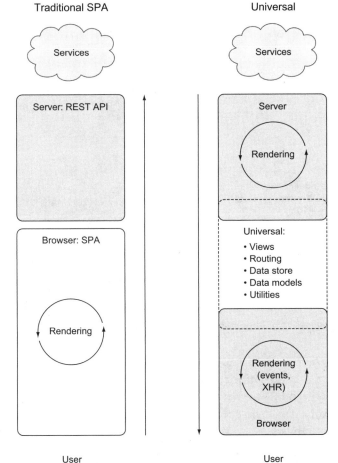

Figure 17.2 Universal HTML generation and code sharing between browser and server vs. no code sharing in a traditional SPA

In a practical application, Universal JavaScript architecture consists of the following:

- Client-side React code for the browser. This can be an SPA or just some simple UIs making AJAX requests.
- A Node.js server generating HTML for the first page on the server and serving browser React code with the same data. This can be implemented using Express and either a template engine or React components as a template engine.
- Webpack to compile JSX for both the server and the browser.

Figure 17.3 shows the model.

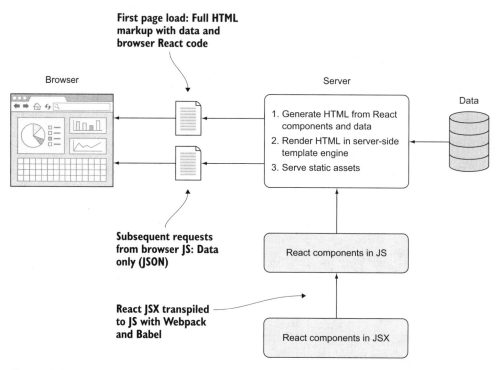

Figure 17.3   Practical application of Universal JavaScript with React, Node, and Express

You may be thinking, "Show me how to use this wonder, Universal JavaScript, already!" All right, let's look at a hands-on example of rendering React components on the server. We'll do so in a gradual way, because several components (as in parts, not React components) are involved in using the Universal JavaScript pattern. You'll need to learn how to do these things:

- *Generate HTML from React components*—You have just React components as input and plain HTML as output: no HTTP(S) servers yet.
- *Render HTML code generated from React components in Express servers*—Similar to the previous item, but now you use React in a template engine for 100% server-side rendering (no browser React yet).

- *Implement and serve React browser files via Express*—Eventually, you'll need an HTTP(S) server, and Express is one of the options. Until now, you've used node-static or Webpack Dev Server. At this point, there's no server-side HTML generation, just serving built/compiled static assets.

In the end, you'll use React to generate server-side HTML while loading browser React at the same time—the Holy Grail of Universal JavaScript. But before you can fly, you need to learn to walk!

17.2 React on Node

Let's start with a basic use case: generating HTML from a Node script. This example doesn't include servers or anything complex, just importing components and generating HTML. Make sure your Node version is at least 6 and your npm version is at least 3.

You need to learn only a handful of methods to generate HTML from React components on the server. First, you need the npm modules `react` and `react-dom`. You can install React and npm following the instructions in appendix A. This example uses React and React DOM version 15.

If you're new to writing server-side Node code, you might wonder where this server-side code goes. It goes in a plain text file; name it index.js. The React component is in email.js (I'll cover non-JSX plain JavaScript for now). Those two files must be in the same folder (ch17/node).

The project structure looks like this:

```
          /node
              /node_modules        ⟵──── Dependencies
              email.js
Node          email.jsx            ⟵──── Email component
code  └─▷    index.js
              package.json
```

First, include the modules in your server-side code in node/index.js.

```
const ReactDOMServer = require('react-dom/server')          Imports the
                                                            ReactDOMServer class
const React = require('react')
const Email = React.createFactory(require('./email.js'))    Creates a function that
...                                                         returns elements of the
                                                            Email class
```

What's up with `createFactory()`? Well, if you just imported email.js, that would be a component class; but you need a React element. Thus you can use JSX: `createElement()` or `createFactory()`. The latter gives a function that, when invoked, will give you an element.

Once you've imported your components, run `renderToString()` from ReactDOM-Server:

```
const emailString = ReactDOMServer.renderToString(Email())
```

Here's the code fragment from index.js:

```
const ReactDOMServer = require('react-dom/server')
const React = require('react')
const Email = React.createFactory(require('./email.js'))

const emailString = ReactDOMServer.renderToString(Email())
console.log(emailString)
// ...
```

Importing JSX

Another approach to use JSX is to convert it on the fly. The `babel-register` library will enhance `require` to do just that so you can configure your `require` once and then import JSX like any other JS files.

To import JSX, you can use `babel-register` as shown here in its index.js, in addition to installing `babel-register` and `babel-preset-react` (use npm to install them):

```
require('babel-register')({
  presets: [ 'react' ]
})
```

Is email.js regular JavaScript? In this case, it has to be. You can "build" JSX into regular JS with Webpack.

> **Listing 17.2   Server-side `Email` (node/email.jsx)**

```
const React = require('react')

const Email = (props)=> {
  return (
    <div>
      <h1>Thank you {(props.name) ? props.name: '' }
        for signing up!</h1>
      <p>If you have any questions, please contact support</p>
    </div>
  )
}

module.exports = Email
```

You'll get strings rendered by React components. You can use these strings in your favorite template engine to show on a web page or somewhere else (such as HTML email). In my case, email.js (ch17/node/email.js) with a heading and a paragraph renders into the following HTML strings with Universal React attributes.

Listing 17.3   node/email.jsx rendered into strings

```
<div data-reactroot="" data-reactid="1" data-react-checksum="1319067066">
  <h1 data-reactid="2">
    <!-- react-text: 3 -->Thank you <!-- /react-text -->
    <!-- react-text: 4 -->
    <!-- /react-text -->
    <!-- react-text: 5 -->for signing up!<!-- /react-text -->
  </h1>
  <p data-reactid="6">If you have any questions, please contact support</p>
</div>
```

What's happening with the attributes `data-reactroot`, `data-reactid`, and `data-react-checksum`? You didn't put them in there; React did. Why? For browser React and Universal JavaScript (discussed in the next section).

If you won't need the React markup that browser React needs (for example, if you're creating an HTML email), use the `ReactDOMServer.renderToStaticMarkup()` method. It works similarly to `renderToString()` but strips out all the `data-reactroot`, `data-reactid`, and `data-react-checksum` attributes. In this case, React is just like any other static template engine.

For example, you can load the component from email.js and generate HTML with `renderToStaticMarkup()` instead of `renderToString()`:

```
const emailStaticMarkup = ReactDOMServer.renderToStaticMarkup(Email())
```

The resulting `emailStaticMarkup` doesn't have React attributes:

```
<div><h1>Thank you for signing up!</h1><p>If you have any questions,
  please contact support</p></div>
```

Although you won't need the browser React for email, you use the original `renderToString()` for the Universal JavaScript architecture with React. Server-side React adds some secret sauce to the HTML in the form of checksums (`data-react-checksum` HTML attributes). Those checksums are compared by the browser React, and if they match, browser components won't regenerate/repaint/rerender unnecessarily. There's no flash of content (which often happens due to rerendering). The checksums will match if the data supplied to the server-side components is *exactly* the same as that on the browser. But how do you supply the data to the components created on the server? As properties!

If you need to pass some properties, pass them as object parameters. For example, you can provide a name (`Johny Pineappleseed`) to the `Email` component:

```
const emailStringWithName = ReactDOMServer.renderToString(Email({
  name: 'Johny Pineappleseed'
}))
```

The full ch17/node/index.js is shown next, with three ways to render HTML—static, string, and string with a property:

```
const ReactDOMServer = require('react-dom/server')
const React = require('react')
const Email = React.createFactory(require('./email.js'))

const emailString = ReactDOMServer.renderToString(Email())
const emailStaticMarkup = ReactDOMServer.renderToStaticMarkup(Email())
console.log(emailString)
console.log(emailStaticMarkup)

const emailStringWithName =
  ReactDOMServer.renderToString(Email({name: 'Johny Pineappleseed'}))
console.log(emailStringWithName)
```

That's how you render React components into HTML in plain Node—no servers and no thrills. Next, let's look at using React in an Express server.

17.3 React and Express: rendering on the server side from components

Express.js is one of the most popular Node.js frameworks—maybe *the* most popular. It's simple yet highly configurable. There are hundreds of plug-ins called *middleware* that you can use with Express.js.

In a bird's-eye view of the tech stack, Express and Node take the place of an HTTP(S) server, effectively replacing technologies like Microsoft IIS (www.iis.net) Apache httpd (https://httpd.apache.org), nginx (www.nginx.com), and Apache Tomcat (http://tomcat.apache.org). What's unique about Express and Node is that they allow you to build highly scalable, performant systems, thanks to the non-blocking I/O nature of Node (http://github.com/azat-co/you-dont-know-node). Express's advantages are its vast ecosystem of middleware and its mature, stable codebase.

Unfortunately, a detailed overview of the framework is out of the scope of this book, but you'll create a small Express app and render React in it. In no way is this is a deep dive into Express.js, but it'll get you started with the most widely used Node.js web framework. Call it an express course in Express if you wish.

> **TIP** As mentioned earlier, appendix A covers how to install both node.js and Express, if you want to follow along with this example.

17.3.1 Rendering simple text on the server side

Let's build HTTP and HTTPS servers using Express and then generate HTML on the server side using React, as shown schematically in figure 17.4. The most basic example of using React in Express as a view engine is to generate an HTML string without markup (checksums) and send it as a response to the request. Listing 17.4 illustrates the /about page rendered from a React component about.js.

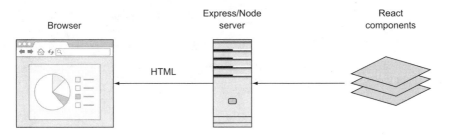

Figure 17.4 The Express/Node server will generate HTML and send it to the browser.

Listing 17.4 Using React on Express to show HTML on a page

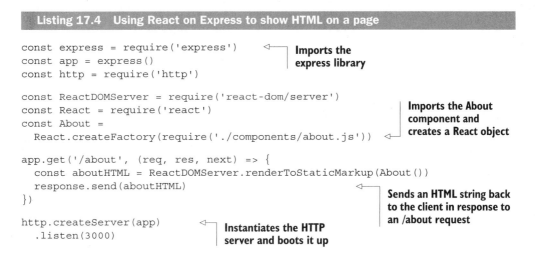

```
const express = require('express')        ◁┐  Imports the
const app = express()                      │  express library
const http = require('http')

const ReactDOMServer = require('react-dom/server')
const React = require('react')                          Imports the About
const About =                                           component and
  React.createFactory(require('./components/about.js'))  ◁ creates a React object

app.get('/about', (req, res, next) => {
  const aboutHTML = ReactDOMServer.renderToStaticMarkup(About())
  response.send(aboutHTML)                      ◁
})                                                 Sends an HTML string back
                                                   to the client in response to
http.createServer(app)       ◁                     an /about request
  .listen(3000)              │ Instantiates the HTTP
                               server and boots it up
```

This will work, but /about won't be a complete page with <head> and <body>. It's better to use a proper template engine (like Handlebars) for the layout and top HTML elements. You also may wonder what app.get() and app.listen() are. Let's look at another example, and all will be revealed.

17.3.2 *Rendering an HTML page*

This is a more interesting example in which you'll use some external plug-ins and a template engine. The idea for the app is the same: serve HTML generated from React using Express. The page will display some text that's generated from about.jsx (see figure 17.5). No thrills, but it's simple, and starting with simple is good.

Create a folder called react-express. (This example is in ch17/react-express.) The end project structure is as follows:

```
/react-express
  /components
    about.jsx
  /views
    about.hbs
  index.js
  package.json
```

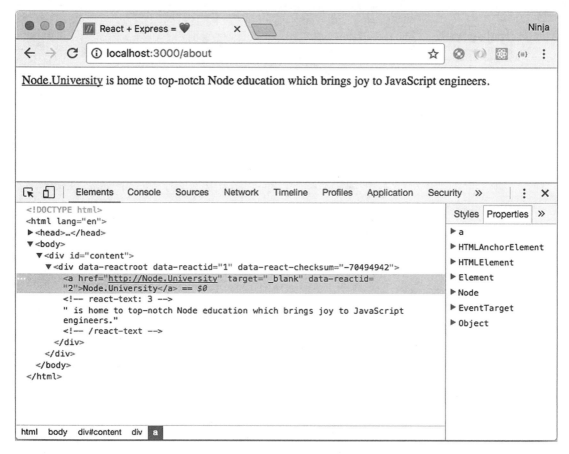

Figure 17.5   Rendering from the React component on the server side

Create package.json with `npm init -y`, and then install Express with npm like this:

```
$ npm install express@4.14.0 --save
```

As with any Node application, open an editor and create a file. Typically, you create a server file named index.js, app.js, or server.js, which you'll later start with the `node` command. In this case, name it index.js.

The file has these parts:

- *Imports*—Requires dependencies such as `express` and its plug-ins
- *Configurations*—Sets certain configuration values such as what template engine to use
- *Middleware*—Defines common actions performed for all incoming requests, such as validation, authentication, compression, and so on
- *Routes*—Defines the URLs handled by this server, such as /accounts, /users, and so on, as well as their actions

- *Error handlers*—Show meaningful messages or web pages when errors happen
- *Bootup*—Starts HTTP and/or HTTPS server(s)

Here's a high-level overview of the Express and Node server file:

```
const express = require('express')          ⟵── Imports modules
const app = express()
const errorHandler = require('errorhandler')
const http = require('http')
const https = require('https')
// Import other modules
// ...

app.set('view engine', 'hbs')               ⟵── Sets configurations

app.get('/',                     ⟵┐  Defines routes (no pure
  // ...                          │  middleware in this project)
)                                │
app.get('/about',
  // ...
)

// ...
                                 ┐  Defines error handlers
app.use(errorHandler)        ⟵──┘  (type of middleware)

http.createServer(app)              ⟵── Boots up the HTTP server
  .listen(3000)

// ...
if (typeof options != 'undefined')
  https.createServer(app, options)  ⟵── Boots up the HTTPS server
    .listen(443)
```

Now let's go deeper. The imports section is straightforward. In it, you require dependencies and instantiate objects. For example, to import the Express.js framework and to create an instance, write these lines:

```
var express = require('express')
var app = express()
```

CONFIGURATION

You set configurations with `app.set()`, where the first argument is a string and the second is a value. For example, to set the template engine to hbs (www.npmjs.com/package/hbs), use this configuration `view engine`:

```
app.set('view engine', 'hbs')
```

hbs (no affiliation with Harvard Business School) is an Express template (or view) engine for the Handlebars template language (http://handlebarsjs.com). You may have worked with Handlebars or a close relative of it, such as Mustache, Blaze, and so on. Ember also uses Handlebars (http://mng.bz/90Q2). It's a common, easy-to-get-started template, which is why you'll use it here.

One caveat: you must install the hbs package in order for Express to properly use the view engine. Do so by executing npm i hbs --save.

MIDDLEWARE

The next section sets up middleware. For example, to enable the app to serve static assets, use the static middleware:

```
app.use(express.static(path.join(__dirname, 'public')))
```

The static middleware is great because it turns Express into a static HTTP(S) server that proxies requests to files in a specified folder (public in this example), just as NGINX or Apache httpd would.

ROUTES

Next are routes, also known as endpoints, resources, pages, and many other names. You define a URL pattern that will be matched by Express against real URLs of incoming requests. If there's a match, Express will execute the logic associated with this URL pattern; this is called *handling* a request. It can involve anything from displaying static HTML for a 404 Not Found page to making a request to another service and caching the response before sending it back to the client.

Routes are the most important part of a web application because they define URL routing and in a way act as controllers in your good-old model-view-controller (MVC) pattern. In Express, you define routes using the app.NAME() pattern, where *NAME* is the name of an HTTP method in lowercase. For example, this is a syntax to GET the / (home page or empty URL) endpoint, which will send back the string "Hello":

```
app.get('/', (request, response, next) => {
  response.send('Hello!')
})
```

For the /about page/route, you can change the first argument (the URL pattern). You can also render the HTML string:

```
app.get('/about', (req, res, next) => {
  response.send(`<div>
  <a href="https://node.university" target="_blank">Node.University</a>
   is home to top-
     notch Node education which brings joy to JavaScript engineers.
</div>`)
})
```

LAYOUT WITH HANDLEBARS

Next you want to render React HTML from the Handlebars template, because Handlebars will provide you with an overall layout including such things as <html> and <body>. In other words, you have React for UI elements and Handlebars for the layout.

Create a new views folder containing this template, called about.hbs:

```
<!DOCTYPE html>
<html lang="en">
  <head>
    <meta charset="utf-8" />
    <title>React + Express = 💜 </title>          Uses a heart 💜
    <meta name="author" content="Azat" />
  </head>
                                          Uses triple curly braces to output
                                          unescaped HTML from the about
  <body>                                  variable (supplied in index.js)
    <div id="content">{{{about}}}</div>
  </body>
</html>
```

RENDERING THE PAGE

In the route (in the file ch17/react-express/index.js), change response.send() to response.render():

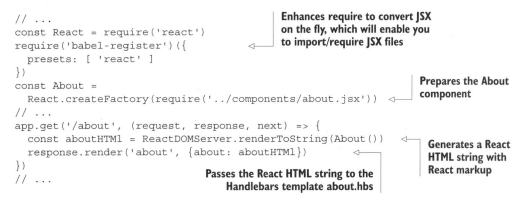

```
// ...
const React = require('react')
require('babel-register')({
  presets: [ 'react' ]
})
const About =
  React.createFactory(require('../components/about.jsx'))
// ...
app.get('/about', (request, response, next) => {
  const aboutHTMl = ReactDOMServer.renderToString(About())
  response.render('about', {about: aboutHTMl})
})
// ...
```

Enhances require to convert JSX on the fly, which will enable you to import/require JSX files

Prepares the About component

Generates a React HTML string with React markup

Passes the React HTML string to the Handlebars template about.hbs

Express routes can render from Handlebars templates, with data such as the about string variable, or send a response in a string format.

> **Do you have to use a different template engine for server rendering and layouts?**
>
> It's possible to use React for layouts, instead of Handlebars. There's an express-react-views library to do that (www.npmjs.com/package/express-react-views). It's only for static markup, not for browser React.
>
> I won't cover it here, because it requires extensive use of dangerouslySet-InnerHTML,[4] doesn't support all HTML, and often confuses beginner Express-React developers. In my humble opinion, there's little benefit to using React for layouts.

---

[4] See chapter 3 or https://facebook.github.io/react/docs/dom-elements.html#dangerouslysetinnerhtml.

HANDLING ERRORS

Error handlers are similar to middleware. For example, they can be imported from a package such as errorhandler (www.npmjs.org/package/errorhandler):

```
const errorHandler = require('errorhandler')
...
app.use(errorHandler)
```

Or you can create them in index.js:

```
app.use((error, request, response, next) => {
  console.error(request.url, error)
  response.send('Wonderful, something went wrong...')
})
```

You trigger an error handler by invoking next(error) in a request handler or middleware. error is an error object, which you can create with new Error('Ooops'), where "Ooops" will become the error message. Here's an example in /about:

```
app.get('/about', (request, response, next) => {
  // ... do weird stuff
  let somethingWeirdHappened = true
  if (somethingWeirdHappened) return next(new Error('Ooops'))
})
```

Don't forget to use return. For more about error handling in Node and Express, check out the Node Patterns course (http://node.university/p/node-patterns) or my post "Node Patterns: From Callbacks to Observer" (http://webapplog.com/node-patterns).

BOOTING UP THE SERVER

Finally, to start your app, run listen() by passing a port number and a callback (optional):

```
http.createServer(app).listen(portNumber, callback)
```

In this example, it looks like this:

```
http.createServer(app)
  .listen(3000)
```

Here's the full server code for ch17/react-express/index.js, to make sure nothing has slipped through the cracks.

Listing 17.5 Full code for React, Express, hbs server

```
const fs = require('fs')
const express = require('express')
const app = express()
const errorHandler = require('errorhandler')
```

```
const http = require('http')
const https = require('https')

const React = require('react')
require('babel-register')({
  presets: [ 'react' ]
})
const ReactDOMServer = require('react-dom/server')
const About = React.createFactory(require('./components/about.jsx'))

app.set('view engine', 'hbs')
app.get('/', (request, response, next)=>{
  response.send('Hello!')
})

app.get('/about', (request, response, next) => {
  const aboutHTMl = ReactDOMServer.renderToString(About())
  response.render('about', {about: aboutHTMl})
})

app.all('*', (request, response, next)=> {
  response.status(404).send('Not found...
➥ did you mean to go to /about instead?')
})
app.use((error, request, response, next) => {
  console.error(request.url, error)
  response.send('Wonderful, something went wrong...')
})

app.use(errorHandler)

http.createServer(app)
  .listen(3000)

try {
  const options = {
    key: fs.readFileSync('./server.key'),
    cert: fs.readFileSync('./server.crt')
  }
} catch (e) {
  console.warn('Create server.key and server.crt for HTTPS')
}
if (typeof options != 'undefined')
  https.createServer(app, options)
    .listen(443)
```

Implements a catchall fallback. You wouldn't believe how many people in my classes implement a server, go to a nonexistent URL, and think there's an error, when in fact they should be viewing /about.

Loads the key and certificate for SSL/HTTPS[5]

Now everything should be ready to run the server with node index.js or its shortcut (node .) to see the server response when you navigate to http://localhost:3000/about. If something is missing or you get errors when you start the server and navigate to the address, refer to the project source code in ch17/react-express.

---

[5] You can look up how to generate them in my post "Easy HTTP/2 Server with Node.js and Express.js," https://webapplog.com/http2-node.

WARNING   The SSL key and certificate are needed for SSL and HTTPS to work. The GitHub code for this example purposely doesn't include server.key and server.crt, because *sensitive information like keys shouldn't be committed to a version-control system.* You should create your own keys by following the instructions at https://webapplog.com/http2-node. If you don't have them, then the example code will only create an HTTP server.

The end result should be a proper HTML page with a header and body. In the body should be React markup such as data-react-checksum and data-reactroot, as shown in figure 17.6.

Why does this example use markup rendering and not static HTML strings or express-react-views? You'll need this markup with checksums later, for the browser React; that's the Universal JavaScript architecture.

In the next section, you'll put together all you've learned about React on the browser, Express, and React on Node to implement a Universal JavaScript architecture.

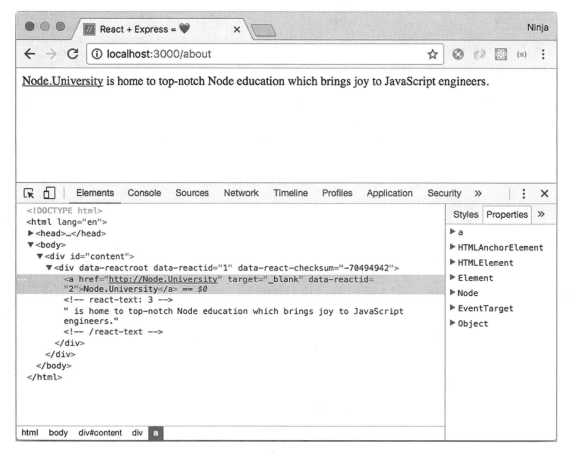

Figure 17.6   Rendering React markup from a Handlebars layout using Express gives you an HTML page.

17.4   *Universal JavaScript with Express and React*

This section combines all the skills from this chapter (and most of the book!). You'll render component(s) on the server, plug them in the template, and enable browser React.

To learn about Universal JavaScript, you'll build a message board with three components: `Header`, `Footer`, and `MessageBoard` (see figure 17.7). The `Header` and `Footer` components will have static HTML to display some text, and `MessageBoard` will have a form to post messages on the board and a list of messages. This app will use AJAX calls to get the list of messages and post new messages to the back-end server, which in turn will use a MongoDB NoSQL database.

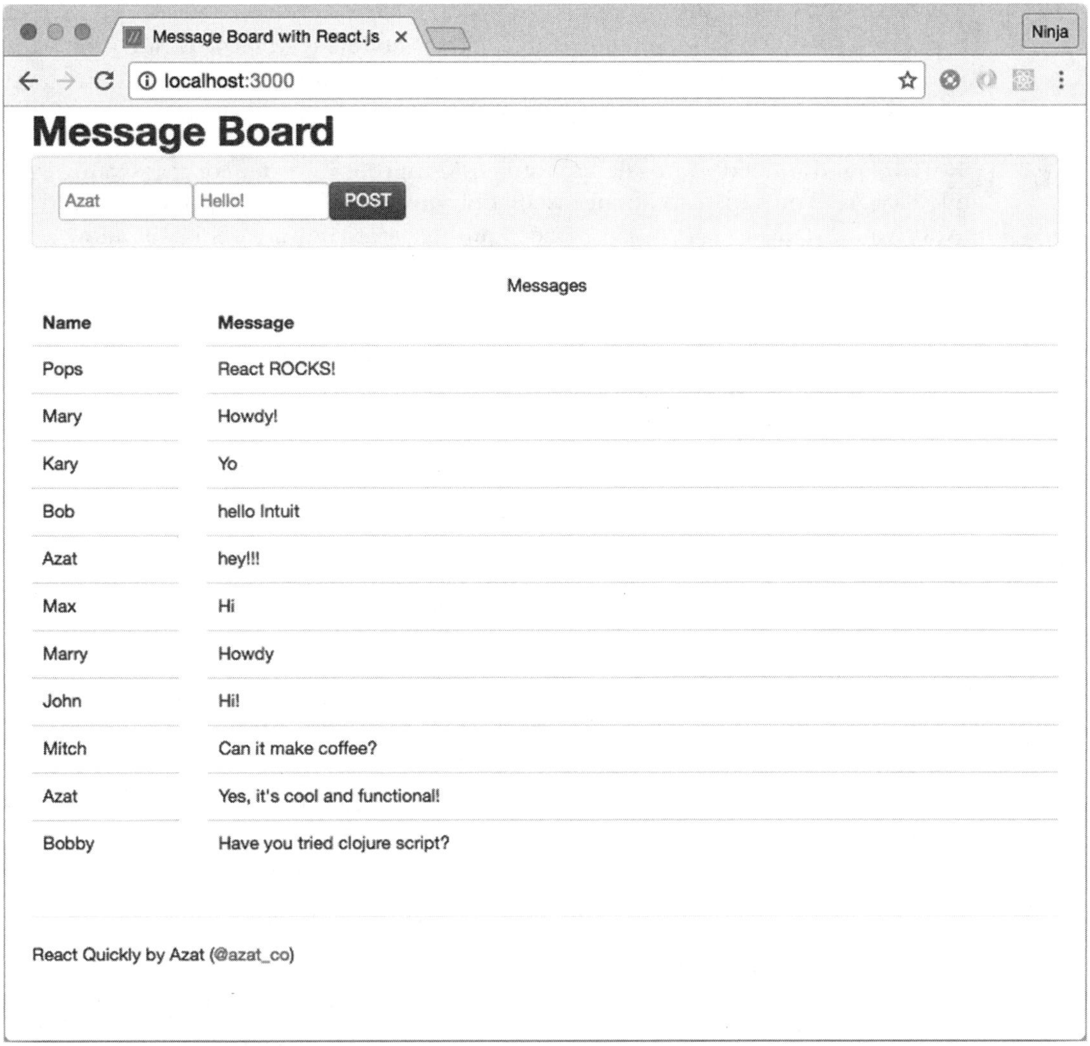

Figure 17.7   **Message board app with a form to post a message and a list of existing messages**

Concisely, for Universal React, you'll need to follow these steps:

1   Set up the server so that it provides data to the template and renders HTML (components and properties), such as index.js.
2   Create a template that outputs data (a.k.a. locals) unescaped, such as views/index.hbs.
3   Include the browser React file (ReactDOM.Render) in the template for interactivity, such as client/app.jsx.
4   Create the `Header`, `Footer`, and `MessageBoard` components.
5   Set up build processes with Webpack, such as webpack.config.js.

A few parts interact with each other: server, components, data, and browser. Figure 17.8 shows a diagram of how they're connected in the message board example. The server acts as a static-assets HTTP server and as an app that renders server-side HTML (first page load only). Browser React code enables interactivity of browser events and subsequent persistence (via HTTP requests to the server) after the initial page load.

> **NOTE**   You also need to install and launch MongoDB in order for this example to work. You can read about installation on its website or in appendix D. After you install MongoDB, run `mongod` and leave it running. This will allow your Express server to connect to it using the magic URL mongodb://localhost:27017/board.

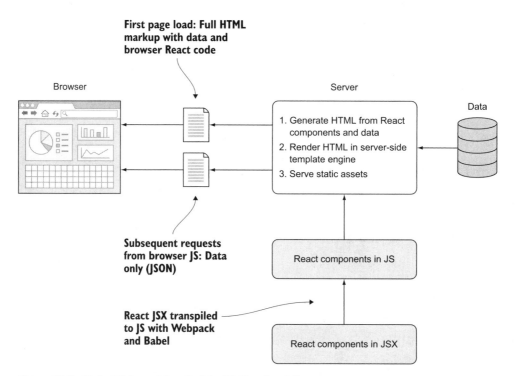

Figure 17.8   Gist of Universal JavaScript with React and Express

17.4.1   *Project structure and configuration*

The project structure is as follows:

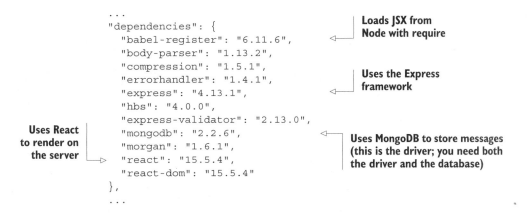

```
/client
   app.jsx                  ⊲—— Client/browser code
/components
   board.jsx                    ⊲─┐ Shared code between the
   footer.jsx                     │ client/browser and server
   header.jsx
/node_modules
/public
   /css
   /js                          ⊲─┐ Compiled and bundled
      bundle.js                   │ by Webpack scripts
      bundle.js.map
/views
   index.hbs
index.js                     ⊲—— Server code
package.json
webpack.config.js
```

The server dependencies include these packages (quoted from package.json):

```
...
"dependencies": {                           ⊲─┐ Loads JSX from
   "babel-register": "6.11.6",                │ Node with require
   "body-parser": "1.13.2",
   "compression": "1.5.1",
   "errorhandler": "1.4.1",                  ⊲─┐ Uses the Express
   "express": "4.13.1",                        │ framework
   "hbs": "4.0.0",
   "express-validator": "2.13.0",
   "mongodb": "2.2.6",                       ⊲─┐ Uses MongoDB to store messages
   "morgan": "1.6.1",                          │ (this is the driver; you need both
   "react": "15.5.4",                          │ the driver and the database)
   "react-dom": "15.5.4"
},
...
```

Uses React to render on the server ⤷ "react": "15.5.4",

Now you can set up the server in message-board/index.js.

> ### Express middleware
>
> I want to say a few words about the middleware used in this project, in case you're new to Express. Express isn't a large framework that does almost everything for you. On the contrary, it's a base foundation layer on top of which Node engineers build custom systems that are virtually their own frameworks. They are fit precisely to the task at hand, which isn't always the case with all-in-one frameworks. You get only what you need with Express and its ecosystem of plug-ins. Those plug-ins are called *middleware* because they use the middleware pattern, with Express implementing the middleware manager.

(continued)

Every Express engineer has favorite middleware packages that they use from project to project. I tend to start with the following and then add more packages if and when I need them:

- compression—Automatically compresses responses using the gzip algorithm. This makes responses smaller and faster to download, which is useful.
- errorhandler—Rudimentary handler for errors such as 404 and 500.
- express-validator—Validates the payload of incoming requests. It's always a good idea to have this.
- morgan—Logs requests on the server. Supports multiple formats.
- body-parser—Enables automatic parsing of JSON and the urlencoded data format into Node/JS objects accessible in request.body.

For information about compression, body-parser, and errorhandler, as well as a list of additional Express middleware, see appendix C, https://github.com/azat-co/cheatsheets/tree/master/express4, or *Pro Express.js* (http://proexpressjs.com).

17.4.2 Setting up the server

Just as you did in the previous examples, you'll implement the server side of things in index.js and then work through the five sections so you can see how it breaks down. First, the following listing shows it in full (ch17/message-board/index.js).

> **Listing 17.6 Server side of the message board app**

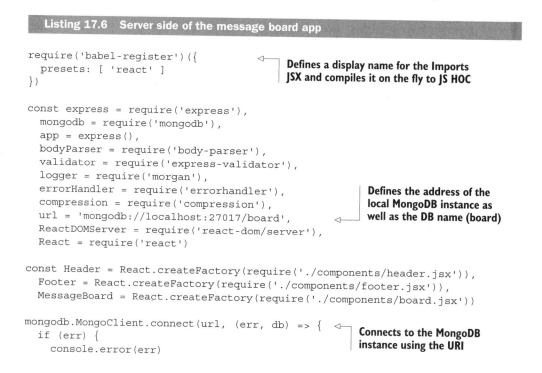

```
require('babel-register')({
  presets: [ 'react' ]
})
```
Defines a display name for the Imports JSX and compiles it on the fly to JS HOC

```
const express = require('express'),
  mongodb = require('mongodb'),
  app = express(),
  bodyParser = require('body-parser'),
  validator = require('express-validator'),
  logger = require('morgan'),
  errorHandler = require('errorhandler'),
  compression = require('compression'),
  url = 'mongodb://localhost:27017/board',
  ReactDOMServer = require('react-dom/server'),
  React = require('react')
```
Defines the address of the local MongoDB instance as well as the DB name (board)

```
const Header = React.createFactory(require('./components/header.jsx')),
  Footer = React.createFactory(require('./components/footer.jsx')),
  MessageBoard = React.createFactory(require('./components/board.jsx'))

mongodb.MongoClient.connect(url, (err, db) => {
  if (err) {
    console.error(err)
```
Connects to the MongoDB instance using the URI

```
    process.exit(1)
  }

  app.set('view engine', 'hbs')

  app.use(compression())
  app.use(logger('dev'))
  app.use(errorHandler())
  app.use(bodyParser.urlencoded({extended: true}))
  app.use(bodyParser.json())
  app.use(validator())
  app.use(express.static('public'))

  app.set('view engine', 'hbs')

  app.use((req, res, next) => {
    req.messages = db.collection('messages')
    return next()
  })

  app.get('/messages', (req, res, next) => {
    // ...
  })
  app.post('/messages', (req, res, next) => {
    // ...
  })

  app.get('/', (req, res, next) => {
    // ...
  })

  app.listen(3000)
})
```

Sets collection as a property of a request object for easier access in other routes and their modularization

CONFIGURATION

Again, you need to use babel-register to import JSX, after installing babel-register and babel-preset-react with npm:

```
require('babel-register')({
  presets: [ 'react' ]
})
```

In index.js, you implement your Express server. Let's import the components using the relative path ./components/:

```
const Header = React.createFactory(require('./components/header.jsx')),
  Footer = React.createFactory(require('./components/footer.jsx')),
  MessageBoard = React.createFactory(require('./components/board.jsx'))
```

For the purpose of rendering React apps, you need to know that Express.js can use pretty much any template engine. Let's consider Handlebars, which is close to regular

HTML. You can enable Handlebars with this statement, assuming app is the Express.js instance:

```
app.set('view engine', 'hbs')
```

The hbs module must be installed (I have it in package.json).

MIDDLEWARE

Middleware provides a lot of functionality for your server that you'd otherwise have to implement yourself. The following are the most essential for this project:

```
        // ...
        app.use(compression())
        app.use(logger('dev'))
        app.use(errorHandler())
        app.use(bodyParser.urlencoded({extended: true}))
        app.use(bodyParser.json())
        app.use(validator())
        app.use(express.static('public'))
        // ...
```

Enables parsing of the incoming JSON data payloads

Enables server logs for requests to help with debugging and development

Enables access to all the files under public, such as bundle.js

SERVER-SIDE ROUTES

In your route—let's say, /—you call render on views/index.handlebars (res.render ('index')), because the default template folder is views:

```
app.get('/', (req, res, next) => {
    req.messages.find({}, {sort: {_id: -1}}).toArray((err, docs) => {
      if (err) return next(err)
      res.render('index', data)
    })
})
```

The req.message.find() call is a MongoDB method to fetch documents. Although you must have MongoDB installed and running for this example to work verbatim (without any changes), I don't like to enforce my database preference on you. It's easy to replace calls to MongoDB with whatever you want. Most modern RDBMS and NoSQL databases have Node drivers; most of them even have ORM/ODM libraries written in Node. Therefore, you can safely ignore my DB call, if you're not planning to use MongoDB. If you do want to use MongoDB, appendix D has a cheatsheet for you. The idea is that in the request handler, you can make a call to an external service (for example, using axios to get Facebook user information) or use a database (MongoDB, PostgreSQL, and so on). How you get the data in Node isn't the focus of this chapter.

The most important thing here with regard to Universal React is res.render() (ch17/message-board/index.js), shown in listing 17.7. This render() method is a special Express feature for templates. It has two arguments. The first is the name of the template: index.hbs, which is in the views directory. The second argument to res.render() is the locals: data that will be used in the templates. All the data is sent (or *combined with* or *hydrated*) to the ch17/message-board/view/index.hbs template (the .hbs extension is optional).

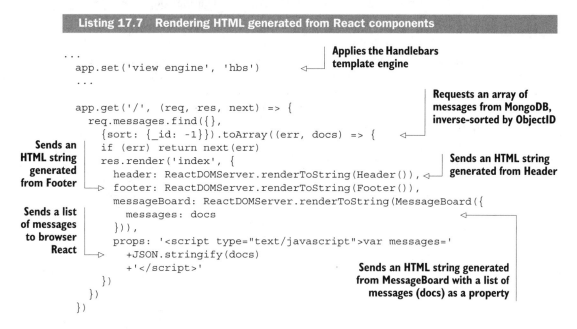

Listing 17.7 Rendering HTML generated from React components

```
...
  app.set('view engine', 'hbs')        ◁——┐  Applies the Handlebars
  ...                                       template engine

  app.get('/', (req, res, next) => {                    Requests an array of
    req.messages.find({},                                messages from MongoDB,
      {sort: {_id: -1}}).toArray((err, docs) => {  ◁——  inverse-sorted by ObjectID
      if (err) return next(err)
      res.render('index', {                                  Sends an HTML string
        header: ReactDOMServer.renderToString(Header()), ◁—— generated from Header
        footer: ReactDOMServer.renderToString(Footer()),
        messageBoard: ReactDOMServer.renderToString(MessageBoard({
          messages: docs                            ◁—————————┐
        })),
        props: '<script type="text/javascript">var messages='
          +JSON.stringify(docs)
          +'</script>'             Sends an HTML string generated
      })                           from MessageBoard with a list of
    })                             messages (docs) as a property
  })
```

Left margin annotations:
- Sends an HTML string generated from Footer
- Sends a list of messages to browser React

At this point, you have an Express server that renders a Handlebars template with three HTML strings from React components. This isn't exciting by itself; you could have done this without React. You could have used Handlebars or Pug or Mustache or any other template engine to render everything, not just the layout. Why do you need React? Well, you'll be using React on the browser, and browser React will take your server HTML and add all the events and states—all the magic. That's why!

You aren't finished with the server yet. You need to implement the two APIs for this example:

- `GET /messages`—Gets a list of messages from a database
- `POST /messages`—Creates a new message in a database

These routes will be used by browser React when it makes AJAX/XHR requests to `GET` and `POST` data. The code for the routes goes in Express, in index.js:

```
app.get('/messages', (req, res, next) => {
  req.messages.find({},
    {sort: {_id: -1}}).toArray((err, docs) => {
    if (err) return next(err)
    return res.json(docs)
  })
})
```

The route to handle creation of messages (POST /messages) will use express-validator to make sure the incoming data is present (notEmpty()). express-validator is convenient middleware because you can set up all kinds of validation rules.

WARNING Input validation is paramount to securing your apps. Developers work with the code and the system: they wrote it, they know how it works, and they know what data it supports. Thus they unconsciously become biased about the data they feed the app, which can lead to loopholes. *Always* sanitize your data server-side. You should consider *every* user to be potentially either a malicious attacker or a negligent person who never reads your instructions and always sends weird data.

The route will also use the reference to the database from req.messages to insert a new message:

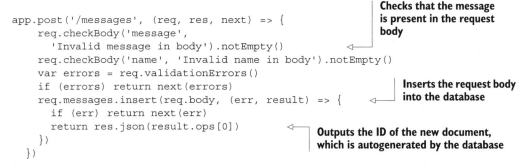

```
app.post('/messages', (req, res, next) => {
    req.checkBody('message',
      'Invalid message in body').notEmpty()          ◄───┘  Checks that the message
    req.checkBody('name', 'Invalid name in body').notEmpty()      is present in the request
    var errors = req.validationErrors()                           body
    if (errors) return next(errors)
    req.messages.insert(req.body, (err, result) => {   ◄───┘  Inserts the request body
      if (err) return next(err)                                into the database
      return res.json(result.ops[0])     ◄───┐  Outputs the ID of the new document,
    })                                        which is autogenerated by the database
  })
})
```

---

node-dev

As mentioned earlier, I recommend using the nodemon tool or something similar, such as node-dev. node-dev monitors for file changes and restarts the server when changes are detected. It can save you *hours* of work! To install node-dev, run this command:

```
npm i node-dev@3.1.3 --save-dev
```

In package.json, you can add the command node-dev . to the start npm script:

```
...
  "scripts": {
    ...
    "start": "./node_modules/.bin/webpack && node-dev ."
  },
  ...
```

The bootup call is primitive compared to the previous section, when you used HTTPS:

```
app.listen(3000)
```

Obviously, you can add HTTPS to it and change the port number or take the port number from environment variables.

Remember, the root / route handles all the GET requests to / or to http://local-host:3000/, in this case. It's implemented in listing 17.7 (ch17/message-board/view/index.hbs). The route uses a template called index in res.render(). Now, let's implement the template.

17.4.3 *Server-side layout templates with Handlebars*

You can use any template engine on the server to render React HTML. Handlebars is a good option because it's similar to HTML, which means little modification is needed when transitioning from HTML to this template engine. Following is the Handlebars index.hbs file:

```
<!DOCTYPE html>
<html lang="en">
  <head>
    <!-- meta tags and CSS -->
  </head>

  <body>
  <div class="container-fluid">
    <!-- header -->
    <!-- props -->
    <!-- messageBoard -->
    <!-- footer -->
  </div>
  <script type="text/javascript" src="/js/bundle.js"></script>
  </body>
</html>
```

You use triple curly braces ({{{...}}}) to output components and properties (unescaped output) such as HTML. For example, {{{props}}} will output a <script/> script tag so you can define a messages variable in it. The index.hbs code to render unescaped HTML string for props is

```
<div>{{{props}}}</div>
```

The rest of the locals (data) are outputted similarly:

```
<div id="header">{{{header}}}</div>
...
<div>{{{props}}}</div>
...
<div class="row-fluid"  id="message-board" />{{{messageBoard}}}</div>
...
<div id="footer">{{{footer}}}</div>
```

Here's how you output an HTML string from the Header component in Handlebars (ch17/message-board/views/index.hbs).

Listing 17.8   Outputting HTML generated by React in Handlebars

```
...
  <div class="container-fluid">
    <div class="row-fluid">
      <div class="span12">
        <div id="header">{{{header}}}</div>
      </div>
    </div>
  ...
```

What about the data? In order to get the benefit of server-side React working together with browser React, you must use the same data on the browser and server when you create React elements. You can pass the data from the server to browser React without needing AJAX calls by embedding the data as a JS variable right in the HTML!

When you pass `header`, `footer`, and `messageBoard`, you can add `props` in the / Express route. In index.hbs, print the values with triple curly braces and include the js/bundle.js script, which will be generated by Webpack later (ch17/message-board/views/index.hbs).

Listing 17.9   Server-side layout to render HTML from React components

```
<!DOCTYPE html>
<html lang="en">
  <head>
    <meta charset="utf-8" />
    <title>Message Board with React.js</title>
    <meta name="description" content="Message Board" />
    <meta name="author" content="Azat Mardan" />
    <meta name="viewport" content="width=device-width, initial-scale=1.0" />
    <link type="text/css" rel="stylesheet" href="/css/bootstrap.min.css" />
    <link type="text/css" rel="stylesheet"
    ➥ href="/css/bootstrap-responsive.min.css" />
  </head>
  <body>
    <div class="container-fluid">
      <div class="row-fluid">
        <div class="span12">
          <div id="header">{{{header}}}</div>        ⟵  Outputs HTML
        </div>                                            generated from the
      </div>                                              Header component
      <div>{{{props}}}</div>          ⟵  Outputs HTML containing a <script>
      <div class="row-fluid">             with a list of messages as an array
        <div class="span12">
          <div id="content">
            <div class="row-fluid"  id="message-board" />{{{messageBoard}}}</div>
          </div>
        </div>
        <div class="row-fluid">
          <div class="span12">
            <div id="footer">{{{footer}}}</div>
```

```
          </div>
        </div>
      </div>
      <script type="text/javascript" src="/js/bundle.js"></script>
    </body>
  </html>
```

Includes browser React

This template includes some Twitter Bootstrap styling, but it's not essential for the project or the Universal JavaScript example. You use a few variables (a.k.a. locals: header, messageBoard, props, and footer) in your templates, which you need to provide in the render() of an Express request handler. As a reminder, this is index.js code that you implemented earlier (listing 17.7, ch17/message-board/view/index.hbs) and that uses the previous template by calling it index, which is a convention for index.hbs:

```
res.render('index', {
  header: ReactDOMServer.renderToString(Header()),
  footer: ReactDOMServer.renderToString(Footer()),
  messageBoard:
    ReactDOMServer.renderToString(MessageBoard({messages: docs})),
  props: '<script type="text/javascript">var messages='+JSON.stringify(docs)+
    '</script>'
})
```

The values will be generated from React components. This way, you'll be using the same components on the server and on the browser. The ability to easily render on the server (with Node) is the beauty of React.

Next, let's move on to variables: props, header, footer, and so on.

17.4.4 Composing React components on the server

You're finally doing what you did in all the previous chapters: creating React components. Isn't it good to get back to something familiar once in a while? Yes. But where do the components come from? They live in the components folder. As I mentioned earlier, the components will be used on the browser and the server; that's why you're putting them in a separate components folder and not creating them in client. (Other options for component folder names are shared and common.)

To expose these components, each of them must have module.exports, which is assigned a value of the component class or a stateless function. For example, you require React, implement the class or a function, and then export Header as follows:

```
const React = require('react')
const Header = () => {
  return (
    <h1>Message Board</h1>
  )
}

module.exports = Header
```

Although there's no mention of React in the code, it's used by JSX.

Declares a stateless component

Exports the stateless component

The message board will use AJAX/XHR calls to get a list of messages and post a new message. The calls are in board.jsx. The file will include MessageBoard. It's your container (smart) component, so the calls are in that component.

It's interesting to look at where you make AJAX calls in MessageBoard: in component-DidMount(), because this lifecycle event will *never* be called on the server (ch17/message-board/components/board.jsx)!

Listing 17.10   Fetching messages and sending a message

```
const request = require('axios')
const url = 'http://localhost:3000/messages'          ◁─┐  Creates a variable for
const fD = ReactDOM.findDOMNode                            the server address. It
...                                                        can be changed later.
class MessageBoard extends React.Component {
  constructor(ops) {
    super(ops)
    this.addMessage = this.addMessage.bind(this)
    if (this.props.messages)
      this.state = {messages: this.props.messages}
  }
  componentDidMount() {
    request.get(url, (result) => {               ◁─┐  Makes a GET request with axios
      if(!result || !result.length){                   and updates the state on success
        return;                                         with the list of messages
      }
      this.setState({messages: result})
    })
  }
  addMessage(message) {
    let messages = this.state.messages
    request.post(url, message)                   ◁─┐  Makes a POST request with
      .then(result => result.data)                    axios and, on success, adds the
      .then((data) =>{                                message to the list of messages
        if(!data){                                     by updating the state
          return console.error('Failed to save')
        }
        console.log('Saved!')
        messages.unshift(data)
        this.setState({messages: messages})
      })
  }
  render() {
    return (
      <div>
        <NewMessage messages={this.state.messages} addMessageCb=
          {this.addMessage} />
        <MessageList messages={this.state.messages} />      ◁─┐
      </div>
    )
  }                              Passes the method to add messages to the
}                              NewMessage representational/dumb component,
                                which will create a form and event listeners
```

You can look up the implementation of NewMessage and MessageList in the same file (ch17/message-board/components/board.jsx); I won't bore you here. They're *representational* components with little or no logic—just the description of the UI in the form of JSX.

You're done with rendering React (and layout) HTML on the server. Now, let's sync up the markup with the browser React; otherwise, no messages would be added—there would be no interactive browser JavaScript events!

17.4.5 *Client-side React code*

If you stopped the implementation at this point, there would be only static markup from the rendering of React components on the server. New messages wouldn't be saved, because the onClick event for the POST button wouldn't work. You need to plug in the browser React to take over where the server's static markup rendering left off.

You create app.jsx as a *browser-only* file. It won't be executed on the server (unlike the components). This is the place to put ReactDOM.render() calls to enable browser React:

```
ReactDOM.render(<MessageBoard messages={messages}/>,
  document.getElementById('message-board')
)
```

You also need to use the global messages as a property for MessageBoard. The messages property value will be populated by the server-side template and {{{props}}} data (see section 17.4.3). In other words, the messages array of messages will be populated from index.hbs when the template gets data (called locals) from the props variable in the Express.js route /.

Failure to provide the same messages property to MessageBoard on the server and on the browser will result in browser React repainting the entire component, because browser React will consider the views to be different. Under the hood, React will use the checksum attribute to compare the data that's already in the DOM (from the server-side rendering) with whatever browser React comes up with. React uses checksum because it's quicker than doing an actual tree comparison (which could take a while).

In the app.js file, you need to require some front-end libraries and then render out components in the DOM (ch17/message-board/client/app.jsx).

> **Listing 17.11   Rendering client React components on the browser**

```
const React = require('react')
const ReactDOM = require('react-dom')

const Header = require('../components/header.jsx')
const Footer = require('../components/footer.jsx')
const MessageBoard = require('../components/board.jsx')

ReactDOM.render(<Header />, document.getElementById('header'))
```

```
ReactDOM.render(<Footer />, document.getElementById('footer'))
ReactDOM.render(<MessageBoard messages={messages}/>,
➥ document.getElementById('message-board'))
```

The browser code is tiny!

17.4.6 *Setting up Webpack*

The final step is setting up Webpack to bundle the browser code into one file, manage dependencies, and convert JSX code. First you need to configure Webpack as follows, with the entry point client/app.jsx, with output set to public/js in the project folder, and using Babel loaders. The devtool setting gets the proper source code lines in Chrome DevTools (not the lines from the compiled JS code):

```
module.exports = {
  entry: './client/app.jsx',
  output: {
    path: __dirname + '/public/js/',
    filename: 'bundle.js'
  },
  devtool: '#sourcemap',
  stats: {
   colors: true,
   reasons: true
  },
  module: {
    loaders: [
      {
        test: /\.jsx?$/,
        exclude: /(node_modules)/,
        loader: 'babel-loader'
      }
    ]
  }
}
```

To convert JSX to JS, you can use babel-preset-react and specify the Babel configs in package.json:

```
...
  "babel": {
    "presets": [
      "react"
    ]
  },
  ...
```

The client-side dependencies (for browser React) like Babel and Webpack in package .json will be development dependencies, because Webpack will bundle everything that's needed into bundle.js. Thus you won't need them at runtime:

```
{
  ...
  "devDependencies": {
    "axios": "0.13.1",
    "babel-core": "6.10.4",
    "babel-jest": "13.2.2",
    "babel-loader": "6.2.4",
    "babel-preset-react": "6.5.0",
    "node-dev": "3.1.3",
    "webpack": "1.13.1"
  }
}
```

TIP Be sure you use the exact versions provided here. Otherwise, all the new stuff that will come out when I'm done writing this paragraph will break the project—and I'm only half joking!

Also, while you're in package.json, add an npm build script (it's optional but more convenient):

```
...
"scripts": {
  ...
  "build": "./node_modules/.bin/webpack"
},
...
```

I personally love to use `watch` for Webpack (`-w`). In package.json, you can add the option `-w` to the npm build script:

```
...
"scripts": {
  "build": "./node_modules/.bin/webpack -w",
  ...
},
...
```

Consequently, every time you run `npm run build`, Webpack will use Babel to convert JSX into JS and stitch all the files with their dependencies into a giant ball. In this case, it will be put in /public/js/app.js.

Thanks to the include in the views/index.hbs template, right before the ending `</body>` tag, the browser code is working (the following line is what's in the template):

```
<script type="text/javascript" src="/js/bundle.js"></script>
```

When I run this default task with `npm run build`, I see these logs:

```
Hash: 1d4cfcb6db55f1438550
Version: webpack 1.13.1
Time: 733ms
```

```
     Asset     Size   Chunks                Chunk Names
   bundle.js  782 kB        0   [emitted]   main
bundle.js.map 918 kB        0   [emitted]   main
      + 200 hidden modules
```

That's a good sign. If you see another message or errors, compare your project with the code on at www.manning.com/books/react-quickly or https://github.com/azat-co/react-quickly/tree/master/ch17.

17.4.7 *Running the app*

That's it as far as rendering React.js components in Express.js apps goes. Typically, all you need are the following (assuming you have a build process and components):

- A template that outputs locals/data unescaped
- A res.render() call to hydrate data to the template and render it (components, properties, and such)
- Inclusion of the browser React file (with ReactDOM.Render) in the template for interactivity

Are you still confused about Universal Express and React? If so, get the tested, working code for the project from www.manning.com/books/react-quickly or https://github.com/azat-co/react-quickly/tree/master/ch17/message-board and poke around. You can remove code in app.js to disable browser React (so there's no interactivity such as mouse clicks), or remove code in index.js to disable server React (slight delay when loading a page).

To run the project, have MongoDB running ($ mongod; for more instructions see appendix D). In the project folder, run these commands:

```
$ npm install
$ npm start
```

Don't forget to either have Webpack running builds in watch mode (npm run build) or restart the app every time you make a change to the browser code.

Open http://localhost:3000 in your browser, and you'll see the message board (see figure 17.9). If you look closely at the way the page is loaded (Chrome DevTools), you'll see that the first load is fast because the HTML is rendered on the server.

When you comment out the code in ch17/message-board/index.js that's responsible for server-side rendering, you can compare the timing by looking at the Network tab. There, notice the localhost resource (first page load and server-side rendering) and the GET XHR call to /messages. My results for the localhost are *much* faster, as shown in figure 17.10.

Of course, the bulk of the total loading time is taken up by bundle.js. After all, it has more than 200 modules! GET /messages doesn't take too long—just a few milliseconds. But still, users will see everything on the page when the localhost call happens. Conversely, without isomorphic/universal code, users will see fully formed HTML only after GET /messages, plus some for browser React to render the HTML client-side.

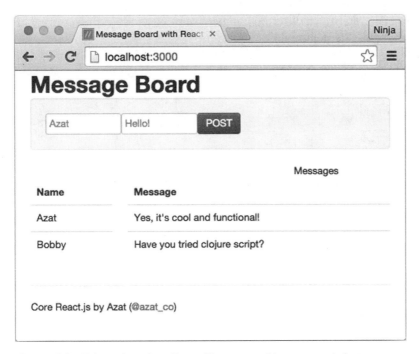

Figure 17.9 Universal app in action, with server and browser rendering

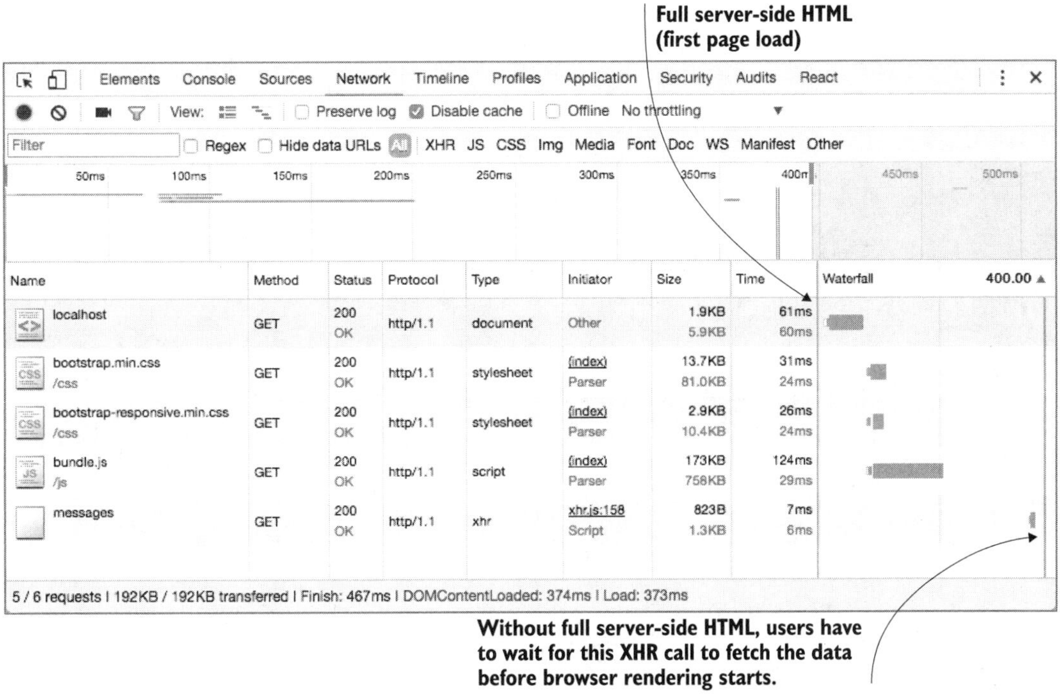

Figure 17.10 Loading the server-side HTML is 10 times faster than complete loading, which is slower due to bundle.js.

Let's inspect the app from a different perspective by comparing Universal versus browser rendering side by side. Figure 17.11 shows the results for localhost. With the Universal

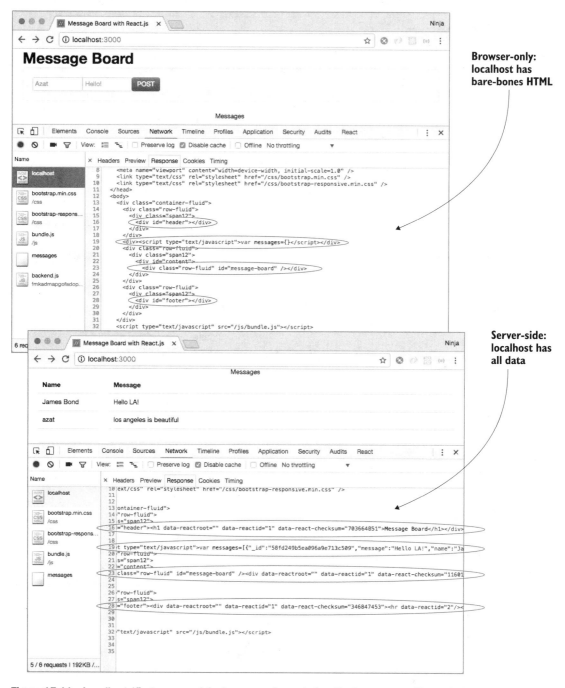

Figure 17.11   Localhost (first response) for browser-only rendering (top) vs. server-side rendering (bottom)

approach, localhost has all the data, and it loads in a mere 20–30 ms. With browser-only React, localhost has only bare-bones, skeleton HTML. So, users will have to wait about 10 times as long. Anything greater than 150 ms is usually noticeable by humans.

You can play around by commenting out the rendering statements in index.js (Express.js) or app.jsx (browser React). For example, if you comment out the server-side `Header` but leave the browser render for `Header` intact, then you may not see `Header` for a few moments before it appears.

Also, if you comment out passing the `props` variable on the server or modify its value, browser React will update the DOM after getting the list of messages for `axios`. React will give you a warning that checksums don't match.

Universal routing and data

Sooner or later, your application will grow, and you'll need to use libraries such as React Router and Redux to route data (covered in chapters 13 and 14). Interestingly, these libraries already support Node, and React Router even supports Express. For example, you can pass React Router routes to Express for server-side support via `match` and `RouterContext`, to render components on the server side:

```
const { renderToString } = require('react-dom/server')
const { match, RouterContext } = require ('react-router')
const routes = require('./routes')
// ...
app.get('/', (req, res) => {
  match({ routes,                          ← Uses a special method from React Router
    location: req.url                      ← Passes the location/URL to the React Router method
    },
    (error,
    redirectLocation,
    renderProps) => {
    // ...
    res
      .status(200)
      .send(renderToString(                ← Renders an HTML string using a special React Router component and properties
        <RouterContext {...renderProps} />
      ))
  })
}
```

Redux has the `createStore()` method (chapter 14), which you can use server-side in Express middleware to provide a data store. For example, for an `App` component, the server-side code with Redux will look like this:

```
const { createStore } = require('redux')
const { Provider } = require('react-redux')
const reducers = require('./modules')
const routes = require('./routes')

// ...
```

(continued)

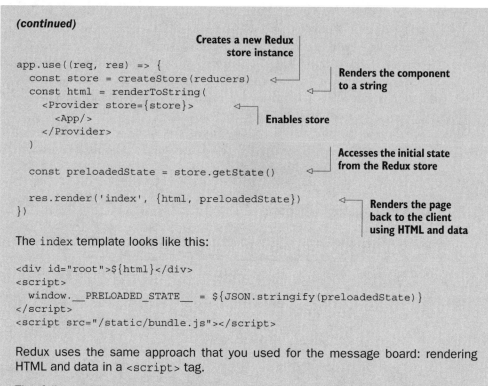

Creates a new Redux store instance

```
app.use((req, res) => {
  const store = createStore(reducers)
  const html = renderToString(
    <Provider store={store}>
      <App/>
    </Provider>
  )

  const preloadedState = store.getState()

  res.render('index', {html, preloadedState})
})
```

Renders the component to a string

Enables store

Accesses the initial state from the Redux store

Renders the page back to the client using HTML and data

The `index` template looks like this:

```
<div id="root">${html}</div>
<script>
  window.__PRELOADED_STATE__ = ${JSON.stringify(preloadedState)}
</script>
<script src="/static/bundle.js"></script>
```

Redux uses the same approach that you used for the message board: rendering HTML and data in a `<script>` tag.

The full example with explanations is at http://mng.bz/F5pb and http://mng.bz/Edyx.

This concludes the discussion of isomorphic or Universal JavaScript. The uniformity and code reuse it provides are tremendous benefits that help developers be more productive and live happier work lives!

17.5   *Quiz*

1   What is the method used to render a React component on the server?

2   Rendering the first page on the server improves performance. True or false?

3   CommonJS and Node.js module syntax, using `require()` (along with Webpack), lets you "require" or import npm modules in browser code. True or false?

4   Which of the following is used to output unescaped strings in Handlebars? `<%...%>`, `{{...}}`, `{{{...}}}` or `dangerouslySetInnerHTML=...`

5   What is the best place to put AJAX/XHR calls in browser React so they won't be triggered on the server?

17.6 Summary

- To use and render React on the server, you need `react-dom/server` and `render-ToString()`.
- The data must be the same to sync server React HTML with browser React. React uses checksums for comparison.
- The difference between `renderToString()` and `renderToStaticMarkup()` is that one has checksums, which allows browser React to reuse the HTML (`renderToString()`), and the other doesn't.
- For Universal JS to work, you render React on the server, supply browser React with the same data, and render browser React components.
- Use triple curly braces `{{{html}}}` to output unescaped HTML content in Handlebars.

17.7 Quiz answers

5 `componentDidMount()`, because it will never be called on server rendering.

4 `{{{...}}}` is the correct syntax. For escaped variables, use `{{data}}` to ensure safer usage.

3 True. You can use the `require()` and `module.exports` syntax right out of the box with Webpack. Just by setting an entry point in the webpack.config.js, you can make Webpack traverse all the dependencies from there and include only the needed ones.

2 True. You get all the data on the first page load without having to wait for bundle.js and AJAX requests.

1 `ReactDOMServer.renderToString()`. `renderToStaticMarkup()` won't render checksums.

18

Project: Building a bookstore with React Router

This chapter covers

- Project structure and Webpack configuration
- The host HTML file
- Creating components
- Launching the project

The project in this chapter focuses mainly on demonstrating how to use React Router, some ES6 features, and Webpack. In this project, you'll build a simple e-commerce storefront for a bookstore (figure 18.1).

You'll learn how to create browser routing, as well as the following techniques for working with React Router:

- How to pass data to a route and access it
- How to access URL parameters
- How to create modal windows with changing URLs
- How to use layouts by nesting routes

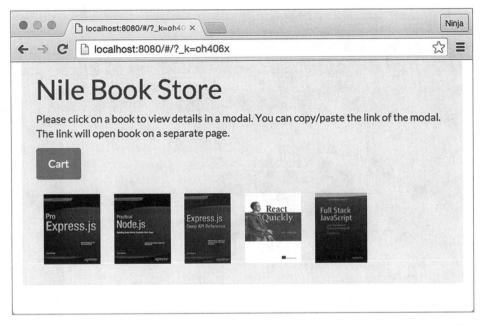

Figure 18.1 Nile Book Store home page with a list of books

To illustrate these techniques, the project includes several screens with different routes:

- *Home (/)*—The storefront with a book list
- *Product page (/product/:id)*—A separate product page
- *Cart (/cart)*—A web page showing the quantities and titles selected by the user
- *Checkout (/checkout)*—A print-ready invoice with the list of books

The product information will come from an array of data set in one of the files (ch18/nile/jsx/app.js; refer to the project structure in the next section). The product page can act as a modal dialog or as a separate page. When you click a product image on the home page, a modal dialog will open; for example, figure 18.2 shows a modal dialog with the detailed view of *React Quickly*.

The URL is /products/3 followed by the hash token to keep track of the state. The link is shareable: if you open it in a new window/tab, it's a normal screen, not a modal dialog (see figure 18.3). Modals are useful when you're navigating through a list and don't want to lose the context by going to a new page. But when you share a direct product link, there's no context or list—you want to focus attention on the product.

The roadmap to implementing the bookstore front end consists of the following steps:

1. Setting up the project with npm, Babel, and Webpack
2. Creating the HTML file
3. Creating the components
4. Launching the project

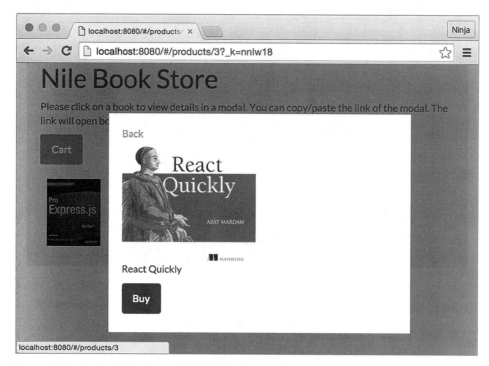

Figure 18.2   Product view in a modal window of the Nile bookstore

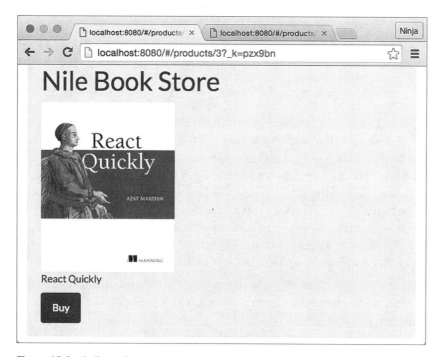

Figure 18.3   A direct link opens the product view in a new window rather than a modal.

I encourage you to implement the items listed in the "Homework" section at the end of the chapter and submit your code to the book's GitHub repository: https://github.com/azat-co/react-quickly.

> **NOTE** To follow along with the project, you'll need to download the unminified version of React and install node.js and npm for compiling JSX. I'm also using Webpack as the build tool. Appendix A covers how to install everything.

> **NOTE** The source code for the project in this chapter is at www.manning.com/books/react-quickly and https://github.com/azat-co/react-quickly/tree/master/ch18. You can also find some demos at http://reactquickly.co/demos.

Let's start with setting up the project.

18.1 Project structure and Webpack configuration

You have a basic understanding of the end result of this project: a front-end web app with URL routing. Time to jump in to the project structure. This is what the folder structure will look like:

```
/css
  bootstrap.css
/images
  ...
/js                        Compiled and
  bundle.js                bundled code
  bundle.js.map
/jsx
  app.jsx                  Shopping cart
  cart.jsx                 component
  checkout.jsx
  modal.jsx
  product.jsx
/node_modules
  ...
index.html                 Host HTML file
package.json
webpack.config.js
```

Entry-point script with App and ReactDOM.render() → points to /js

Modal component → points to modal.jsx

I've abridged the contents of the images and node_modules folders for the sake of brevity. This is a front-end-only application, but you need package.json to install dependencies and tell Babel what to do. The following listing shows those dependencies in full, in package.json.

Listing 18.1 Nile Book Store project dependencies and setup

```
{
  "name": "nile",
  "version": "1.0.0",
  "description": "",
  "main": "index.js",
```

```
  "author": "Azat Mardan",                    Creates the npm script for building
  "license": "MIT",                               the assets with watch mode
  "scripts": {
    "build": "node ./node_modules/webpack/bin/webpack.js -w"   ◁────────┐
  },
  "babel": {
    "plugins": [                            Adds a JSX plug-in
      "transform-react-jsx"         ◁────┘  for Babel
    ],
    "presets": [                      ┌─ Adds the ES6/ES2015-to-ES5
      "es2015"                  ◁──┤   conversion (to support old
    ],                              │  browsers)
    "ignore": [
      "js/bundle.js",
      "node_modules/**/*.js"   ◁────┐  Excludes dependencies
    ]                               │  from Babel
  },
  "devDependencies": {
    "babel-core": "6.3.21",
    "babel-loader": "6.4.1",
    "babel-plugin-transform-react-jsx": "6.3.13",
    "babel-preset-es2015": "6.3.13",
    "history": "4.0.0",              ◁────┐  Installs the history library to
    "react": "15.5.4",                    │  be used with React Router
    "react-addons-test-utils": "15.2.1",
    "react-dom": "15.5.4",
    "react-router": "2.8.0",
    "webpack": "2.4.1",
    "webpack-dev-server": "1.14.0"
  }
}
```

After starting with the standard project properties, the `scripts` command points to the local installation of Webpack. This way, you're using the same version as in the devDependencies property. The build creates the bundle.js file and starts the Webpack development server on port 8080. You don't have to use it; you can instead build manually each time there's a change and use `node-static` (https://github.com/cloudhead/node-static) or a similar local web server:

```
"scripts": {
    "build": "node ./node_modules/webpack/bin/webpack.js -w"
  },
```

The next line is required for Babel v6.x, because without it Babel won't do much. You're telling Babel to use the JSX transformer and ES2015 presets:

```
  "babel": {
    "plugins": [
      "transform-react-jsx"
    ],
    "presets": [
      "es2015"
    ],
```

The next Babel config isn't optional. It excludes some files from the Babel loader, such as certain node_modules folders and files:

```
"ignore": [
  "js/bundle.js",
  "node_modules/**/*.js"
]
},
```

NOTE Next, you'll define dependencies. You need to use the *exact* version numbers shown here, because I can't guarantee that future versions will work. Given the speed at which React and Babel are developing, there will most likely be changes. But there's nothing wrong with using slightly older versions to learn the concepts, as you're doing in this book.

The devDependencies are for development, as the name suggests, and aren't part of production deployment. This is where you put Webpack, Webpack Dev Server, Babel, and other packages. Please double-check that you're using the exact versions listed here:

```
...
"devDependencies": {
  "babel-core": "6.3.21",
  "babel-loader": "6.4.1",
  "babel-plugin-transform-react-jsx": "6.3.13",
  "babel-preset-es2015": "6.3.13",
  "history": "4.0.0",
  "react": "15.5.4",
  "react-addons-test-utils": "15.2.1",
  "react-dom": "15.5.4",
  "react-router": "2.8.0",
  "webpack": "2.4.1",
  "webpack-dev-server": "1.14.0"
  }
}
```

Now that you've defined the project dependencies, you need to set up the Webpack build process so you can use ES6 and transform JSX. To do this, create the file webpack.config.js in the root directory, with the following code (ch18/nile/webpack.config.js).

Listing 18.2   Webpack configuration for the Nile store

```
module.exports = {
  entry: "./jsx/app.jsx",
  output: {
    path: __dirname + '/js',
    filename: "bundle.js"
  },
  devtool: '#sourcemap',
  stats: {
```

```
      colors: true,
      reasons: true
    },
    module: {
      loaders: [
        {
          test: /\.jsx?$/,
          exclude: /(node_modules)/,
          loader: 'babel-loader'
        }
      ]
    }
}
```

Run npm i (short for npm install), and you're finished with the setup. Next, you'll create an HTML file that will hold skeleton <div> elements for React components.

18.2   *The host HTML file*

The HTML for this project is very basic. It has a container with the ID content and includes js/bundle.js (ch18/nile/index.html).

Listing 18.3   Host HTML file

```
<!DOCTYPE html>
<html>
  <head>
    <link href="css/bootstrap.css" type="text/css" rel="stylesheet"/>
  </head>
  <body>
    <div class="container-fluid">
      <div id="content" class=""></div>
    </div>
    <script src="js/bundle.js"></script>
  </body>
</html>
```

Now you can do a quick test to see whether the build and development processes work:

1   Install all the dependencies with $ npm install. Do this just once.
2   Put console.log('Hey Nile!') in jsx/app.jsx.
3   Run the app with $ npm run build. You can leave it running, because the -w will rebuild the file on changes.
4   Start your local web server from the project root. You can use node-static or webpack-dev-server, which you included in package.json.
5   Open the browser at http://localhost:8080.
6   Open the browser console (such as Chrome DevTools). You should see the "Hey Nile!" message.

18.3   Creating components

Onward to building the app, assuming you were able to see the message. You'll begin by importing the modules using ES6 modules and destructuring. Simply put, *destructuring* is a way to define a variable from an object by using the same name as one of the object's properties. For example, if you want to import accounts from user.accounts and declare accounts (see the repetition?), then you can use {accounts} = user. If you're not sure about destructuring, refer to the ES6 cheatsheet in appendix E.

18.3.1   Main file: app.jsx

The first file to write is app.jsx, where you set up the main imports, book information, and routes. Minus the component code, which we'll get to in a moment, app.jsx looks like this (ch18/nile/jsx/app.jsx).

Listing 18.4   Main app file

```
const React = require('react')
const ReactDOM = require('react-dom')
const { hashHistory,          ◁──── Imports the
   Router,                          hash history
   Route,
   IndexRoute,
   Link,                      Imports objects
   IndexLink               ◁── from React Router
} = require('react-router')

            ┌ const Modal = require('./modal.jsx')
  Imports   │ const Cart = require('./cart.jsx')
components  │ const Checkout = require('./checkout.jsx')
            └ const Product = require('./product.jsx')          A small array of book data so
                                                                you don't need to work with
const PRODUCTS = [                                        ◁──── a database in this example
   { id: 0, src: 'images/proexpress-cover.jpg',
      title: 'Pro Express.js', url: 'http://amzn.to/1D6qiqk' },
   { id: 1, src: 'images/practicalnode-cover.jpeg',
      title: 'Practical Node.js', url: 'http://amzn.to/NuQ0fM' },
   { id: 2, src: 'images/expressapiref-cover.jpg',
      title: 'Express API Reference', url: 'http://amzn.to/1xcHanf' },
   { id: 3, src: 'images/reactquickly-cover.jpg',
      title: 'React Quickly',
      url: 'https://www.manning.com/books/react-quickly'},
   { id: 4, src: 'images/fullstack-cover.png',
      title: 'Full Stack JavaScript',
      url: 'http://www.apress.com/9781484217504'}
]

const Heading = () => {               ◁──┐
   return <h1>Nile Book Store</h1>       │  Both of these components are
}                                        │  implemented as stateless.
                                         │
const Copy = () => {                   ◁──┘
```

```
    return <p>Please click on a book to view details in a modal. You can
➡ copy/paste the link of the modal. The link will open the book on a
➡ separate page.</p>
  }

  class App extends React.Component {
    ...
  }

  class Index extends React.Component {
    ...
  }

  let cartItems = {}
  const addToCart = (id) => {
    if (cartItems[id])
      cartItems[id] += 1
    else
      cartItems[id] = 1
  }

  ReactDOM.render((
    <Router history={hashHistory}>
      <Route path="/" component={App}>
        <IndexRoute component={Index}/>
        <Route path="/products/:id" component={Product}
          addToCart={addToCart}
          products={PRODUCTS} />
        <Route path="/cart" component={Cart}
        cartItems={cartItems} products={PRODUCTS}/>
      </Route>
      <Route path="/checkout" component={Checkout}
        cartItems={cartItems} products={PRODUCTS}/>
    </Router>
  ), document.getElementById('content'))
```

The cartItems object holds the current items in the shopping cart. It's empty initially.

After you import everything at the top of the file, you hardcode the products into an array; each object has `id`, `src`, `title`, and `url`. Obviously, in the real world you'd get this data from the server, not have it in the browser JavaScript file:

```
const PRODUCTS = [
  { id: 0, src: 'images/proexpress-cover.jpg',
    title: 'Pro Express.js', url: 'http://amzn.to/1D6qiqk' },
  { id: 1, src: 'images/practicalnode-cover.jpeg',
    title: 'Practical Node.js', url: 'http://amzn.to/NuQ0fM' },
  { id: 2, src: 'images/expressapiref-cover.jpg',
    title: 'Express API Reference', url: 'http://amzn.to/1xcHanf' },
  { id: 3, src: 'images/reactquickly-cover.jpg',
    title: 'React Quickly',
    url: 'https://www.manning.com/books/react-quickly'},
  { id: 4, src: 'images/fullstack-cover.png',
    title: 'Full Stack JavaScript',
    url: 'http://www.apress.com/9781484217504'}
]
```

You implement the next component as stateless using ES6 fat arrows. Why not have it as an <h1> in a render? Because doing it this way, you can use it on multiple screens. You use the same stateless style for Copy. It's just static HTML, so you don't need anything extra, not even properties:

```
const Heading = () => {
  return <h1>Nile Book Store</h1>
}

const Copy = () => {
  return <p>Please click on a book to view details in a modal. You can
    copy/paste the link of the modal. The link will open the book on a
    separate page.</p>
}
```

The two main components, App and Index, come next, followed by the cartItems object, which holds the current items in the shopping cart. It's empty initially. addTo-Cart() is a simple function—in a server-side version, you'd use Redux to persist the data to the server and sessions so a user could come back to the shopping cart later:

```
let cartItems = {}
const addToCart = (id) => {
  if (cartItems[id])
    cartItems[id] += 1
  else
    cartItems[id] = 1
}
```

Finally, here's the ReactDOM.render() method you use to mount the Router component. You need to pass the history library to React Router. As I mentioned earlier, it can be the browser or hash history (this project is using the latter):

```
ReactDOM.render((
  <Router history={hashHistory}>
    <Route path="/" component={App}>
      <IndexRoute component={Index}/>
      <Route path="/products/:id" component={Product}
        addToCart={addToCart}
        products={PRODUCTS} />
      <Route path="/cart" component={Cart}
        cartItems={cartItems} products={PRODUCTS}/>
    </Route>
    <Route path="/checkout" component={Checkout}
      cartItems={cartItems} products={PRODUCTS}/>
  </Router>
), document.getElementById('content'))
```

Passes a method to add the book to the shopping cart

Uses the Index component in IndexRoute

Passes a list of items in the cart and a list of all products as cartItems and products properties

Defines Checkout outside of App so the header isn't rendered

For the /products/:id route, the Product component route gets the addToCart() function to facilitate buying a book. The function will be available in this.props .route.addToCart because whatever property you pass to Route will be available in this.props.route.NAME in the component. For example, products will become this.props.route.products in Product:

```
<Route path="/products/:id" component={Product} addToCart={addToCart}
  products={PRODUCTS} />
```

The /checkout route is outside of App, so it doesn't have a header (see figure 18.4). If you recall, path and the route structure can be independent:

```
<Route path="/checkout" component={Checkout}
  cartItems={cartItems} products={PRODUCTS}/>
```

![Browser window showing localhost:8080/#/checkout with an Invoice table]

Invoice	
Pro Express.js	1
Practical Node.js	2
React Quickly	1
Total: 4	

Figure 18.4   An invoice shouldn't have the header shown on other views.

In this case, by putting Checkout outside of App, Checkout isn't App's child. You can click Back to navigate back to the app from the invoice/checkout screen.

THE APP COMPONENT

Now you can implement the App component! It's the main component because it's the entry point for Webpack and because it provides the layout for most of the views; renders child components such as Product, the product list, and Cart; and shows a modal dialog. Remember ReactDOM.render()? Here's the gist, which shows that App is the root component of the app:

```
ReactDOM.render((
  <Router history={hashHistory}>
    <Route path="/" component={App}>
      <IndexRoute component={Index}/>
      <Route path="/products/:id" component={Product} .../>
```

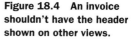
App is the granddaddy of
Product, Cart, and Index.

```
    <Route path="/cart" component={Cart} .../>
  </Route>
  // ...
</Router>
), document.getElementById('content'))
```

Unlike the stateless components, which were just functions, this component is the real deal (ch18/nile/jsx/app.jsx).

Listing 18.5   App component

```
class App extends React.Component {
  componentWillReceiveProps(nextProps) {
    this.isModal = (nextProps.location.state &&
      nextProps.location.state.modal)
    if (this.isModal &&
      nextProps.location.key !== this.props.location.key) {
      this.previousChildren = this.props.children
    }
  }
  render() {
    console.log('Modal: ', this.isModal)
    return (
      <div className="well">
        <Heading/>
        <div>
          {(this.isModal) ? this.previousChildren :
            this.props.children}

          {(this.isModal)?
            <Modal isOpen={true} returnTo=
              {this.props.location.state.returnTo}>
              {this.props.children}
            </Modal> : ''
          }
        </div>
      </div>
    )
  }
}
```

Uses the state passed in Link (implemented in Route)

Saves the children in previousChildren to render

Displays the content of old children (home page) if modal; otherwise, displays children defined in the Router structure

Displays a modal with book details

Recall that `componentWillReceiveProps()` takes the following properties as its argument. This method is a good place to determine whether this view is modal:

```
class App extends React.Component {
  componentWillReceiveProps(nextProps) {
    this.isModal = (nextProps.location.state &&
      nextProps.location.state.modal)
```

The following condition checks whether you're on a modal screen or a nonmodal screen. If it's modal, you assign children as previous children. The `isModal` Boolean determines whether the screen is modal based on state, which comes from the location property set in the Link element (you'll see an example in the Index component):

```
if (this.isModal &&
  nextProps.location.key !== this.props.location.key) {
  this.previousChildren = this.props.children
}
}
```

In the render() function, note that it doesn't matter whether Heading is just a function (stateless component). You can render it like any other React component:

```
render() {
  console.log('Modal: ', this.isModal)
  return (
    <div className="well">
      <Heading/>
```

And the ternary expression renders either this.previousChildren or this.props .children. React Router populates this.props.children from other nested routes/components, such as Index and Product. Remember that App is used by almost all of the app's screens. By default, you want to render this.props.children when working with React Router:

```
<div>
  {(this.isModal) ? this.previousChildren: this.props.children}
```

If you didn't have the isModal condition, and you output this.props.children every time, then when you clicked a book image to open the modal, you'd always see the same content, as shown in figure 18.5. Obviously, this behavior isn't what you intend. For this reason, you render the previous children, which in the case of a modal window is the home page. You can reuse a modal link with state.modal equal to true (shown later, in the Index component). As a result, you'll see the modal on top of the current context.

Finally, you can render the modal in another ternary expression. You're passing isOpen and returnTo:

```
      {(isModal)?
        <Modal isOpen={true} returnTo={this.props.location.state.returnTo}>
          {this.props.children}
        </Modal> : ''
      }
    </div>
  </div>
  )
}
}
```

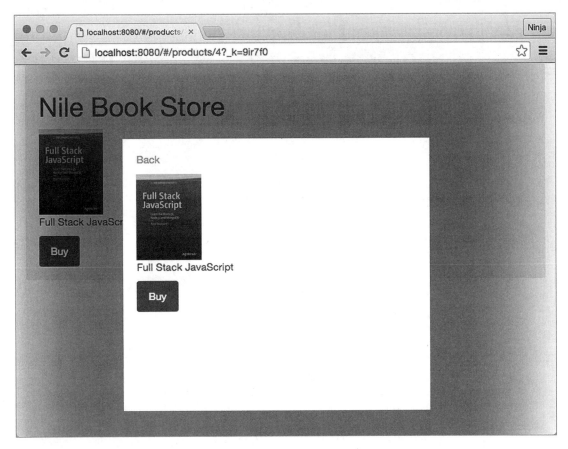

Figure 18.5 If you don't check for `isModal` and use `previousChildren`, the list of books isn't shown.

THE INDEX COMPONENT

Continuing with nile/jsx/app.jsx, the next component is the home page. If you'll recall, it shows the full list of books. The code is shown next (ch18/nile/jsx/app.jsx).

Listing 18.6 `Index` component for the home page

```
class Index extends React.Component {
  render() {
    return (
      <div>
        <Copy/>
        <p><Link to="/cart" className="btn btn-danger">Cart</Link></p>
        <div>
          {PRODUCTS.map(picture => (
            <Link key={picture.id}
              to={{pathname: `/products/${picture.id}`,
                state: { modal: true,
```

> **Adds the link to the shopping cart with Link** → (points to the `<Link to="/cart"...` line)

> **Uses ES6 interpolation (string template) to create a product URL** → (points to the `to={{pathname: ...}` line)

> **Shows a modal window** → (points to the `state: { modal: true,` line)

```
                         returnTo: this.props.location.pathname }
                }
              }>
              <img style={{ margin: 10 }} src={picture.src} height="100" />
            </Link>
          ))}
        </div>
      </div>
    )
  }
}
```

In the map() iterator, you render links to the book modals. These links will open in a separate, nonmodal view when you navigate to them directly:

```
{PRODUCTS.map(picture => (
    <Link key={picture.id}
      to={{pathname: `/products/${picture.id}`,
        state: { modal: true,
          returnTo: this.props.location.pathname }
        }
      }>
```

You can pass any property to the component associated with the /products/:id route (that is, Product and its parent, App). The properties are accessible in this.props .location.NAME, where NAME is the name of the property. You used state.modal earlier, in the Modal component.

The <img> tag uses the src attribute to render the book image:

```
              <img style={{ margin: 10 }} src={picture.src} height="100" />
            </Link>
          ))}
        </div>
      </div>
    )
  }
}
```

That's it for the app.jsx file. The next component to implement is the Cart component; it will live in its own file, because it's not closely related to the application the way App is a layout of the bookstore.

18.3.2 *The Cart component*

The /cart route, rendered by Cart, displays the list of books and their quantity in the shopping cart, as shown in figure 18.6. The Cart component uses cartItems to get the list of books and their quantity. Notice the ES6 style for the render() function (nile/jsx/cart.jsx).

Listing 18.7 Cart component

```
const React = require('react')
const {
  Link
} = require('react-router')

class Cart extends React.Component {
  render() {
    return <div>
      {(Object.keys(this.props.route.cartItems).length == 0) ?
        <p>Your cart is empty</p> : ''
      }
      <ul>
        {Object.keys(this.props.route.cartItems).map((item,
          index,
          list)=>{
          return <li key={item}>
            {this.props.route.products[item].title}
            - {this.props.route.cartItems[item]}
          </li>
        })}
      </ul>
      <Link to="/checkout"
        className="btn btn-primary">
        Checkout
      </Link>
      <Link to="/" className="btn btn-info">
        Home
      </Link>
    </div>
  }
}

module.exports = Cart
```

Iterates and renders each item in a shopping cart

Adds navigation to the checkout, which displays a print-ready invoice

Adds navigation to the storefront to let the user make more purchases

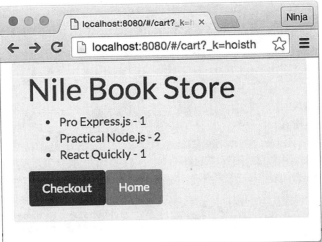

Figure 18.6 Shopping cart

Cart uses `this.props.route.products`, which is a list of products. This works because in app.js, you defined the `route` property:

```
<Route path="/cart" component={Cart}
  cartItems={cartItems} products={PRODUCTS}/>
```

If you're using Redux (chapter 14), you won't need to manually pass properties such as `products`, because `Provider` will populate the data store in children automatically.

18.3.3 *The Checkout component*

Next is `Checkout`, shown in figure 18.7. This is the only component outside the `App` route. To refresh your memory, this is the routing from app.js:

```
ReactDOM.render((
  <Router history={hashHistory}>                          App route:
    <Route path="/" component={App}>              ←────   main layout
      <IndexRoute component={Index}/>
      <Route path="/products/:id" component={Product}
        addToCart={addToCart}
        products={PRODUCTS} />
      <Route path="/cart" component={Cart}
        cartItems={cartItems} products={PRODUCTS}/>
    </Route>                                              Checkout route is
    <Route path="/checkout" component={Checkout}   ←────  outside of the App route
      cartItems={cartItems} products={PRODUCTS}/>
  </Router>
), document.getElementById('content'))
```

As you can see, `App` and `Checkout` are on the same level of the hierarchy. Thus, when you navigate to /checkout, the `App` route is *not* triggered. There's no layout. (Interestingly, it's possible to nest the URLs but keep the components out of the nested structure: for example, by setting /cart/checkout. You won't do that here, though.)

Figure 18.7 `Checkout` doesn't need a header.

The print-ready invoice uses a Twitter Bootstrap table and table-bordered styles. Again, you use ES6's const (remember, object properties can change) and function syntax (nile/jsx/checkout.jsx).

Listing 18.8 Checkout component

```
const React = require('react')
const {
  Link
} = require('react-router')


class Checkout extends React.Component {
  render() {
    let count = 0
    return <div><h1>Invoice</h1><table className="table table-bordered">
      <tbody>
      {Object.keys(this.props.route.cartItems).map((item, index,
        list)=>{
        count += this.props.route.cartItems[item]
        return <tr key={item}>
          <td>{this.props.route.products[item].title}</td>
          <td>{this.props.route.cartItems[item]}</td>
        </tr>
      })}
      </tbody></table><p>Total: {count}</p></div>
  }
}

module.exports = Checkout
```

Iterates and renders each item in the shopping cart → (points to the `Object.keys(...).map(...)` block)

Uses a list of products passed in the route to pull a title → (points to the `<td>{this.props.route.products[item].title}</td>` line)

Exports the class ⟵ (points to `module.exports = Checkout`)

Now you need to implement the Modal component.

18.3.4 *The Modal component*

This component renders its children in a modal dialog. Recall that in App, the code uses Modal like this:

```
{(this.isModal) ?
  <Modal isOpen={true} returnTo={this.props.location.state.returnTo}>
    {this.props.children}
  </Modal> : ''
}
```

Modal takes children from App's this.props.children, which in turn is defined in app.js, in <Route>. Here's a reminder of the routing structure:

```
ReactDOM.render((
  <Router history={hashHistory}>
    <Route path="/" component={App}>
      <IndexRoute component={Index}/>
      <Route path="/products/:id" component={Product}
```

```
        addToCart={addToCart}
        products={PRODUCTS} />
      <Route path="/cart" component={Cart}
        cartItems={cartItems} products={PRODUCTS}/>
    </Route>
    <Route path="/checkout" component={Checkout}
      cartItems={cartItems} products={PRODUCTS}/>
  </Router>
), document.getElementById('content'))
```

This is how you can view a product page both as a standalone and as a modal. Components nested under the App route are its children, depending on the URL (nile/jsx/modal.jsx).

Listing 18.9   Modal component

```
const React = require('react')
const {
  Link
} = require('react-router')

class Modal extends React.Component {
  constructor(props) {
    super(props)
    this.styles = {
      position: 'fixed',
      top: '20%',
      right: '20%',
      bottom: '20%',
      left: '20%',
      width: 450,
      height: 400,
      padding: 20,
      boxShadow: '0px 0px 150px 130px rgba(0, 0, 0, 0.5)',
      overflow: 'auto',
      background: '#fff'
    }
  }
  render() {
    return (
      <div style={this.styles}>
        <p>
          <Link to={this.props.returnTo}>
            Back
          </Link>
        </p>
        {this.props.children}
      </div>
    )
  }
}

module.exports = Modal
```

Defines styles as an instance attribute of the class

Uses a fixed position (along with top, right, left, bottom) to float the modal in the middle in a detached mode

Notice the camelCase for boxShadow, which in CSS is box-shadow.

Applies styles to make a modal view

The modal window displays an individual `Product` component because that's what's nested under `App` in routing and because the `Product` route has the URL path /product/:id, which you used along with `state` set to `modal true` in `Index` (product list).

18.3.5 *The Product component*

The `Product` component uses the property from its route to trigger actions (`this.props.route.addToCart`). The `addToCart()` method in app.js puts a specific book in the shopping cart (if you're using Redux, then this dispatches the action). You trigger `addToCart()` with the browser `onClick` event handler and a local method in `Product` called `handleBuy()`, which triggers the method `addToCart` from app.js. To summarize: `onClick → this.handleBuy → this.props.route.addToCart → addToCart()` (app.js). As a reminder, `addToCart()` is as follows:

```
let cartItems = {}
const addToCart = (id) => {
  if (cartItems[id])
    cartItems[id] += 1
  else
    cartItems[id] = 1
}
```

Of course, if you're using Redux or Relay, then you'll use their methods. This example keeps things simple with a plain array acting as a data store and a single method.

Now let's look at the `Product` component itself. As always, you start by importing React and defining the class; then you take care of the event and render. Here's the full code for `Product` (nile/jsx/product.jsx) with the most interesting parts noted.

Listing 18.10 Individual product information

```
const React = require('react')
const {
  Link
} = require('react-router')

class Product extends React.Component {          Binds the function to
  constructor(props) {                           make sure you have the
    super(props)                                 proper value of this
    this.handleBuy = this.handleBuy.bind(this)  ◁
  }
  handleBuy (event) {                                Passes the book ID to
    this.props.route.addToCart(this.props.params.id)  ◁  the function in app.jsx
  }
  render() {
    return (
      <div>                                    Pulls the image path and
        <img src={this.props.route.products[    filename from the list of
    ➥ this.props.params.id].src}          ◁     products using this book's ID
          style={{ height: '80%' }} />
        <p>{this.props.route.products[this.props.params.id].title}</p>
```

```
        <Link
          to={{
            pathname: `/cart`,
            state: { productId: this.props.params.id}
          }}
          onClick={this.handleBuy}
          className="btn btn-primary">
            Buy
        </Link>
      </div>
    )
  }
}
```

<!-- annotation -->
Triggers the function
when the Buy button
is clicked

```
module.exports = Product
```

You can also send a state to `Cart` in the `Link` component:

```
<Link
  to={{
    pathname: `/cart`,
    state: { productId: this.props.params.id}
  }}
  onClick={this.handleBuy}
  className="btn btn-primary">
    Buy
</Link>
```

Recall that `Product` is used by the modal indirectly: `Modal` doesn't render `Product`. Instead, `Modal` uses `this.props.children`, which has `Product`. Thus, `Modal` can be considered a passthrough component. (See chapter 8 for more about `this.props` `.children` and passthrough components that use it.)

18.4   Launching the project

That's all for the bookstore. You've used some ES6 features and passed around states with React Router. Now, run the project by building it with `npm run build`, starting a local web server (WDS or `node-static`), and navigating to http://localhost:8080/nile, assuming you have a static web server running in a parent folder that has a nile folder (the URL path depends on where you launched the static web server).

You should see the home page with a grid of book covers. When you click a cover, a modal window appears; click the Buy button to add the book to the cart, which appears on the /cart and /checkout pages. Enjoy!

18.5   Homework

For bonus points, do the following:

- Abstract (copy/paste) `Index` and `App` into separate files, away from app.js, and rename `App` as `Layout`.
- Move the data to persistent storage such as MongoDB or PostgreSQL.

- Change the hash URL to hash-less by using a history API alongside the custom Express server (which you'll need to implement). Refer to the Netflix clone with hash-less URLs in chapter 15 for inspiration.
- Add unit tests for `Product` and `Checkout` using Jest.

Submit your code in *a new folder under ch18* as a pull request to this book's GitHub repository: https://github.com/azat-co/react-quickly/.

18.6 Summary

- The `Link` component is imported from `react-router` and can be used to pass state, as in `<Link to={{pathname: '/product', state: { modal: true }}}>`.
- The React Router state is available in `this.props.location.state`.
- You can pass properties defined in `<Route name={value}>`, and they'll be available in `this.props.route.name`.

Watch this chapter's introduction video by scanning this QR code with your phone or going to http://reactquickly.co/videos/ch19.

Project: Checking passwords with Jest

19

This chapter covers

- Project structure and Webpack configuration
- The host HTML file
- Implementing a strong password module
- Creating Jest tests
- Implementing the `Password` component and UI

This project focuses on building a UI, working with modules, and testing with Jest, along with other React-related techniques such as component composition, ES6 syntax, state, properties, and so on. Recall that chapter 16 dealt with testing; you used a password widget as an example of unit testing and UI testing. In this project, you'll build the widget itself to check, verify, and generate new passwords. Along the way, I'll explain testing again, here and there, in an expanded format.

The widget has a Save button that's disabled by default but becomes enabled when the password is strong enough (according to the preset rules), as shown in figure 19.1. In addition, the Generate button lets you create a strong (according to the criteria) password. As each rule is satisfied, it's crossed out. There's also a Show Password check box that hides/shows the password, just as in most macOS interfaces (see figure 19.2).

406

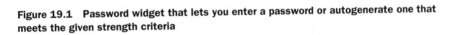

Figure 19.1   Password widget that lets you enter a password or autogenerate one that meets the given strength criteria

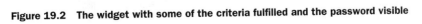

Figure 19.2   The widget with some of the criteria fulfilled and the password visible

The parent component is called `Password`, and the child components are listed here:

- `PasswordInput`—Input field for the password
- `PasswordVisibility`—Check box to toggle the password's visibility
- `PasswordInfo`—List of criteria that must be met before you can save the password
- `PasswordGenerate`—Button to generate a password that satisfies all the criteria

The widget is built using a single parent component. You provide the password-strength rules to the component as properties, so the component is highly customizable. I'll bet you can use it in your own apps with some customization!

NOTE   To follow along with this project, you'll need to install Node.js and npm to compile JSX. This example also uses Webpack as a build tool and, of course, Jest as the test engine. Appendix A covers how to install everything.

NOTE   Because parts of this project were first introduced in chapter 16, the source code is in the ch16 folder; you can find it at www.manning .com/books/react-quickly and https://github.com/azat-co/react-quickly/ tree/master/ch16. You can also find some demos at http://reactquickly .co/demos.

Let's start by setting up the project.

19.1 *Project structure and Webpack configuration*

This is what the complete folder structure looks like. Begin by creating a new project folder named password:

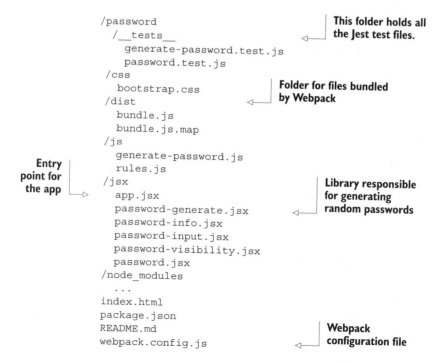

The __tests__ folder is for Jest tests. The css folder contains my Twitter Bootstrap theme, called Flatly (https://bootswatch.com/flatly). The js and jsx folders have libraries and components, respectively. And js/generate-password.js is the library responsible for generating random passwords.

The dist folder contains the compiled JSX files with source maps. That's where Webpack will put the concatenated file and its source map. Here, *dist* is short for *distribution*; it's a commonly used name, along with js or build. I used it here to introduce some variety and show you how to customize Webpack configs.

Don't forget that to avoid having to install each dependency with the exact version manually, you can copy package.json from the following listing to the password folder and then run npm install in it (ch16/password/package.json).

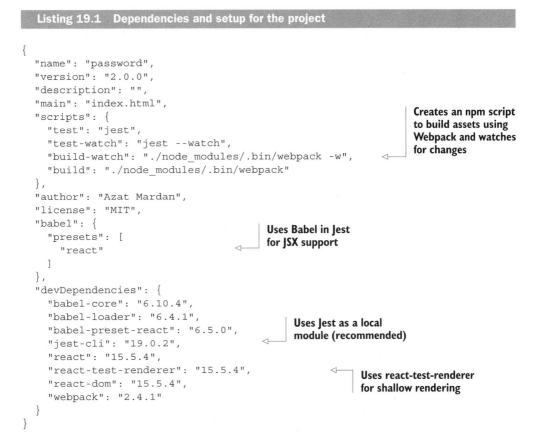

Listing 19.1 Dependencies and setup for the project

```
{
  "name": "password",
  "version": "2.0.0",
  "description": "",
  "main": "index.html",
  "scripts": {
    "test": "jest",
    "test-watch": "jest --watch",
    "build-watch": "./node_modules/.bin/webpack -w",      <--  Creates an npm script to build assets using Webpack and watches for changes
    "build": "./node_modules/.bin/webpack"
  },
  "author": "Azat Mardan",
  "license": "MIT",
  "babel": {
    "presets": [
      "react"                                              <--  Uses Babel in Jest for JSX support
    ]
  },
  "devDependencies": {
    "babel-core": "6.10.4",
    "babel-loader": "6.4.1",
    "babel-preset-react": "6.5.0",
    "jest-cli": "19.0.2",                                  <--  Uses Jest as a local module (recommended)
    "react": "15.5.4",
    "react-test-renderer": "15.5.4",                       <--  Uses react-test-renderer for shallow rendering
    "react-dom": "15.5.4",
    "webpack": "2.4.1"
  }
}
```

The interesting thing here is the scripts section, which you'll use for testing, compilation, and bundling:

```
"scripts": {
  "test": "jest",
  "test-watch": "jest --watch",
```

```
    "build-watch": "./node_modules/.bin/webpack -w",
    "build": "./node_modules/.bin/webpack"
},
```

Recall that in the Nile store in chapter 18, you used `transform-react-jsx`:

```
"babel": {
  "plugins": [
    "transform-react-jsx"
  ],
```

But in this project, you use the React preset. It's just another way to accomplish the same thing. You can use a preset or a plug-in. Presets are a more modern approach and are used in more docs and projects.

The test script (npm `test`) is for running Jest tests manually. Conversely, the `test-watch` script keeps Jest running in the background. `test-watch` is launched with npm run `test-watch` because only `test` and `start` don't require run. You run `test-watch` once, and Jest (in watch mode) will notice any source code changes and rerun the tests. Here's an example of the output:

```
PASS  __tests__/password.test.js
 PASS  __tests__/generate-password.test.js

Test Suites: 2 passed, 2 total
Tests:       3 passed, 3 total
Snapshots:   0 total
Time:        1.502s
Ran all test suites.

Watch Usage
 › Press o to only run tests related to changed files.
 › Press p to filter by a filename regex pattern.
 › Press t to filter by a test name regex pattern.
 › Press q to quit watch mode.
 › Press Enter to trigger a test run.
```

So far, you've defined the project dependencies. Next, you need to set up the Webpack build process so you can transform JSX to JS. To do this, create the webpack .config.js file in the root directory with the following code (ch16/password/webpack.config.js).

Listing 19.2   Webpack configuration

```
module.exports = {
  entry: './jsx/app.jsx',          ← Sets an entry point for the project
                                      (there can be multiple points)
  output: {
    path: __dirname + '/dist/',
    filename: 'bundle.js'
  },
  devtool: '#sourcemap',           ← Sets up the source maps to see the
                                      correct source line numbers in DevTools
```

```
    stats: {
     colors: true,
     reasons: true
    },
    module: {
      loaders: [
        {
          test: /\.jsx?$/,
          exclude: /(node_modules)/,      Applies Babel, which will use
          loader: 'babel-loader'    ◁──┘  Babel configs from package.json
        }
      ]
    }
}
```

Now you can define configs to build your project in webpack.config.js. The entry point is the app.js JSX file in the jsx folder, and the destination is the dist folder. Also, configs will set the source maps and the Babel loader (to convert JSX into JS).

The build will be called with ./node_modules/.bin/webpack, or with ./node_modules/.bin/webpack -w if you want the tool to monitor file changes. Yes, with -w (watch), you can make Webpack rebuild on every file change—that is, each time you click Save in Notepad (I don't like IDEs). Watch is great for active development!

You can create more than one webpack.config.js by specifying a different filename with --config:

```
$ ./node_modules/.bin/webpack --config production.config.js
```

Each config file can use a new script in package.json for convenience.

The bottom line is that Webpack is easy and fun to work with because it supports CommonJS/Node modules by default. There's no need for Browserify or any other module loaders. With Webpack, it's like writing a Node program for browser JavaScript!

19.2 The host HTML file

Next, create the index.html file. It has a container with ID content and includes dist/bundle.js (ch16/password/index.html).

Listing 19.3 Host HTML file

```
<!DOCTYPE html>
<html>

  <head>
    <link href="css/bootstrap.css" rel="stylesheet" type="text/css"/>
  </head>

  <body class="container">
    <h1>Password Input Widget</h1>
    <div id="password"></div>
```

```
        <script src="dist/bundle.js" ></script>
    </body>
```
◁─┐ **Loads the bundled**
   │ **application**

```
</html>
```

Now you should be set up and ready to start developing. It's a good idea to test in increments during development so the area in which you look for bugs is as small as possible. So, perform a quick test to see if the setup is working correctly, just as you did in chapter 18. Do something along these lines:

1 Install all the dependencies with `npm install`. Do this just once.
2 Put `console.log('Painless JavaScript password!')` into jsx/app.jsx.
3 Run the app with `npm start`. You can leave it running, because `-w` will rebuild the file when there are changes.
4 Start a local web server from the project root.
5 Open the browser at http://localhost:8080.
6 Open the browser console (such as Chrome DevTools). You should see the "Painless JavaScript password!" message.

19.3 *Implementing a strong password module*

The strong-password module is a generate-password.js file sitting in password/js. The test for the file will be in password/__tests__/generate-password.test.js. This module will return random passwords when invoked. The passwords will contain a good mix of different types of characters:

- *Special characters*—!@\#$%^&*()_+{}:"<>?\[]\',./`~
- *Lowercase*—abcdefghijklmnopqrstuvwxyz
- *Uppercase*—ABCDEFGHIJKLMNOPQRSTUVWXYZ
- *Numbers*—0123456789

These categories, along with length and randomness, will ensure that the password is secure enough. Using TDD/BDD, let's implement the tests first.

19.3.1 *The tests*

Begin with the tests in generate-password.test.js. Remember that you store them in the __tests__ folder so Jest can find them (ch16/password/__tests__/generate-password.test.js).

Listing 19.4 Tests for the password module

```
const generatePassword = require('../js/generate-password.js')
const pattern = /^[A-Za-z0-9\!\@\#\$\%\^\&\*\(\)\_\+\{\}\:\"\<\>\?\\\|\
➥ [\]\/'\,\.\`\~]{8,16}$/

describe('method generatePassword', ()=>{
    let password, password2
```
◁─┐ **Defines a RegEx pattern**
   │ **for a password that**
   │ **meets all criteria**

```
it('returns a generated password of the set pattern', ()=>{
  password = generatePassword()
  expect(password).toMatch(pattern)
})
```
Tests that the newly generated password matches the pattern

```
it('return a new value different from the previous one', ()=>{
  password2 = generatePassword()
  expect(password2).toMatch(pattern)
  expect(password2).not.toEqual(password)
})

})
```
Tests that invoking the method returns a new password

You start by declaring the password variable and importing generate-password.js. The regular expression checks the content and length of the password. It's not perfect, because you don't check that each password has at least one of those characters, but it'll do for now:

```
let password,
  password2,
  pattern = /^[A-Za-z0-9\!\@\#\$\%\^\&\*\(\)\_\+\{\}\:\"\'\<\>\?\\|
    ⇒ \[\]\/'\,\.\`\~]{8,16}$/
```

Write in the test suite describe the noun method generatePassword. That's what you're going to test: it's the function exported in the generate-password.js module.

Implement the test suite it with the code to unit-test via the BDD-style expect statements, as described in chapter 16. At a minimum, check against a regular-expression pattern for the password:

```
describe('method generatePassword', () => {
  it('returns a generated password of the set pattern', ()=>{
    password = generatePassword()
    expect(password).toMatch(pattern)
  })
  it('returns a new value different from the previous one', ()=>{
    password2 = generatePassword()
    expect(password2).not.toEqual(password)
  })
})
```

What if the password isn't different each time you invoke generatePassword()? What if it's hardcoded in generate-password.js? That would be bad! So, the second test suite expects the second generated password to be different.

19.3.2 The code

You'll implement a strong-password module in js/generate-password.js so you can TDD/BDD it right away—that is, you'll write the test first and only then write the code. Here's a versatile password generator that uses three sets of characters to satisfy the strong-password criteria:

```
const SPECIALS = '!@#$%^&*()_+{}:"<>?\|[]\',./`~'
const LOWERCASE = 'abcdefghijklmnopqrstuvwxyz'
const UPPERCASE = 'ABCDEFGHIJKLMNOPQRSTUVWXYZ'
const NUMBERS = '0123456789'
const ALL = `${SPECIALS}${LOWERCASE}${UPPERCASE}${NUMBERS}`

const getIterable = (length) => Array.from({length},
  (_, index) => index + 1)
```
Adds +1 to avoid 0 as a value, and uses an implicit return

```
const pick = (set, min, max) => {
  let length = min
  if (typeof max !== 'undefined') {
    length += Math.floor(Math.random() * (max - min))
  }
  return getIterable(length).map(() => (
    set.charAt(Math.floor(Math.random() * set.length))
  )).join('')
}
```
Defines the pick function, which returns chars from a set between min and max

Creates an iterable element with empty strings

Shuffles chars to get randomness

```
const shuffle = (set) => {
  let array = set.split('')
  let length = array.length
  let iterable = getIterable(length).reverse()
  let shuffled = iterable.reduce((acc, value, index) => {
    let randomIndex = Math.floor(Math.random() * value)
    [acc[value -1], acc[randomIndex]] = [acc[randomIndex], acc[value - 1]]
    return acc
  }, [...array])
  return shuffled.join('')
}
```
Reverses the iterable to get a value from max to min

Applies the reducer to get the shuffled array

```
module.exports = () => {
  let password = (pick(SPECIALS, 1)
    + pick(LOWERCASE, 1)
    + pick(NUMBERS, 1)
    + pick(UPPERCASE, 1)
    + pick(ALL, 4, 12))
  return shuffle(password)
}
```
Defines the rules to satisfy the widget

The exported function (assigned to `module.exports`) calls the `shuffle()` method, which *randomly* moves characters around in the string. `shuffle()` takes the password generated by `pick()`, which uses sets of characters to make sure the generated password includes at least one of a certain group of characters (numbers, uppercase letters, specials, and so on). The final part of the password consists of more random elements from the union set `ALL`.

You can run the unit test for password/__tests__/generate-password.js with the command `jest __tests__/generate-password.test.js` or `npm test __tests__/generate-password.test.js` executed from the project root (password folder). It should pass with a message similar to the following:

```
jest __tests__/generate-password.test.js

 PASS __tests__/generate-password.test.js
  method generatePassword
    ✓ returns a generated password of the set pattern (4ms)
    ✓ return a new value different from the previous one (2ms)


Test Suites: 1 passed, 1 total
Tests:       2 passed, 2 total
Snapshots:   0 total
Time:        1.14s
Ran all test suites matching "__tests__/generate-password.test.js".
```

19.4 Implementing the Password component

The next logical thing is to work on the main component, Password. According to TDD, you again must start with a test: a UI test, in this case, because you want to test behavior like clicking.

19.4.1 The tests

Create a UI test file called __tests__/password.test.js. We already covered this file in chapter 16, so I'll present the full example here with some comments (ch16/password/ __tests__/password.test.js).

Listing 19.5   Spec for the `Password` component

```
describe('Password', function() {
  it('changes after clicking the Generate button', (done)=>{
    const TestUtils = require('react-addons-test-utils')        ◁─┐ Includes the
    const React = require('react')                                │ libraries
    const ReactDOM = require('react-dom')
    const Password = require('../jsx/password.jsx')

    const PasswordGenerate = require('../jsx/password-generate.jsx')
    const PasswordInfo = require('../jsx/password-info.jsx')
    const PasswordInput = require('../jsx/password-input.jsx')
    const PasswordVisibility = require('../jsx/password-visibility.jsx')

    const fD = ReactDOM.findDOMNode

    let password = TestUtils.renderIntoDocument(<Password       ◁─┐
      upperCase={true}
      lowerCase={true}          Creates a React component thanks to JSX
      special={true}           support from the babel-jest package (part of Jest:
      number={true}               https://github.com/facebook/jest/tree/master/
      over6={true}                                      packages/babel-jest)
      />
    )

    let rules = TestUtils.scryRenderedDOMComponentsWithTag(password,
      'li')                     ◁─┐
    expect(rules.length).toBe(5)    │ Gets the list items (<li>)
```

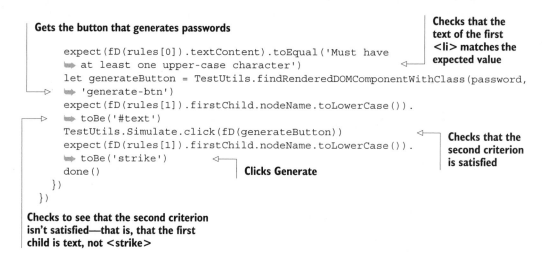

Gets the button that generates passwords

Checks that the text of the first `<li>` matches the expected value

```
    expect(fD(rules[0]).textContent).toEqual('Must have
 ➥ at least one upper-case character')
    let generateButton = TestUtils.findRenderedDOMComponentWithClass(password,
 ➥ 'generate-btn')
    expect(fD(rules[1]).firstChild.nodeName.toLowerCase()).
 ➥ toBe('#text')
    TestUtils.Simulate.click(fD(generateButton))
    expect(fD(rules[1]).firstChild.nodeName.toLowerCase()).
 ➥ toBe('strike')
    done()
  })
})
```

Clicks Generate

Checks that the second criterion is satisfied

Checks to see that the second criterion isn't satisfied—that is, that the first child is text, not `<strike>`

You can extend this test case to check that all the properties and rules pass; this is homework (see the "Homework" section at the end of this chapter for more ideas). It's a good idea to have another suite and provide a different mix of properties, and then test for that as well.

That's it! Your test should fail (npm test or jest) with an error:

```
Error: Cannot find module '../jsx/password.jsx' from 'password.test.js'
```

That's normal for test-driven development because we write tests before apps. The main thing you need to do now is to implement the Password component.

19.4.2 The code

Next, you'll create the Password component with some initial state. The state variables are as follows:

- strength—The object with the strength "meter" (that is, the set of rules, each of which is set to true or false depending on whether the criterion is met)
- password—The current password
- visible—Whether the password input field is visible
- ok—Whether the password meets all the rules and you can allow the user to save it (enables the Save button)

Imagine that a few days after you implement this widget, a developer from another team wants to use your component but with slightly stricter password criteria. The best approach is to *abstract* (a fancy word for *copy and paste*) the code with the password criteria (rules) into a separate file. You'll do this before proceeding with password.jsx.

Create a file called rules.js (ch16/password/js/rules.js). This file will implement password rules that you can use in password.jsx to perform validation and show warning messages. Keeping the rules separate will make it straightforward to change, add, or remove rules in the future.

Listing 19.6   Rules for password strength

```
module.exports =  {
  upperCase: {
    message:  'Must have at least one upper-case character',
    pattern: /([A-Z]+)/
  },
  lowerCase: {
    message: 'Must have at least one lower-case character',
    pattern: /([a-z]+)/
  },
  special:{
    message: 'Must have at least one special character (#$@!&%...)',
    pattern: /([\!\@\#\$\%\^\&\*\(\)\_\+\{\}\:\"\<\>\?\\|\[\]\/'\,\.\`\~]+)/
  },
  number: {
    message: 'Must have at least one number',
    pattern: /([0-9]+)/
  },
  'over6': {
    message: 'Must be more than 6 characters',
    pattern: /(.{6,})/
  }
}
```

Basically, you have a bunch of rules, each of which has the following:

- A key, such as over6
- A message, such as Must be more than 6 characters
- A regular-expression pattern, such as /(.{6,})/

Now, on to password.jsx. You need to do the following:

- Render with the upperCase, lowerCase, special, number, and over6 rules.
- Check that the rules have been rendered (length is 5).
- See that rule 1 isn't satisfied.
- Click the Generate button.
- See that rule 2 is satisfied.

Let's implement the component. You import dependencies and create the component with initial state (ch16/password/jsx/password.jsx).

Listing 19.7   Implementing the Password component

```
const React = require('react')
const ReactDOM = require('react-dom')
const generatePassword = require('../js/generate-password.js')

const rules = require('../js/rules.js')

const PasswordGenerate = require('./password-generate.jsx')
const PasswordInfo = require('./password-info.jsx')
const PasswordInput = require('./password-input.jsx')
```

```
const PasswordVisibility = require('./password-visibility.jsx')

class Password extends React.Component {
  constructor(props) {
    super(props)
    this.state = {strength: {}, password: '', visible: false, ok: false}
    this.generate = this.generate.bind(this)
    this.checkStrength = this.checkStrength.bind(this)
    this.toggleVisibility = this.toggleVisibility.bind(this)
  }
  ...
}
```

Next, you implement a method to check for the password strength:

```
checkStrength(event) {
  let password = event.target.value
  this.setState({password: password})
  let strength = {}
```

The following code block goes through each property (upperCase, over6, and so on) and checks the current password using the regular-expression pattern in rules. If the criterion is met, the property in the strength object is set to true:

```
Object.keys(this.props).forEach((key, index, list)=>{
  if (this.props[key] && rules[key].pattern.test(password)) {
    strength[key] = true
  }
})
```

this.setState() is asynchronous, so you use a callback to provide logic that relies on the updated state. In this case, you check that the number of properties in the strength object (this.state.strength) is equal to the number of rules (props). It's a rudimentary check; checking each property in a loop would be a more robust solution, but this code works for now. You set ok to true if the numbers match (that is, if all the rules for password strength are satisfied):

```
this.setState({strength: strength}, ()=>{
  if (Object.keys(this.state.strength).length ==
    Object.keys(this.props).length) {
    this.setState({ok: true})
  } else {
    this.setState({ok: false})
  }
})
```

The next method hides and shows the password field. This is a useful feature when you're generating a new password, because you may want to save the password (or need help remembering it):

```
toggleVisibility() {
  this.setState({visible: !this.state.visible}, ()=>{
  })
}
```

Next is the `generate()` method, which creates random passwords using the js/generate-password.js module. Setting `visible` to `true` ensures that users can see the newly generated password. Right after the password is generated, you call `checkStrength()` to check its strength. Typically, the conditions will be satisfied, and users will be able to proceed by clicking Save:

```
generate() {
  this.setState({visible: true, password: generatePassword()}, ()=>{
    this.checkStrength({target: {value: this.state.password}})
  )
}
```

In the `render()` function, `Password` processes the rules and renders a few other React components:

- `PasswordInput`—Password input field (`input`)
- `PasswordVisibility`— Password visibility toggle (`input` with type `checkbox`)
- `PasswordInfo`—The list of rules for password strength (`ul`)
- `PasswordGenerate`—Password-generation button (`button`)

You begin by processing the rules and determining which of them are satisfied (`isCompleted`). Instead of passing the context in `_this` or using the `bind(this)` pattern, you use fat-arrow functions `()=>{}`. There's no big difference; choose one approach or the other, and use it.

Object.keys flattens your hash table into an array by giving you an array of keys of that object. You can iterate over that array of keys with `map()` and construct a new array with objects that have `key`, `rule`, and `isCompleted`:

```
render() {
  var processedRules = Object.keys(this.props).map((key)=>{
    if (this.props[key]) {
      return {
        key: key,
        rule: rules[key],
        isCompleted: this.state.strength[key] || false
      }
    }
  })
  // return ...
```

IMPLEMENTING PASSWORD'S RENDER() FUNCTION
Once your array of processed rules is ready, you can begin rendering the components. Remember that `for` is a special word in JavaScript. That's why you need to use `class-Name`, not `class` (ch16/password/jsx/password.jsx).

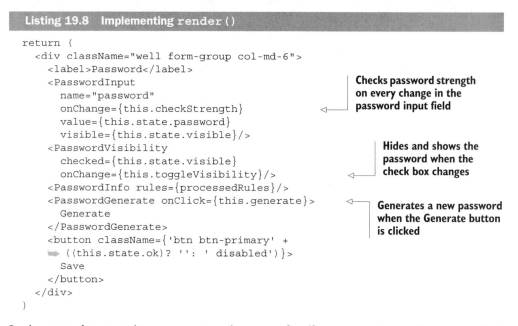

```
return (
  <div className="well form-group col-md-6">
    <label>Password</label>
    <PasswordInput
      name="password"
      onChange={this.checkStrength}
      value={this.state.password}
      visible={this.state.visible}/>
    <PasswordVisibility
      checked={this.state.visible}
      onChange={this.toggleVisibility}/>
    <PasswordInfo rules={processedRules}/>
    <PasswordGenerate onClick={this.generate}>
      Generate
    </PasswordGenerate>
    <button className={'btn btn-primary' +
      ((this.state.ok)? '': ' disabled')}>
      Save
    </button>
  </div>
)
```

Listing 19.8 Implementing render()

- Checks password strength on every change in the password input field
- Hides and shows the password when the check box changes
- Generates a new password when the Generate button is clicked

Let's cover the most important parts in more detail. PasswordInput is a controlled component (for a detailed comparison between controlled and uncontrolled components, see chapter 5). You listen on every change with the this.checkStrength callback, which uses e.target.value, so there's no need for refs:

```
<PasswordInput name="password" onChange={this.checkStrength}
  value={this.state.password}  visible={this.state.visible}/>
```

Similar to PasswordInput, PasswordVisibility is a controlled component, and the event handler for change is this.toggleVisibility:

```
<PasswordVisibility checked={this.state.visible}
  onChange={this.toggleVisibility}/>
```

You pass the processedRules object to the list of rules, and the PasswordGenerate button triggers this.generate:

```
<PasswordInfo rules={processedRules}/>
<PasswordGenerate onClick={this.generate}>Generate</PasswordGenerate>
```

The Save button is disabled and enabled based on the this.state.ok value. Don't forget the space before disabled, or you'll get the btn-primarydisabled class instead of two classes, btn-primary and disabled:

```
<button className={'btn btn-primary' +
      ((this.state.ok)? '': ' disabled')}>Save</button>
    </div>
  )
}})
```

The other components, in listings 19.9 (ch16/password/jsx/password-generate.jsx), 19.10 (ch16/password/jsx/password-input.jsx), and 19.11 (ch16/password/jsx/password-visibility.jsx), are *dumb components*. They just render classes and pass properties.

Listing 19.9 `PasswordGenerate` component

```
const React = require('react')
class PasswordGenerate extends React.Component{
  render() {
    return (
      <button {...this.props} className="btn generate-btn">
        {this.props.children}</button>
    )
  }
}
module.exports = PasswordGenerate
```

Listing 19.10 `PasswordInput` component

```
const React = require('react')
class PasswordInput extends React.Component {
  render() {
    return (
      <input className="form-control"
        type={this.props.visible ? 'text' : 'password'}
        name={this.props.name}
        value={this.props.value}
        onChange={this.props.onChange}/>
    )
  }
}

module.exports = PasswordInput
```

Listing 19.11 `PasswordVisibility` component

```
const React = require('react')
class PasswordVisibility extends React.Component {
  render() {
    return (
      <label className="form-control">
        <input className=""
          type="checkbox"
          checked={this.props.checked}              ◁— Controls the component with a property value
          onChange={this.props.onChange}/> Show password   ◁— Triggers even on the parent via the property
      </label>
    )
  }
}

module.exports = PasswordVisibility
```

Let's look at `PasswordInfo` for a moment (ch16/password/jsx/password-info.jsx). It takes the processed `rules` array and iterates over that property. If `isCompleted` is true, you add `<strike>` to the `<li>`. `<strike>` is an HTML tag that applies a strikethrough line to text. This is what you check for in the password.test.js test, too.

Listing 19.12 `PasswordInfo` **component**

```
const React = require('react')
class PasswordInfo extends React.Component {
  render() {
    return (
      <div>
        <h4>Password Strength</h4>
        <ul>
          {this.props.rules.map(function(processedRule, index, list) {
            if (processedRule.isCompleted)
              return <li key={processedRule.key}>
                <strike>{processedRule.rule.message}</strike>
              </li>
            else
              return <li key={processedRule.key}>
              ➥ {processedRule.rule.message}</li>
          })}
        </ul>
      </div>
    )
  }
}

module.exports = PasswordInfo
```

> **Checks for rule satisfaction via a property**

> **Uses the text provided in rules.js via a property**

You're finished with the password.jsx file! Now you have everything ready to rerun the test. Don't forget to recompile with `npm run build` or `npm run build-watch`. If you followed everything to a T, you should see something like this after you run `npm test`:

```
Using Jest CLI v0.5.10
 PASS  __tests__/generate-password.test.js (0.03s)
 PASS  __tests__/password.test.js (1.367s)
2 tests passed (2 total)
Run time: 2.687s
```

Good job—you can pat yourself on the back!

19.5 *Putting it into action*

To see the widget in action, you need to do one more tiny step: create jsx/app.jsx, which is an example file for the component. Here's how to render the `Password` widget in your app:

```
const React = require('react')
const ReactDOM = require('react-dom')
```

```
const Password = require('./password.jsx')

ReactDOM.render(<Password
    upperCase={true}
    lowerCase={true}
    special={true}
    number={true}
    over6={true}/>,
  document.getElementById('password'))
```

You can run the files like any other front-end app. I prefer node-static (https://github.com/cloudhead/node-static), or you can see an online demo at http://reactquickly.co/demos. Notice how the Save button becomes active when all the rules are satisfied, as shown in figure 19.3.

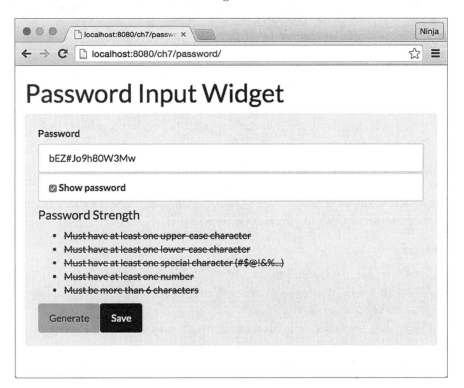

Figure 19.3 The Save button is enabled when all the strength criteria are met.

CI and CD

The best software engineering practice doesn't stop at writing and running tests locally. The tests are much more valuable when combined with the deployment process and automated. These processes, called *continuous integration* (CI) and *continuous deployment* (CD), are great for speeding up and automating software delivery.

(continued)

I highly recommend setting up CI/CD for anything more than a prototype. There are plenty of good software-as-a-service (SaaS) and self-hosted solutions out there. With the tests in this project, setting up a CI/CD environment won't take long. For example, with AWS, Travis CI, or CircleCI, all you need to do is configure your project in terms of the environment it should run in and then provide a test command such as `npm test`. You can even integrate those SaaS CIs with GitHub so that you and your team can see CI messages (pass, fail, how many failures, and where) on GitHub pull requests.

Amazon Web Services offers its own managed services: CodeDeploy, CodePipeline, and CodeBuild. For more information on these AWS services, refer to Node University: https://node.university/p/aws-intermediate. If you prefer a self-hosted solution instead of a managed solution, take a look at Jenkins (https://jenkins.io) and Drone (https://github.com/drone/drone).

19.6   Homework

For bonus points, try the following:

- Test any scenario you can think of: for example, enter only a lowercase character (such as *r*), and see that the lowercase criterion has been satisfied but not the other criteria.
- Sign up for a free account with a cloud SaaS CI provider (AWS, Travis CI, CircleCI, and so on), and set up the project to run in the cloud CI environment.

Submit your code in *a new folder under ch16* as a pull request to this book's GitHub repository: https://github.com/azat-co/react-quickly.

19.7   Summary

- Jest test files are stored in the __tests__ folder by convention.
- You can use regular or shallow rendering with either `react-dom/test-utils` or `react-test-renderer/shallow`.
- Jest (v19) tests can be written using JSX because Jest will convert JSX automatically.
- To enable automatic test reruns (recommended for development), use `jest --watch`.

Watch this chapter's introduction video by scanning this QR code with your phone or going to http://reactquickly.co/videos/ch20.

Project: Implementing autocomplete with Jest, Express, and MongoDB

This chapter covers

- Project structure and Webpack configuration
- Implementing the web server
- Adding the browser script
- Creating the server template
- Implementing the autocomplete component

The goal of this project is first of all to combine many of the techniques you've learned throughout this book, such as component composition, states, form elements, and testing, as well as how to fetch data from an API server and store and how to implement a simple Express server and Universal React rendering. You've already done most of these things in the book, but repetition is the mother of learning—especially intermittent repetition!

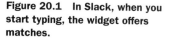

Figure 20.1   In Slack, when you start typing, the widget offers matches.

In this chapter, you'll build a well-rounded component and supply it with a back end. This little project is close to the sort of real-life projects you'll most likely perform on the job.

In a nutshell, this project will guide you through building an autocomplete component that's visually and functionally similar to the one in Slack (a popular messaging app) and Google (a popular search engine), as shown in figure 20.1. For simplicity's sake, the widget will work with the names of rooms in a chat application.

The autocomplete widget, shown in figure 20.2, has the following:

1 *Input field*—Always appears but is empty initially
2 *List of options, filtered according to the entered characters*—Appears when there's at least one match
3 *Add button*—Appears when there are no matches

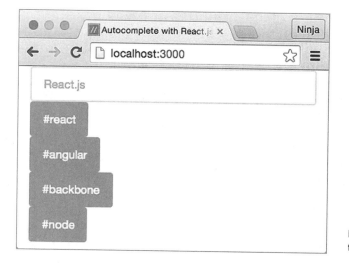

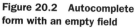

Figure 20.2   Autocomplete form with an empty field

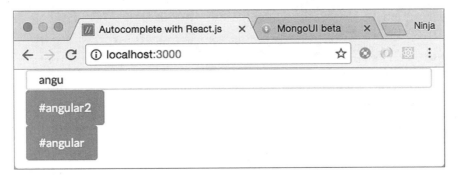

Figure 20.3 Typing angu filters the matches and shows only *angular* and *angular2*.

Room names are filtered using the entered characters as the first characters of each option. A simple comparison autocompletes the name of a room (see figure 20.3). For example, if you have rooms named *angular, angular2*, and *react*, and you type angu, then only *angular* and *angular2* will be shown as a match, not the *react* option.

What if there are no matches? There's a way to add a new option using the Add button. For convenience, the Add button is shown only when there are no matches (see figure 20.4). This button lets you *persist* (save permanently in the database) the new input.

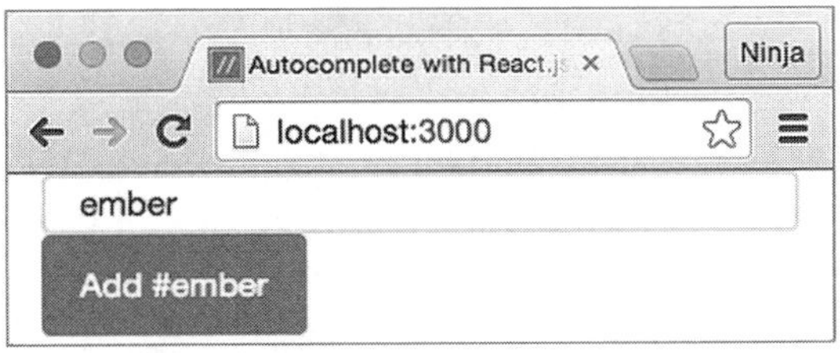

The new option is saved to the database via an XHR call to the REST API. You can use this new room name in future matches (see figure 20.5), just like the initial list of room names.

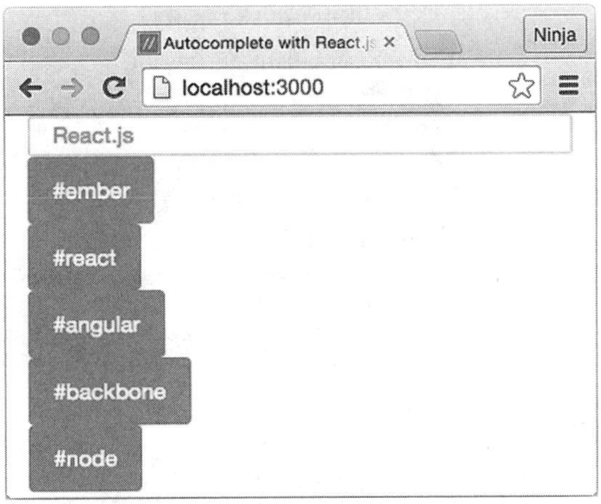

To implement this autocomplete widget, you need to do the following:

- Install dependencies.
- Set up the build process with Webpack.
- Write tests using Jest.
- Implement an Express REST API server that connects to MongoDB and also acts as a static server for the widget example.
- Implement an Autocomplete React component.
- Implement the example using Autocomplete and Handlebars.

![Figure 20.4 screenshot showing browser with "ember" typed and an "Add #ember" button]

Figure 20.4 The Add button is shown only when there are no matches.

![Figure 20.5 screenshot showing browser with "React.js" typed and a list: #ember, #react, #angular, #backbone, #node]

Figure 20.5 The room name has been saved and now appears in the list.

You'll render the React components on the server, test them with Jest, and make AJAX/XHR requests with `axios`.

> **NOTE**   The source code for the examples in this chapter is at www.manning .com/books/react-quickly and https://github.com/azat-co/react-quickly/ tree/master/ch20. You can also find some demos at http:// reactquickly.co/demos.

Let's start by setting up the project.

20.1   *Project structure and Webpack configuration*

To give you an overview of the tech stack, in this project you'll use the following technologies and libraries:

- Node.js and npm for compiling JSX and downloading dependencies such as React
- Webpack as a build tool
- Jest as the test engine
- Express to act as a web server, and MongoDB accessed using the native MongoDB Node.js driver to hold the autocomplete options
- Handlebars for the layout

Why Handlebars and not React for everything?

I prefer to use Handlebars for the layout for several reasons. First, React makes it painstakingly difficult to output unescaped HTML; it uses a weird syntax that involves the word `dangerously`. But this is what you need to do for Universal React and server-side rendering. Yes, the unescaped HTML can expose an app to cross-site scripting attacks,[1] but you're rendering on the server, so you control the HTML string.

The second reason is that Handlebars more naturally renders things like `<!DOCTYPE html>`. React can't do it as naturally because React is meant more for individual elements than entire pages.

Third, React is for managing state and automatically maintaining the view in accordance with the state. If all you're doing is rendering a static HTML string from a React component, why bother with React? It's overkill. Handlebars is similar to HTML, so it's easy to copy and paste existing HTML code without having to think twice about JSX and React gotchas that may bite you in the tail when you're converting HTML to React.

Finally, my personal experience explaining code functionality to other developers and to students in my courses and workshops has shown that some people have a harder time understanding the structure when React components are used for layout on the server and other React components are used for views on both the client and server.

---

[1]   A cross-site scripting (XSS) attack is characterized by attackers injecting malicious code into legitimate websites that users trust but that contain XSS vulnerabilities. For example, an attacker can post a message with some bad code that includes `<script>` elements on a vulnerable forum that isn't sanitizing and/or escaping the post text. All visitors to the forum will end up executing the malicious code. For more on XSS, see Jakob Kallin and Irene Lobo Valbuena, "Excess XSS: A Comprehensive Tutorial on Cross-Site Scripting," https://excess-xss.com.

Appendix A covers the installation of these tools, so I won't bore you by duplicating that information. Go ahead and create a new project folder named autocomplete. This is what the folder structure will look like:

```
/autocomplete
  /__tests__
      autocomplete.test.js
  /node_modules
  /public
    /css
       bootstrap.css
    /js
       app.js
       app.js.map
  /src
    app.jsx
    autocomplete.jsx
  /views
    index.handlebars
  index.js
  package.json
  rooms.json
  webpack.config.js
```

Folder for front-end/client static files (alternative names: static, dist, client, build, and so on)

Compiled bundle file (alternative names: bundle.js and script.js)

Source code in JSX (alternative names: jsx, components, and source)

An entry point: that is, the main front-end script file, which uses the Autocomplete component

Autocomplete component

Handlebars template to render HTML layout on the server side

Seed data for MongoDB

The __tests__ folder is for Jest tests. As should now be familiar to you, the node_modules folder is for Node.js dependencies (from npm's package.json). The public, public/css, and public/js folders contain the static files for the application.

On naming

Naming is paramount to good software engineering because a good name provides a crucial piece of information. It can tell you a lot about the script, file, module, or component without you having to read the source code, tests, or documentation (which may not exist!).

Just as you've gotten familiar with putting JSX files into the jsx folder and using build as a destination folder for compiled files, I've started to use other names. That's because you'll encounter many different conventions. Each project will probably have a different structure; the structure may vary a lot or a little. As a developer, it's your job to be comfortable with configuring tools such as Webpack and libraries such as Express to work with any names. For that reason, and to add variety, in this chapter I use public instead of build (plus public is a convention for static files served by Express), src instead of jsx (you may have other source files, not just JSX, right?), and so on.

The public/js/app.js file will be bundled by Webpack from the dependencies and the JSX source code src/app.jsx. The source code for the Autocomplete component is in the src/autocomplete.jsx file.

The views folder is for Handlebars templates. If you feel confident about your React skills, you don't have to use a template engine; you can use React as the Node.js template engine!

In the root of the project, you'll find these files:

- *webpack.config.js*—Enables build tasks
- *package.json*—Contains project metadata
- *rooms.json*—Contains MongoDB seed data
- *index.js*—With the Express.js server and its routes for the API server (GET and POST /rooms)

Don't forget that to avoid installing each dependency with the exact version manually, you can copy the package.json file from the following listing (ch20/autocomplete/package.json) to the root folder, and run npm install.

Listing 20.1 Dependencies and setup for the project

```
{
  "name": "autocomplete",
  "version": "1.0.0",
  "description": "React.js autocomplete component with Express.js, and
  ➥ MongoDB example.",
  "main": "index.js",
  "scripts": {
    "test": "jest",
    "start": "npm run build && ./node_modules/.bin/node-dev index.js",
    "build": "./node_modules/.bin/webpack",
    "seed": "mongoimport rooms.json --jsonArray --collection=rooms
    ➥ --db=autocomplete"
  },
  "keywords": [
    "react.js",
    "express.js",
    "mongodb"
  ],
  "author": "Azat Mardan",
  "license": "MIT",
  "babel": {
    "presets": [
      "react"
    ]
  },
  "dependencies": {
    "babel-register": "6.11.6",        Lets you import and transpile
    "body-parser": "1.13.2",           JSX on the server side
    "compression": "1.5.1",
    "errorhandler": "1.4.1",           Express server-side
    "express": "4.13.1",               web framework
    "express-handlebars": "2.0.1",
    "express-validator": "2.13.0",     Library to connect to
    "mongodb": "2.0.36",               the MongoDB database
```

Express plug-in (middleware) for logging HTTP requests

```
      "morgan": "1.6.1"
    },
    "devDependencies": {
      "axios": "0.13.1",
      "babel-core": "6.10.4",
      "babel-loader": "6.2.4",
      "babel-preset-react": "6.5.0",
      "jest-cli": "13.2.3",
      "node-dev": "3.1.3",
      "react": "15.5.4",
      "react-dom": "15.5.4",
      "webpack": "1.13.1"
    }
  }
```

Of course, using the same versions as in this book is important if you want to have a working app in the end. Also, don't forget to install the dependencies from package .json using npm i.

The scripts section is interesting:

```
"scripts": {
    "test": "jest",
    "start": "./node_modules/.bin/node-dev index.js",
    "build": "./node_modules/.bin/webpack",
    "seed": "mongoimport rooms.json --jsonArray --collection=rooms
    ➥ --db=autocomplete"
},
```

test is for running Jest tests, and start is for building and launching your server. You also add seed data for the room names, which you can run with $ npm run seed. The database name is autocomplete, and the collection name is rooms. This is the content of the rooms.json file:

```
[ {"name": "react"},
  {"name": "node"},
  {"name": "angular"},
  {"name": "backbone"}]
```

When you run the seed command, it prints something like this (MongoDB must be running as a separate process):

```
> autocomplete@1.0.0 seed /Users/azat/Documents/Code/
➥ react-quickly/ch20/autocomplete
> mongoimport rooms.json --jsonArray --collection=rooms --db=autocomplete

2027-07-10T07:06:28.441-0700    connected to: localhost
2027-07-10T07:06:28.443-0700    imported 4 documents
```

You've defined the project dependencies, and now you need to set up your Web-pack build process so you can use ES6 and transform JSX. To do this, create the webpack.config.js file in the root directory with the following code (ch20/autocomplete/webpack.config.js).

Listing 20.2   Webpack configuration

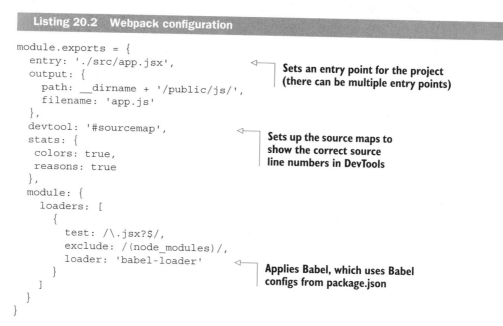

```
module.exports = {
  entry: './src/app.jsx',                      Sets an entry point for the project
  output: {                                    (there can be multiple entry points)
    path: __dirname + '/public/js/',
    filename: 'app.js'
  },
  devtool: '#sourcemap',
  stats: {                                     Sets up the source maps to
   colors: true,                               show the correct source
   reasons: true                               line numbers in DevTools
  },
  module: {
    loaders: [
      {
        test: /\.jsx?$/,
        exclude: /(node_modules)/,
        loader: 'babel-loader'                 Applies Babel, which uses Babel
      }                                        configs from package.json
    ]
  }
}
```

There's no difference between this Webpack config file and those in the other projects you've built so far. It sets up Babel for transpiling JSX files and identifying where the bundled JavaScript will be saved.

20.2   *Implementing the web server*

In this project, rather than a host HTML file, you need to write a simple web server to receive requests based on what the reader has typed so far and respond with a list of suggestions. It will also render the control on the server side and send the respective HTML to the client. As noted earlier, the example uses Express as the web server. The index.js file defines the web server and has three sections:

- Importing libraries and components
- Defining the REST API for receiving requests
- Rendering the control on the server side

We'll look at each section in turn. First is the most straightforward bit: the imports. The following listing shows the components and libraries the server needs (ch20/autocomplete/index.js).

Listing 20.3   Components and libraries for the web server

```
                    const express = require('express'),      Defines and imports using a comma-style
Instantiates          mongodb = require('mongodb'),          (multiline) declaration (analogous to
the Express           app = express(),                       having const on each line)
app
```

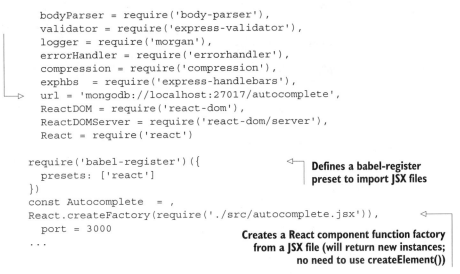

```
                bodyParser  = require('body-parser'),
                validator   = require('express-validator'),
                logger      = require('morgan'),
                errorHandler = require('errorhandler'),
                compression = require('compression'),
                exphbs   = require('express-handlebars'),
                url = 'mongodb://localhost:27017/autocomplete',
                ReactDOM = require('react-dom'),
                ReactDOMServer = require('react-dom/server'),
                React = require('react')

          require('babel-register')({
            presets: ['react']
          })
          const Autocomplete  = ,
          React.createFactory(require('./src/autocomplete.jsx')),
            port = 3000
          ...
```

Sets the MongoDB connection string to the local database

Defines a babel-register preset to import JSX files

Creates a React component function factory from a JSX file (will return new instances; no need to use createElement())

The next section continues with index.js and discusses connecting to the database and middleware.

20.2.1 Defining the RESTful APIs

The index.js file has GET and POST routes for /rooms. They provide RESTful API endpoints for your front-end app to supply the data. The data in turn will come from a MongoDB database, which you can see with an npm script (npm run seed), assuming that you have it in package.json and that you have the rooms.json file. But before fetching data from the database, you need to connect to it and define the Express routes (ch20/autocomplete/index.js).

Listing 20.4   RESTful API routes

```
mongodb.MongoClient.connect(url, function(err, db) {
  if (err) {
    console.error(err)
    process.exit(1)
  }
  app.use(compression())
  app.use(logger('dev'))
  app.use(errorHandler())
  app.use(bodyParser.urlencoded({extended: true}))
  app.use(bodyParser.json())
  app.use(validator())
  app.use(express.static('public'))
  app.engine('handlebars', exphbs())
  app.set('view engine', 'handlebars')

  app.use(function(req, res, next){
    req.rooms = db.collection('rooms')
    return next()
```

Connects to MongoDB

Terminates the current process with an error code

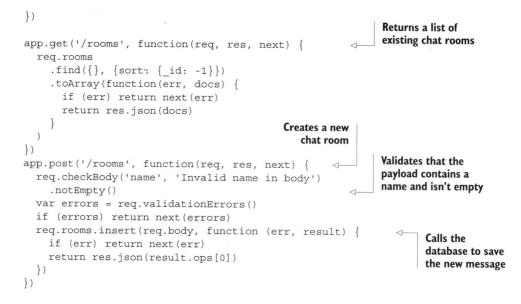

```
})
app.get('/rooms', function(req, res, next) {          ←  Returns a list of
  req.rooms                                                existing chat rooms
    .find({}, {sort: {_id: -1}})
    .toArray(function(err, docs) {
      if (err) return next(err)
      return res.json(docs)
    }
  )
})
                                          Creates a new
                                            chat room
app.post('/rooms', function(req, res, next) {         ←  Validates that the
  req.checkBody('name', 'Invalid name in body')          payload contains a
    .notEmpty()                                    ←      name and isn't empty
  var errors = req.validationErrors()
  if (errors) return next(errors)
  req.rooms.insert(req.body, function (err, result) {  ←  Calls the
    if (err) return next(err)                             database to save
    return res.json(result.ops[0])                        the new message
  })
})
})
```

If you need to brush up on the Express.js API, there's a convenient cheatsheet in appendix C.

20.2.2 Rendering React on the server

Finally, index.js contains the / route, where you render React on the server by hydrating components with the room objects (ch20/autocomplete/index.js).

Listing 20.5 Server-side React

```
app.get('/', function(req, res, next){                    Creates the Autocomplete
  var url = 'http://localhost:3000/rooms'                         React element
  req.rooms.find({}, {sort: {_id: -1}}).toArray(function(err, rooms){
    if (err) return next(err)
    res.render('index', {
      autocomplete: ReactDOMServer.renderToString(Autocomplete({  ←
        options: rooms,
        url: url
      })),                                          Passes the URL of the API
      data: `<script type="text/javascript">        to fetch and create names
        window.__autocomplete_data = {
          rooms: ${JSON.stringify(rooms, null, 2)},        ←
          url: "${url}"
        }                                    Uses stringify parameters
      </script>`                               to prettify the output
    })
  })
})
```

- **Passes the names of rooms as the options property** → `options: rooms,`
- **Passes data from the server to the browser code to ensure that Universal React works properly** → `data:` script block

There are two properties for the Autocomplete component: options and url. options contains the names of the chat rooms, and url is the URL of the API server (http://localhost:3000/rooms in this case). The `Autocomplete` component will be rendered on the browser as well.

20.3 Adding the browser script

The browser script is an example of how someone might use the autocomplete widget; it will be run only on the browser. The file is very short. You just create an element with `options` and `url` properties (ch20/autocomplete/src/app.jsx).

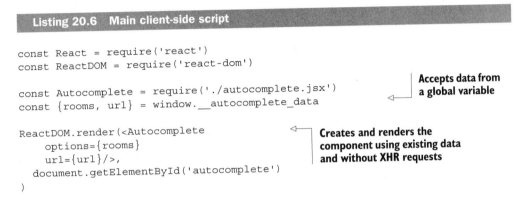

Listing 20.6 Main client-side script

```
const React = require('react')
const ReactDOM = require('react-dom')

const Autocomplete = require('./autocomplete.jsx')     Accepts data from
const {rooms, url} = window.__autocomplete_data        a global variable

ReactDOM.render(<Autocomplete              Creates and renders the
    options={rooms}                        component using existing data
    url={url}/>,                           and without XHR requests
  document.getElementById('autocomplete')
)
```

The global `__autocomplete_data` is provided via the data local (*local* is the term for template data in Express lingo) using the `<script>` tag in the / route.

Listing 20.7 Express app rendering data for browser React

```
res.render('index', {          Uses a script element to "print"
  // ...                       JavaScript in the Handlebars
  data: `<script type="text/javascript">    template index.hbs
         window.__autocomplete_data = {
           rooms: ${JSON.stringify(rooms, null, 2)},   Converts data from an
           url: "${url}"                               object into a string to
         }                                             print it
       </script>`
```

The `<script>` HTML tag is injected into the index.hbs template (the .hbs file extension is assumed by Express, so it's optional). Next, you'll implement this template.

20.4 Creating the server template

In the index.handlebars file, you can see the `props` and `autocomplete` locals being output.

Listing 20.8 Host markup page

```
<!DOCTYPE html>
<html lang="en">
  <head>
```

```
    <meta charset="utf-8" />
    <title>Autocomplete with React.js</title>
    <meta name="description" content="React Quickly: Autocomplete" />
    <meta name="author" content="Azat Mardan" />
    <meta name="viewport" content="width=device-width, initial-scale=1.0" />
    <link type="text/css" rel="stylesheet" href="/css/bootstrap.css" />
  </head>

  <body>
    <div class="container-fluid">
        <div>{{{data}}}</div>                            ◁─── Renders the <script> tag
        <div class="row-fluid">                               containing the list of names
          <div class="span12">                                and the URL for the API
            <div id="content">
              <div class="row-fluid"                                    Renders static HTML
                 id="autocomplete" />{{{autocomplete}}}</div>  ◁─── with Universal
          </div>                                                   React's checksum
        </div>
      </div>
      <script type="text/javascript" src="/js/app.js"></script>   ◁───┐
    </body>                                                            │
</html>                          Applies the client script that will activate
                                browser React and use __autocomplete_data
                                        (see the previous section)
```

The work for running the autocomplete example is done. Obviously, it will be powered by the Autocomplete component. Next, you'll finally start implementing it.

20.5   *Implementing the Autocomplete component*

The Autocomplete component is self-sufficient, meaning it isn't just a view component but can also fetch from and save to the REST API. It has two properties: options and url. In accordance with TDD, let's start coding the Autocomplete component with tests.

20.5.1   *The tests for Autocomplete*

According to the principles of TDD/BDD, you should begin with tests. The __tests__/autocomplete.test.js file lists room names and then renders the component into autocomplete:

```
                            Hardcodes rooms data
                            for the room names
const rooms = [              ◁───
    { "_id" : "5622eb1f105807ceb6ad868b", "name" : "node" },
    { "_id" : "5622eb1f105807ceb6ad868c", "name" : "react" },
    { "_id" : "5622eb1f105807ceb6ad868d", "name" : "backbone" },
    { "_id" : "5622eb1f105807ceb6ad868e", "name" : "angular" }
  ]
const TestUtils = require('react-addons-test-utils'),
  React = require('react'),
  ReactDOM = require('react-dom'),                          Saves the fD object for
  Autocomplete = require('../src/autocomplete.jsx'),        convenience (less typing
  fD = ReactDOM.findDOMNode              ◁───               means fewer errors)
```

```
const autocomplete = TestUtils.renderIntoDocument(
  React.createElement(Autocomplete, {
    options: rooms,
    url: 'test'
  })
)
const optionName = TestUtils.findRenderedDOMComponentWithClass(autocomplete,
  'option-name')
  ...
```

Uses TestUtils from react-addons-test-utils to render the Autocomplete component

Gets the input field by the class option-name

You get the input field, which has an `option-name` class. These room options will match the input-field value.

Now you can write the actual tests. You can get all the `option-name` elements from the widget and compare them against the number 4, which is the number of rooms in the rooms array:

```
describe('Autocomplete', () => {
  it('have four initial options', () => {
    var options = TestUtils.scryRenderedDOMComponentsWithClass(
      autocomplete,
      'option-list-item'
    )
    expect(options.length).toBe(4)
  })
```

The next test changes the input-field value and then checks for that value and the number of the offered autocomplete option. There should be only one match, which is react:

```
it('change options based on the input', () => {
    expect(fD(optionName).value).toBe('')
    fD(optionName).value = 'r'
    TestUtils.Simulate.change(fD(optionName))
    expect(fD(optionName).value).toBe('r')
    options = TestUtils.scryRenderedDOMComponentsWithClass(autocomplete,
      'option-list-item')
    expect(options.length).toBe(1)
    expect(fD(options[0]).textContent).toBe('#react')
  })
```

The last test changes the room name field to ember. There should be no matches, only the Add button:

```
it('offer to save option when there are no matches', () => {
    fD(optionName).value = 'ember'
    TestUtils.Simulate.change(fD(optionName))
    options = TestUtils.scryRenderedDOMComponentsWithClass(
      autocomplete,
      'option-list-item'
    )
```

```
    expect(options.length).toBe(0)
    var optionAdd = TestUtils.findRenderedDOMComponentWithClass(
      autocomplete,
      'option-add'
    )
    expect(fD(optionAdd).textContent).toBe('Add #ember')
  })
})
```

20.5.2 *The code for the Autocomplete component*

Finally, it's time to write the Autocomplete component (ch20/autocomplete/
src/autocomplete.jsx). It includes the input field, the list of matching options, and
the Add button to add a new option when there are no matches. The component performs two AJAX/XHR calls: to retrieve a list of options and to create a new option.
There are two methods:

- filter()—Happens on every new input in the <input> field. Takes the current
  input and the list of options, and sets the state to a new list that contains only
  options that match the current input.
- addOption()—Happens on a button click or Enter press for the Add button.
  Takes the value, and sends it to the server.

This is how the Autocomplete component looks at a high level:

```
const React = require('react'),
  ReactDOM = require('react-dom'),
  request = require('axios')

class Autocomplete extends React.Component {
  constructor(props) {
    ...
  }
  componentDidMount() {                    Fetches the list of
    ...                                    options from the server
  }
  filter(event) {                     Filters the list to leave only the
    ...                               options matching the input
  }
  addOption(event) {                  Adds a new option persistently by
    ...                               making an XHR call to the server
  }
  render() {
    return (                                         Captures the option
      <div ...>                                      value by tracking the
        <input ... onChange={this.filter}>           browser event
        </input>
        {this.state.filteredOptions.map(function(option,
      ➥ index, list) {
          ...                                Prints the list of matching
        })}                                  (filtered) options
        ...
        <a ...onClick={this.addOption}>
```

Calls the add
method when
the button (a
link) is clicked →

```
                 Add #{this.state.currentOption}
               </a>
          ...
        </div>
      )
    }
  }

    module.exports = Autocomplete
```

Now let's start from the beginning of the file. Begin by importing the libraries in the CommonJS/Node.js style; thanks to Webpack, this is bundled for the browser's consumption. The `fD` alias is for convenience:

```
const React = require('react'),
  ReactDOM = require('react-dom'),
  request = require('axios')

const fD = ReactDOM.findDOMNode
```

`constructor` sets the state and bindings. You set `options` from properties. `filteredOptions` will initially be the same as all the options, and the current option (input-field value) is empty. As the user types characters, `filteredOptions` will become narrower and narrower, to match the entered letters.

In `componentDidMount()`, you perform the GET request using the `axios` (request variable) library. It's similar to jQuery's `$.get()`, but with promises:

```
class Autocomplete extends React.Component {
  constructor(props) {
    super(props)
    this.state = {options: this.props.options,
      filteredOptions: this.props.options,
      currentOption: ''
    }
    this.filter = this.filter.bind(this)
    this.addOption = this.addOption.bind(this)
  }
  componentDidMount() {                                        Blocks fetching
    if (this.props.url == 'test') return true   ◁────┘        for the test
    request({url: this.props.url})
      .then(response=>response.data)
      .then(body => {
        if(!body) {
          return console.error('Failed to load')
        }
        this.setState({options: body})          ◁────┐        Sets the result
      })                                               │        to options
      .catch(console.error)
  }
  ...
```

The `filter()` method is called on every change of the `<input>` field. The goal is to leave only the options that match user input:

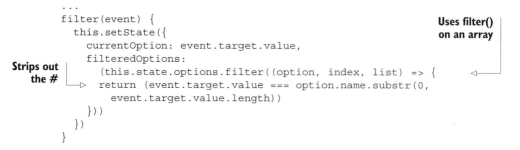

```
...
filter(event) {
  this.setState({
    currentOption: event.target.value,
    filteredOptions:
      (this.state.options.filter((option, index, list) => {
        return (event.target.value === option.name.substr(0,
        event.target.value.length))
      }))
  })
}
```

Strips out the #

Uses filter() on an array

The `addOption()` method handles the addition of a new option, in the event that there are no matches, by invoking the store's action:

```
addOption(event) {
  let currentOption = this.state.currentOption
  request
    .post(this.props.url, {name: currentOption})
    .then(response => response.data)
    .then((body) => {
      if(!body){
        return console.error('Failed to save')
      }
      this.setState({
        options: [body].concat(this.state.options)
      },
      () => {
        this.filter({target: {value: currentOption}})
      }
      )
    })
    .catch(error=>{return console.error('Failed to save')})
}
```

Uses axios to make a POST request

Uses Array.concat() to create a new array instead of Array.push(), because mutating state directly is a bad practice

Calls the filter() method in the callback of setState() to ensure that the new value is saved to the state when filter() runs

Finally, the `render()` method has a controlled component, `<input>`, with an `onChange` event listener, `this.filter`:

```
...
render() {
  return (
    <div className="form-group">
      <input type="text"
        onKeyUp={(event) => (event.keyCode==13) ? this.addOption() : ''}
        className="form-control option-name"
        onChange={this.filter}
        value={this.currentOption}
        placeholder="React.js">
      </input>
```

onKeyUp can be written as a method, not necessarily as an anonymous inline function, right in {}.

The list of filtered options is powered by the filteredOptions state, which is updated in the filter() method. You iterate over it and print _id as keys and links with option.name:

Uses the map() method to display the list of filtered options

```
{this.state.filteredOptions.map(function(option, index, list){
    return <div key={option._id}>
        <a className="btn btn-default option-list-item"
            href={'/#/'+option.name} target="_blank">
            #{option.name}
        </a>
    </div>
})}
...
```

Displays the name of an option with #, as in Slack

Uses a URL as a value for the anchor tag for each option

The last element is the Add button, which is shown only when there's no filtered-Options (no matches):

Hides the button when there are matches

```
...
{(()=>{
    if (this.state.filteredOptions.length == 0 &&
        this.state.currentOption!='')
        return <a className="btn btn-info option-add"
            onClick={this.addOption}>
            Add #{this.state.currentOption}
        </a>
})()}
</div>
    )
  }
}
```

Prompts to add the currently typed value as an option

Uses addOption as an onClick event handler

You're using CommonJS syntax, so you can declare the Autocomplete component and export it like this:

```
module.exports = Autocomplete
```

You're finished. Good job, mate!

20.6 *Putting it all together*

If you've followed along through the steps, you should be able to install the dependencies with this command (if you haven't done so already):

```
$ npm install
```

Then, launch the app as follows (you must have started MongoDB first with $ mongod):

```
$ npm start
```

The tests will pass after you run this command:

```
$ npm test
```

There's also npm run build, without the watch (you'll need to rerun it on changes). npm start runs npm run build for you.

Optionally, you can seed the database with $ npm run seed. Doing so populates MongoDB with names from ch20/autocomplete/rooms.json:

```
[ {"name": "react"},
  {"name": "node"},
  {"name": "angular"},
  {"name": "backbone"}]
```

That's all for the Autocomplete component. Now, run the project by building it with npm run build and navigating to http://localhost:3000, assuming you have MongoDB running in a separate terminal. Although 127.0.0.1 is an alias, you must use the same domain localhost as the browser location to avoid CORS/Access-Control-Allow-Origin issues, because JavaScript will call the localhost server.

You should see the component with names (if you seeded the database) on the page. When you type characters in the input field, the selection will be filtered according to matches in the input. When there are no matches, click the Add button to add the room to the database; it will immediately appear in the list.

Mongo and MongoUI

If you ever need to manipulate the data in MongoDB directly, the mongo shell (a.k.a. REPL) is available via the mongo command in the terminal. It automatically connects to the locally running instance on port 27017 (you must have one running; to do so, use mongod). Once in the mongo shell, you can perform all kinds of operations like creating a new document, querying a collection, dropping a database, and so on. The advantage is that you can use the mongo shell anywhere, even on a remote server without a GUI.

But there's a lot of typing involved when working with the mongo shell, and typing is slow and error-prone. Therefore, I built a better tool called MongoUI (https://github.com/azat-co/mongoui), which you can use to query, edit, add documents, remove documents, and do other things in a browser by clicking with your trackpad instead of typing copious amounts of JSON (MongoDB is JavaScript and JSON-based).

MongoUI allows you to work with MongoDB via a user-friendly web interface. This figure shows the names of the rooms in my rooms collection in the autocomplete database.

(continued)

The MongoDB web interface

Install MongoUI with `npm i -g mongoui`, launch it with `mongoui`, and then open in the browser at http://localhost:3001. Oh, and MongoUI is built with React, Express, and Webpack. Enjoy!

The end result of this autocomplete example is shown in figure 20.6. You can open the Network tab and click Localhost to make sure the server-side rendering is working (that is, that the data and HTML for names are there).

If for some reason your project isn't working, there may be a new version or a typo in your code. Refer to the working code at www.manning.com/books/react-quickly or https://github.com/azat-co/react-quickly/tree/master/ch20.

Figure 20.6 Inspect the localhost response by clicking Network (1) and Localhost (2) to ensure that server-side rendering (3) is working properly.

20.7 Homework

For bonus points, do the following:

- Add a test for a Remove button, which is as an X icon next to each option name.
- Add the Remove button as an X icon next to each option name. Implement an AJAX/XHR call, and add a REST endpoint to handle deletion.

- Enhance the matching algorithm so that it will find matches in the middle of names. For example, typing ac should show *react* and *backbone*, because both of them contain the letters *ac*.
- Add a Redux store.
- Implement GraphQL instead of a REST API back end.

Submit your code in *a new folder under ch20* as a pull request to this book's GitHub repository: https://github.com/azat-co/react-quickly.

20.8 *Summary*

- Curly braces output unescaped HTML in Handlebars, whereas in React you need to use __html to dangerously set inner HTML.
- `findRenderedDOMComponentWithClass()` tries to find a *single* component by its CSS class name, and `scryRenderedDOMComponentsWithClass()` finds *multiple* components by their CSS class name (see chapter 16).
- `babel-register` lets you import and use JSX files: `require('babel-register')` `({presets:['react']})`.
- MongoUI is an open source, web-based interface built on React for developing and administering MongoDB databases. You can install it with `npm i -g mongoui` and run it with `mongoui`.

appendix A
Installing applications used in this book

In this appendix, you'll find installation instructions for the following applications (valid as of May 2017):

- React v15
- Node.js v6 and npm v3
- Express v4
- Twitter Bootstrap v3
- Browserify
- MongoDB
- Babel

Installing React

You can download React in a myriad of ways:

- Hotlink to the file on a content-delivery network (CDN) such as Cloudflare: https://cdnjs.cloudflare.com/ajax/libs/react/15.5.4/react.js or https://cdnjs .cloudflare.com/ajax/libs/react/15.5.4/react-dom.js (full list: https://cdnjs .com/libraries/react).
- Download the file from a React website such as http://facebook .github.io/react/downloads.html or https://github.com/facebook/react.
- Use npm (see the next section), as in `npm install react@15 react-dom@15`. You don't need to be concerned about rendering React on servers right now. react.js is in node_modules/react/dist.
- Use Bower (http://bower.io) with `bower install --save react`.
- Use Webpack/Grunt/Browserify/Gulp to bundle from npm modules.

Installing Node.js

If you're unsure whether you have Node.js and npm, or you don't know what version you have, run these commands in your Terminal/iTerm/bash/zsh/command line:

```
$ node -v
$ npm -v
```

Most of the time, npm comes with Node.js, so follow the instructions for Node.js to install npm. The easiest way to install Node and npm is to go to the website and pick the right architecture for your computer (Windows, macOS, and so on): https://nodejs.org/en/download.

For macOS users who already have Ruby (which typically comes with Mac computers), I highly recommend using Homebrew. That's what I use, because it allows me to install other developer tools like databases and servers. To get brew on your Mac, run this Ruby code in your terminal (I promise this will be the last time we use Ruby in this book!):

```
$ ruby -e "$(curl -fsSL
➥ https://raw.githubusercontent.com/Homebrew/install/master/install)"
```

Now you should have brew installed; go ahead and update its registry and install Node.js along with npm. The latter comes with Node.js, so as I mentioned earlier, no additional commands are necessary:

```
$ brew update
$ brew install node
```

Another great tool that will let you switch between Node versions effortlessly is Node Version Manager (nvm, https://github.com/creationix/nvm):

```
$ curl -o- https://raw.githubusercontent.com/creationix/nvm/v0.32.1/install.sh
➥ | bash
$ nvm install node
```

That's it. You should be able to see the versions of Node and npm. If you want to upgrade your npm, use the npm command:

```
$ npm i -g npm@latest
```

To upgrade Node, use nvm or a similar tool like nave or n. For example, in nvm this command will also reinstall packages to the new version:

```
$ nvm install node --reinstall-packages-from=node
```

If npm gives you permission errors when you install a module/package, then make sure the npm folder has the proper permissions (be sure you understand what this command does before you run it):

```
$ sudo chown -R $USER /usr/local/{share/man,bin,lib/node,include/node}
```

Installing Express

Express is a local dependency just like React, meaning each project must install it. The only way to install Express is with npm:

```
npm i express@4 -S
```

The -S adds the entry to package.json.

In no way is this is a deep dive into Express.js, but it'll get you started with the most widely used Node.js web framework. First, install it with npm, like this:

```
$ npm install express@4.13.3
```

Typically, you'd create the server file index.js, app.js, or server.js, which you'll later start with the node command (for example, node index.js). The file has these parts:

- Imports
- Configurations
- Middleware
- Routes
- Error handlers
- Bootup

The imports section is trivial. In it, you require dependencies and instantiate objects. For example, to import the Express.js framework and create an instance, write these lines:

```
var express = require('express')
var app = express()
```

In the configurations section, you set configurations with app.set(), where the first argument is a string and the second is a value. For example, to set the template engine to Jade, use the configuration view engine:

```
app.set('view engine', 'jade')
```

The next section is for setting up middleware, which is similar to plug-ins. For example, to enable the app to serve static assets, use the static middleware:

```
app.use(express.static(path.join(__dirname, 'public')))
```

Most important, you define routes with the app.NAME() pattern. For example, this is the syntax for the GET /rooms endpoint taken from ch20/autocomplete:

```
app.get('/rooms', function(req, res, next) {
  req.rooms.find({}, {sort: {_id: -1}}).toArray(function(err, docs){
    if (err) return next(err)
    return res.json(docs)
  })
})
```

Error handlers are similar to middleware:

```
var errorHandler = require('errorhandler')
app.use(errorHandler)
```

Finally, to start your app, run `listen()`:

```
http.createServer(app).listen(portNumber, callback)
```

Of course, there's more to Express.js than this brief introduction. Otherwise, I wouldn't have written a 350-page book on the framework (*Pro Express.js*; Apress, 2014, http://proexpressjs.com)! If you want to hear from a different author(s), then consider *Express in Action* by Evan M. Hahn (Manning, 2016, www.manning .com/books/express-in-action). The framework is powerful but flexible and can be configured without requiring much magic.

If building Express.js apps isn't your core competency, or if you know how to do it but need a refresher, check out my Express.js cheatsheet in appendix C or view a graphical version of it at http://reactquickly.co/resources.

Installing Bootstrap

You can get Twitter Bootstrap from the official website: http://getbootstrap.com. This book uses v3.3.5. You have several options:

- Download an archive of minified JavaScript and style files without docs, ready for use without modification: https://github.com/twbs/bootstrap/releases/ download/v3.3.5/bootstrap-3.3.5-dist.zip.
- Download the source code in Less (https://github.com/twbs/bootstrap/ archive/v3.3.5.zip) or Sass (https://github.com/twbs/bootstrap-sass/archive/ v3.3.5.tar.gz). These are ideal for tweaking.
- Link from a CDN. You'll get better performance due to caching, but this approach requires the internet to run.
- Install Bootstrap with Bower.
- Install Bootstrap with npm.
- Install Bootstrap with Composer.
- Create your own version of Bootstrap by selecting only the components you need: http://getbootstrap.com/customize.
- Use a Bootstrap theme to get swappable looks without much work. For example, Bootswatch offers Bootstrap themes at https://bootswatch.com.

To link from a CDN, include these tags in your HTML file:

```
<!-- Latest compiled and minified CSS -->
<link rel="stylesheet"
  href="https://maxcdn.bootstrapcdn.com/bootstrap/3.3.5/css/bootstrap.min.css">

<!-- Optional theme -->
```

```
<link rel="stylesheet"
href="https://maxcdn.bootstrapcdn.com/bootstrap/3.3.5/css/
➥ bootstrap-theme.min.css">

<!-- Latest compiled and minified JavaScript -->
<script src=
   "https://maxcdn.bootstrapcdn.com/bootstrap/3.3.5/js/bootstrap.min.js">
   ➥ </script>
```

For Bower, npm, and Composer, run these terminal commands, respectively, in your project folder (one for each package manager):

```
$ bower install bootstrap
$ npm install bootstrap
$ composer require twbs/bootstrap
```

For more information, see http://getbootstrap.com/getting-started.

Installing Browserify

Browserify lets you package npm modules into front-end bundles, ready for use in the browser. Basically, you can turn any npm module (usually only for Node) into a front-end module.

> **NOTE** If you're using Webpack, you won't need Browserify.

First, install Browserify with npm:

```
$ npm install -g browserify
```

As an example, let's use ch16/jest. Go to that folder, and create a script.js file to include the generate-password.js library. The contents of script.js can be as minimal as this:

```
var generatePassword = require('generate-password')
console.log(generatePassword())
console.log(generatePassword())
```

Save script.js, and run this command in your terminal or command prompt:

```
$ browserify script.js -o bundle.js
```

Inspect bundle.js, or include it in index.html:

```
<script src="bundle.js"></script>
```

Open the index.html file in your browser, and inspect the console; it will show two random passwords. The source code is in ch16/jest.

Installing MongoDB

The easiest way to install MongoDB is to go to www.mongodb.org/downloads#production and choose the appropriate package for your system.

On macOS, you can use brew and run these commands:

```
$ brew update
$ brew install mongodb
```

Don't install mongodb globally with npm. It's a driver, not a database, so it belongs with other dependencies in the local node_modules folder.

This book uses version 3.0.6, so use later (or older) versions at your own risk. They haven't been tested to work with the book's examples.

Most often, you'll need to create a /data/db folder with the proper permissions. You can do that or pass any other custom folder to the mongod command with --dbpath. For example:

```
$ mongod --dbpath ./data
```

Once the database is running (mongod), play with code in the shell, which is mongo:

```
$ mongo
> 1+1
> use autocomplete
> db.rooms.find()
```

Here's an explanation of some of the most commonly used shell commands:

- > show dbs—Shows databases on the server
- > use DB_NAME—Selects the database DB_NAME
- > show collections—Shows collections in the selected database
- > db.COLLECTION_NAME.find()—Performs a find query on the collection named COLLECTION_NAME to find any items
- > db.COLLECTION_NAME.find({"_id": ObjectId("549d9a3081d0f07866fdaac6")})— Performs a find query on the collection named COLLECTION_NAME to find the item with ID 549d9a3081d0f07866fdaac6
- > db.COLLECTION_NAME.find({"email": /gmail/})—Performs a find query on the collection named COLLECTION_NAME to find items with an email property matching /gmail
- > db.COLLECTION_NAME.update(QUERY_OBJECT, SET_OBJECT)—Performs an update query on the collection named COLLECTION_NAME to update items that match QUERY_OBJECT with SET_OBJECT
- > db.COLLECTION_NAME.remove(QUERY_OBJECT)—Performs a remove query for items matching the QUERY_OBJECT criteria on the COLLECTION_NAME collection
- > db.COLLECTION_NAME.insert(OBJECT)—Adds OBJECT to the collection named COLLECTION_NAME

Check out my MongoDB cheatsheet in appendix D, or view a graphical version of it at http://reactquickly.co/resources. In addition to the most-used MongoDB commands, it includes Mongoose (Node.js ODM) methods. Enjoy!

Using Babel to compile JSX and ES6

Babel is mostly for ES6+/ES2015+, but it can also convert JSX to JavaScript. By using Babel for React, you can get extra ES6 features to streamline your development.

ES6 is finalized, but its features—as well as the features of future versions of ECMAScript—may not be fully supported by all browsers. To use cutting-edge new features like ES Next (https://github.com/esnext/esnext) or to use ES6 in older browsers (IE9), get a compiler like Babel (https://babeljs.io). You can run it as a standalone tool or use with your build system.

To use Babel as a standalone CLI tool, first create a new folder. Assuming you have Node.js and npm installed, run this command to create package.json:

```
$ npm init
```

Open the package.json file, and add `babel` lines in JSON. You can place them in any order as long as `babel` is a top-level property. This tells Babel to use React and JSX to transform the source files. The setting is called a *preset*. Without it, the Babel CLI won't do anything:

```
"babel": {
"presets": ["react"]
},
```

Install both Babel CLI v6.9.0 and React preset v6.5.0 with npm. In your terminal, command prompt, or shell, execute these commands:

```
$ npm i babel-cli@6.9.0 --save-dev
$ npm i babel-preset-react@6.5.0 --save-dev
```

You can use this command to check the version:

```
$ babel --version
```

There are Babel plug-ins for Grunt, Gulp, and Webpack (http://babeljs.io/docs/setup). Here's a Gulp example. Install the plug-in:

```
$ npm install --save-dev gulp-babel
```

In gulpfile.js, define a `build` task that compiles src/app.js into the build folder:

```
var gulp = require('gulp'),
  babel = require('gulp-babel')

gulp.task('build', function () {
  return gulp.src('src/app.js')
    .pipe(babel())
    .pipe(gulp.dest('build'))
})
```

For more about Webpack and Babel, see chapter 12.

Node.js and ES6

You can compile Node.js files with a build tool or use the standalone Babel module `babel-core`. Install it as follows:

```
$ npm install --save-dev babel-core@6
```

Then, in Node.js, call this function:

```
require('babel-core').transform(es5Code, options)
```

Standalone browser Babel

Babel v5.x has a standalone browser file that you can use for in-browser transformation (development only). It was removed in 6.x, but some folks created a `babel-standalone` module to fill the gap (https://github.com/Daniel15/babel-standalone). You can use that or the older version's files—for example, from Cloudflare CDN:

- *Unminified version*—http://mng.bz/K1b9
- *Minified version*—http://mng.bz/sM59

Or you can build your own standalone browser file using a build tool like Gulp or Webpack. This way, you can pick only the things you need, such as the React transformer plug-in and ES2015 presets.

appendix B
React cheatsheet

When you develop your own projects, searching on the internet for React documentation and APIs or going back to this book's chapters to find a single method isn't efficient. If you'd like to save time and avoid the distractions lurking everywhere on the Net, use this React cheatsheet as a quick reference.

Print-ready PDF available

In addition to the text version presented here, I've created a *free* beautifully designed, print-ready PDF version of this cheatsheet. You can request this PDF at http://reactquickly.co/resources.

Installation

React

- ```<script src="https://unpkg.com/react@15/dist/react.js"></script>```
- ```$ npm install react --save```
- ```$ bower install react --save```

React DOM

- ```<script src="https://unpkg.com/react-dom@15/dist/react-dom.js"></script>```
- ```$ npm install react-dom```
- ```$ bower install react-dom --save```

Rendering

ES5

```
ReactDOM.render(
    React.createElement(
      Link,
      {href: 'https://Node.University'}
    )
  ),
  document.getElementById('menu')
)
```

ES5+JSX

```
ReactDOM.render(
  <Link href='https://Node.University'/>,
  document.getElementById('menu')
)
```

Server-side rendering

```
const ReactDOMServer = require('react-dom/server')
ReactDOMServer.renderToString(Link, {href: 'https://Node.University'})
ReactDOMServer.renderToStaticMarkup(Link, {href: 'https://Node.University'})
```

Components

ES5

```
var Link = React.createClass({
  displayName: 'Link',
  render: function() {
    return React.createElement('a',
      {className: 'btn', href: this.props.href}, 'Click ->', this.props.href)
  }
})
```

ES5 + JSX

```
var Link = React.createClass({
  render: function() {
    return <a className='btn' href={this.props.href}>Click ->
      this.props.href</a>
  }
})
```

ES6 + JSX

```
class Link extends React.Component {
  render() {
    return <a className='btn' href={this.props.href}>Click ->
      this.props.href</a>
  }
}
```

Advanced components

Options (ES5)

- *Type validation in development mode*—propTypes object
- *Object of default properties*—getDefaultProps function()
- *Object of the initial state*—getInitialState function()

ES5

```
var Link = React.createClass ({
  propTypes: { href: React.PropTypes.string },
  getDefaultProps: function() {
    return { initialCount: 0 }
  },
  getInitialState: function() {
    return {count: this.props.initialCount}
  },
  tick: function() {
    this.setState({count: this.state.count + 1})
  },
  render: function() {
    return React.createElement(
      'a',
      {className: 'btn', href: '#', href: this.props.href,
        onClick: this.tick.bind(this)},
      'Click ->',
      (this.props.href ? this.props.href : 'https://webapplog.com'),
      ' (Clicked: ' + this.state.count+')'
    )
  }
})
```

ES5 + JSX

```
var Link = React.createClass ({
  propTypes: { href: React.PropTypes.string },
  getDefaultProps: function() {
```

```
      return { initialCount: 0 }
    },
    getInitialState: function() {
      return {count: this.props.initialCount};
    },
    tick: function() {
      this.setState({count: this.state.count + 1})
    },
    render: function() {
      return (
        <a onClick={this.tick.bind(this)} href="#" className="btn"
          href={this.props.href}>
          Click -> {(this.props.href ? this.props.href :
          ➥ 'https://webapplog.com')}
          (Clicked: {this.state.count})
        </a>
      )
    }
  })
```

ES6 + JSX

```
export class Link extends React.Component {
  constructor(props) {
    super(props);
    this.state = {count: props.initialCount};
  }
  tick() {
    this.setState({count: this.state.count + 1});
  }
  render() {
    return (
      <a onClick={this.tick.bind(this)} href="#" className="btn"
        href={this.props.href}>
        Click -> {(this.props.href ? this.props.href :
          'https://webapplog.com')}
        (Clicked: {this.state.count})
      </a>
    )
  }
}
Link.propTypes = { initialCount: React.PropTypes.number }
Link.defaultProps = { initialCount: 0 }
```

Lifecycle events

- componentWillMount function()
- componentDidMount function()
- componentWillReceiveProps function(nextProps)
- shouldComponentUpdate function(nextProps, nextState)→ bool
- componentWillUpdate function(nextProps, nextState)
- componentDidUpdate function(prevProps, prevState)
- componentWillUnmount function()

Sequence of lifecycle events (inspired by http://react.tips)

Mounting	Updating component properties	Updating component state	Using `forceUpdate()`	Unmounting
`getDefaultProps()`				
`getInitialState()`				
`componentWillMount()`				
	`componentWillReceiveProps()`			
	`shouldComponentUpdate()`	`shouldComponentUpdate()`		
	`componentWillUpdate()`	`componentWillUpdate()`	`componentWillUpdate()`	
`render()`	`render()`	`render()`	`render()`	
`componentDidMount()`	`componentDidUpdate()`	`componentDidUpdate()`	`componentDidUpdate()`	
				`componentWillUnmount()`

Special properties

- `key`—Unique identifier for an element to turn arrays/lists into hashes for better performance. For example: `key={id}`.
- `ref`—Reference to an element via `this.refs.NAME`. For example: `ref="email"` will create a `this.refs.email` DOM node or `ReactDOM.findDOMNode(this.refs.email)`.
- `style`—Accepts an object for camelCased CSS styles instead of a string (immutable since v0.14). For example: `style={{color: red}}`.
- `className`—HTML `class` attribute. For example: `className="btn"`.
- `htmlFor`—HTML `for` attribute. For example: `htmlFor="email"`.
- `dangerouslySetInnerHTML`—Sets inner HTML to raw HTML by providing an object with the key `__html`.
- `children`—Sets the content of the element via `this.props.children`. For example: `this.props.children[0]`.
- `data-NAME`—Custom attribute. For example: `data-tooltip-text="..."`.

propTypes

Types available under `React.PropTypes`:

- `any`
- `array`
- `bool`
- `element`
- `func`
- `node`
- `number`
- `object`
- `string`

To make a property required (warning only), append `.isRequired`.

More methods:

- `instanceOf(constructor)`
- `oneOf(['News', 'Photos'])`
- `oneOfType([propType, propType])`

Custom validation

```
propTypes: {
  customProp: function(props, propName, componentName) {
    if (!/regExPattern/.test(props[propName])) {
      return new Error('Validation failed!');
    }
  }
}
```

Component properties and methods

Properties

- `this.refs`—Lists components with a `ref` property.
- `this.props`—Lists any properties passed to an element (immutable).
- `this.state`—Lists states set by `setState` and `getInitialState` (mutable). Avoid setting state manually with `this.state=....`
- `this.isMounted`—Flags whether the element has a corresponding DOM node.

Methods

- `setState(changes)`—Changes state (partially) to `this.state`, and triggers a rerender
- `replaceState(newState)`—Replaces `this.state`, and triggers a rerender
- `forceUpdate()`—Triggers an immediate DOM rerender

React add-ons

As npm modules:

- `react-addons-css-transition-group` (http://facebook.github.io/react/docs/animation.html)
- `react-addons-perf` (http://facebook.github.io/react/docs/perf.html)
- `react-addons-test-utils` (http://facebook.github.io/react/docs/test-utils.html)
- `react-addons-pure-render-mixin` (http://facebook.github.io/react/docs/pure-render-mixin.html)
- `react-addons-linked-state-mixin` (http://facebook.github.io/react/docs/two-way-binding-helpers.html)
- `react-addons-clone-with-props`
- `react-addons-create-fragment`
- `react-addons-css-transition-group`
- `react-addons-linked-state-mixin`
- `react-addons-pure-render-mixin`
- `react-addons-shallow-compare`
- `react-addons-transition-group`
- `react-addons-update` (http://facebook.github.io/react/docs/update.html)

React components

- *Lists of React components*—https://github.com/brillout/awesome-react-components and http://devarchy.com/react-components
- *Material-UI*—Material design React components (http://material-ui.com)
- *React Toolbox*—React components that implement the Google Material Design specification (http://react-toolbox.com)

- *JS.Coach*—Opinionated catalog of open source JS (mostly React) packages (https://js.coach)
- *React Rocks*—Catalog of React components (https://react.rocks)
- *Khan Academy*—Collection of reusable React components (https://khan.github.io/react-components)
- *ReactJSX.com*—Registry of React components (http://reactjsx.com)

appendix C
Express.js cheatsheet

When you develop your own projects, searching on the internet for React documentation and APIs or going back to this book's chapters to find a single method isn't efficient. If you'd like to save time and avoid the distractions lurking everywhere on the Net, use this Express cheatsheet as a quick reference.

Print-ready PDF available

In addition to the text version presented here, I've created a *free* beautifully designed, print-ready PDF version of this cheatsheet. You can request this PDF at http://reactquickly.co/resources.

Installing Express.js

- $ `sudo npm install express`—Installs the latest Express.js locally
- $ `sudo npm install express@4.2.0 --save`—Installs Express.js v4.2.0 locally, and saves it to package.json
- $ `sudo npm install -g express-generator@4.0.0`—Installs the Express.js command-line generator v4.0.0

Generator

Usage

$ `express [options] [dir]`

Options

- `-h`—Prints usage information
- `-V`—Prints the express-generator version number
- `-e`—Adds EJS engine support; defaults to Jade if omitted
- `-H`—Adds hogan.js engine support
- `-c <library>`—Adds CSS support for `<library>` (`less`|`stylus`|`compass`); defaults to plain CSS if `-c <library>` is omitted
- `-f`—Generates into a non-empty directory

Basics

- `var express = require('express')`—Includes a module
- `var app = express()`—Creates an instance
- `app.listen(portNumber, callback)`—Starts the Express.js server
- `http.createServer(app).listen(portNumber, callback)`—Starts the Express.js server
- `app.set(key, value)`—Sets a property value by key
- `app.get(key)`—Gets a property value by key

HTTP verbs and routes

- `app.get(urlPattern, requestHandler[, requestHandler2, ...])`—Handles GET method requests
- `app.post(urlPattern, requestHandler[, requestHandler2, ...])`—Handles POST method requests
- `app.put(urlPattern, requestHandler[, requestHandler2, ...])`—Handles PUT method requests
- `app.delete(urlPattern, requestHandler[, requestHandler2, ...])`—Handles DELETE method requests
- `app.all(urlPattern, requestHandler[, requestHandler2, ...])`—Handles all method requests

- `app.param([name,] callback)`—Processes URL parameters
- `app.use([urlPattern,] requestHandler[, requestHandler2, ...])`—Applies middleware

Requests

- `request.params`—Parameter middleware
- `request.param`—Extracts one parameter
- `request.query`—Extracts a query string parameter
- `request.route`—Returns a route string
- `request.cookies`—Accesses cookies; requires `cookie-parser`
- `request.signedCookies`—Accesses signed cookies; requires `cookie-parser`
- `request.body`—Reads a payload; requires `body-parser`

Request-header shortcuts

- `request.get(headerKey)`—Reads `Value` for the header key
- `request.accepts(type)`—Checks whether the type is accepted
- `request.acceptsLanguage(language)`—Checks the language
- `request.acceptsCharset(charset)`—Checks the character set
- `request.is(type)`—Checks the type
- `request.ip`—Reads an IP address
- `request.ips`—Reads IP addresses (with `trust-proxy` on)
- `request.path`—Reads a URL path
- `request.host`—Accesses a host without a port number
- `request.fresh`—Checks freshness
- `request.stale`—Checks staleness
- `request.xhr`—Checks for XHR/AJAX-y requests
- `request.protocol`—Returns an HTTP protocol
- `request.secure`—Checks whether `protocol` is `https`
- `request.subdomains`—Reads an array of subdomains
- `request.originalUrl`—Reads the original URL

Response

- `response.redirect(status, url)`—Redirects a request
- `response.send(status, data)`—Sends a response
- `response.json(status, data)`—Sends JSON, and forces proper headers
- `response.sendfile(path, options, callback)`—Sends a file
- `response.render(templateName, locals, callback)`—Renders a template
- `response.locals`—Passes data to the template

Handler signatures

- `function(request, response, next) {}`—Request-handler signature
- `function(error, request, response, next) {}`—Error-handler signature

Stylus and Jade

Install Jade and Stylus:

```
$ npm i -SE stylus jade
```

Apply the Jade template engine:

```
app.set('views', path.join(__dirname, 'views'))
app.set('view engine', 'jade')
```

Apply the Stylus CSS processor:

```
app.use(require('stylus').middleware(path.join(__dirname, 'public')))
```

Body

```
var bodyParser = require('body-parser')
app.use(bodyParser.json())
app.use(bodyParser.urlencoded({
    extended: true
}))
```

Static

```
app.use(express.static(path.join(__dirname, 'public')))
```

Connect middleware

```
$ sudo npm install <package_name> --save
```

- `body-parser` (https://github.com/expressjs/body-parser)—Accesses a request payload
- `compression` (https://github.com/expressjs/compression)—Compresses using Gzip
- `connect-timeout` (https://github.com/expressjs/timeout)—Cuts off requests after a specified time
- `cookie-parser` (https://github.com/expressjs/cookie-parser)—Parses and reads cookies
- `cookie-session` (https://github.com/expressjs/cookie-session)—Uses a session via a cookies store
- `csurf` (https://github.com/expressjs/csurf)—Generates a token for Cross-Site Request Forgery (CSRF)
- `errorhandler` (https://github.com/expressjs/errorhandler)—Uses development error handlers

- express-session (https://github.com/expressjs/session)—Uses a session via an in-memory or another store
- method-override (https://github.com/expressjs/method-override)—Overrides HTTP methods
- morgan (https://github.com/expressjs/morgan)—Outputs server logs
- response-time (https://github.com/expressjs/response-time)—Shows the response time
- serve-favicon (https://github.com/expressjs/serve-favicon)—Serves a favicon
- serve-index (https://github.com/expressjs/serve-index)—Serves a directory listing and files as a file server
- serve-static (https://github.com/expressjs/serve-static)—Serves static content
- vhost (https://github.com/expressjs/vhost)—Uses a virtual host

Other popular middleware

- cookies (https://github.com/jed/cookies) and keygrip (https://github.com/jed/keygrip)—Parse cookies (analogous to cookie-parser)
- raw-body (https://github.com/stream-utils/raw-body)—Uses a raw payload/body
- connect-multiparty (https://github.com/superjoe30/connect-multiparty)—Processes file uploads
- qs (https://github.com/ljharb/qs)—Parses query strings with objects and arrays as values
- st (https://github.com/isaacs/st) and connect-static (https://github.com/andrewrk/connect-static)—Serve static files (analogous to staticCache)
- express-validator (https://github.com/ctavan/express-validator)—Performs validation
- less (https://github.com/emberfeather/less.js-middleware)—Processes LESS files into CSS
- passport (https://github.com/jaredhanson/passport)—Authenticates requests
- helmet (https://github.com/evilpacket/helmet)—Sets security headers
- connect-cors (https://npmjs.com/package/cors)—Enables cross-origin resource sharing (CORS)
- connect-redis (http://github.com/visionmedia/connect-redis)—Connects to Redis

Resources

- *Express Foundation* free online course, https://node.university/p/express-foundation
- *Pro Express* (Apress, 2014), my comprehensive book on Express.js, http://proexpressjs.com
- Express.js posts on my blog, https://webapplog.com/tag/express-js

appendix D
MongoDB and
Mongoose cheatsheet

When you develop your own projects, searching on the internet for React documentation and APIs or going back to this book's chapters to find a single method isn't efficient. If you'd like to save time and avoid the distractions lurking everywhere on the Net, use this MongoDB cheatsheet as a quick reference.

Print-ready PDF available

In addition to the text version presented here, I've created a *free* beautifully designed, print-ready PDF version of this cheatsheet. You can request this PDF at http://reactquickly.co/resources.

MongoDB

- `$ mongod`—Starts the MongoDB server (`localhost:27017`)
- `$ mongo` (connects to the local server by default)—Opens the MongoDB console

MongoDB console

- `> show dbs`—Shows databases on the server
- `> use DB_NAME`—Selects the database `DB_NAME`
- `> show collections`—Shows collections in the selected database
- `> db.COLLECTION_NAME.find()`—Performs a find query on the collection named `COLLECTION_NAME` to find any items
- `> db.COLLECTION_NAME.find({"_id"-ObjectId("549d9a3081d0f07866fdaac6")})`—Performs a find query on the collection named `COLLECTION_NAME` to find the item with ID 549d9a3081d0f07866fdaac6
- `> db.COLLECTION_NAME.find({"email": /gmail/})`—Performs a find query on the collection named `COLLECTION_NAME` to find items with an `email` property matching `/gmail`
- `> db.COLLECTION_NAME.update(QUERY_OBJECT, SET_OBJECT)`—Performs an update query on the collection named `COLLECTION_NAME` to update items that match `QUERY_OBJECT` with `SET_OBJECT`
- `> db.COLLECTION_NAME.remove(QUERY_OBJECT)`—Performs a remove query for items matching `QUERY_OBJECT` criteria on the `COLLECTION_NAME` collection
- `> db.COLLECTION_NAME.insert(OBJECT)`—Adds `OBJECT` to the collection named `COLLECTION_NAME`

Installing Mongoose

- `$ sudo npm install mongoose`—Installs the latest version of Mongoose locally
- `$ sudo npm install mongoose@3.8.20 --save`—Installs Mongoose v3.8.20 locally, and saves it to package.json

Mongoose basic usage

```
var mongoose = require('mongoose')
var dbUri = 'mongodb://localhost:27017/api'
var dbConnection = mongoose.createConnection(dbUri)
var Schema = mongoose.Schema
var postSchema = new Schema ({
  title: String,
  text: String
})
var Post = dbConnection.model('Post', postSchema, 'posts')
Post.find({},function(error, posts){
  console.log(posts)
  process.exit(1)
})
```

Mongoose schema

- `String`
- `Boolean`
- `Number`
- `Date`
- `Array`
- `Buffer`
- `Schema.Types.Mixed`
- `Schema.Types.ObjectId`

Create, read, update, delete (CRUD) Mongoose example

```
// Create
var post = new Post({title: 'a', text: 'b')
post.save(function(error, document){
  ...
})

// Read
Post.findOne(criteria, function(error, post) {
  ...
})

// Update
Post.findOne(criteria, function(error, post) {
  post.set()
  post.save(function(error, document){
    ...
  })
})

// Delete
Post.findOne(criteria, function(error, post) {
  post.remove(function(error){
    ...
  })
})
```

Mongoose model methods

- `find(criteria, [fields], [options], [callback])`, where callback has error and documents arguments—Finds a document
- `count(criteria, [callback])`, where callback has error and count arguments—Returns a count of documents with matching criteria
- `findById(id, [fields], [options], [callback])`, where callback has error and document arguments—Returns a single document by ID
- `findByIdAndUpdate(id, [update], [options], [callback])`—Executes MongoDB's `findAndModify()` to update a document by ID

- `findByIdAndRemove(id, [options], [callback])`—Executes MongoDB's `findAndModify()` to remove a document by ID
- `findOne(criteria, [fields], [options], [callback])`, where `callback` has error and document arguments—Returns a single document
- `findOneAndUpdate([criteria], [update], [options], [callback])`—Executes MongoDB's `findAndModify()` to update document(s)
- `findOneAndRemove(id, [update], [options], [callback])`—Executes MongoDB's `findAndModify()` to remove a document
- `update(criteria, update, [options], [callback])`, where `callback` has error and count arguments—Updates documents
- `create(doc(s), [callback])`, where `callback` has error and `doc(s)` arguments—Creates a document object, and saves it to the database
- `remove(criteria, [callback])`, where `callback` has an error argument—Removes documents

Mongoose document methods

- `save([callback])`, where `callback` has error, doc, and count arguments—Saves the document
- `set(path, val, [type], [options])`—Sets a value on the document's property
- `get(path, [type])`—Gets the value of a property
- `isModified([path])`—Checks whether a property has been modified
- `populate([path], [callback])`—Populates a reference
- `toJSON(options)`—Gets JSON from the document
- `validate(callback)`—Validates the document

appendix E
ES6 for success

This appendix provides a quick introduction to ES6. It describes the 10 best features of the new generation of the most popular programming language—JavaScript:

1 Default parameters
2 Template literals
3 Multiline strings
4 Destructuring assignment
5 Enhanced object literals
6 Arrow functions
7 Promises
8 Block-scoped constructs: `let` and `const`
9 Classes
10 Modules

> **NOTE** This list if highly subjective. It's in no way intended to diminish the usefulness of other ES6 features that didn't make it on the list only because I wanted to limit the number to 10.

Default parameters

Remember when we had to use statements like these to define default parameters?

```
var link = function (height, color, url) {
    var height = height || 50
    var color = color || 'red'
    var url = url || 'http://azat.co'
    ...
}
```

Print-ready PDF available

In addition to this essay, I've created a *free* beautifully designed, print-ready ES6/ES2015 cheatsheet. You can request this PDF at http://reactquickly.co/resources.

This approach was fine until the value wasn't 0. When you have 0, there may be a bug. A 0 value defaults to the hardcoded value instead of becoming the value itself, because 0 is falsy in JavaScript. Of course, who needs 0 as a value (#sarcasmfont)? So we ignored this flaw and used the logical OR. No more! In ES6, you can put the default value right in the signature of the function:

```
var link = function(height = 50, color = 'red', url = 'http://azat.co') {
    ...
}
```

This syntax is similar to Ruby. My favorite, CoffeeScript, has this feature, as well—and has had it for many years.

Template literals

Template literals or interpolation in other languages is a way to output variables in a string. In ES5, you had to break the string like this:

```
var name = 'Your name is ' + first + ' ' + last + '.'
var url = 'http://localhost:3000/api/messages/' + id
```

In ES6, you can use the new syntax ${NAME} in the back-ticked string:

```
var name = `Your name is ${first} ${last}.`
var url = `http://localhost:3000/api/messages/${id}`
```

Do you wonder if you still can use template-literal syntax with Markdown? Markdown uses back-ticks for inline code blocks. That's a problem! The solution is to use two, three, or more back-ticks for Markdown code that has back-ticks for string templates.

Multiline strings

Another bit of yummy syntactic sugar is the multiline string. In ES5, you had to use one of these approaches:

```
var roadPoem = 'Then took the other, as just as fair,\n\t'
    + 'And having perhaps the better claim\n\t'
    + 'Because it was grassy and wanted wear,\n\t'
    + 'Though as for that the passing there\n\t'
    + 'Had worn them really about the same,\n\t'

var fourAgreements = 'You have the right to be you.\n\
    You can only be you when you do your best.'
```

In ES6, you can use back-ticks:

```
var roadPoem = `Then took the other, as just as fair,
    And having perhaps the better claim
    Because it was grassy and wanted wear,
    Though as for that the passing there
    Had worn them really about the same,`

var fourAgreements = `You have the right to be you.
    You can only be you when you do your best.`
```

Destructuring assignment

Destructuring can be a harder concept to grasp, because some magic is going on. Let's say you have simple assignments where the keys/objects properties/attributes house and mouse are the variables house and mouse:

```
var data = $('body').data(),        ◁┐  data has the properties
  house = data.house,                  │  house and mouse.
  mouse = data.mouse
```

Here are some other examples of destructuring assignments (from Node.js):

```
var jsonMiddleware = require('body-parser').json

var body = req.body,                ◁┐  body has a username
  username = body.username,            │  and password.
  password = body.password
```

In ES6, you can replace the previous ES5 code with these statements:

```
var { house, mouse} = $('body').data()     ◁┐  You'll get the house and
                                              │  mouse variables.
var {json} = require('body-parser')

var {username, password} = req.body
```

This also works with arrays. Crazy!

```
var [col1, col2]  = $('.column'),
   [line1, line2, line3, , line5] = file.split('\n')
```

The first line assigns the 0 element to col1 and the 1 element to col2. The second statement (yes, the missing line4 is intentional) produces the following assignment, where fileSplitArray is the result of file.split('\n'):

```
var line1 = fileSplitArray[0]
var line2 = fileSplitArray[1]
var line3 = fileSplitArray[2]
var line5 = fileSplitArray[4]
```

It may take you some time to get used to the destructuring assignment syntax, but it's a sweet sugarcoating—no doubt about that.

Enhanced object literals

What you can now do with object literals is mind blowing! We went from a glorified version of JSON in ES5 to something closely resembling classes in ES6.

Here's a typical ES5 object literal with some methods and attributes/properties:

```
var serviceBase = {port: 3000, url: 'azat.co'},
    getAccounts = function(){return [1,2,3]}

var accountServiceES5 = {
  port: serviceBase.port,
  url: serviceBase.url,
  getAccounts: getAccounts,
  toString: function() {
    return JSON.stringify(this.valueOf())
  },
  getUrl: function() {return "http://" + this.url + ':' + this.port},
  valueOf_1_2_3: getAccounts()
}
```

If you want to be fancy, you can inherit from serviceBase by making it the prototype with the Object.create() method:

```
var accountServiceES5ObjectCreate = Object.create(serviceBase)
var accountServiceES5ObjectCreate = {
  getAccounts: getAccounts,
  toString: function() {
    return JSON.stringify(this.valueOf())
  },
  getUrl: function() {return "http://" + this.url + ':' + this.port},
  valueOf_1_2_3: getAccounts()
}
```

I know, accountServiceES5ObjectCreate and accountServiceES5 are *not* identical, because one object (accountServiceES5) has the properties in the *proto* object (see

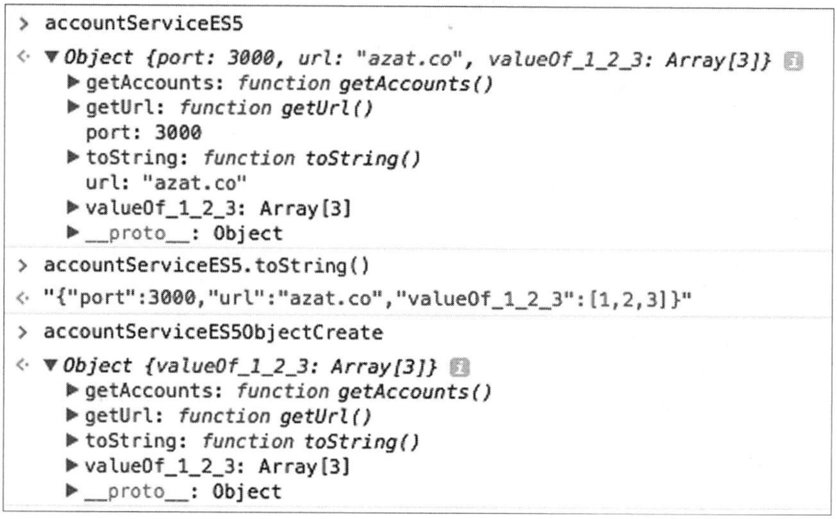

```
> accountServiceES5
⟨· ▼ Object {port: 3000, url: "azat.co", valueOf_1_2_3: Array[3]} ⓘ
      ▶ getAccounts: function getAccounts()
      ▶ getUrl: function getUrl()
        port: 3000
      ▶ toString: function toString()
        url: "azat.co"
      ▶ valueOf_1_2_3: Array[3]
      ▶ __proto__: Object
> accountServiceES5.toString()
⟨· "{"port":3000,"url":"azat.co","valueOf_1_2_3":[1,2,3]}"
> accountServiceES5ObjectCreate
⟨· ▼ Object {valueOf_1_2_3: Array[3]} ⓘ
      ▶ getAccounts: function getAccounts()
      ▶ getUrl: function getUrl()
      ▶ toString: function toString()
      ▶ valueOf_1_2_3: Array[3]
      ▶ __proto__: Object
```

Figure E.1   Objects in ES5

figure E.1). But for the sake of the example, we'll consider them similar. In the ES6 object literal, there are shorthands for assignment: getAccounts: getAccounts, becomes just getAccounts, without the colon.

Also, you set the prototype in the __proto__ property, which makes sense (not '__proto__' though—that would be just a property):

```
var serviceBase = {port: 3000, url: 'azat.co'},
    getAccounts = function(){return [1,2,3]}
var accountService = {
    __proto__: serviceBase,
    getAccounts,
```

In addition, you can invoke super in toString():

```
toString() {
    return JSON.stringify((super.valueOf()))
    },
    getUrl() {return "http://" + this.url + ':' + this.port},
```

And you can dynamically create keys, object properties, and attributes such as valueOf_1_2_3 with the ['valueOf_' + getAccounts().join('_')] construct:

```
[ 'valueOf_' + getAccounts().join('_') ]: getAccounts()
}
console.log(accountService)
```

The resulting ES6 object with __proto__ as the serviceBase object is shown in figure E.2. This is a great enhancement to good-old object literals!

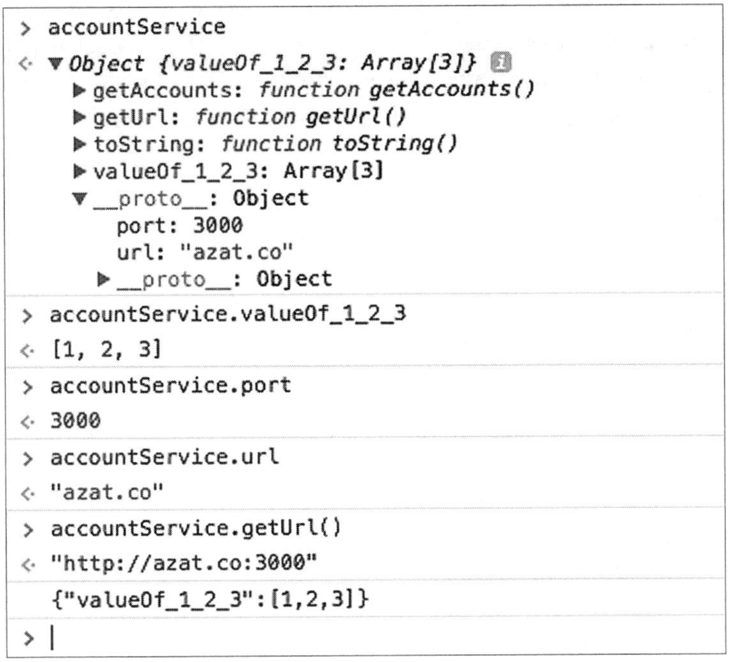

```
> accountService
⌄ ▼ Object {valueOf_1_2_3: Array[3]} 🛈
     ▶ getAccounts: function getAccounts()
     ▶ getUrl: function getUrl()
     ▶ toString: function toString()
     ▶ valueOf_1_2_3: Array[3]
     ▼ __proto__: Object
        port: 3000
        url: "azat.co"
        ▶ __proto__: Object
> accountService.valueOf_1_2_3
⌄ [1, 2, 3]
> accountService.port
⌄ 3000
> accountService.url
⌄ "azat.co"
> accountService.getUrl()
⌄ "http://azat.co:3000"
  {"valueOf_1_2_3":[1,2,3]}
> |
```

Figure E.2 The ES6 object literal extends from `serviceBase` and defines methods and attributes.

Arrow functions

This is probably the feature I wanted the most. I love the fat arrows in CoffeeScript, and now we have them in ES6. First, arrow functions save space and time because they're short:

```
const sum = (a, b, c) => {
  return a + b + c
}
```

Fat arrows are also amazing because they make this behave properly. this has the same value as in the context of a function—this doesn't mutate. The mutation typically happens each time you create a closure.

Using arrow functions in ES6 means you don't have to use that = this, self = this, _this = this, and .bind(this). For example, this code in ES5 is ugly:

```
var _this = this
$('.btn').click(function(event){
  _this.sendData()
})
```

This ES6 code is better:

```
$('.btn').click((event) => {
  this.sendData()
})
```

Sadly, the ES6 committee decided that having skinny arrows is too much of a good thing, and they left us with a verbose function() instead. (Skinny arrows in CoffeeScript work like the regular function in ES5 and ES6.)

Here's another example that uses call to pass the context to the logUpperCase() function in ES5:

```
var logUpperCase = function() {
  var _this = this

  this.string = this.string.toUpperCase()
  return function () {
    return console.log(_this.string)
  }
}


logUpperCase.call({ string: 'es6 rocks' })()
```

In ES6, you don't need to mess around with _this:

```
var logUpperCase = function() {
  this.string = this.string.toUpperCase()
  return () => console.log(this.string)
}


logUpperCase.call({ string: 'es6 rocks' })()
```

Note that you can mix and match the old function with => in ES6 as you see fit. And when an arrow function is used with a one-line statement, it becomes an expression: that is, it will implicitly return the result of that single statement. If you have more than one line, you need to use return explicitly.

This ES5 code, which creates an array from the messages array,

```
var ids = ['5632953c4e345e145fdf2df8','563295464e345e145fdf2df9']
var messages = ids.map(function (value) {
  return "ID is " + value                    ⟵── Explicit return
});
```

becomes this in ES6:

```
var ids = ['5632953c4e345e145fdf2df8','563295464e345e145fdf2df9']
var messages = ids.map(value => `ID is ${value}`) //    ⟵── Implicit return
```

Notice that this code uses string templates. Another feature I love from CoffeeScript!

Parentheses (()) are optional for single parameters in an arrow function's signature. You need them when you use more than one parameter. In ES5, the following code has function() with an explicit return:

```
var ids = ['5632953c4e345e145fdf2df8', '563295464e345e145fdf2df9'];
var messages = ids.map(function (value, index, list) {
  return 'ID of ' + index + ' element is ' + value + ' '   ⟵── Explicit return
})
```

And the more eloquent version of the code in ES6 uses parentheses around the parameters and an implicit return:

```
var ids = ['5632953c4e345e145fdf2df8','563295464e345e145fdf2df9']
var messages = ids.map((value, index, list) =>
  `ID of ${index} element is ${value} `)          ⟵— Implicit return
```

Promises

Promises have historically been a controversial topic. There were many promise implementations with slightly different syntaxes: Q, Bluebird, Deferred.js, Vow, Avow, and jQuery Deferred, to name just a few. Other developers said we didn't need promises and could use async, generators, callbacks, and so on. Fortunately, ES6 now has a standard `Promise` implementation.

Let's consider a trivial example of delayed asynchronous execution with `setTimeout()`:

```
setTimeout(function(){
  console.log('Yay!')
}, 1000)
```

This code can be rewritten in ES6 with `Promise`:

```
var wait1000 =  new Promise(function(resolve, reject) {
  setTimeout(resolve, 1000)
}).then(function() {
  console.log('Yay!')
})
```

It can also use ES6 arrow functions:

```
var wait1000 =  new Promise((resolve, reject)=> {
  setTimeout(resolve, 1000)
}).then(()=> {
  console.log('Yay!')
})
```

So far, we've increased the number of lines of code from three to five without any obvious benefit. The benefit comes if you have more nested logic in the `setTimeout()` callback. The following code

```
setTimeout(function(){
  console.log('Yay!')
  setTimeout(function(){
    console.log('Wheeyee!')
  }, 1000)
}, 1000)
```

can be rewritten with ES6 promises:

```
var wait1000 =  ()=> new Promise((resolve, reject)=>
  {setTimeout(resolve, 1000)})

wait1000()
    .then(function() {
```

```
        console.log('Yay!')
        return wait1000()
    })
    .then(function() {
        console.log('Wheeyee!')
    });
```

Still not convinced that promises are better than regular callbacks? Me neither. I think that once you get the idea of callbacks, there's no need for the additional complexity of promises. Nevertheless, promises are available in ES6 for those who adore them; and they do have a fail-and-catch-all callback, which is a nice feature. See James Nelson's post "Introduction to ES6 Promises: The Four Functions You Need to Avoid Callback Hell" for more about promises (http://mng.bz/3OAP).

Block-scoped constructs: let and const

You may have already seen the weird-sounding `let` in ES6 code. It isn't a sugarcoating feature; it's more intricate. `let` is a new `var` that lets you scope a variable to blocks. You define blocks with curly braces. In ES5, blocks did *nothing* to variables:

```
function calculateTotalAmount (vip) {
  var amount = 0
  if (vip) {
    var amount = 1
  }
  { // More crazy blocks!
    var amount = 100
    {
      var amount = 1000
      }
  }
  return amount
}

console.log(calculateTotalAmount(true))
```

The result is 1,000. Wow! That's a bad bug. In ES6, you use `let` to restrict the scope to the blocks. Variables are function-scoped:

```
function calculateTotalAmount (vip) {
  var amount = 0 // Probably should also be let, but you can mix var and let
  if (vip) {
    let amount = 1 // First amount is still 0
  }
  { // more crazy blocks!
    let amount = 100 // First amount is still 0
    {
      let amount = 1000 // First amount is still 0
      }
  }
  return amount
}

console.log(calculateTotalAmount(true))
```

The value is 0, because the if block also has let. If it had nothing (amount=1), then the expression would have been 1.

When it comes to const, things are easier; it creates a read-only reference, and it's block-scoped like let. (*Read-only* means you can't reassign the variable identifier.) const works on objects as well; their properties can change.

Suppose you have a constant url, like this: const url="http://webapplog.com". Reassigning it with const url="http://azat.co" will fail in most browsers— although the documentation states that const doesn't mean immutability, if you try to change the value, it won't change.

To demonstrate, here's a bunch of constants that are okay because they belong to different blocks:

```
function calculateTotalAmount (vip) {
  const amount = 0
  if (vip) {
    const amount = 1
  }
  { // More crazy blocks!
    const amount = 100
    {
      const amount = 1000
    }
  }
  return amount
}

console.log(calculateTotalAmount(true))
```

In my humble opinion, let and const overcomplicate the language. Without them, we had only one behavior; but now there are multiple scenarios to consider.

Classes

If you love object-oriented programming, then you'll love this feature. It makes writing classes and inheriting from them as easy as liking a comment on Facebook.

Creating and using classes in ES5 was a pain because there was no class keyword (it was reserved but did nothing). In addition, lots of inheritance patterns like pseudo-classical,[1] classical,[2] and functional just added to the confusion, pouring gasoline on the fire of the JavaScript wars.

I won't show you how to write a class (yes, there are classes; objects inherit from objects) in ES5, because there are many flavors. Let's look at an ES6 example. The ES6 class uses prototypes, not the function factory approach. Here's a baseModel class in which you can define a constructor and a getName() method:

---

[1] See Ilya Kantor, "Class Patterns," http://javascript.info/class-patterns.
[2] See Douglas Crockford, "Classical Inheritance in JavaScript," www.crockford.com/javascript/inheritance .html.

```
                   class baseModel {
                     constructor(options = {}, data = []) {        ←──── Class constructor
                       this.name = 'Base'
                       this.url = 'http://azat.co/api'
                       this.data = data
                       this.options = options
         Class   ┌     }
       method   └──→  getName() {
                       console.log(`Class name: ${this.name}`)
                     }
                   }
```

Notice that this code uses default parameter values for options and data. Also, method names no longer need to include the word function or a colon (:). The other big difference is that you can't assign properties (this.NAME) the same way as methods—that is, you can't say name at the same indentation level as a method. To set the value of a property, assign a value in the constructor.

AccountModel inherits from baseModel with class NAME extends PARENT_NAME. To call the parent constructor, you can effortlessly invoke super() with parameters:

```
class AccountModel extends baseModel {
  constructor(options, data) {
    super({private: true}, ['32113123123', '524214691'])    ←┐ Calls the parent
    this.name = 'Account Model'                              │ constructor method
    this.url +='/accounts/'                                  │ with super
  }
}
```

If you want to be fancy, you can set up a getter like this, and accountsData will be a property:

```
class AccountModel extends baseModel {
  constructor(options, data) {
    super({private: true}, ['32113123123', '524214691'])
    this.name = 'Account Model'
    this.url +='/accounts/'
  }
  get accountsData() {          ←┐ Calculated
    // ... make XHR             │ attribute getter
    return this.data
  }
}
```

How do you use this abracadabra? It's easy:

```
let accounts = new AccountModel(5)
accounts.getName()
console.log('Data is %s', accounts.accountsData)
```

In case you're wondering, the output is

```
Class name: Account Model
Data is %s 32113123123,524214691
```

Modules

As you may know, JavaScript had no support for native modules before ES6. People came up with AMD, RequireJS, CommonJS, and other workarounds. Now there are modules with `import` and `export` operands.

In ES5, you use `<script>` tags with an immediately invoked function expression or a library like AMD, whereas in ES6 you can expose a class with `export`. I'm a Node.js guy, so I use CommonJS, which is also a Node.js module syntax.

It's straightforward to use CommonJS on the browser with the Browserify bundler (http://browserify.org). Let's say you have a `port` variable and a `getAccounts` method in an ES5 module.js file:

```
module.exports = {
  port: 3000,
  getAccounts: function() {
    ...
  }
}
```

In the ES5 main.js file, you'd `require('module')` that dependency:

```
var service = require('module.js')
console.log(service.port) // 3000
```

In ES6, you use `export` and `import`. For example, this is the library in the ES6 module.js file:

```
export var port = 3000
export function getAccounts(url) {
  ...
}
```

In the ES6 main.js importer file, you use the syntax `import {name} from 'my-module'`:

```
import {port, getAccounts} from 'module'
console.log(port) // 3000
```

Or you can import everything as a `service` variable in main.js:

```
import * as service from 'module'
console.log(service.port) // 3000
```

Personally, I find ES6 modules confusing. Yes, they're more eloquent, but Node.js modules won't change anytime soon. It's better to have only one style for browser and server JavaScript, so I'll stick with CommonJS/Node.js style for now. In addition, support for ES6 modules in browsers isn't available as of this writing, so you'll need something like jspm (http://jspm.io) to use ES6 modules.

For more information and examples, see http://exploringjs.com/es6/ ch_modules.html. And no matter what, write modular JavaScript!

Using ES6 today with Babel

To use ES6 today, use Babel as part of your build process. There's more information on Babel in chapter 3.

Other ES6 features

There are many other noteworthy ES6 features that you probably won't use (at least, not right away). Here they are, in no particular order:

- New math, number, string, array, and object methods
- Binary and octal number types
- Default rest spread
- For of comprehensions (hello again, mighty CoffeeScript!)
- Symbols
- Tail calls
- Generators
- New data structures like Map and Set

ECMAScript improves productivity and reduces mistakes. It will continue to evolve. Learning never stops. Take advantage of these resources:

- ES6 cheatsheet, http://reactquickly.co/resources
- *Understanding ECMAScript 6* by Nicolas Zakas (Leanpub, 2017), https://leanpub .com/understandinges6
- *Exploring ES6* by Axel Rauschmayer (Leanpub, 2017), http://exploringjs .com/es6.html
- ES6 course, https://node.university/p/es6
- ES7 and ES8 course, https://node.university/p/es7-es8

index

React in Action
by Mark Tielens Thomas

ISBN: 9781617293856
300 pages
$44.99
November 2017

RxJS in Action
by Paul P. Daniels and Luis Atencio

ISBN: 9781617293412
352 pages
$49.99
July 2017

Functional Programming in JavaScript
How to improve your JavaScript programs using
functional techniques
by Luis Atencio

ISBN: 9781617292828
272 pages
$44.99
June 2016

For ordering information go to www.manning.com

MORE TITLES FROM MANNING

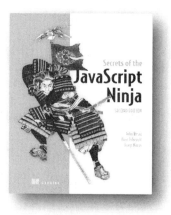

Secrets of the JavaScript Ninja,
Second Edition
by John Resig, Bear Bibeault, and Josip Maras

    ISBN: 9781617292859
    464 pages
    $44.99
    August 2016

Angular 2 Development with TypeScript
by Yakov Fain and Anton Moiseev

    ISBN: 9781617293122
    456 pages
    $44.99
    December 2016

Angular in Action
Covers Angular 2
by Jeremy Wilken

    ISBN: 9781617293313
    310 pages
    $44.99
    November 2017

For ordering information go to www.manning.com